Lal Ded of ... Saint Poetess

A Catalogue of Lal Vakhs

(Revised Edition)

Compiled By:

Sham S Misri (M.Sc.)
Sarla Gurtoo Misri (M.A. B.Ed.)

Introduction		16
Birth and Life of Lal Ded		22
Legends		26
Death		39
Vakhs		41
SM1.	Aaguruyee Ratak Saari Saari Tarakh	45
SM2.	Aaguryei Grazum	46
SM3.	Aami Pana Sodras Naavi Chhas Lamaan	47
SM4.	Aanchari Bichari Vechar Wonoon	48
SM5.	Anchaar Hanzani Hund Gyome Kanan	49
SM6.	Aarus Nerineh Modur Sheerai	50
SM7.	Aasa Bol Padenam Saasa	51
SM8.	Aasas Kuni Sapdas Saithaa	51
SM9.	Aasi Pondaiiy Zamaiy Zoasi	53
SM10.	Aasi Aes Ta Asii Aasav	54
SM11.	Aatali Paatali Kogam Teelith, Ye guura	56
SM12.	Aatheim Ta Shee-Thiem Mai-Ti Havtam	57
SM13.	Aayas Ti Suidooye Gach Ti Suidooye	58
SM14.	Aayas watey Gayas Naa watey	59
SM15.	Anderiy Aayas Chandry Gaaran	60
SM16.	Abhyasse Kinee Vekass Phollum	61
SM17.	Abhyassee Sovekaas Lye Vathoo	62
SM18.	Avistar Pothyan Chhi Ha Mali Paraan	63
SM19.	Akooie Omkar Yeli Lye Onum	64
SM20.	Akuy Omkaar Yus Naabi Daray	65
SM21.	Anaahata Kha-Swaruup Shuunyaalay	66

SM22.	Andariy Aayas Chandrie Gaaraan	67
SM23.	Ander Aasit Nebar Chondoom	68
SM24.	Atha Ma Baa Traavoon yi Khar Baa	69
SM25.	Atchan Aai Ta Gatchhun Gatchhey	70
SM26.	Attanech Sun Dith Thavan Mattan	71
SM27.	Avtal, Pevtal Kogam Teelith	72
SM28.	Azapa Gayatri Hamsa Hamsa Zapith	73
SM29.	Aayas Kami Dishi Ta Kami Vatey	74
SM30.	Achun Hu Na Prakash Kunay	75
SM31.	Andariy Aayas Chandrie Gaaraan	76
SM32.	Babri Langas Mushuk No mooray	77
SM33.	Bhaan Gole Tai Prakash Aao Zoonai	79
SM34.	Brahm Burzas Peth Watnovuum	80
SM35.	Broonth Kali Aasan Tithi Keran	81
SM36.	Buthi Kya Jaan Chhukh Vondi Chhukh Kani	82
SM37.	Chaalun Chhai Vuzmal Ta Tratai	83
SM38.	Chei Deev Gartas Ti Darthi Sazakh	84
SM39.	Challa Cheita Vondas Bhiiy Mo Bar	85
SM40.	Chammer Chatter Rath Simhasan	86
SM41.	Chandaan Looses Pani Panas	87
SM42.	Chaandanas Gyaanaprakaashas	88
SM43.	Charmoon Chatith Detuth Pon Paanas	89
SM44.	Chas Kenh Na Ta Assas Kenhniiy	90
SM45.	Che Kavo Logui Chui	92
SM46.	Chei Naa Bo Naa Daiyey Naa Dyaan	93
SM47.	Chet Aanadas Gyaan Prakaashas	94

SM48.	Cheth Amar Peth Thavizai	95
SM49.	Cheth Novui Chandram Novuy	96
SM50.	Cheth Torugh Gagana Bramvoom	98
SM51.	Cheth Torugh Vagi Hyath Rotom	100
SM52.	Chondmakh Bona Ta Bei Chon Deeshan	101
SM53.	Chandoom Ta Chondum Tren Deeshan	102
SM54.	Chui Kuni Tai Choi Naa Kunai	103
SM55.	Dachinis Oberas Zayoon Zaanhaa	104
SM56.	Dhama Dhama Mana Omkar Parnovum	105
SM57.	Damaa Dam Kormas Daman Haale	106
SM58.	Dhaman Basti Ditto Dil	107
SM59.	Deshi Aayas Dash Dishi Teelith	108
SM60.	Dihichi Lari Daari Bar Troprim	109
SM61.	Den Chezitai Razoon Aasi	110
SM62.	Dhobi Yeli Chavnas Dhobi Kani Pathie	112
SM63.	Dilkis Baagas Dour Kar Haesil	113
SM64.	Diluk Khur-Khura Meh Mali Kustam Manuk Kotur Maray	114
SM65.	Dhith Karith Raza Pherina	115
SM66.	Deev Vata Deever Vata	116
SM67.	Doad Kyah Zaani Yas No Baney	117
SM68.	Doh Tara Duniyas Lol Borum	118
SM69.	Dokh Chein Travith Mokh Wuch Haras	119
SM70.	Dwaadashaanta Manddal Yas Diivas Thaji	121
SM71.	Dhami Dyunthum Shabnam Pyomut	122
SM72.	Dhami Aasis Lokutai Kuur	123
SM73.	Dami Aasses Loukutai Kura-Jawan Kuur	124

SM74.	Dami Deetham Gaej Dazwani	125
SM75.	Dhami Deethum Nad Vahvani	126
SM76.	Gaal Kadinam Bol Parinam	127
SM77.	Gaatula Akh Vuchum Bwachi Suity Maran	128
SM78.	Gafilo Haquk Kadum Tul	129
SM79.	Gagan Chei Bhutal Chei	130
SM80.	Gaggan Paith Bhutal Shiv Yeli Dyunthum	131
SM81.	Gaytrei Azappa Challa Aki Tajim	133
SM82.	Gita Paraan Paraan Kouni Moodukh	134
SM83.	Gwarai Mole Tai Gwarai Maeji	135
SM84.	Guru Chu Ishwar, Gurui Maheshwar	136
SM85.	Gratta Chu Pheraan Zeari Zearey	137
SM86.	Guras Maal Pew Aamein Naatan	138
SM87.	Guru Kath Hridiyas Manz, Bag Ratam	139
SM88.	Guru Monui Lallishuri Guru	140
SM89.	Gwar Shabdas Yus Yatchh Patchh Barey	141
SM90.	Gwaran wonnum Kunui Vachun	142
SM91.	Gwaras Precheome Sassi Latey	144
SM92.	Gyaan Marg Chaai Haak Vair	146
SM93.	Gyanaek Ambar Puurith Tane	147
SM94.	Haa Manushi Kav Chuy Logmoot Parmas	148
SM95.	Haa Manushi! Kya Ze Chukh Vothaan Seki Loor	149
SM96.	Haasa Bole Padinam Saasa	150
SM97.	Hacivi Haarinji Pyatsuv Kaan Gom	151
SM98.	Hai Gura Parameshwaraa	152
SM99.	Ham Ham Karaan Gondum Ta Moroom	153

SM100.	Heh Nish Hah Draav Shah Kya Gavi	155
SM101.	Hu Kus Ta Bo Kus Teliwan Che Kus	157
SM102.	Hyath Karith Raaj Pheri-Naa	162
SM103.	Haii Hung Naad Zan Wazaan	163
SM104.	Ho'nd Maarrtyan Ya Kath	164
SM105.	Kaalan Kaal Zole Udwiiy Chei Gole	165
SM106.	Kaamas Saitee Priyei No Barem	166
SM107.	Kaayas Ander Roodum Achit	167
SM108.	Kaayas Bal Choi Maayas Zaagun	168
SM109.	Kachul Ta Maval Kath Kuit Chhui	169
SM110.	Kalamie Parum Ti Kalamie Sorum	170
SM111.	Kaman Sanna Neindar Tai Kamsana Woodie	171
SM112.	Kandeev Grah Teez Kandan Vaanas	172
SM113.	Kandyav geh te'zy kandyav vanvaas	173
SM114.	Kando Karakh Kandi Kandey	174
SM115.	Kanptha Chetan Gamnas	175
SM116.	Karmook Kul No Choi Banith Gachoon	176
SM117.	Karum Zu Kaaran Tre Kombith	177
SM118.	Kath Ha Vanai Kath Ha Vanai	178
SM119.	Katha Boozam Ta Katha Karem	179
SM120.	Kavo Chook Tsetaan Anine Vachh	180
SM121.	Kenchan Dithitum Torai Aalav, Kenchav Rachie	181
SM122.	Kenchan Dithitum Ore Aalav …Khev Totie	182
SM123.	Kenchan ranei chhai sahaz boonie, nerav nebar shuhul karav	183
SM124.	Kenchan Mali Dithuth Yeti Kya Tatai	184
SM125.	Kenchan Ditith Gulal Yechie	185

SM126.	Kenchas Pyath Kyah Chui Nachun	186
SM127.	Kenh Chiy Nenderi Hatte Vudiy	187
SM128.	Kenh-Chan Ranei Chai Sahaz Boonie	188
SM129.	Kheth Ti Moodhee Na Kheth Ti Moodhee	189
SM130.	Khaith Gandith Shami Naa Manas	190
SM131.	Khyana Khyana Karaan Kun No Vaatakh	191
SM132.	Kol Ta Mol Kath Kuit Choei	192
SM133.	Kosoom Bagas Heut Mai Achoon	193
SM134.	Kriya Karem Dharm Karum	193
SM135.	Kunirey Bozakh Kuni No Rozakh	195
SM136.	Kus Bub Tai Kousi Mougi	196
SM137.	Kus Marri Tai Kasu Maaran	197
SM138.	Kusoo Dengi Tai Kusoo Zaagi	198
SM139.	Kyaah Kara Paantsan Dahan Ta Kahan	199
SM140.	Kyah Bodhukh Moh Bhav Sodur Daarie	200
SM141.	Kyah Kara Kangri Pan Chein Karinyam	201
SM142.	Kokalee Sath Kol Gachan Paatali	202
SM143.	Kus Push Tai Kus Poshaanee	204
SM144.	Kush Posh Tel Diiph Zal Naa Gatshe	205
SM145.	Kyah Bodhukh Moh Bhav Sodur Daarie	206
SM146.	La Illah Il-Lalah Sahi Korum	207
SM147.	Leka Ta Thoka Paith Sheri Hetcham	208
SM148.	Lal Bo Draayas Kapsi Poshie Sachie	209
SM149.	Lal Bo Draayas Lolarey	210
SM150.	Lal Buh Lusis Chaaran Ta Gaaraan	211
SM151.	Lalith-Lalith Vaday Boh Vay	212

SM152.	Lal Boh Chaayas Somana Baag Baras	213
SM153.	Lal Bo Draayas Dooray Dooray	215
SM154.	Lal Bo Draayas Shiv Gaarney	216
SM155.	Lal Mai Dopukh Look Haand Krainee	218
SM156.	Lalli Gwar Brahmand Peth Kani Vuchum	219
SM157.	Lattan Hund Maaz Laaryom Vattan	220
SM158.	Lolaki Naar Lolli Lallenovum	221
SM159.	Loluki Vokhla Vaalinj Pishim	222
SM160.	Loob Maarun Sahaz Vyatsaarun	223
SM161.	Laachari Bichaari Pravad Karoom	224
SM162.	Larah Lazam Manz Maidaanas	225
SM163.	Lazz Kaase Sheet Niwaree	227
SM164.	Maarith Panch Boot Tim Phal Handi	228
SM165.	Madh Pyome Sendi Zallookyoot	229
SM166.	Manai Dengi Tai Akul Zaagi	230
SM167.	Mannas Gonn Chhui Chanchal Aasun	231
SM168.	Mandachi Hanz Hankal Kar Cheneim	232
SM169.	Manas Graaiye Chaje Pazikooe Ann Khoyome	233
SM170.	Manas Saethi Manai Gandoom	234
SM171.	Mandas Dudur Tai Vadris Sukray	235
SM172.	Mansai Maan Bhav-Saras	236
SM173.	Marookh Maar Paanch Bhoot	237
SM174.	Methya Kapat Asath Trovum	238
SM175.	Muuda Kraiy Chy Na Daarun Ta Paaroon	239
SM176.	Mudas Gyaanach Kath No Wanizay	240
SM177.	Mudas Gyaanach Kath No Vanizey -Seki Shaathas	241

SM178.	Moodas Pranvoon Chuie Moi Waal Chaidoon	242
SM179.	Mun Choor Maroon Gandun Neshkal	243
SM180.	Muudh Zanith Ta Pashith Laag	244
SM181.	Mal wondi Zolum	245
SM182.	Mal Vonda Zolum, Jigar (Kam) Morum	246
SM183.	Mann Posh Tai Yach Pushaani	247
SM184.	Maryam Na Kunh Ta Mara Na Kansi	248
SM185.	Mayas Hu Na Prakash Kunay	249
SM186.	Mokris Zan Mal Chollum Manas	250
SM187.	Na Pyaayas Na Zaayas	251
SM188.	Na Rozie Vandha Tai Na Retkoului	252
SM189.	Na Lal Zaayas Na Lal Pyaayas	254
SM190.	Naar Gachi Chaalun Ta Aar Gachi Galoon	255
SM191.	Naath Naa Paan Naa Paraznovoom	256
SM192.	Nabad Boaras Attagand Dyol Gome	257
SM193.	Nabisthans Chai Prakrath Zalvani	259
SM194.	Nabisthans Chet Zal Wani	260
SM195.	Nafsui Myon Chhui Husituiy	262
SM196.	Nafus Dituth Orai Meenith	263
SM197.	Nath Buvno Rannie Mangay	264
SM198.	Nav Trapraviith Deh Shomrawith	265
SM199.	Niyam Karooth Garbaa	267
SM200.	Omui Chu Voth Path Omui Chui Sorun	268
SM201.	Omai Akui Achhur Porum	269
SM202.	Omkaar Ye'li Layi O'num	270
SM203.	Omuy Aadi Tai Omuy Sorum	271

SM204.	Ora Ti Paanai Yora Ti Paanai, Poat Waannai	272
SM205.	Ora Ti Panai Yora Ti Panai, Paanai Paanas	273
SM206.	Ore Ti Yorie Yore Ti Orie	274
SM207.	Omkar Shreer Kewal Zonum	275
SM208.	Paanai Aasakh Ti Paanai Kaasakh	276
SM209.	Paanai Aasakh Ta Paanai Kaasakh	277
SM210.	Paanas Laagith Roovuk Meei Cheii	278
SM211.	Panchav Nishi Paanch Ravim	280
SM212.	Pannai Aav Paanas Saetee	281
SM213.	Par Ta Paan Yemi Somui Mone	282
SM214.	Paraan Paraan Zev Taal Phojim	283
SM215.	Paras Ha Mali Parum Ti Panas Vonum	284
SM216.	Parith Ti Boozith Brahmin Cheitan	285
SM217.	Parun Svalab Paaloun Dvarlab	286
SM218.	Parun Polum Apuruy Porum	287
SM219.	Patnaech San Dith Thavan Mattan	288
SM220.	Pawan Poorith Yus Ani Vagi	289
SM221.	Pawan Ta Praan Somui Dyunthum	290
SM222.	Poorak Kumbak Reechak Karome	292
SM223.	Pota Zooni Vathith Mot Bolnovum	293
SM224.	Praanas Saetee Lye Yeli Karem	294
SM225.	Pranvuni Lookan Chuk Pranaan	295
SM226.	Prath Tirthan Gatchhaan Sanyasii	296
SM227.	Praan Ta Rohoon Kunooi Zonoom	297
SM228.	Raajas Boj Yemi Kartal Tuji	298
SM229.	Raaza-Hams Aasith Loguth Koloiye	299

SM230.	Rangas Manz Chuie Byon Byon Labun	300
SM231.	Rav Matt Thali Thali Tapeetan	301
SM232.	Ravan Manz Ravun Ravoom	302
SM233.	Raavnas Manz Raavun Rovum, Raavnas Kenh Ne…	303
SM234.	Rozani Aayas Gachoon Gachoom	306
SM235.	Rut Ta Krut Soruy Pazyam	307
SM236.	Sabur Chui Zuer Marech Ti Noonie	308
SM237.	Sahazas Sham Ta Dam No Gachay	309
SM238.	Sahib Chu Behith Paane Vaanas	311
SM239.	Sidh Maali Sidho Sedh Kathan Kan Thav	312
SM240.	Samsar Hav Mali Yaarivu Jungul	313
SM241.	Samsar Niyiam Taev Tachhi	314
SM242.	Samsaaras Aayas Tapasii	315
SM243.	Samsaras Manz Bagh Kath Shayei Rozay	316
SM244.	Sani Khota Soun Chui Mann Kui Samandar	317
SM245.	Saras Saetee Sodaa Korum	318
SM246.	Sehni Hund Shikar Vaskav Zaani	319
SM247.	Sheel Ta Maan Chhui Kranjli Poonie	320
SM248.	Shevan Chattith Shashikal Vuzum	322
SM249.	Shiliyaz Hunz Dutma Bazum	323
SM250.	Shishiras Vuth Kus Ratte	324
SM251.	Shiv Chui Zawiul Zaal Wahraavith	325
SM252.	Shiv Chhui Thali Thali Rozaan	326
SM253.	Shiv Gur Tay Keshav Palns	328
SM254.	Shiv Shiv Karaan Hamsa-Gath So'rith	329
SM255.	Shiv Shiv Karan Shiv No Toshay	330

SM256.	Shiv Ta Shakhti Katyoo Deenthim	331
SM257.	Shiv Vaa Keshava Vaa Zin Vaa	332
SM258.	Sirius Hu Na Prakash Kunay	333
SM259.	Shran Ti Dyan Kya Sana Kari	334
SM260.	Shuunyuk Maedaan Kodum Paanas	335
SM261.	Shunikie Maidaan Waar Waar Pakzai	337
SM262.	Shurah Ta Dah Yus Sumrith Khaarai	338
SM263.	Shai Aases Ta Shai Chhas	339
SM264.	Sinhki Salali Yudvai Mul Kasak	340
SM265.	Soi Kul No Dodha Saet Sagizey	341
SM266.	Soi Mata Roopi Payee Diyay	342
SM267.	Soman Gaaroon Manz Yeth Kanday	343
SM268.	Sootas Ta Saatas Pachas Na Rumas	344
SM269.	Swargas Feeras Bergas Bergas	345
SM270.	Sorgus Mazun Kya Chui Basuni	347
SM271.	Swarg Jamma Praavith Alakh Prowum	348
SM272.	Sarafas Nish Kahvacha Kharoon	349
SM273.	Sat Sangye Paviter Doroom	351
SM274.	Sone Drav Dehion Ta Mal Gose Wathit	353
SM275.	Sone Thaav Thaij Tai Hosh Thav Phokas	354
SM276.	Taeer Slilas Khot Tiiy Taeeray	356
SM277.	Tala Chhui Zyus Ta Petha Chhukh Nachaan	357
SM278.	Tana Mana Gayas Bo Tas Kunui	358
SM279.	Tanthur Gali Tai Manthur Mochai	359
SM280.	Tatav Prakash Anath So Wani Paaniiye	361
SM281.	Tember Paiyes Kuv No Chagin	362

SM282.	Tim Chi Na Manush Tim Che Reshi	363
SM283.	Tori Ti Panai, Yori Ti Panai	364
SM284.	Treshi Bochhi Mo Kreshi–Naavun	366
SM285.	Trei Nengi Sara Asari-Saras	367
SM286.	Tulkatur Shishar- Gaanth Sheen Sharanita Mani	368
SM287.	Tyoth Modur Ta Myuuth Zahar	369
SM288.	Vakh, Maanas, Kwal, Akwal Naa Ate	370
SM289.	Vadneh Saeti Gaash Ho Mare	371
SM290.	Vakh Sedhee Chuie Dith Mokhas Beethim	372
SM291.	Wathoo Rannya Archoon Sakhar	374
SM292.	Waawech Graaya Paanas vuchhim	375
SM293.	Wuchaan Bu Chas Saras Andar	376
SM294.	Yas Na Kenh Kaan Tai Chonoi Yas Toroi	377
SM295.	Yath Saras Sirini Phole Na Vechee	378
SM296.	Yav Taeer Chali Tim Ambar Heta	380
SM297.	Yehiie Shiila Chyii Piitthas Ta Pattas	381
SM298.	Yi Kyah Aasith Yi Kyuth Rang Gome	382
SM299.	Yi Yi Karum Kara Pyatrum Paanas	383
SM300.	Ye Kyah Aasith Ye Kyuth Rang Gome	384
SM301.	Yem Ho Tundhey Bar Tal Zagan	385
SM302.	Yemai Shei Chei Timay Shei Mei	386
SM303.	Yemi Lodui Chone Kaamani Dushaar	388
SM304.	Yemi Kar Khamas Taleh Kin Zaagi	389
SM305.	Ye'my Luub Manmath Mad Tsuur Morun	390
SM306.	Yihay Maaira-Ruup Pay Diye	391
SM307.	Yot Ba Gayas Tati Os Sui	392

SM308.	Yus Hav Mali Haidyam Gelyam Maskhara Karyam	393
SM309.	Yi yi Karum Suy Archun	394
SM310.	Zagtas Ander Kaetyah Paalim	395
SM311.	Zal Ho Mali Lusui Na Pakaan Pakaan	396
SM312.	Kus Ha Mali Lusie Na Pakan Pakan	396
SM313.	Zal Paeth Pakun Thakun Loukan	397
SM314.	Zal Thamuno Hutva Turnavano	397
SM315.	Zanam Pravith Karam Sovoom	398
SM316.	Zanam Pravith Vebhov No Chondoom	399
SM317.	Zanuni Zaayaay Ruty Tay Kutiy	400
SM318.	Zaanahaa Naaddi-Dal Mana Ra'ttith	400
SM319.	Zain Mali Zaino, Angan Angan	402
SM320.	Zuv yeli dangi Aun kati rochie	404

Miscellaneous and Relevant 405

1) Lal Ded Spiritualism and Mysticism 405
2) Lal Ded and six great signs of spiritualism 407
3) Lal Ded and the concept of Shunya (Nothingness) 408
4) Lal Ded and Aum (Om) Emphasis 410
5) Lal Ded and Cosmic vision 418
6) Lal Ded as a wandering preacher 419
7) Lal Ded and her trials and tribulations 420
8) Lal Ded as social reformer 421
9) Lal Ded and Shaivism 422
10) Lal Ded had three discourses with Guru 424
11) Lal Ded-14th Century a turning point in the history of Kashmir 429
12) Lal Ded – The main contribution of Rishi Movement 430

13)	*Lal Ded and Yoga (Yogini)*	*433*
14)	*Yogic powers of Lal Ded*	*435*
15)	*Lal Ded and Kashmiri language*	*436*
16)	*Lal Ded and Lullaby- (Lal Songs)*	*438*
17)	*Lal Ded Ignored by Historians*	*445*
18)	*New Vakhs*	*445*
	Notes	*447*

About The Author(s) 458

About The Book 461

Android App 461

References 462

Other Books by The Same Author(s) 464

Acknowledgements 465

Introduction

A Kashmiri saying:
Kani phol ti nuni phol gav dariyavas. Kani phol dop, "bu -golus." Nuni phol von, "yusuy gol ti Sui gol."
A pebble and a piece of salt fell into the river. The pebble said, "I am dissolving." The piece of salt replied, " The one which has actually dissolved has perished." Was the original inhabitant of Kasheer a 'Nuni phol?' I wonder!
The Kashmiri Pandits have been the original inhabitants of Kashmir since times immemorial. Though their recorded history is 5000 years only but as per the latest archaeological excavations done at Semthan (near Bijbehara) it is established that the Aadhi Maanav (supposed to be the real ancestors of Kashmiri Pandits) were living in Kashmir even 85, 000 years ago.
Kashmir, rightly called the crown of India, has been creative not only in producing great kings, philosophers, historians, and poets who not only shone like luminaries in the firmament, but also in producing a women of extra-ordinary talents and rare gifts called Lalleshwari, an ascetics of the most sublime and exalted order with a halo of 'Divineness'. Lalleshwari, more popularly called by the homely name of Lal Ded (Mother Lal) was one of those master spirits, who took birth at periodic intervals in this world to deliver a message of truth and peace, urging the humanity to follow higher ideals of life and shun the frivolities of mortal earthly existence. She was an apostle of goodness and a follower of the 'Shaiva philosophy'.

The political and cultural crisis that erupted in Kashmir in 1989 has brought about drastic changes in the Kashmiri Pandit identity. So much so, that Lalla, who embodies a Kashmiri identity, a sharp battle had been fought around her by various claimants, under the banners of authenticity and historicity.
History can be horrible, appalling hard to learn. The trouble is it keeps on 'changing.' In math's, two and two is usually four and in science water is always made up of Oxygen and hydrogen. But in History things are not that simple. In history a "fact" is sometimes not a fact at all. Really it is just someone's 'opinion'. And opinions can be different for different people. For example, at some point one writer had said about Lal Ded-

that she was not a Kashmiri Brahmin girl, thus creating confusion in minds of the common people.

It had also been said that she accepted Islam and was a follower of Shah Hamadan who took refuge in Kashmir from Timur's persecution. All non-sense and gibberish! There are plenty of evidence to establish that Kashmir enjoyed a wonderful status for being a habitat of rishis harboring a strong and sound original tradition of Rishi-cult with its root systems entrenched in the Vedic age. In terms of history, Sufism in its essence was foreign to Kashmir. It was introduced in the religious environment of Kashmir by the Muslim followers and propagandists. Most of them sought protection in Kashmir when they were under harassment and persecution in their native lands for their indulgence in politics and routine affairs. Some distorted ideas were floated about Lal Ded as being a Muslim which is quite twaddle. In 1885, a Muslim scholar Pir Ghulam Hasan summed up the argument in his Tarikh-i-Hasan "The Hindus say that she is one of them. The Muslims claim that she belongs to them. The truth is that she is among the chosen of God. May god's peace is upon her."

At another time one more author had perhaps more knowingly than innocently re-introduced an Islamized name for Lal Ded. A similar campaign was spearheaded at the inaugural function of Lal Ded Hospital, Srinagar, which was initially named as Lalla Arifa Hospital by the powers that be. An elderly person sitting in the audience challenged the mind-boggling and unhistorical references to Lal Ded. The function presided over by Sheikh Abdullah, Chief Minister of Jammu & Kashmir, was factually disrupted by the dynamic involvement of an elderly man leaning against his walking stick. The Sheikh initially hesitated but later changed his mind under a wave of protest by several indisputable and unquestionable intellectuals including Pt Jaya Lal Koul and Prof. P. N Pushup, professors of eminence, distinction, and classical vintage. The Sheikh had to order formation of a committee to have a second look at the Lalla Arifa nomenclature. On the suggestions and advice of the committee the Islamized nomenclature was dropped.

The night of January 19, 1990, will remain the most unforgettable one in the memory of every Kashmiri Pandit men and women. That nightstands singled out as the harbinger of the terrible catastrophe which engulfed the panic-stricken unlucky community. That night flood gates broke open and the war cries inciting the Muslims that it was time they came out into the streets to welcome the ringing of the dawn of a new and Islamic order. That night seemed to be fated to ring out the life of every Kashmiri Pandit child, man, and woman. That night signaled that all was over with them. That night tolled the knell of what Kashmir and oft-quoted Kashmiriyat symbolized. No male Muslim man or child stayed back in doors but streamed out to swell the crowds whose shouts of 'death to India', death to Kafirs ranted the skies from the entire valley of Muslim dominated Kashmir. That night in the pall of darkness the land of rishis would get saturated with the warm blood of Kafirs. That night demons veiled as neighbors', friends, co-workers came out in true colours. A sea change had swept over the so-called peace-loving Kashmiri Muslims. Some Muslims, high and the low, rubbed shoulders in wild anger in their common war against the Hindus. The poor pandits were quietly sitting with their arms and legs near their body. At this moment they were together indoors while their fate hung in balance. They read the clear writing on the wall; their days in their native land were now numbered. The panic had started and there was gloom on every Pandits face. They must catch time by the forelock to escape the imminent doom. The Tenth migration was surely in the offing.

Similar situations were created in the past when Hindus of Kashmir were humiliated, but then a saintly voice like that of Lal Ded was heard. It was she who united the disheartened and demoralized Hindus by her very presence in the valley then.

Lal Ded had taken this life form with a mission partly for herself and partly for showing a path of deliverance to the suffering masses that were experiencing the worst of their time in Kashmir. She succeeded in her mission but had to face lots of hardships till she was recognized as the ultimate savior of the people at large. The suffering of the people didn't end totally so she continued to be worried. It's the same worry that she's referring to in her Vakh

Shiv chuy thali thali rozan.
Mo zan Hiund tu musalman
Truk ay chuk pan panun parzanav,
Suy chay sahibas sati zaniy zan.

Lalleshwari was very liberal in her associations with all kinds of people. She was revered equally by the people of all faith. To her all faiths were equally authentic ways of God. She taught them the ultimate way of living, extending all love and compassion to everyone high and low, rich, and poor and doing everything in the Lord's name so that nothing wrong is committed. It was her prime concern to create bridges of understanding between man and man who had been warring with each other consequent upon the exploitation based on caste and community by some vested interests. She succeeded in her mission such that both Hindus and Muslims of Kashmir considered her as a sincere messenger from God to show them the path for settlement and the way towards truth. All such messengers of God are above all such distinctions. They do not nourish any kind of hatred between man and man. They bring all types of people together who for some worldly reasons are brought on the war path by some vested interests. Lalleshwari was one among the towering personalities of the world who had come to strengthen the bonds of humanity in her own region besides giving those lessons to make their lives purposeful. Her message did cut through the man-made barriers of religions. Hindus as well as Muslims became her pupil with equal passion. Her appeal was humanistic and not sectarian. Her move towards uniting the communities was positive and not of negative rejection. Her Clarion call to understand human values in those days won for her the esteem and praise of Hindus and Muslims alike. The edge of ruthless conversion got blunted. It was an achievement on her part in uniting the lost children of one God. She happened to be a Rishika (knowledgeable woman seer of the Vedic lore) of the fourteenth Century, who realized Shiva as the Divine being.

Conflict between Hindu and Islamic cultures in Kashmir Valley resulted in continuous political reverses for the Hindus, but at the social level there was a happy interchange between the two communities. A process of synthesis between Islam and Vedanta (Kashmir Shaivism in the Valley) started preparing the ground for the development of Sufism. In Kashmir, Sufis were given the name of Rishis by the common people. Sheikh Nur-ud-Din, the founder of the Rishi Order, known as Alamdar-i-Kashmir or the Standard Bearer of Kashmir, was also called Nunda Rishi.

Lal Ded was revered by all sections of society and even by Nund Rishi who was greatly influenced by her. Lal Ded's spiritual powers along with Nund Rishi's became the shield against growing violence committed by the Sultan's of that time who were using forced and violent methods for conversion. Lalleshwari the Shaivite saint of Kashmir had nothing directly to do with the politics of the time. That beauty of the valley is now gone. Lal Ded had a mission to perform. Her life and sayings were mainly responsible in molding the character of her people and setting up tradition of love and tolerance which is not characterized in the state of Kashmir today.

From the valley of Kashmir in northern India, the principles of Shaivism were first written down in the ninth century. Shaivism represents a basic view on the Universe. It seems that the gods had to somehow restore their energies to the Primitive Force, the Source from which everything emerged in the very beginning. Shakti represents the force of transformation and regeneration, an extraordinary growing force that may lead to ecstasy.

In the Shiva cosmology, the whole universe is considered to have emerged and sustained by two forces, opposed in term of polarity: Shiva (masculine) and Shakti (feminine). She is the colossal force, who supports the biologic, psychic, affective and mental processes of the human being. In Kashmir Shaivism this phenomenal world (Shakti) is real, and it exists and has its bearing in consciousness (chit). In contrast Advaita holds that this phenomenal world is illusion Maya.

With such wonderful Shaivism thoughts in Kashmir, there was complete harmony during the Hindu rule. The idea of conversion was unknown and non-existent. In the Kashmiri culture, Hindu places of worship and prayer places had never been misused as centers of preaching and propagating intolerance. There was no religious bias and hatred to other faiths and creeds. There was no inciting and illegal agitation. There was no religious place for arms and ammunition, or for providing safe shelter to sinners and criminals.

Kashmir has been the place of birth of Kashmiri Pandits. It has been the valley of Sufis and saints. With the sparkling rivers, the splendid gardens, and snow-capped peaks it had taken a heavenly look making Kashmir famous world over. Those who wanted rest and amusement found the same in the Valley of Kashmir. This has been the place where Lal Ded, the great saint and poetess was born. It is also said that Lal Ded was reincarnation of goddess Sharda.

Before the birth of Lalleshwari or Lal Ded, there was destruction of temples and images in Kashmir by Muslim zealots. Hindu worship was driven to the privacy of the home or of 'natural' images - rocks, or ice formations, or springs. In this troubled period of political uncertainty and changing social values, the people of the Valley were subjected to the impact of Islam. From a close contact between the two religions and their deep influence on each other, there resulted the evolution of what may be called Medieval Reformers or Mystics. It was during this period that the rich religious and philosophic traditions of Kashmir produced several mystics and saints. Foremost among them was the great mystic "seer", Lalleshwari, popularly known as Lal Ded (Mother Lalla).

Lal Ded was the pioneer in creating the mystic poetry called *'Vatchun'* and verses called Lal Vakhs. The Lal Vakhs are the earliest composition of verses in Kashmiri literature. These verses are important mechanisms of modern Kashmiri language. The vakhs of Lal Ded have come down to us through folk tradition of Kashmir. Her vakhs are freely quoted by speakers as maxims on appropriate occasions.

Sham S. Misri
Claremont Av.
London, U.K.

Birth and Life of Lal Ded

Little is historically known about Lal Ded's life. It is believed that she was born of a well-to-do Kashmiri Brahman family at Pandrethan, a small village at four miles from Srinagar. Her father's name was Cheta Bhat who lived in the fourteenth century near Pampore. Cheta Bhat was also known by the name Chander Bhat and was a peasant living from hand to mouth.

There is uncertainty about her date of birth. Some clues point out that she was born in the middle of the 14th century when Sultan Alau-ud-Din became the third Muslim king of Kashmir. However, Pir Ghulam Hassan, Persian chronicler writes: "The saintly lady Lalla Arifa, a mystic of the highest order, was brought to light in the year A.D.1300-01. It is said that this virtuous lady was born in a Brahmin family in the village of Sempor. During the early days of her life, she was under the influence of an extraordinary spell of ecstasy…she was married at Pampore…"

A thorough research conducted has shown, various dates and places given by different authors.

About her birth, most of the authors have agreed for three dates. The three Birth dates are.

A.D. (1300-01); A.D. (1334-35); and A.D. (1346-47).

The Places of birth are two:

Sempor (near Pampur); and Pandrethan.

After extensive study and intensive research work, on 'LAL DED ' in 1973 Prof. J.L. Koul opines that the dates of birth and death of Lalleshwari was sometime between (b 1317-20 A D) & (d 1387-90 A D). These dates seem to be in compatibility and in agreement with the circumstantial evidence and hence more authentic and nearest the truth.

Lal Ded was a mystic poet from the valley of Kashmir. She spread her philosophy of love. People have called her a saint and a Sufi singer. From her childhood she grasped the atmosphere of piety and religion. One does not know how she looked. But it is said that she walked about with her hair let loose and utterly unclad. Lal Ded had a protruded belly, and her belly would hang down, covering the lower parts of her body. In fact, 'Lal 'is a Kashmiri word which means a Hanging Belly. During her lifetime and later, both the Hindu and Muslim communities have claimed her as their own.

Although Kashmiri historians produced a lot of records of Kashmir in the recent past between the 15th and 17th centuries but none of them mentions Lal Ded. She is not mentioned even in well-known Sanskrit historical chronicles like Rajatarangini in which Kalhana recorded events up to 1151 AD and which Jonaraja extended up to 1445 AD and Jaina Rajatarangini which chronicles events from 1459 to 1486 AD. Nor do the chronicles written in Persian during succeeding centuries until about 1746 make any mention of her. It may be that because all these were chronicles of kings and their political events, so, their scope was limited. Lal Ded also, in none of her vakhs mentions contemporary political or court event. Probably, as a village lady, she did not know about what went on at the palace.

When Lal was twelve years of age, she got married to Sona Bhat having nick name Nica Bhatt, a Brahman boy of Drangbal near Pampur. She was treated cruelly by her mother-in-law. It is sometimes said that her Mother-in-law was the stepmother of her husband. According to a custom of the Brahmans of Kashmir, a bride was usually given a new name on her marriage, therefore, Lal Ded was known as Padmavati in her husband's home. But her maiden name continued to be used by her family and friends. Her marriage was sad and unhappy.

Her mother-in-law often incited her son against his wife. Legend has it that her mother-in-law who nearly starved her-off treated her cruelly. Lal Ded's mother-in-law was cunning and tricky. Lalleshwari would not utter a word of protest, against strange ways of ill-treatment from her mother-in-law but take every care to shield her husband as well as mother--in-law and their honours.

It is said that her father-in-law was kind and friendly to her. One day, her father-in-law accidentally found out the truth. He got annoyed with his wife and scolded her. This incident invited more curses on Lal Ded. Her mother-in-law poisoned the ears of her son with all sorts of stories. The husband started treating her badly. This was perhaps the turning point in her life. Lal Ded though a natural seeker faced a disastrous crisis in life. Her marriage got fractured. As a result, agitation, conflict, misery, and uncertain future were the leading factors in her mind. She looked around and saw herself in a dilemma of misery. She became restless and something screamed out in her. "Where is release from human misery?" Ultimately, the cruelties of worldly life led her to renunciation. She left home at the age of twenty-four. She renounced the world and set out in quest of the Truth. It was an inner call, the call that comes to one who is prepared for it. She plunged into torturous harshness but all in vain. She says:

"Passionate, with longing in mine eyes,
Searching wide, and seeking nights and days,
Lo! I beheld the Truthful One, the wise,
Here in mine own House to fill my gaze".

Her passion for God set fire to all she had. She had drunk a cup of God intoxicating drink.

Her vakhs confirm and establish that she engaged herself with Jap, tap, and dhyana, as the common yogic practices to calm her mind which was deeply agitated and extremely disturbed.

Perhaps, it took time for her fame to spread, and it was only long afterwards when she became a legend that chroniclers felt it necessary to mention her in their records. The name of Lal Ded is first mentioned in 1654 by Baba Dawud Mushkati in his Asrarul-Abrar a theological document, (The secret of the Pious). Then, her mention was in Waqiate Kashmir completed in 1746. Some names give evidence to her life and to her miracles. Her astonishing life and the amazing vakhs that she sang go beyond time. People believe that "her sayings echo and re-echo to this day". The extraordinary love contained in her vakhs has the power to move one even today.

The great mystic Sheikh Noorud Din Noorani (1377-1438 A.D.) was her immediate successor. He mentions Lal Ded's name in one of his emotions and confirms her way of life. One Kashmiri folk story recounts that as a baby, Nunda Rishi refused to be breast-fed by his mother. It was Lal Ded who breast-fed him. Later, he became her disciple in the mystic lore and experience.

The saying:
Zena yeli na mandchok
Chana kyazi chuk mandachan

When you did not feel shy of getting born, why do you feel shy of feeding milk?

Lal Ded was one of those who wandered in the wilderness of love, sobbing and lamenting. According to Nunda Rishi's saying:

'Tas Padmanporich Lallay
Emi galli amrit pevo
Tami Shiv vuch thali thalay
Tithuy meh var ditoo divoo'

The Lala of Padmanpora, Gulp by gulp Amrit who drank, who saw Shiva face to face everywhere? Grant me too that boon O Lord Siva!

Lal Ded was a country girl. She was a born saint. Even as a child, born and bred up in a religious atmosphere she had shown signs of strange spiritual feeling. From quite young age Lalleshwari slowly and steadily resorted to secret spiritual practices deep Sadhana and yoga in isolation and privacy. This perhaps may not have worked. Later, a highly talented and reputed scholar yogi of the time, Siddha Sri Kanth (Sedha Mol) of Srinagar became her guru. He taught her certain spiritual disciplines during the early years of her life at her father's house. Her guru introduced such practices to her that over a period she came to realize their very important role and value in attaining identity with Shiva.

Siddha Srikanth whom she calls 'omniscient' subsequently phrased her spiritual evolution through debates and discourses coupled with all grades of Shaiva-practices.

Legends

Many legends and stories remain about Lalla. All of them may not be factually accurate but they do throw light on the social and communal beliefs of her time and of later times.

There is a persistent legend that when Lal Ded left her husband's home, she wandered naked, dancing and singing in ecstatic frenzy. She did not care about her personal appearance because she was convinced that the true self was the spirit within: The Guru gave me but one precept-From without, go within, this saying I took to heart, And, naked, I began to dance. It is also said that Lal's guru acknowledged that she had outstripped him in meditation. On one occasion…

1. There is a legend which tells that once when her Guru, Siddha Shrikantha, was having his early morning bath in the river, he noticed that a little above where he was takin a bath, Lalla was cleaning and scrubbing the outside of an earthen pot filled with dirt. He was angry and forcefully protested with her. "What use this scrubbing the pot while the dirt inside it is not removed?" Lalla was quick to retort. She angrily replied: What profits it to bathe to cleanse the body while the inner self is not purified?"

Lalla had outstripped the need to perform rituals and ceremonies as also the need to worship icons and images. Indeed, she upbraided those who felt satisfied with these externalities of religion: O fool! True action does not reside in fasts or religious rituals. And again, the god is stone, the temple is stone. From top to bottom, all is one, O priest! Whom do you worship? Make your mind and your life one. And again, Devotee and ascetic Wander from temple to temple to find that God Who is in themselves.

The Guru, Siddha Shrikantha, undertook a 40-day strict and serious penance of fasting and self-humiliation. It was a loss of face for him.

2. One morning Lalla came to his Guru's house and enquired where he was. On being told that he was engrossed and absorbed in his meditation, Lalla observed with gentle irony, "Yes, watching his horse being kicked at the meadow of Nandamarg (Ava Nandamarg chis divan guris taaph)." There is slight variation of her remark, viz, "Yes, feeding salt to his horse at Nandamarg (Ava Nandamarg divan guris nun)."

Shrikantha overheard her remarks and felt embarrassed, because his mind had indeed strayed into watching his horse being kicked by some other horse at the meadow where it had been sent for summer months.

Then, it is said, she gave him demonstration of what the penance should really be. She placed an earthen pot on her head and another under her feet; and with fading of the moon, her body waned till, on the fifteenth night of dark fortnight (amavas), nothing was left of her except a little quantity of 'trembling quicksilver'. Then, with the waxing moon her body waxed, and, on the full moon night, she was herself again.

In wonderment her Guru asked: "What was the quicksilver like substance in the pot trembling all the time?"

"It was I," replied Lalla.

The Guru admitted that the disciple had far out stripped the master and her instructor - (gav tsath gwaras khasith).

3. It was Lalla's habit to rise early and go to the ghat with an earthen pitcher under her arm. Before collecting water, she would spend time on ablutions and yogic exercises like breath control etc., while going across to the temple of Natakeshaw Bhairaw. One day, the mother-in-law had hinted and suggested to her son that Lalla was not faithful to him. And then one morning, her husband waited for Lalla to return. With the firm resolve Nika Bhat, her husband wanted to shove her out of his home. He got his evil and devilish form and hid his stick behind the door. As Lal Ded approached, her husband, Nika Bhat struck the pitcher. And another miracle occurred. It is believed that the pitcher broke into pieces, but the water content remained intact in a frozen state. Lalla filled each household pots with water till not a drop more was needed.

After filling all the vessels at home, she asked her mother-in-law if there were any other vessels to be filled. On getting a negative reply, Lalleshwari threw the remaining water out at a place which later came to be known as Lalla-Trag (marsh). The marsh still exists but has now gone dry.

4. This spring has now dried up but to this day it is called Lalla Trag (Trag means "pond"). As the historian Pir Ghulam Hassan has stated, this spring went dry in 1925-26.

The miracle of the pitcher turned out to be a turning point in Lalla's relationship with her in-laws. And, now she was in her much more important relationship with the Supreme Consciousness. By this time most probably she had still to receive the 'word', the supernatural, rather cryptic, or mysterious light from her guru as to what course she should adopt to know the Eternal in her own Self. She left her in-laws for good and took to wandering as an ascetic, a saint in search of Enlightenment. The story goes that she wandered almost naked like a mad person who does not care for any formality of dress. The legend goes that her lull (in Kashmiri), or belly protruded forward bent itself to cover her private parts. People therefore forgot her original maiden's name of Lalita (shortened to Lalla in Kashmir) and began to call her Lalla Ded, the' Grandmother Lal' with the belly hanging down.

5. One tells of how Lalla, had ignored the normal convention of dress, choosing to wander around naked, was teased by several children. A nearby cloth merchant scolded the children for their disrespect to Lal Ded. It was Lalla who asked the merchant for two lengths of cloth, equal in weight. The merchant obliged her. That day as she walked around naked, she wore a piece of cloth over each shoulder. As she walked, and as she met with respect or scorn (disrespect), she tied a knot in one or another.

In the evening, she brought the cloth back to the merchant. She then asked him to weigh them again. The cloths were equal in weight, no matter how many knots were in each. Respect and scorn have no weight of their own. Smiling, Lalla said to the shopkeeper: "I shall not feel distressed or hurt.

"A Kashmiri saying which means that it is best to be self-dependent, even if they hurl a thousand abuses at me."

She thus brought home to the vendor, and her disciples, that mental balance and sympathy should not be shaken by the manner people greeted or treated a person.

While she was affectionately called Lal Ded, she would sometimes be teased and mocked at and even called names ('Lalla Ma'tch, the mad Lalla) by street urchins.

6. Legend has it that her mother-in-law who nearly starved her-off treated her cruelly. The story goes like this that LAL had always a stone in her plate covered with a thin layer of rice so that it would look like a

big heap. "LAL" never uttered a word against her ill treatment. Later, LAL "relinquished her married life and became a wandering mystic.

7. Once on a festive occasion while filling a pitcher at the riverbank, she was asked by her girlfriends what the festivity and merriment at her home was all about. She said, "Whether they slaughter a ram or a lamb, Lalla will never miss her shingle".
Lalla replied this in a vakh:
"Ho'nd maarrtyan ya kath
Lalli nalavath tsali'nas zanh."
(They may kill a big lamb, or a small one Lalla will have the large pebble on her plate). Lal's father-in-law over-heard her remark and that day, when food was served to her, he verified the truth of it.

8. It is said that when Nund Rishi (Later named Sheikh Nur Ud din Wali), an eminent saint of Kashmir was born, he would not suck his mother's breast. It so happened that one-day Lal Ded chanced to come that way. She patted the baby with the words:
'Yina mandachokh na khena chukh mandachan.'
It means you were not ashamed to be born and yet you are ashamed to suck your mother's breast. And with these words Lal Ded told him to draw milk from the breast of his mother, which he did.

9. Lal Ded used to wander in rags in half nude attire. She was a contemporary of "Shah-i-Hamdan." A popular tradition in Kashmir bears it from generation to generation that when "Lal" saw Shah-i-Hamdan" she cried out ---- "After all I have seen a man" thereafter she is reported to have clothed herself and greatly associated herself with Shah-i-Hamdan.

10. It is said that Lal Ded lived for some time at the village of Khampor, ten miles south of Srinagar on the, then, main road to Shopian. She saw Mir Sayyid Ali Hamadani approaching from the other side. Suddenly, she ran to the nearby shop of a grocer to hide herself, saying "Here is a man going!" But the grocer turned her away and she rushed into the baker's shop. Before the baker knew what it was all about, she jumped into the hot oven. Bewildered, poor baker put the lid on the oven and fell down unconscious. But Lal Ded came out "attired in beautiful dress" to meet the Sayyid unabashed.

There is a Kashmir saying, viz.

Ayi vanis ti gayi kandras
Came to visit a grocer but went to a baker's shop (instead). The story is about Lal Ded, Kashmiri saint, who wanted to bless a shopkeeper, but blessed a baker instead. The proverb means to give benefit to someone in place of someone else.

11. There is another legend according to which Lalla's mother-in-law used to taunt, scold, and insult her on the slightest pretext. She was accused of not knowing how to spin yarn, even though she, in fact, spun yarn as fine as the lotus stalk. Since there was no electricity available those days, Lal Ded used to spin the wheel even under moon light. While spinning the charkha Lal Ded used to sing songs of her beloved God. Although Lal Ded was making good quality of the yarn, but still her mother-in-law was not satisfied. The spinning wheel was finally thrown into the pond. It is said that Lal Ded also jumped into the pond. But a miracle happened Lal Ded survived and soon lotus plants bloomed from that pond. The miracle was expressed in the following verse!

Bahan variyan yander kot Lallay
Bahi vahaer laayin sarsai voth
Nadir tai Pamposh khaet thali thaley
Tith paeth tothtou mea baley.

For twelve years Lal Ded operated the spinning wheel. After twelve years she jumped into a pond. From the pond lotus plants grew and lotus flowers bloomed.

Lal Ded was also reproached for being shy and reserved. She did not mix with the young daughters-in-law of the neighborhoods and did not join in their fun and frolic.

12. There is an anecdote relating to the prophecy which Lal Ded makes on one occasion. Most of the Persian chronicles have mentioned it.

It is said that once Shihab ud din, the elder son and heir apparent of Sultan Alau ud din, had gone on hunting with his companions, Malik Jindar, Adarsh Rawal, and Akhtaji. On the way they felt very thirsty. Quite unexpectedly, there issued forth from a mountain defile Lalla Arifa bearing a cup of sherbet in her hand. She offered the drink to the prince. He accepted it and after he drank of it, offered it to Adarsh Rawal, who, in turn, handed it over to Malik Jindar. The Malik, however, did not leave any of it for the third companion. Thereupon, Lal Ded prophesied that the prince would become a renowned king. Adarsh would be his prime minister, Malik his commander in chief. But the third companion would die before they reached home. The prophecy came to pass. This is perhaps the only anecdote that finds corroboration to Jonaraja's Rajatarangini with slight modification.

13. Once an open-air performance was held at Pampore. Many people had come to attend the show. Lal Ded's father-in-law too was there, and he saw her attending nude among the spectators. He reprimanded her and led her into his house to put on some clothes and cover her shame. Lal Ded protested, saying that there were no human beings about, only goats and sheep. She asked her father-in-law to look out from the window. He saw and was dumbfounded. There were only sheep and goats there. For, hath it not been said that whoever is engrossed only is material pursuits is but an animal or indeed a block of wood or lump of stone.

14. Pandit Anand Koul (1868-1941), has gathered strange legend relating to her birth. In previous birth of hers, Lal Ded was married to a man living at Pandrethan where she gave birth to a son. On the 11th day of her confinement at the ceremony called kāhnethar, she said to the family priest, Siddha, "How is the newborn baby related to me?"

"Why," said he, "He is your son."

"No," She replied, "I shall presently die and be born as a filly at the village of Marhom with such and such marks. Should you be curious to know the answer to my query, you may come to village Marhom after a year."

After a year, Siddha went to the village and found the filly with the characteristic marks. On enquiry the filly told him that she was about to die and be reborn as a pup at Vejibehara after six months and he could have the answer there. Thereupon, all upon a sudden, a tiger rushed from a nearby bush and killed the filly. His curiosity very much awakened, Siddha pursued her not only at Vejibehara, where he recognized the pup with the recognizable marks and where he was again asked to meet her in another birth somewhere else, but, so on with six births of her. Then, seventh time she was reborn in the same family at Pandrethan in which she had died on the eleventh day of her confinement. When she was twelve years of age, she was married to a young man in a Brahmin family surnamed Nica Bhatt, living at Drangabal Mahal at Pampore, the ancient Padmapura founded in A.D. 812-849 by Padma, minister of king Ajatapida. It was while the marriage ceremony was on at her father's house that the bride Lalla whispered to Siddha: "The boy who was born to me in a previous birth you know of is the bridegroom here." Siddha remembered and was amazed.

A woman tells us the story of one of our mysterious women. "He could never shut the bedroom door completely, in case his mother called for water or God knows what."

The story is now known in detail. When a man and women are alone, he makes sure that the room is darkened, the windows shut, the curtains down, doors bolted, as if he is ashamed of being a married man. All openings are secure. In silence he makes love to his wife, one hand on her mouth, and he consumes her with hunger. But he is like a man under siege, a man chased. In the night he looks at her and is possessed by her luminescence and her hair and her nakedness. When morning comes and he draws the curtains from the windowpanes and opens all the windows and doors he has closed the night before, he can see her teeth and her nakedness stretched across the bed. He hears his mother calling him, and when he remembers his need in the night it makes his stomach turn.

Then he has a great urge to flee and free himself. So, he makes some derogatory remarks and snips off all the brief threads of the night. She goes about her work, a complete woman, and she forgives his dilemma and his incompleteness. During the day they work like normal ones, each has their own routine to attend to. It is as if they do not know each other, and they do not exchange a word unless it is essential. During the day he ministers to his mother completely, no divided loyalties, a free man. Only then, at night, hiding in the dark, can he feel free to be with his wife.

The time comes before him to choose between right and wrong, but his mind is locked, and he is not free. He must give up one for the other. In the absence of wisdom, he is guided solely by destiny, and he makes his selfish choice. He slides under his mother's quilt; it has all the designs on it. But that was a long time ago; and you can hardly make out those designs now. Her bony knees are tucked up under her leathery wrinkled and withered breast. Her eyes are small, sticky, flat and open like a fish.

She does not ask, but he has come to some conclusion and is ready with a verdict. "Her nipples are small, and she has hair on her face," he says.

His mother makes a short breathless sound which signifies that she has known it all along. "And that is not all; her head seems to be on fire all the time." And then one night she thought I (HUSBAND) was sleeping, and she called a tiger from the wooden ceiling and rode off into the night".

The old woman lets out a quick breath, a gasp and her knuckles turn white as she tries to sit upright.

"I have heard of such things," she says with fear in her voice. She thinks she knows the wretched truth, something she had a feeling about all along. The very son she sought to protect is sleeping with a demon.

Things go from bad to worse. The son lingers more and more in the kitchen, where mother spends all her time. He tells his mother astonishing things.

"She rolls herself into a small ball and glows like mercury, and if I try to look at her, she darts about the room and finally comes to rest only when I close my eyes and cover my head. I can't see but I know, just as I know it is morning even before I open my eyes. I see the sky come down through the window into the room and she lets it in through her ring as she holds it between her thumb and forefinger. In the morning she goes about her business, milks the cow, feeds the birds and she goes to the river to bathe, but she never leaves the room. She is there all the time, I know because she has a light around her, even in the dark and it never leaves our room."

The mother listens and now she thinks she must do something. He has let his mother into a sacred circle where she is forbidden. As a result, everything now is dark and misleading to the old woman. Uncomprehending, she beats her breast silently, looking out at the mountains and up at the sky to see if they understand.

She whispers to her son, "A witch. What are we to do now?" They are mother and son again, united against the unknown.

The mother had anticipated that a daughter-in-law would cause discord in their perfect dead father-mother homestead. She pulls her quilt around her; she is overcome with dreadful certainty. Her blindness is about to wreak havoc upon them, but she cannot bring herself to make the right choice.

When you see the fresh richly colored embroidery on the quilt, she, a young woman then, slept soundly under it. Her lips were red, her eyes heavy from sleep, her limbs tired, and her youthful face hidden from her black hair. On one night, it was very cold outside, and she had slept as if dead. She felt someone pull her long hair, which had fallen onto the wooden floor and her heart turned to ice. She sat up, but her husband tore her out of bed. She grasped the edge of the bed, and her quilt, but he pushed her down to the floor.

When she tried to resist, he dragged her across the floor, and she pulled her quilt to cover her nakedness. He dragged her out of the room and threw her out of the room. Then he went into their bedroom followed by a woman who closed the door behind them.

They said that after that wife ran around naked except for her stomach, which covered her because it had grown immense folds of lotus like petals.

That is what some people said. But the woman with the lotus petals was someone else, a divine poet who wandered in the valley, singing about the unity of all mankind, purifying, and preparing herself for her union with God. It seems whenever people saw the mystic Lal Ded, all that was revealed to them was their own shame and nakedness, while she sang songs which covered the souls of multitude that followed her with a permanent indigo dye.

Her (Lalla) stomach had grown immense from the child that she was carrying. She picked herself up, tended her bruised knees and then to the infant at her breast, and she tolerated. The little creature looked up at her adoringly and held her finger tight, and she held onto him and closes the door behind him. The mother's blood has turned and cherished him beyond her dreams. She grew old in her husband's house, making herself useful as a maid to her husband and his concubine. She brought up her only child, and together they watched her husband and her concubine die of the same disease.

Now the son is marriageable, and his mother has her pride. She finds a girl for her son. Once the bride, another woman's child, another young woman, has entered their house she must be fed, which is bad enough, but to nurture a sorceress? She watches her son at night as he follows his wife into his bedroom and closes the door behind him. The mother's blood has turned to venom, she cannot hold it within her. The girl should be returned to her parents.

The old woman should make sure that her son is not suffering from disease of nerves. Her son allows her to physically enter their living quarters, creeping into the door at night and hiding behind the trunks of silver, silk, Pashmina and other valuables, the girl has brought as dowry. The daughter in law is the only daughter of a great sage, and he has given her everything.

"I knew her father had a lot to hide when I saw the trunks she brought," She had told her son. The old woman slides in behind the trunks and hides there.

When all is quiet and son pretends to sleep the bride gets up from the bed, opens her hair, and shaking it loose, lets it fall around her shoulders as he sits on the floor in the middle of the room. Her eyes are closed as he weaves her legs intricately. Very steadily a small circle of fire emanates from her head until a full column of flames shoots straight up from her head to the ceiling and through it upward to the heavens. The flames are of blinding white brilliance, but nothing catches fire as the column sweeps upwards.

The mother-in-law, preoccupied all her life with only her own anatomical constrictions, and denials, is blinded by what she has seen. She holds her hand to the wall; she has turned to stone, as it were. She comes to slowly, but her brain is feverish now, the ideal place destruction to germinate. The fire that has started there will burn everything down.

She tells herself," My son is a naïve and practices no such medications or austerities. He cannot stand up to this level of magic. She is not the proper wife for him. What shall I do, what shall I do now to protect him, is it too late?" She sits down in helplessness; something must be done."

Next morning, still muttering under her breath, angry and sightless, armed with the necessary incomprehension she suspiciously makes sarcastic remarks to the young woman. She hopes to provoke an outburst that will justify her actions. The son shrinks and trembles in a corner of the kitchen.

"The marriage was mother's idea," he says to himself. "So, let her deal with it."

Their relatives' sense that something is wrong and come in like predators sniffing a fresh kill, ready to tear the carcass apart still further.

The young woman is unperturbed. When she walks it looks as if there is an inch of space between her feet and the ground. She is serene in the face of all ignorance around her, nothing else except God and her karma exist for her; it is as if she cannot hear or see anything else.

The next she is gone.

The son looks for the light she used to leave behind, but his room is dark now, and empty. The room has become a space enclosed by walls; it is not even a place anymore. He knows then that he has heard her, but he has not listened; he has looked at her, but he has not seen her. He cries like a child, but his head is small, and his mind has been nailed down too soon in his life and it cannot fly.

His mother consoles him. She says, "A man's heart is like a bird, it wants to sing on every branch. There are other branches, keep your heart within you."

The son looks at his mother vacantly. He does not tell her that his entire being has flown away and all she is looking at is his body. When he looks at his mother that is all he can see as well.

The old woman has scattered everything to the winds. The young woman has broken every tradition and returned to her father, who is her spiritual mentor as well. When he sent his daughter out in the world, he had mixed oil and water, thinking he is just a father, and she is just a daughter. Now she has come back to him to resume her meditations, purified of anything that might weigh her down.

The husband tosses and turns in his bed and looks out at the sky, which stays outside. He awakes with cold sweats at night and feels as though he is permanently in a cold hard desert. He refuses to come out of his room. In desperation his mother pleads with him and together they go to the girls' father's house to bring her back. But at her father's door they are told it is too late, and they are returned away.

The mother and son return to their home and live the rest of dying lives in the blindness with which they covered their eyes.

15. One day Lal Ded came to the temple where Siddha Shrikantha, her guru, was engaged in worship and prayers. He saw her and asked what she wanted. She replied that she had come to the temple for privacy, to ease herself. He had her out at once to a spot some distance away. But Lalla began to dig there and unearthed some idols. Wherever the guru took her, she unearthed idols, to his amazement. This legend was interpreted by the chronicler Pir Ghulam Hasan to mean that her aim was to show that God is everywhere hence no place is more sacred than any other. This was to the utter amazement of her guru.

16. Most of the time Lal Ded would remain aloof. When Lalla went to fetch water from the river each morning, she used to meditate at a quiet spot away from home. She used to be scolded for loitering and was even accused of disloyalty to her husband. It is possible that her husband was already angered by her sexual coldness towards him.

There is a saying ascribed to her, viz.

Na zayas ta na pyayas, na kheyam hand na shonth

("I did not become pregnant or give birth, nor did I eat the food given to a pregnant woman.")

However, the truth was soon found out, and what was suspected to be a secret assignment turned out to be her daily meeting with God on whom she used to meditate at a quiet spot away from her home. She unusually would get up early in the morning and go on her daily chore of fetching water from the nearby river. The legend has it that she used to cross the river, of course, without her feet dipping into the water to the shrine of Nata Keshava Bhairava at the ghat of Zinypor village. Here she held her daily communication with God. Once, when after her meditation as usual, she quietly entered the compound of her house with the pitcher of water on her head, her husband in his rage at her conduct struck the pitcher of water on her head with a stick. The earthen pot broke into pieces but the water in it stood frozen on her head till she filled all pots in the kitchen.

This incident seems to have betrayed her. Her miraculous powers became known, her fame spread, and crowds of visitors came for her darshan. It was time she left her home. This she now did, in utter disregard of her personal appearance.

There is a pushy legend that when Lal Ded left her husband's home, she wandered naked, dancing and singing in ecstatic frenzy. She did not care about her personal appearance because she was convinced that the true self was the spirit within: The Guru gave me but one teaching.
"From without withdraw your gaze within,
And fix it on the innermost Self."
I, Lalla, took to heart this one precept,
And, therefore naked I began to dance.
It is also said that Lal's guru acknowledged that she had outstripped him in meditation.
Based on her vakh:
Gurun vonnum kunoi vachun
Nebreh dopnum ander achun
Sui gov Lali vakh te vochun
Towai hotum nangai nachun
The legend has grown and become persistent that she wandered naked, dancing and singing in ecstatic passion.

17. Pandit Anand Kaul relates that sometimes Mir Sayyid Ali Hamadani, Lal Ded and Nund Rishi would meet to converse on spiritual subjects. He gives instances of their playing at the game of blind man's bluff; at making predictions of what a gathering would bring. And, even at showing off their occult powers- all these to the advantage of Lal Ded.

18. There is a legend associated with her mahasamadhi, getting freed from the mortal coil of her body, and getting blissfully merged with that which shall last forever-the Infinite Soul, Lalla's Siva. When claimed by both the Hindus and the Muslims alike, Lalla performed a postmortem miracle. There arose a flame of light from her dead body and without anyone realizing what was happening, it vanished into the void.
"Shoonyas shoonyaa meelith gav".
Grierson notes Lal Ded's fondness for the expression 'Shoonyas shoonyaa meelith gav' (Shunya becomes merged with Shunya).

Death

Lalleshwari lived a life of purity guided by the discipline of the doctrine and principles of yogic philosophy. With passage of time, her experiences matured, knowledge deepened, and she got transformed into a careful and a cautious yogini of the highest order. During her lifetime Lalleshwari became the supreme mistress of Yoga.

Towards the late seventies or eighties of the fourteenth Century A. D. Lalleshwari is said to have gone to Bijbehara town in Anantnag district in South Kashmir. A dispute is said to have arisen between the Hindus and the Muslims, the former wanting to cremate the body according to Hindu rites whereas the latter wanted to bury it according to the Muslim code. Appreciating the sentiments, the spirit of the yogini is said to have asked those present to bring two large washbasins. The body is said to have sat inside one and inverted the other over her head. Thereafter the body is stated to have shrunk slowly till the two washbasins overlapped.

It is there that her soul is said to have left her physical body to merge into the Supreme Soul. When she gave up her soul, it buoyed up like a flame of light in the air and then disappeared.

After some time, those present are said to have ventured to remove the upper washbasin. They found there nothing but a liquid formation. Half of the liquid is said to have been taken by the Hindus for cremation and the other half by the Muslims for burial adjacent to the local Jama Masjid.

The Hindus called her Lalleshwari and the Muslims Lalla Arifa. But both called her Lal DED (Grandmother or Grandma). The exact date of her death is not known. According to Noor Namas and Rishi Namas she died around 1377 A.D. during the reign of sultan Shihab –ud-Din. Lalleshwari did not preach any religion, she even ignored ritual. She projected a way of life quite in harmony without cultural traditions. So, Lal lived on as a wandering ascetic absorbed in God consciousness seeking and seeing God everywhere (Shiv tsorun thali thale). She seems to have been unmindful of Hindu caste taboos regarding food and drink (*anas khyanas kya chum dvesh*); she disregarded the ceremonial pieties and outward observance. She hated meat, unlike the Brahmins of Kashmir; and unlike both Hindus and Muslims, spoke vehemently against the killing of innocent sheep even as a sacrifice to the Deity.

Lal Ded passed away, leaving a shadow behind. It is a matter of surprise that no monument to this saintly figure has been erected to mark the place where her body was cremated or laid to rest.

Maryam na kanh ta mara na kansi
Mara nich ta lasa nich

Alike for me is life and death; Happy to live, happy to die, I mourn for none, none mourns for me. Lalla reminds us of Raza hams: Royal swan who is supposed to sing melodiously at the point of his death. Drawing an analogy - You were as intelligent as the Royal Swan. How is it? You have turned mute now. O! Someone has robbed you of something within. How is it? All the organs of body have ceased to function. The brain itself has ceased to respond to the impulses of mind. Now nothing can be swallowed, so choking has come about. Ah! The essence of life 'the soul' has gone off unnoticed. Like the grinding stone mill stopping and the grains choked and the miller running away with the grains unnoticed.

Thus Lal-Ded explains when the end of life comes about the soul departs along with the accumulated fruit of action (Karma) and is drawn to such a state which is suitable to it.

Vakhs

The vakhs of Lal Ded have come down to us through oral tradition. The vakhs that are available have not been arranged in any clear-cut basis. Lal Ded was neither a preacher nor a reformer. She did not have disciples. Her influence pervaded all state of Kashmiri life. She did not create a movement. Her vakhs became part of oral lore traversing families, generations, even religions.

Her poems (called vakhs) or Lal Vakhs have been translated by many renowned persons. Some of them are as follows:

1. Pt. Baskar Razdan 18th Century

Lal Ded's vakhs were translated in Sanskrit for the first time in 18th century, by Pt. Baskar Razdan of Kashmir. It is the first book on Lal Vakhs. It was written in Sharda script. This Sanskrit book of Lal vakhs became the bed rock for the western Indologists to understand the inner spirit of Lalleshwari. She expressed her experiences in her native language 'Kashmiri'.

Lal Ded has played a significant role as the maker of Kashmiri language and literature. Though Kashmiri has had a much longer history, and Kalhana records what is said to be "the earliest specimen "of Kashmiri, yet we can find good reason to admire Lal Ded as the originator or the founder of modern Kashmiri. Her poetry is modern because it comes to us alive even today. Indeed, she helped Kashmiris to discover our mother tongue. Before her, Kashmiri verse was written to assist the memory. It was a sort of pattern of letters, ideas, or associations which assists in remembering something like a device, such as a formula or rhyme, used as an aid in remembering and memorizing mysterious doctrine. But, in Lal Ded's vakh it is used to express aspiration and experience, thought, and feeling. She opened new channels of communication between the common people themselves. Lal Ded's Kashmiri poetry she has an extraordinary force of originality.

2. Pt. Makand Ram Shastri (1914)

Lal Ded's sayings were written one more time in 1914 by Pt. Makand Ram Shastri from the oral speech of Dharmdas Darvesh of Handwara.

3. Sir George A. Grierson 1920.

When Pt. Makand Ram Shastri prepared the manuscript, he passed them on to Sir George A. Grierson who published the vakhs as Vakyani in 1920. "LAL" used to out-pour her soul in rhythmic notes which formed the first poetic composition of Kashmiri poetry celled VAKH. These were first edited by Sir George A. Grierson. Both Muslims and Pandits have a reverence for memory of "Lal Ded" in their hearts.

4. Sir Richard Temple (1924)

In 1924 Sir Richard Temple published "The Word of Lal - the Prophetess", rendering these sayings of Lal Ded into English. He also explained her philosophy. In his voluminous work 'The Word of Lalla' Sir Richard Temple bafflingly characterizes her as Shaiva-Yogini based on contents of her vakhs which he has admirably translated into the idiom of English. Lalla Ded's Vakhs form is that she was a yogini of the highest order. Being Shaivite to the core she had deeply penetrated the spiritual imagination of Kashmiris as a Shaiva-yogini. In the words of Sir Richard Temple, Lal Ded's poetry is 'aflame with the red fire of a thought that burns.' She did not compose her vakhs as a deliberate contribution to literature or philosophy; she did not sing them nor write them for devotional singing. Her vakhs were short and an outburst of her life.

5. Prof B.N. Parimu- in his monumental studies on Lalla Ded clearly calls her the forerunner of the Bhakti Movement in India. As yoga and Bhakti are not mutually contradictory to each other, Lalla carefully practiced Bhakti yoga.

6. Prof. Jayalal Kaul says: "Lal Ded enriched the thought and literature of Kashmir and the Kashmiri poetry. "His book on Lal Ded contains 224 vakhs. Prof. Jia Lal Kaul has sorted out the vakhs of Lal Ded from the works of Grierson & Anand Koul +Wanchoo's works +Parimoo's works on Lal Ded.

7. Pandit Anand Koul Bamzai wrote "Lalla Yogeshwari: Her Life and Sayings", adding 75 more vakhs (sayings) to the list. Lal Ded found the Supreme Light in her own soul. She realized that the Supreme Self (God) and-her own soul was one. One can trace out the ascent of her own self to the Supreme self from her own verses'.

Sheila Trisal wrote Life sketch of Lalla Yogeshwari. Many of the vakhs have been collected and published by Dr. Grierson, Dr. Barnett, Sir

Richard Temple and Pandit Anand Koul and apart from the consideration that they explain the Saiva philosophy of Kashmir.

Lal Ded's Vakh are mainly the outpourings of her soul. Her Vakhs are an expression of her inner experience. The Vakh is mostly a four-line stanza, complete and independent in itself, a few are put in form of questions and answers. Each line of Lal Ded's Vakh completes the sense and has completeness and gives the Vakh the edge of a proverb. Lal Ded's vakhs put together make her biography, the biography of a saint. The vakhs tell her spiritual life story, her philosophy, and her outlook of life. Her vakhs give a clear message to mankind. Lalla was a yogini. She straddled yoga and tantra, Kashmiri Shaivism, and the solo 'Soul'. Her verses taught universal brotherhood and oneness of God. Her vakhs had jugglery of words.

Lal Ded's vakhs are remarkable for clarity and coherence, depth of thought. Sometimes her vakhs are cryptic, embodying rare spiritual experiences, rather than like the devotional songs. She lived the truth she found for herself and made no compromise with convention or custom. That is why her influence has been durable and widespread. Lal's poems are charged with an overjoyed devotion. The idiomatic power of Lalla's mind in her poems is glorious manifestos of clarification. There are many instances where Lal Ded speaks of energy, the expressiveness, of phrase and metaphor charged with memorable associations. This is also with the imagery drawn naturally from the familiar surroundings of the countryside. The ferry across the river, the creaky bridges on the causeway, the bloom of a cotton flower, the kailyard, the saffron field, Water, snow and ice, the washer man striking clothes on the washing stone, the mulling of puttoo (woolen cloth) tweed in the big stone mortar with fuller's earth, shepherds and their flock, the sowing and the harvesting, the tawny bullock, the goldsmith's refining of gold using crucible and chemicals etc.

Lal Ded did not establish any cult or sect. Her predecessors had contributed to the great Shiva philosophy and remained limited within a small cult. Lalleshwari was a thought-provoking saint-poetess and a profound Shaivite philosopher. She was a deep thinker, creative artist, and the builder of the Kashmiri language. She has been and continues to be an unmatched sage, seer, sadakh par excellence.

Lal Ded lived and wandered as an ascetic. She had been seeking and seeing God everywhere. Many remember Lal Ded as a saint. She was a seer in the literal sense of the word and laid great stress upon direct seeing and experience. Her devotees heard the vakhs memorized them and circulated them by word of mouth to those who were fellow seekers. With passage of time language changed and many words became difficult to understand.

The Vakhs of Lal Ded convey Yoga philosophy and Saivism. They are open and of high thought and spiritual truth. Most of the vakhs are precise, appropriate, and sweet. Some of Her vakhs are difficult to understand as the language has undergone so many changes. Her vakhs are relevant not only for the Kashmiri culture but also for the entire human civilization. Her each Vakh is now being analyzed by literary world at the national and global level so that the same can be utilized for the betterment of society. It is astonishing that what Lal Ded had said 700 years ago looks innovative even today. The vakhs of Lal Ded had a charismatic power to impact her listeners that people heard her and formed her sayings into chants and verses which continue to be sung even today.

SM1. Aaguruyee Ratak Saari Saari Tarakh

Aaguruyee ratak saari saari tarakh
Ad kow moodo pathak zanh
Aaguras ander shiv ta shakhtee woochak
Woochak ta heichak tasund naav

Aaguruyee=source. ratak=clasp, grip, hold; saari saari tarak=cautiously tread the path; ad.kow = then; moodo=unaware, ignorant; pathak = drown; zanh=never ever; aagurus ander = at source; shiv ta shakhtee woochak= you will see shiv and shakhtee; heichak tasund naav = you will learn more about Lord's grace.

In totality, Lalla says that she has observed all that is pure and shinning. She wants all the people of vision and stature to go to the source of 'purity and love.' She wants the spirit of man to soar to the new heights. She cautions to move with care to avoid dangerous routes of big black holes and deep fissures, which cannot be seen by ordinary eyes. She urges all men of faith, to see the Lord Along with His consort 'Shakti ' mingled up together, two bodies and one soul. To learn more and more about Lord's grace, she desires those men should widen the understanding of knowledge.

SM2. Aaguryei Grazum

Aaguryei grazum
Woogwaani dour sogum
Orkai karapaayi zagat woozum
Yore ti kenh mai sorroom no

Aaguryei grazum= I was blessed eternally, so the inspiration came to me directly from the source of divinity; Woogwaani dour sogum= I didn't make any personal efforts to seek for the water for the field of my devotion; Orkai karapaayi zagat woozum= the water of realization came of its own to quench my thirst. It was only with the grace of my Lord that I was able to create such a wide influence among my people; Yore ti kenh mai sorroom no= I didn't myself contribute even a bit in this direction.

Lal Ded was overjoyed over the victory of her soul. Some great thoughts smashed her mind. As she was drunk to her fill with the glories of the Lord, she expressed her thought, through brilliant words. She says, "I roared at the source of the Bliss. I quenched my thirst with the Nectar of His making. I visualized the universe of my own thoughts. To mingle with the infinite, it was all His benign grace. All the Truth has emanated from Him and none of my individual efforts has helped me to gain access to that high state of divine consciousness. It is His blessings alone have helped me.

Lalleshwari was a mystic. She had a glorious past life with rich Karmas. Here in this Vakh she makes assertions of her personal divine attributes saying she didn't need make any vigorous efforts to achieve goals. She had come to this world with enough divine support of her past Karma to make fast strides in her celestial development. Here it's clear that her development was already complete in her previous life and that she had taken this life only with a special mission which she performed with all success.

SM3. Aami Pana Sodras Naavi Chhas Lamaan

Aami pana sodras naavi chhas lamaan
Kati bozi daie myon meti diyi taar
Aamen taakyan ponyi zan shemaan
Zuv chhum bramaan ghar gatchhaha

Aami Pana= untwisted thread; Sodras=the sea of life, which is difficult to cross after death; Naavi Chhas Lamaan= tow I, my boat; Kati Bozi = Will hear; Dyii=God; Meone=mine; Meti=to me; Deyee Taar=carry across; Aamen= unbaked; Takyan= clay plates; Poien=water; Zan Shaman=gets lost; Zuw=soul; Chhum Bramaan= has a temptation to merge; Ghar Gachh Ha= unite with His Divine grace.

Often Lal's vakhs point to what she observed in her real life around her. There are some vakhs which convey the state of her mind when she has a deep sense of sadness and solitude. It seems she had developed a harsh sense of emptiness within her and in the world about her.

With a loose spun (raw) thread I (Lalla) am towing my boat upon the sea; would my God hear my prayer and sail me safe across. She feels alone, towing her boat upon the sea with a rope of untwisted thread; she is towing the boat of her life with a loose thread in the open sea. Oh! She wishes the God Almighty would hear her prayer to help her safe across. Her efforts are like water in the plates of unbaked clay, whirling and wasting, her dizzy soul. The unbaked pots melt away. They leak when water is poured in. She has a temptation to merge with His Divine grace. Would God grant her to reach her home!

SM4. Aanchari Bichari Vechar Wonoon

Aanchari bichari vechar wonoon
Pran ta ruhan haieve maa
Pranas buzith mazza chahoon
Nadir chui tai haiew maa

Aanchari Bichari= blessed lady of Anchar lake; Vechar= expression to a new idea; Wonoon=said; Praan=Onion, allegorically the exhale and inhale; Ruhoon=Garlic allegorically soul, or Rooh; Haieve Maa=may you buy; Pranas Buzith Mazza Chahoon= The intake of momentary pleasures of the world like "Nadir' the stem of Lotus flower is quite different to Roohn or sense of experiencing the existence of soul.

No wonder, the blessed lady of Anchar lake has given expression to a new idea, that is if there is anybody who likes to purchase 'Onion' and 'Garlic' vegetables bitter is taste but with enough food value, quite opposite to Nadir stem of lotus flower since Lal-Ded is referring to onion and garlic that is symbolically, majestic soul and exhale and inhale of breath. As such she wants to enjoy the delight and pleasure of her mind and experiencing the thrill of her final merger with the celestial waves of cosmos with the inhale and exhale of breath, by virtue of which one observes the pure existence, pure consciousness, and pure thought. The intake of momentary pleasures of the world like "Nadir' the stem of Lotus flower is quite different to *Roohn* or sense of experiencing the existence of soul.

SM5. Anchaar Hanzani Hund Gyome Kanan

Anchaar hanzani hund gyome kanan
Nadir chiv tai haieev maa
Tee booz trukaiv tim rood vanan
Chainun choi tai cheeniv maa

Anchaar=a Lake in Kashmir; Hanzani=a boat lady; Hund Gyome Kanan=heard a loud call, kan means ear; Nadir= a vegetable that grows in a lake, lotus stem; Chiv=are in my possession; Tai Haieev Maa=may you buy; Tee=that; Booz=heard; Trukaiv=intelligent people; Tim=they; Rood Vanan= wise continued saying; Chainun Cho Tai Cheeniv Maa =may feel if you like to.

(Lalleshwari was a wonderful artist capable of creating situations far above human notion. Another meaning of 'wanan' is forest, but this meaning does not appear to fit here).

One Day Lal Ded heard the loud call of the Boat woman of Anchar Lake. In her call she was addressing if there was anybody who wanted to purchase the 'Nadir', stem of Lotus flower. Nadur is a vegetable delicious in taste and grows in a lake. The neighbours, intelligent ones, on listening to the cry, got a different notion. E.g., is there anybody who wants to purchase momentary pleasures of the world. The very thought widened their limited understanding. As such, they thought for acquiring peace and contentment, so this whim produced in them a longing, for renunciation, right thought, and right tranquility.

SM6. Aarus Nerineh Modur Sheerai

Aarus nerineh modur sheerai
Ner veerus nerineh shuriya naav
Moorkhas paznun chui hastis kashoun
Yes, ha mali daandas beh chaav!

Aarus=plums and peach fruits of Rosaceae family of drupe- 'fruits' in the genus prunus; modur =sweet; moorkhas=a dud, duffer; paznun=futile to teach; Hastis kashoun= scratching an elephant. Daandas=bull; beh chaav=determined in an obstinate or unthinking way.

Lal Ded tries to explain that it is difficult to deal with a person who is headstrong. Such people point where they are foolishly or irrationally stubborn; obstinately opinionated, especially in refusing to consider alternatives. Basically, they are hard to work with because they believe they have all the answers, regardless of the facts or opinions. Giving an example of an elephant, who, when scratched feels unaffected. It is hard to convince a fool.

SM7. Aasa Bol Padenam Saasa

Aasa bol padenam saasa
Mey mani vasa kheedna hiyae
Bu yod sahaz shanker bakt aasaa
Mokris saasa mal kya peyye

Aasa bol padenam saasa=to mock and call names; mey=I, me; Bu=me, I; yod=if; sahaz= true; Shanker bhakaz= devotee of Shiva, Shanker; mal= dirt.

Let them mock at me and call me names. If a true devotee of Siva I am, I shall not feel distressed or hurt, because a few ashes cannot make a mirror dirty, the ashes can serve rather as polish.

SM8. Aasas Kuni Sapdas Saithaa

Aasas kuni sapdas saithaa
Nazdeek aasith gyas dour
Zahir batin kunuy deenthum
Gaam khait chait chowanzah choor

Aases kuni=I was the only child; spades saithaa=I got association with lots of people; nazdeek aasith=I was nearer to tha Lord in my childhood;gyas dour= with advancing age I gradually distanced from my Lord's grace;Zahir batin kunny deunthum= with my advancement in spiritual awakening I began seeing Him unique and alone within and without what touched me above all was his simplicity, His beautiful generous unconcern for everything in the Universe; Gaaem khaith chaith chuvanzah chour= the negative influences of human animal instincts, 54 in all.

I was born, as the only child of my parents and gradually spread up to become one with all, I developed a consciousness that gave me dignity and assurance I was surprised to find myself spread up far and wide I was fairly intoxicated with joy, as I saw Him unique and alone within and without what touched me above all was his simplicity, His beautiful generous unconcern for everything in the Universe.

I grieve over the indecision of my mind. It betrays me in keeping my concentration tight in the moments I enjoy the thoughtless state of my mind. This is due to fifty-four thieves which are eating me up within. Fifty-four thieves are the bad instincts, which have gained entrance in our body, i.e. (1) Lust; (2) Greed; (3) Anger; (4) Attachment; (5) Conceit; (6) Ego; (7) Wisdom plus five senses; plus, five organs; plus, mind of the body =18 multiplied by the common factor (i) purity (Satu gun), (ii) Activity (Raju gun), (iii) Inertia (Tams gun) in the body: Total $18 \times 3 = 54$

The purpose of unfolding her personal experience is essentially to make the seeker aware about the hurdles in the path of all spiritual development as the enemies here are none but those who are the part of one's earthly existence.

SM9. Aasi Pondaiiy Zamaiy Zoasi

Aasi pondaiiy zamaiy zoasi
Netee karayei snaan tirthan.
Vohare vhariyas nonuy aasee,
Nishi chuy ta paraz naav tan.

Aasi pondaiiy= laughing and sneezing; zamaiy zoasi = coughing, yawning; Netee=regularly; karayei snaan tirthan= bathing in sacred springs; Vohare vhariyas=throughout the year; nonuy aassee= going about unclothed, He is to be seen in all these activities all the year round. He is close to you as yourself; Nishi chuy ta= He is about you all the time; paraz naav tan=recognize Him.

Shiva is by our side. Shiva is not away from us. Spiritual life is to live like the lotus petal amidst water. Only a man of realization feels that Shiva is abiding in the human consciousness. In the happiness of His bewitching presence, I am mad for joy. I am laughing, sneezing, coughing, and yawning in sheer freedom of joy. I come to the spring of Love, for a daily bath, as if I am on a pilgrimage. Now, I am going about quite naked, and unclothed in His grace, throughout the year. He is within me, yet He is beyond my recognition. Vedas say: The River is an object of veneration. A Tirtha is associated with river, the water resource. Here, '*Vohare vhariyas nonuy aasee*' means remaining vivid in all manifestations, keeping nothing hidden. So is Shiva, everywhere.

SM10. Aasi Aes Ta Asii Aasav

Assi aes ta asii aasav
Assee dore kari path wath
Shivas sori na zyon ta marun
Ravas sori na atgath

Assi aes= we had an existence in the past; assee aasav = in time future, we shall be; Assee Dore Kari path wath= throughout the ages, we have been; Shivas sori Na zuen ta marun= Forever Siva creates, dissolves, and creates again; Ravas=the sun; atgath= sun rises and sets, coming and going; Ravas sori Na atgath= forever the sun rises and sets; atgath=coming and going, the immortal soul shuttles between life and death; It's we who came and went through the aeons. Shiva must create and destroy perpetually, Forever the sun must rise and set.)

Lal-Ded says: We had an existence in the past. We shall survive in the future too. Each moment of our life is a debt. We have existed throughout the ages in various creative forms: Then dissolve and are reborn again and again. Both the spiritual and physical powers of man are divine. It is in man's own hands to attain his Goal of righteousness, and then only one comes nearer and nearer to God.

The sun continues to rise, and the sun continues to set- for all times to come.

Here it refers to the idea when the individual self is lost; the universal self in found. Likewise, the sun moves from west to east and again from east to west and then at one time sun dies and night comes and then at another moment it is born again and again.
Here she means to say that the same people who lived in the past and would repeat their existence in the future too because they fail in their essential purpose again and again and are sent back repeatedly. Thus, there is no end to this cycle of birth and death.

This fact equates equally to the rising and setting of Sun which has been nourishing all existence unendingly and without fail. This coming and going endlessly seems to be obviously of no practical purpose except the great display of the Lord's big game or Maya and the human being an important element of this whole drama of life. Lalleshwari wants to awaken man to the real purpose of life instead of wasting this rare opportunity. Shiva, the universal Lord too has been creating and destroying numerous forms since time immemorial without a fault as the Sun has been setting and rising continuously.

SM11. Aatali Paatali Kogam Teelith, Ye guura

Aatali paatali kogam teelith
Ye guraa ti guraa agoor akhand
Aaseen gajra taseen kajra
Rahadha bakhta, tum kone baba chal
Aagura rakhai bangalai par
Changa gadaa barkhaa, tum lab ja, ja ja

Aatali paatali= in the space; kogam= an ordinary creature; teelith= wander.

I wandered, through the space, as an ordinary creature of this world without any delusion. Oh Lo! I saw the grace of the Lord, mingled up with the grace of my Guru (Master) with all magnificence. This was the fusion of two great souls, without any duality or discord. O! I have become part of their eminence. I seem to be a stranger to myself. My attainment is due to my infinite faith and detached love, like that of the legendary love of "Rhada" for "Lord Krishna." So, no one should object to my moves, for I am a free Soul to wander anywhere to seek His benign grace I see my master at the top of my head or Sahasraras. Lalla talks of release of hormones that reduced her to nothingness and thus she mingled with the nothings of the Cosmos. She tells the blessed ones to arise awake and go for finding the bliss of Super Consciousness that she has met with.

SM12. Aatheim Ta Shee-Thiem Mai-Ti Havtam

Aatheim ta shee-thiem mai-ti havtam
Gyan kathan chuie manook soz
Kenchan chuie nar ta narolliiye prantam
Saadas yech chui ati mo roze

Aatheim ta shee-thiem mai-ti havtam=O Lord! I have failed to understand my uneasiness about knowing the truth; Gyan kathan chuie manook soz=some unseen force is attracting me towards you. Kenchan chuie nar ta narolliiye prantam=some attain thoughtless state of mind and live always in communion with the Lord and His grace. Saadas yech chui ati mo roze=some people pose as saints who are like dreadful ghosts and haunt people every now nad then, their company should be avoided.

Some invisible lines of forces are attracting me towards your grace. I want to merge with your perfection. Bless me with mystic truths. Widen my limited knowledge. Listening to discourses and pious thoughts bring unheard music and immense peace. Some blessed ones have become the (incarnation) living form of the divine spirit. They are realized souls. They live always in unity with the Lord and His grace. Some pose as saints. They are like dreadful ghosts. They haunt people every now and then. Their company be avoided.

SM13. Aayas Ti Suidooye Gach Ti Suidooye

Aayas ti suidooye gach ti suidooye
Saidis hole mai kareim kyah
Bo tas assas aguriiy veduyei
Vedis ta vendas kareim kyah

Aayas ti suidooye= I was born a pure soul; gach ti suidooye= straight I shall return; Saidis hole mai kareim kyah= how would the divine justice harm a sinless soul like me, how can the crooked lead me astray?; Bo assas tas aguriiy veduyei= her simple sinless life with the help of good past karmas earned her the awakening of self, Agarai veyzay =known from beginning; Vedis ta Vendas kareim kyah= her going back too would be smooth without any burdens whatsoever, He knows me from the beginning of time, and loves me. She adds further that that her smooth travel through this hectic life was the outcome of her being already highly liberated with enough awakening of self.

I was born like a rose. It will ever bloom and shall leave this world like a Yogi. I lived a simple poverty-stricken life. Surely, no harm can come to me: He knows me from the beginning of time and loves me. There is nothing that a crooked man can do to me. I killed my ego and vanity. For me there is nothing in this world that has any value in it. There is nothing that can change the course of my life, for I am indifferent to both lowliness and greatness. I was conscious of His eminent presence from the very beginning of my life, as such my safety and realization are guaranteed from moment to moment from one of sheer ecstasy to another of acute depression. I know Him well. He lives within the core of my heart. There is nothing that can wean me away from Him.

SM14. Aayas watey Gayas Naa watey

Aayas watey gayas naa watey
Semanz svathi lusum doh
Vuchum chandas haar na atey
Ath naavi taaras dim kayah buh

Aayas=I came; watey=by the highway; gayas=returned; naa=not; svath=Setu, the embankment, Semanz svathi lusum doh=I was caught in the mid-way, I could not complete my journey, to reach the goal and see the Divine, I could not cover the distance of Svath;Vuchum=I saw; Chandas=pocket; Har= penny, a cowrie, Har has second meaning also that is Hari (Shiv); Nav=boat; Taras=to cross, what to ferryman?' Naavi- Taar'=my journey to Divine awareness could not be completed within that designated hour. Since I had to reach, the other alternative was of the naavi taar that is taking help of the boatman to carry me across. Hence the state of helplessness was felt by Lal Ded. Buh=me.

By the highway I came, by the highway I return not; searching the pockets, not a penny there, what to pay the ferryman to take across. I was born to travel along the road of righteousness. But to my bad luck could not go through it in the right manner. I am held up in the halfway on the embankment of life's stream. The day has passed, and the darkness has spread. I can't see anything beyond. I find myself lost. I must cross life's river, what shall I pay to boatman? I am with empty pockets. For, the good actions done in this world are the only coins accepted by the Boatman to carry across. As I have earned nothing of that sort, so with empty pocket, I weep for joy. O' Lord! How will I go across!

Lal Ded feels helpless and lonely, like one who, when the day is done and the light fails, finds herself on a ramp with shaky bridges, and a long way to go and her pockets empty, not a cowrie to pay the ferryman to take her across the board river. This she has expressed in the following Vakh:

SM15. Anderiy Aayas Chandry Gaaran

Anderiy aayas chandry gaaran
Garaan aayes hehyan hee,
Paanai vuchhum bihith dukanas,
Paanai panas atha daaran,
Chei hai naaran chei hai maaran
Chei hai naaran yim kamo veih

Andariy aayas= I searched within; chandrie=moon; chandrie gaaran=like Mystic Moon; Gaaraan aayas heiyan hee= for like seeks out the like, Thou art all this and this and this; Chei=thou;Chei Naaraan= there is none else but Thee Narayana; chei maaraan= form of 'Shiva', as a 'destroyer'; chei ath- daaraan= I now see you as a 'beggar' asking Humbly for charitable relief;yim kam veih= What then is the meaning of Thy sport, Of Thy creation's wondrous forms.

I searched within, I saw my Lord as the owner of a big shop, then I saw Him begging humbly for a relief, then I saw Him as Lord Narayana, and after a moment I saw Him in the form of Lord Shiva (the destroyer). I recognized the creation's wondrous colours where the supreme being is in various forms.

SM16. Abhyasse Kinee Vekass Phollum

Abhyasse kinee vekass phollum
So-praksh zonum yohoie deh
Prakash dyana mokh yei dorum
Sokhoi boroom koroom tee

Abhyasse=repeated practice; Prakash=light; Prakash dyana mokh yei dorum=my face got a shine of uninterrupted brightness; Sokhoi boroom= I experienced the ecstasy, heaven; koroom tee= merged with God.

I pursued spiritual practice and acquired the means; to gain the knowledge of divine reality, by virtue of which I realized a situation, where persons and nature nestle together in a state of glory. So, I landed in the realm of divine ecstasy. My body became the personification of celestial light, with all pervading visionary gleam. My face got a shine of uninterrupted brightness. I experienced the bliss of understandings of Truth. The passion of God realization set fire to all; I had and thus, illumined my path to merge with the Supreme of Supreme.

SM 16 A Adha Lal bu vatches Prakash Dhaam

Adha Lal bu vatches Prakash Dhaam
Adha Lal mey pravim Param Gath
Vuchhum ta dyonthum Shili Kani Vath
Ba kos Lal ta mey kya naav

Then I Lalla arrived at the illuminated abode,
Then I Lalla attained the absolute state,
Then I realized that it was just a mass of stone before me,
Who am I Lalla and what is my name?

SM17. Abhyassee Sovekaas Lye Vathoo

Abhyassee sovekaas lye vathoo
Gagnas sagun maili sami chrata
Shunya gol ta anamay motai
Yuhoy updesh chui bhatta

Abhyassee= repeated practice; Abhyassee sovekaas lye vathoo= Practice constantly to absorb the manifested; Gagnas=space, Gagnas sagun maili sami chrata (tsrata)= The world of form merges into the void; Shunya gole= the unearthly Void dissolves, Infinite energy is in the Shunya or Akashya; ta anaamai mochai= the indescribable Supreme alone remains; Shunya gole ta anaamai motai= The void dissolves, the One indescribable remains;Yohai updesh chui=this is the Truth to gain; Bhatta= the Kashmiri Pandit (Brahmin) is often so called, Yohai updesh chui bhatta= This is the truth to learn, O Batta!

Self-evolution is the focal point for the human being. Through constant practice, one gets merged with the infinite self. It means that one gets merged with the formless Gagana or Akasha or space. By repeatedly doing spiritual exercises with devotion and zeal, the seeker will feel and enjoy the delight of conversion of his state of body from. He will land in the realm of happiness. From the saguna world, of forms and qualities, he merges in the vastness of the Void. In that state one observes this universe lifted to merge with the Cosmos. The world at large and the vastness of the space have lost its identity. Then the ethereal void dissolves and the insignificant "Supreme" alone remains. This o! Intelligent one! O Bhatta is the Truth to gain. Lal Ded affirms with great authority that this alone is the Upadesha or a well-meaning instruction. Lal Ded with her Yogic experiences wants to share with all those who are close to her thoughts.

SM18. Avistar Pothyan Chhi Ha Mali Paraan

Avistar pothyn chei ha mali paran
Yeth tota paraan 'Raama' panjaras
Gita paraan ti hiitha labaan
Parem Gita ti paran chhes

Avistar=those who read without thinking; Avistar poothen chei ha mali paran=An uninterested person reads on sacred books without end; Yeth tote paran 'Ram' panjras= just a parrot continues reciting Ram, Ram in his cage as taught by his keeper; Gita paran ti heethalaban= he reads only to boast of being a prolific reader of the Holy Scriptures; Parem Gita ti paran chas= admonishes people who only for the sake of gaining a reputation of being prolific readers of scriptures read Gita again and again.

Lalleshwari. In her vakh assails about empty bookish knowledge. The Pandits are churning water, she says, how can they hope to obtain butter from it? They read the Gita as a pretension, just as the parrot repeats the name of Rama in the cage. It makes them only more and more self-conceited. Even after reading it they remain as ignorant as ever. I too have read the Gita and am still reading it.
(Another version) Last two lines change.
>   **Pur pur karan zal du Mandan**
>   **Budeokh timni ahambav**

It is easy to read and to recite. It is hard to practice what one reads. And, reading seeks out the Self within. Lal Ded had spent whole life in reading the holy texts and to understand them. It meant going deep into the meaning of the holy texts. Lalleshwari, it seems had read and learnt enough of Gita by doing the truest Sadhana that helped her achieving the heights of her development. She emphasized that by constant practice, not by books, conviction grew in her heart about God, who is Consciousness-Bliss. Some people read the holy books for hours together, just as a parrot crams 'Ram', not knowing what he is cramming.

SM19. Akooie Omkar Yeli Lye Onum

Akooie omkar yeli lye onum
Vohee korum pananui paan
Shu wath travith sath marg rotum
Teli lal bo vachas prakash sathan

Akooie= single; Omkar= the supreme word 'OM'; yeli= when; lye onum= I tuned with the cosmic consciousness; vohee= red hot coal; panoonai paan= my whole body; shu-wath= bad thoughts; sath-marg= the path of radiance; rotum= attained, acquired; vachas (vatches)= reached; Prakash sathan= the path of radiance.

When I was tuned with the cosmic consciousness and became one with the energy levels of the supreme word 'Omkaar', my whole body blared as red-hot coal. 1 bade goodbye to all the intermittent bad thoughts that otherwise would have come to my mind and betook myself to the path of radiance and gleam, which straightaway landed me to the abode of light or Prakash sthaan.

Prakash sthaan is a place in the higher dimensional space called Hyper Space beyond Milky Way where many suns of the region focus their light to make it or keep it to a state of dazzling light and radiations. It is in the heart of Lagoon-Nebula which lies 5000 (five thousand) light years away in the direction of Constellation Sagittarius. Central Hot Star O-Herschel-36 is the primary Source of radiation.

SM20. Akuy Omkaar Yus Naabi Daray

Akuy Omkaar yus naabi darey
Komboi Brahmaandas sum garay.
Akooie manthir yus chaitas karay,
Tas saas manthir kyaah zan karay.

Akuy=one; Omkaar=AUM; yus=who so ever; naabi dhare=naval constantly beats; Kombooi-Brahmaannddas sum garai= lit, Brahma's egg, the universe, used also of Brahmarandhra in the crown of the head, a bridge between the manipura cakra and brahma-randhra, with Omkaar as the mantra; Akooie manter= by making mind one with this mighty spell 'OM'; chaitas karai=memorizes; Tas saas manter kyaah zan karai= What need has he for a thousand other spells?

A person, who concentrates on the monosyllable AUM at the naval, with Pranayama, retains breath upto the Brahmanda. For him, there is no need to recite the thousand Mantras.

It is said that no mantra is complete without AUM. The practice of the mantra AUM without a Guru is discouraged. A reason; as soon as the letter 'AUM' is uttered, it creates energy levels or celestial wave form in a person. Therefore, he, whose navel constantly beats with these energy levels, created by none other than one 'Omkaar'. AUM echoes and reverberates. Shri Krishna in the Gita says:" I am vibrant Monosyllable in all the sounds. That Monosyllable is AUM."

This AUM builds a bridge or directs a wave form, between his own and cosmic consciousness, by making mind one with this mighty spell. It requires no other spell or mantra than already set forth.

So, what need has he for a thousand other spells. Focus on the MANTRA 'OM' and release the energy levels which become all universal from the centre of the body to the cosmic sky.

SM21. Anaahata Kha-Swaruup Shuunyaalay

Anaahat kha-swaruup shunyalay
Yas nav na varan na guthr na ruup
Aham vimarsha naad-bindu yas voan
Suy diiva ashwavaar peytth cheyddeys (khotus).

Anaahata kha-swaruup shuunyaalay = who is the eternal 'Anaahata; The unimpaired sound, the void of the sky; Yas naav na varan= who has no name'; na guthr na ruup =who has no gotra, nor form; the One with no name nor family nor caste;Aham vimarsha Naada-Binduy yas voan= who is Pure, who is "Naad-Bindu",(Nada representing Shakti and Vindu, Siva) and represents supreme Paramasiva; Just the Self-aware Sound and the Dot eternal; Suy Diiva ashwavaar peytth ceyddeys (khotus)= He is the God who mounts the horse, that God alone will mount this horse.

He who is the eternal 'Anaahata', The ever-unobstructed sound of OM; Whose is the all-permeating (spread through) form of the ghostly sky; Whose dwelling is the vast inspiring Void; Who has no name, caste, gotra, nor form; Who is Pure, Undifferentiated Self-awareness; Who is "Nada-Bindu", the Light and the Sound. And the Dot, mystically represented by the semicircle and the bindu (dot) of the anunasika of the Syllable OM as it is written. The meaning of nada-bindu (Nada representing Shakti and Vindu, Siva) represents the ultimate Supreme, Paramasiva. He is the God who mounts the horse.

O! Blessed Seeker, the gracious Lord has no shape, colour, sound or form. He is beyond time and space, yet He is all pervading. He has no name, no cast, no creed, no colour, nor any form, yet He is the Omnipresent, Omnipotent, and Omniscient and even then, He has neither ego nor any conceit. His form is like a subtle sound or a spark of light, yet He is the Nucleus of everything that exists in the universe. Since, He is the Supreme, amongst the Supremes; He is the Lord to be worshiped, for all times to come.

(Another version) Last line changes: *Soi deev tai archun kas*

SM22. Andariy Aayas Chandrie Gaaraan

Andariy aayas chandrie gaaraan,
Gaaraan aayas heiyan hih.
Chei hai Naaraan chei maaraan,
Chei ath- daaraan, yim kam veih.

Andariy aayas= I searched within; chandrie=moon; chandrie gaaran=like mystic Moon; Gaaraan aayas heiyan hee= for like seeks out the like, Thou art all this and this and this; Chei=thou;Chei Naaraan= there is none else but Thee Narayana; chei maaraan= form of 'Shiva', as a 'destroyer'; chei ath- daaraan= I now see you as a 'beggar' asking Humbly for charitable relief;yim kam veih= What then is the meaning of Thy sport, Of Thy creation's wondrous forms.'Vih'=vih in Kashmiri language stands for different sensations.

I searched within for the Mystic Moon, for like seeks out the 'like', but with, little success. Thou art all this and this and this; there is no one else but Thee. She saw the Narayana, the lord of Lords and after a pause she saw him in the form of 'Shiva', as a 'destroyer' then again, the next moment she saw him as a 'beggar' asking humbly for charitable relief. As such she saw His bewitching presence in all these forms. O! My 'Lord', what is this. Lal-Ded does not murmur against the Lord and 'His' wondrous pastime, nor does she grumble against man. It is fully evident that Lal-Ded recognized the existence of a supreme being in various forms viz. Narayana, 'Shiva', and then in the form of a beggar-asking humbly for a charitable relief. What then is the meaning of Thy sport, Of Thy creation's wondrous forms?

(Another version)

SM23. Ander Aasit Nebar Chondoom

Ander aasit nebar chondoom
Panenyan ragan kornam soath
Dyan kini diiye zagi kewal zonum
Rang gov sangas meelith kheth.

Ander aasit=Lord seated inside; nebar chondoom= I seek Him in the external world; I sought Him outside though my Lord was already seated inside my heart. On this realization I felt joyful and contented. Upon meditating deeper, I felt His non-dual holy presence everywhere and myself becoming one with Him. This celestial meet presented a wonderful scene – a single spark becoming the fire, a single drop, an ocean."

It is a wonder that the Lord is seated in the corners of my breast, yet I seek Him in the external world. There are seats of infinite powers and energy hidden inside of spine, fibers which can be awakened by the process of exhale and inhale. They have an infinite power which has revealed to me, the truth of 'His' existence. That consciousness assured me that other than soul or Atman or 'Lord' nothing exists. As such I enjoy spiritual bliss and freedom from cycles of life and death. Oh, new awakening has kindled my mind and now I live in Truth and in 'His' jocund company. How this all realization has come about, I don't know.

SM24. Atha Ma Baa Traavoon yi Khar Baa

Atha ma baa traavoon yi khar baa
Yuth na lok hanz kong waari khyee
Tati kus baa dari thar baa
Yeti nanis kartal payee

Atha ma baa traavoon=do not let loose; yi khar baa =this donkey, here it means your mind; Yooth Na=lest; look hanz=some other person's; Kong waari khyee= damage others' saffron fields; Tati koos baa=who will there; dari thar baa= none will bear his back to suffer for you, punishment for the damage done; Yeti nanis kartal payee= none will bear his back to suffer sword cuts for you.

Lal Ded says-Never let loose your mind and develops control over your senses, lest you may trespass the beautiful Saffron fields (illusion) of others. Then no one other than you will have to suffer the consequences, may be in the form of sword cuts of severe blows, for the wrong actions undertaken by you.

SM25. Atchan Aai Ta Gatchhun Gatchhey

Atchan aai ta gatchhun gatchhey
Pakun gatchhey dhyen kyo raath
Yorai aai ta torai gatchhun gatchhey
Kenh na ta kenh na ta kenh na ta kyah

Atchhan aay= forever we come; gatchhun gachhey = forever we go; pakun=travel, move; then kyo raath =day and night; yorai=whence; aai=come; torai=there; khen na ta kenh=there is something mysterious that we need to know, nothingness.

From infinite we come and to infinite we must merge. There is surely some energy or force which binds us with eternity. So, where from we have emerged, there we must merge back for 'Energy' can neither be created nor destroyed. As the total quantum of energy and matter is stated to be constant, interestingly Cosmos is known as Universe signifying unity, harmony pattern and the integrated wholeness. So, Lal Ded says, "there is something; "there is something," "energy or force which binds us with eternity," "whole is this, whole is that, take whole from the whole, yet whole remains." This is the mystery that haunts me. Lal Ded feels that we seem to be bound to the ever-recurring wheel of birth and death. The following Vakh explains it. In this Vakh Lal Ded says: Something is there for us to know, a certain mystery here abides, and it cannot all be meaningless. *See the beauty of the Vakh: Note the use of 'gatchhey' modal verb form with MV 'gatchuu' [to go].*

Atchyan aai ta gatchhun gatchhey [should go]
Pakun gatchhey dhyen kyo raath [should walk]
Yorai aai ta torai gatchhun gatchhe [should go]
We have been coming and going for ever, we should move on day and night, from where we come should return to the same, there is surely something mysterious that we need to know.

SM26. Attanech Sun Dith Thavan Mattan

Attanech sunn dith thavan mattan
Loob buchie bolan gyanich kath
Phaet phaet nayran tim kateh vatan
Trukui mali chookh pur kadh kath

Attanech =thereof; sunn dith =having taken stolen goods, booty, swag, pillage; thavan mattan=store it in your own muths, big earthen pots, hide the booty in these vessels; Loob buchie =lust and greed for money; bolan gyanich kath=the deceitful, dishonest and crafty people will speak of knowledge, awareness; Phaet phaet nayran =they make a show off, they make a deliberate or pretentious display of one's abilities or accomplishments; tim kateh vata=how can they gain consciousness; Trukui mali chookh=intelligent you are; pur kadh kath=understand the true path to realization and consciousness.

It has been always difficult to translate some of the vakhs of Lal Ded because of the corruption in the language, what she had said and how they look to us in the present form. However, to me it means Lal Ded wanted to give a caution to recognize a sincere person from a fraudulent person who is simply interested in loot and plunder for his own benefit. Such crafty persons boast of knowledge, and make deliberate and pretentious display of their accomplishments, duping the common folk who follow them. Such people have only lust and greed for money and can never reach their spiritual goals nor can they lead a common man to right consciousness.

SM27. Avtal, Pevtal Kogam Teelith

Avtal, pevtal kogam teelith
Yeli kaar yetee kar, lagi gobind khanda
Yeman gajra timan gao shara
Raadha yo bakhta chet bavit atma

One must know that all pure knowledge is in the Soul which manifests itself when the disturbing elements are annihilated. When the soul is freed from the weight which keeps it down, it rises to the top of the universe.

Lalla says: All that lives must die. To conquer evil, one must live a life of virtue, morality and must arouse the consciousness of the soul. Those who live a life of satisfaction, must strive for peace. She says there is no higher achievement than peace. Let us be pure and spiritually strong. Then automatically the understanding is widened. To develop such a sincerity, one must develop powerful, love and faith. Lalla gives an example of the legendary Love of "Radha" for Her Love "Lord Krishna." Then only imperfection merges with the perfection and the spirit mingles with the infinite.

SM28. Azapa Gayatri Hamsa Hamsa Zapith

Azapa gayatri hamsa hamsa zapith
Aham travith suyi adu rath
Yem trov Aham su ruud paanai
Buh nu aasun chui opdeesh

Azapa gayatri hamsa hamsa zapith=Gayatri is to be invoked with 'Hamsa'; the reversed Soham Mantra. That is 'Ajapa-japa'. It is the constant vibration of AUM, through our breathing system. It is the creative idea of the Absolute. The sound of Aum is the seed force that evolves in all its expansion. Aum is the transparency of the Divine effulgence, the brightness, the luminosity, the radiance of Soham and Hamsah; yemi trov=whosoever shuns; Aham=ego; Aham or ego is to be shunned during constant japa; there should not be any trace of egotism that 'I am the Karta'-the performer but being the instrument of the Divine. Ajapa Gayatri is beyond transmutation. It is verily, AUM In every soul, as reflux of the Divine.

While in meditation, in complete silence and composed manner, filled with divine qualities of love, mercy, purity, justice, knowledge and truth, keep watch over your inhalation and exhalation and its sounds, "SOO" and "HAM", but actually the breath is already doing the SOO-HAM but without any concentration of mind, that is why it is not producing the required effect, both these sounds, SOO-HAM, which are distinctly audible in silence, produce the frequencies, which produce the energy levels of the order of celestial waves. So, in this state where SOO-HAM sound produces divine ecstasy, the evil instinct of conceit or ego, automatically vanishes off. Thoughtless state of mind comes only by renouncing the EGO. This is the directive of truth to the Seeker. It is an existence which flows eternally with peace, freshness, purity, and bliss.

SM29. Aayas Kami Dishi Ta Kami Vatey

Aayas kami dishi ta kami vate
Gatchha kami deyshi kava zaana vath.
Antidaay lagimay tatey,
Channis phokas kanh ti no saath.

Aayas=came; kami dishi=from which direction, from what place or source, from where; kami vate =which way, fall into decay or decline; Gatchha=to go; kava zaana=do not know; vath= way; antidaay=the end of it all; Chanis=empty; phookas=breath.

Whence I have come and by which way, I do not know. Wither I shall go, and, by which way, I also do not know that. Where I to know the end of it all, and gain the knowledge of the truth, (it would be well, for otherwise), Life here is but an empty breath.

SM30. Achun Hu Na Prakash Kunay

Achun hu na prakash kunay
Kothen hu na tirth kanh
Chundus hu na bandav kunay
Khuneh hu na sukh kanh

Achun= eyes; Prakash= light; kunay= nowhere; kothen= knees; tirth= pilgrimage; chundus= pocket; bandav= friend; sukh= comfort.

Sid Mol says: No, light parallels the light of One's eyes; no pilgrimage is there, like the one, on one's knees; no relative's better than one's own pocket, and no comfort is there, like a warm blanket.

In another version it is:
SM 30 A

Moyas hue na prakaash kuney
Zyes hue na tirth kanh
Dhyes hue na baandav kuney
Lye's hue na sokh kanh

There is no light better than that of the universe, there is no pilgrimage better than worship, there is no friend better than God, there is no satisfaction better than devotion.

SM31. Andariy Aayas Chandrie Gaaraan

Andariy aayas chandrie gaaraan,
Gaaraan aayas heiyan hee.
Chei naaraan chei maaraan,
Chei ath- daaraan, yim kam veih.

Andariy= within; aayas=came; chandrie= the moon; gaaraan=search

I searched within for the Mystic Moon, for like seeks out the 'like', but with, little success. Thou art all this and this and this; there is no one else but Thee. She saw the Narayana, the lord of Lords and after a pause she saw him in the form of 'Shiva', as a 'destroyer' then again, the next moment she saw him as a 'beggar' asking humbly for charitable relief. As such she saw His bewitching presence in all these forms. O! My 'Lord', what is this. Lal-Ded does not murmur against the Lord and 'His' wondrous pastime, nor does she grumble against man. It is fully evident that Lal-Ded recognized the existence of a supreme being in various forms viz. Narayana, 'Shiva', and then in the form of a beggar-asking humbly for a charitable relief. What then is the meaning of Thy sport, Of Thy creation's wondrous forms?

SM31A

Aarbalan manz naagraad rovukh
Saada rovukh chooran manz
Moodagaran gwar pandit rovukh
Raaz hans rovukh kaawan manz

Amid the rocks, the fountain is lost; among the thieves, the saint is lost; among the ignorant and fools, the wise teacher is lost; and, among the crows the royal swan is lost.

SM32. Babri Langas Mushuk No mooray

Babri langas mushuk no maray
Honie basti kofoor kya neray
Man yud gwarhein feri zeray
Nata shaleh tongev kya neri

Babri = Babri Beoul/Basil Seeds; Kan Sherbat or Babri tresh is a very popular beverage of the Kashmir. langas=branch, a twig of basil; mushuk=fragrance; no=not; maray=die; Honie basti=the covering of dog's skin; kofoor= fragrance; kya neray= can't get; mun=mind; yud=if; gwarhein = tame, train, search; feri zeray= can conquer; nata=otherwise; shaleh= The jackal (Canis aurcus), Kashmiri name = Shal, that is found in all villages and in waste lands. They come out during night and howl. Their tail is long, and skin is sometimes used as fur. The black-backed jackal is about the size of domestic dog. It grows to 27 to 33 inches shoulder to rump, with a tail length of about 10 inches. tongev=howling,

In this Vakh Lal Ded makes a judgement that a basil which is considered one of the healthiest herbs; best when fresh, exuding a sweet, earthy aroma that indicates not only the promise of pleasantly pungent flavor, but an impressive list of nutrients. Vitamin K, essential for blood clotting, is one of them. As against, the covering of dog's skin which has invasive and offensive smell and is useless; On the contrary, mind, if trained and tamed can accomplish the unconquerable and unattainable quickly. Otherwise, nothing can be attained by just howling like jackals.

The Jackals, wolves and foxes are a type of canine, animals that are related to dogs.

Why does a wolf sound like? The wolf Sounds. Wolves will even howl in response to something that just sounds like a howl, like a train whistle, fire, or police car siren or even a human howling!

Such howls, though social in nature, also serve to defend the pack's territory against other wolves; and why do wolves howl? When one is "to communicate to other wolves that this is their territory, or stay away," the wolves' howl. They also howl to find fellow pack members when they're apart—gray wolf howls can carry for miles—and for social purposes, such as maintaining relationships within members of the pack.

SM33. Bhaan Gole Tai Prakash Aao Zoonai

Bhaan gole tai prakash aao zoonai
Chander gole tai motai chet
Chet gole tai kenh ti naa kunai
Gai bur bwah sowa vesergith keth

Lal Ded during her wanderings in the space experiences the thrill of the moments of Sun set and the appearance of the Moon on the Earth. She refers to the moments when the Moon enters phase of darkness. Then only the 'Chit' consciousness exists. She further says that when consciousness also fades away, there is the mass conversion of the body form into celestial wave form. In other words, the state of mingling of the spirit with cosmic radiance takes place and everything is reduced to nothingness. Lal says, I mingle with the nothingness of Cosmos.

SM34. Brahm Burzas Peth Watnovuum

Brahm burzas peth watnovuum
Chet chay tari saeet dopmus lum
Hamsu travith soo hum porum
Dopnum Lalli atathi shrum

Brahm burzas peth watnovoom= with meditation and breath exercise I was able to advance my consciousness up to the crown of my head; Chet chay tari saeet dopmus lum=with consciousness, I succeeded in movement of Praana; Hamsu travith soo hum Paroom= improving the sound of breath from Hamsoo to Sooham, an advanced meditative process in breath exercise ; Dopnum Lalli atathi shrum= after achieving higher consciousness, It's a feeling of extreme ecstasy never before experienced by the seeker, everything seems clothed in a strange celestial luminance and the presence of the Lord Shiva is felt vividly everywhere.Lalleshuri stops here and adheres to the position and enjoys the ecstasy of the new development.

With the courtesy and grace of my Master (Guru), I was able to concentrate the sum of the energies "spirit," within the body at the top of my brain, with the aid of proper rhythmic breathing exercises, and with the energy released by the completely absorbed mind. I was able to enter into thoughtless state of mind and after endorsing complete surrender to His divine will, I heard the master's direction "Lalla! Try to absorb yourself in this spell, with full concentration without any vacillation". So, I got completely absorbed in the divine ecstasy, with the thoughtless state of mind and thus was able to illuminate my path to join His benign grace.

SM35. Broonth Kali Aasan Tithi Keran

Broonth kali aasan tithi keran
Tang choonthi papan cheran saet
Maaji kori athvas karith neran
Doh den baranai gaeran saeth
Vetha hokhan tai henar grazan
Teli ho mali aasi vander raj

Broonth kali=in future, in odd times; aasan=will be; tithi keran=such conditions; there will be some odd times in the history of mankind; tang=pear; choonth (tsoonth) =apple; papan=ripen; cheran(tcheran)=apricot; when pears apples and apricots will ripe together at the same time (though they have different seasons to ripe);maaji=mothers; kori daughters; athvas karith= collaborate together; neran=go out; doh den baranai garean saeth= mothers and their daughters will collaborate together and will come out of their houses and they will enjoy their lives with the strangers; vetha the rivers; hokhan=will dry up; henar grazen= brooks will roar; Teli ho mali aasi vander raj=then chimp and ape like people will rule.

Lal-Ded sounds a prophecy, with insight giving picture of horror in which our future generations will be put to. The fruits like pears and apples will ripe along with apricots. (Usually apricots ripen in May-June and pears and apples ripen in the month of August-September). The mothers will move hand in hand along with their daughters to sell their chastity. They will spend days with strangers of little repute. The rivers will dry up and streams will roar with floods. Then Baboon type people will rule the world. The life will be full of greed, hatred, violence, and falsehood.

SM36. Buthi Kya Jaan Chhukh Vondi Chhukh Kani

Buthi kya jaan chhukh vondi chhukh kani
Aslech kath zanh sani no
Paraan lekhaan vuth ongeja gaji
Andrim dui zanh chaji no

Buthi kya jaan chhukh =apparently, by face you are charming; vondi chu kani=in reality you are stone hearted; Aslech kath=in reality; zanh sani no=you are not able to accept the reality, nobody will deeply think; Paraan lekhan vuth ongeja gaji = you have reduced your lips and your finger while reading and writing; Andrim=inside; dui zanh chaji no=but your malice is still there.

Apparently, a look on you tells me you are charming and fascinating. But you are stone hearted person. You are unaware of the reality that you have reduced your lips and your finger while reading and writing. But your inner malice is still there.

SM37. Chaalun Chhai Vuzmal Ta Tratai

Chaalun chhai vuzmal ta tratai
Chaalun chhui mandinyean gatakaar
Chaalun chhui paan-panun kadun grattai
Heti maali santush vaati paanai.

Chaalun= (chaalun or tsaalun) to tolerate; vuzmal= lightning; tratai = thunder; chaalun chhu mandinyean gattakaar =patience to face darkness at noon; chaalun chu paan-panun kaddun grattay = Patience to go through a grinding-mill; Heyti maali santuush=doubt not whatever befalls; vaati paanai=will come to you.

Be ready to tolerate the lightning and cloudbursts,
Be ready to bear sudden darkness at noon,
Be ready to crush your body between two grinding wheels,
Accept it all with patience, the contentment will come to you.
Resilience: to stand in path of lightening; resilience to walk when darkness falls at noon; resilience to grind yourself fine in the turning mill; resilience will come to you. Patience to tolerate lightning and thunder, patience to face darkness at noon, Patience to go through a grinding-mill --O! Dear only patience will bring forth happiness, contentment, and peace unto you.

SM38. Chei Deev Gartas Ti Darthi Sazakh

Chei deev gartas ti darthi sazakh
Chei deev ditith kranzan praan
Chei deev thani rosti vazakh
Kus zaani deev choon parmaan

Chei(tsei) deev='O' God! gartas ti darthi sazak= You are everywhere; Chei deev ditith krenzan pran= You have given life and energy to evry person; Chai deev=Thou God; thane =sound of a bell; rosti vazak= Your echo is in the whole universe; Kus zani deev choon parmaan= the whole creation hums with Thy silent sound. -

O God! How great are you! You are everywhere. You have given life and energy to every person. Your echo is in the whole universe. Your seat is everywhere. Thou dost pass through all shapes and forms, thou breathe life into all frames, and the whole creation hums with Thy silent sound-The Anahata naad, the 'AUM. Who can measure the Immeasurable, O Lord!

SM39. Challa Cheita Vondas Bhiiy Mo Bar

Challa cheita vondas bhiiy mo bar
Choon cheenit karaan paaniiy anaad
Udwiiy zaanakh khuved hari
Kar kewal tasoond taruk naad

Challa cheita vondas bhiiy mo bar= Have no fear, O restless mind; Choon cheenit karaan paaniiy anaad= The Eternal One takes thought for you; Udwiiy zaanakh khuved hari= He knows how to fulfil your wants; Kar kewal tasoond taruk naad= His Name will lead you safe across.

If you have a real desire and zeal, to mingle your imperfection with the perfection of the Lord, try to absorb in His celestial wave form and crave for His grace alone.

Lal Ded was a genius of a Yogini and poetess of eminence. In the Vakh she talks of her enlightened experience on the path of self-recognition and the 'thrill of self-consciousness' and widening vision. Here she addresses the mind: Have no fear, O restless mind, and The Eternal One takes thought for you. He knows how to fulfil your wants. Then cry to Him alone for help, His Name will lead you safe across. She calls the mind with different names- 'O' blessed mind, you are the innovation of the Lord. Be fearless, have patience, success is yours. Keep faith in Him and that faith calls out the divinity within. His Lordship knows how to fulfill your needs. Then cry for His mercy alone. He will come to your help. His unseen hands will convey you safe and will lead you to happiness.

SM40. Chammer Chatter Rath Simhasan

Chammer chatter rath simhasan
Hiad natya ras tula prakh
Kyah manith yeti sethur asvun
Kow zan kaasi marnaen shainkh

Chammer= A royal fly whisk; chatter=sunshade; rath=chariot; simhasan=throne; Hiad = gaiety, cheerfulness; Natya ras= joys of theatre; tula prakh=a bed of softest down. Kyah manith yeti sethur asvuon=Which of these do you think will last forever? Kow zan kaasi marnaen shainkh=How then will you overcome the fear of death?

A happy combination of events! Conjuncture of time, King emperor sitting on Royal Chariot; Now, seated on Royal Throne, with pleasures of Theatre and company of beautiful dancing girls and then lying on a beautiful cushion type bed. Such is a person's mind that he cannot be happy even enjoying the entire King's luxury. Lal Ded has observed that none of these symbols of rank and power go with man when he is dead. Since there is nothing in this world that has any permanence, then how do I know, as to how to put off the fear of death?

SM41. Chandaan Looses Pani Panas

Chandaan luoses pani panas
Chapith gyanas votum na konch
Lai karmas ti vachis althanas
Bari bari baneh ti chavan neh konch

Chanddaan luoses Pani panas = Searching the Self, I wearied myself; chapith gyanas votum Na kaanh = secret mind, beyond knowledge; Lay karmas=approached through meditation and love; vatsas=reached; alsthaanas= the abode of the Supreme; Bari Bari baana= I found wine jars in great quantities; chavan na kaanh= none desiring to drink from them.

Lalla says while searching the Self, I wearied myself; I got tired in search of Him. Who without hard labour can get the fruit of his hard work? I stopped searching, and love led me to the door. There I found wine jars aplenty, but none desiring to drink from them.

In search of God Lal reached "Amrit Bhavan"-Sahasra. People reach there by power of Yoga. Lala regrets that very few people reach this stage and reach salvation. She says that this Amrit is available, but few to drink.

Lal Ded says: I exhausted myself seeking my Lord inside and outside I could not find his hidden self as no such search or knowledge could find him. Then I concentrated on him with deepest love and devotion which took me slowly to the abode of my Lord. Strangely there I found lots of jars filled with plenty of wine but none ready to drink.

SM42. Chaandanas Gyaanaprakaashas

Chaandanas gyaanaprakaashas,
Yimav choun tim zivantay-mukt;
Veyshmas samsaaranis paashas,
Abodhy gaenddaah sheyth-sheyth dith.

Chidananda = Hindu god Shiva; gyaanaprakaashas= of Pure Consciousness and Light of Knowledge; Yimav choun=those who realized; zivantay-mukt= who, while alive, has found release from ever-recurring birth and death; Veyshmas samsaaranis pashas= it seems to be "dark. to swallow the sun; Abodhy=ignorant; gaenddaah=add knot to knot; sheyth-sheyth dith= in hundreds.

They, who have known the Supreme Self, Cidaananda Jnaanaprakaasha, (compact of the Bliss of Pure Consciousness and Light of Knowledge Absolute) - They are the Jivan-mukta-s (who, while alive, has found release from ever-recurring birth and death). The ignorant add knot to knot, in hundreds, to the tangled web of samsara, its recurrent birth, its recurrent death.

SM43. Charmoon Chatith Detuth Pon Paanas

Charmoon chatith detuth pon paanas
Tiuth kyah wawooth pholee sui
Moodas updesh gow reeunz domatas
Kani daands gore aaparith rove

Charmoon =skin, hide; chatith=finished, cut off, Charmoon Chatith= bonds of desire and conceit; detuth=to give; pon=pegs; panus =self; Detuth Pon Paanas= you are pegged; tituth kya=what was it; wawooth=sown;tiiuth Kyah wawooth=what have you sown; pholee Sui=bear rich harvest; Moodas=fool; updesh=counsel; Gow Reeunz Domatas= like the balls thrown inside a dome, rebounding back but not hitting the mark; reeunz domatas=a difficult task,; kani=stone; dandas=bull; Kani Daands=stone bull;gore=sweet molasses; aaparith=fed; Gore Aaparith=feed sweet molasses; Rove=lost, waste of feed.

You are pegged to the bonds of desire and conceit. You only care your own body which you pegged to desire. What is it you have sown, that would bear a rich harvest? As it is very difficult to counsel a fool, it is like the balls thrown inside a dome rebounding back but not hitting the mark, or it is like feeding a lifeless stony bull with sweet molasses which results in wasting all the feed. Or it is like feeding a lifeless stony bull as one cannot expect a yield of milk from a stony bull.

SM44. Chas Kenh Na Ta Assas Kenhniiy

Chas kenh na ta assas kenhniiy
Kenhas kenh gome tarith kenh
Shiv poozoom ta woochum naaraan
Bo tas praraan chenoom na prah

Chas kenh Na= I think my existence has a purpose; assas kenhniiy=I had a past; Kenhas kenh gome tarith kenh=my faith is power of my truth; Shiv poozoom=I worshipped Shiva; woochum Naaraan=found Narayana; Bo Tas Praraan= I have lived through a magnificent moment;chenoom na prah=I crave of His benign blessing.

I do not think my existence is purposeless; even I had existed in the past. O, wonder: How the Truth has magnified the power of my faith which has made my realization pure shining and bright I worshiped the 'Shiva' the 'Lord destroyer' with devotion and zeal but found Him merged in the colour form and spirit of 'Narayana,' the Lord Preserver, O! Wonder my foolery has gone off, I see the truth 'Shiva' and 'Narayana'. They are in fact one in all and all in one. I have thus realized the Lord in all forms and in all names. O Lord! I have just lived through a glorious moment. It has been the best moment of my life. It both touches and teaches; I am longing for His grace and crave of His benign blessing.

Lalla's concept of nothingness (Shunya) is essentially a Kashmir Shaivism concept. To her Supreme Shiva is the universal Lord. He is the absolute truth of the universe. He is the single consolidated self of the cosmic whole. The universe as such should be understood as the personification of the Lord Shiva and nothing beyond His holy influence also termed as nothingness or Shunya. Supreme-Shiva is the absolute master of the universe. The universe is personified with all the attributes of a creator, preserver, and destroyer (Shiva).

"I belong to nothingness (Shunya) of now and was the same in my previous life too. Being nothing is my achievement as I'm an integral part of the universal nothingness. When I worship Shiva I find Narayana, (as Lord Vishnu). To her both were one. This is true for such an awakened soul. This is also because the concept of duality had vanished from her perception.

(Another version) Last line changes:

Chas kenh na ta assas kenhniiy

Kenhas kenh gome tarith kenh

Shiv poozoom ta woochum naaraan

Kenh nish kenh nata kenh goam tirth khet.

SM45. Che Kavo Logui Chui

Che kavo logumuti chui
Kavu chui logmuth parmus,
Kavo goi apzis pazrukh broonth,
Dashi bodh lashi bour hur mashuiy,
Ha yina gachi zena marnukie broonth

Che=you; kavo= how; logumuti chui=have applied; Parmus=God, Shiva; Kavo goi=why have you; apzis=falsehood, fiction; pazrukh=truthfulness, honesty; broonth=resemblance,similarity; Dashi bodh lashi bour hur mashuiy, Dashi=ten, bodh= a bundle, Dashi bodh is a bundle of ten, also bodh=wisdom; lashi bour= lashi is a kind of wood which burns quickly; lash also means defeat, destruction, ruin; bour=burden; mashuiy= forgotten; Hur=a grass bed, the place where a mother gives birth to a child; Mashuiy=forgot; Ha yina gachi=an alarm is given!a sort of warning, Lest you feel; Zena=birth, lifespan; marnukie=death,demice; broonth=resemblance,sembelance.

In this vakh Lal Ded Lal reminds and gives an alarm to the common masses by saying:
you have never cared to be realistic, and pragmatic to Shiva.
You are taking falsehood for reality; both appear same to you.
You have forgotten the ten elements given to you at the time of you birth to be your insight, and perception.
You take your birth and life span to remain forever, and forget death and its similarity, impressions, and traces, and forget Shiv.

SM46. Chei Naa Bo Naa Daiyey Naa Dyaan

Chei naa bo naa daiyey naa dyaan
Gaiiy paanai sarv krai mashith
Aneyaa deeuthuk kenh na, anee
Gyei sath liiye per pashith

Chei naa= neither thou; Bo naa= nor I; daiyey=He, almighty; dyaan=meditation; Gaiiy paanai sarv krai mashith = Even the All-Creator is forgot; Aneyaa deeuthuk= the ignorant blind cannot see, (They) saw Other than all these, the Absolute, the Relationless (Ananvaya, blind) "kenh na anee"; sat= the whole objective universe, the good become absorbed in Him. Sath is said to mean 'the Seven Worlds'.

I moved aimlessly and wanted to have His kind presence; I undertook deep meditation; in this peaceful state, I found myself lost and the duality between me and Him as 'I' and 'mine' or 'you' and 'yours' had gone. Now there is nothing to consider upon. Even the All-Creator is forgotten. His grace, which was following me, has ceased to be. Alas! The ignorant, as a blind cannot see His grace. This is the misfortune. But the pure, the wise, having seen merge in the Supreme. This is the mystery that haunts me.

SM47. Chet Aanadas Gyaan Prakaashas

Chet aanadas gyaan prakaashas
Yemove chuine timan zeewant mukht
Vishvas samsaarnis paashayas
Abodh shat shat gand dittee

Chet= consciousness; Aanadas=delightful, divine; gyaan=visionary; prakaashas=gleam, shine; yemove chuine= those who realize; shat shat= hundreds; gand= knots.

When mind becomes potentially divine, visionary gleam automatically comes. One sees the Lord in its splendid form. Thus, one can render himself immune to life and death cycle as such one becomes entitled to immortality and eternal bliss. Ah, I wonder over the sad state of people, who get themselves trapped, in the tenuous web of this world and bind themselves with hundreds of knots (attachments). It is necessary to arouse their consciousness to overcome the evil. I cannot imagine a more interesting life than this.

SM48. Cheth Amar Peth Thavizai

Cheth amar peth thavizai
Ta travith lagzi zore
Tati nashekui chei sunderzai
Doda shur ti kochi no muuray

Cheth=consciousness, mind; Mind is the most inert organ in the body and should be activated; peth thavizai=to keep on; Doda shur= suckling baby; kochi = mother's lap.

Mind is the most inert organ in the body and should be activated. Keep your mind intent upon the path that leads to immortality. Should it wander away from the path, it will fall into evil ways. Be firm with it and have no fear; for mind is like a suckling baby, which tosses restless even in its mother's lap.

In the state of enlightenment, keep the concentration of mind intact and remain firm in the attempt, with devotion and zeal. At this stage do not invite any doubt, or indecision of mind. For, the mind is like a little baby in the lap of his mother, indecisive and wavering every now and then. Thus, watch the void which is nothing but a celestial wave form merging with the ethereal void. That is the essential nature of purity. This direction of Lalla holds the promise of unifying all the "diversion" forces acting on the mind during the process of meditation as such cravings are to be kept under restraint, for when cravings seize a person, the soul is shattered.

SM49. Cheth Novui Chandram Novuy

Cheth novuy chandram novuy
Zal mea deunthum navam novuy
Yena pytta Lalli mei tan mann novuy
Tana Lal bu navam novuy chhas!

Cheth (tseth) novei = the mind, is ever new; Chandram novie = the ever-changing moon is new; Zalmay dyuuthum= the ever new shoreless expanse of waters that I have seen; Zalmay dyuuthum=I saw "waste of waters" at the time of pralaya, destruction of the Universe as explains Grierson; navam novuy =ever since new the shore less waters; Yena Lalli Mei = since I, Lalla; tan man novei = have worn my body and mind, (emptied it of dead yesterdays and tomorrows unborn); Tana Lal Boah navam novei ches= I live in the ever-present Now, and all things are forever new and new to me.

Since, I am blessed with celestial eyes; I bear the power to abandon the imprisonment of my Soul. Now, I am a liberated Soul as such, I see the mind is new. The moon light appears of different nature; the water in the open Seas is delightful hence new. Ever since I, Lalla, have cleansed my body and mind with celestial water, I live in altogether new state of mind. Lo! I am transformed into something new, where I have eyes to wonder, but lack tongue to praise. So, Lalla shines in eternal wisdom and infinite delight. She has acquired omniscience boundless vision, infinite strength, perfect bliss, and existence without form.

The superb poetic composition of this Vakh is has a strange jugglery of words for their diverse meaning and expression.

When Lalla had her body and soul washed of all her sins past and present, she felt relaxed and refreshed. She had shed all the egos and needless emotions. Having got exposed to the ultimate truth about her Lord, she felt her consciousness (Cheth) as ever new.

She felt the ever-changing moon as new for her. She felt quite new freed of my past burdens. In her ecstasy of achievement Lal Ded felt herself completely transformed. She felt the whole world along with her own self looked entirely renewed. She saw everything new, beautiful, and fresh. The world after realization seemed to her as quite new and fresh. She saw the new world with striking light everywhere. There was profuse grace of the Lord Shiva everywhere. The world she saw had abundance of everything, with no cares of the world, no disease, no death, and no suffering.

SM50. Cheth Torugh Gagana Bramvoom

Cheth torugh gagana bramvoon
Nemishi aki chandi yozan lach
Cheetan vagi bodh yemi ratith zone
Praan apaan sandarith pakach

Cheth=consciousness; Chitta twarug= the steed of mind; gagana bramavon= speedeth over the sky; torugh gagana bramvoom= I directed the steed of my thought (consciousness) around the whole universe and in a moment I was back; Nemishi aki chandi yozan lac= It can travel millions of yojnas (about five miles) in an instant faster than sound and light, through space, land and water; Nimishi aki tsandhi= in the twinkling of the eye; yuuzan lach= hundred thousand leagues traverseth he; Cheetan vagi bodh yemi ratith zon= One can achieve this extra-ordinary faculty by exercising restraint on one's mind, a man of discrimination can control the curvetting steed; Praan apaan sandarith pakach= exercising restraint on one's mind along with proper regulation of Praan and Apaan in a particular systematic direction, the wheels of praana and apraana, guide his chariot aright.

The steed of mind, in the twinkling of an eye, travels an infinite distance, far away in the COSMOS. A man of vision and stature, who can control, this fast-moving steed can guide his chariot like a guided missile on the wheels of energy levels, to the destination of his realization, by proper course of breathing. The mind-horse gallops over the skies, momently traverses a million miles, Consciousness-bridle will hold it in check; control the wings of the airs that go up and down.

Human thought is the controller of all activities whatever a human being indulges into in his life. She claims to have the capacity of moving at a lightning speed around the cosmos at her will and says further that all human beings can achieve this faculty with a proper control of their thought which is the fastest medium of travel. To control one's mind is truly an excruciating process because the ordinary man has his mind shifting to numerous locations without notice and with highest speed. To obtain the concentration of thought on a single point for some time or even longer is not easy. This is the first step of Yoga and the first requirement in any spiritual advancement.

SM51. Cheth Torugh Vagi Hyath Rotom

Cheth torugh vagi hyath rotom *1
Cheth miliwith dashnaad vav
Twai shesikal veglith wacham
Schoonis shoonia meelith gav

Cheth=mind; torugh vagi hyath rotom= I reined in the steed of the mind, and, by constant practice; Cheth miliwith= brought together the praana-s; Dashnaad waaw= ten different senses; Twai shesikal=then the mystic moon; veglith wacham= Then the nectar of the Mystic Moon flowed down; Schoonis shoonia meelith gav= the void merged in the Void. (The mind-horse I reined in and put on course, holding him still with the ten air-channels. The mystic moon melted and downwards flowed. And the void was absorbed into the void!)

I controlled the reins of the mind and by consistency in Sadhana, created the energy levels to vibrate the ten different senses within the body, resulting in the modulated frequency of the required order, which had an effect of releasing the hormones in the specific remote sensors of the brain cells and in the ductless glands of the brain. These hormones keep the seeker in the state of perpetual bliss and when produced in abundance are responsible for creating enough energy, to change the state of the body into the wave form of requisite wavelength of celestial waves of cosmos. Thus, the body merges with the Super Consciousness.

I reined in the steed of the mind, and, by constant practice, brought together the prana-s coursing the ten nadis. Then the nectar of the Mystic Moon flowed down, gradually spreading my whole being, and the void merged in the Void. The stilled mind merged in Pure Consciousness

SM52. Chondmakh Bona Ta Bei Chon Deeshan

Chondmakh bona ta bei chon deeshan
Neab ta nishaan lobmai na kuney
Prachome, saidan saadan bei tap reshan
Tim boozith lagi vadni ti rewanae
Dhab yeli ditnum fikrun ti andheshan
Ada yeti lobmakh pananey garey

Chondmakh(tchhondmakh)=I searched you; bona=in the underworld; ta bei chon(tson) deeshan=I explored all the three worlds (sky, earth and the underworld) in search of my Lord Shiva; Naib ta nishaan lobmas na koonai=I found no clue; Prachome, saidan saadan bei tap reshan= I asked people both ordinary and awakened; Tim Boozith lagi rewanae= all of them responded with sheer ignorance; Ad ho maali karnam dyyaa ditnum darshunai= I persisted till the miracle happened that my Lord was gracious enough to present His glorious self before me; Saar nai so de shaan panai paan naa kunai= I drank deep the holy nectar and learnt to my surprise that He was omnipresent and omniscient and observed everything closely though hidden from the public view.

"I sought for the Lord and went beyond this world and travelled to three different universes in the Milky Way. I did not find any trace of His existence. On my return, I tried to see saints and Hermits, absorbed in meditation. They all expressed their ignorance. Tears rolled down their cheeks, while expressing their failure. Then lo! Within the moon shine, I found exceeding peace in environment round. I had a vision, with a wonderful celestial wakening light around. I saw Him in person with all His grace and grandeur watching everything round. Although He watches everything, yet is invisible for the world, just to keep the sanctity of His grace".

(Another version)

SM53. Chandoom Ta Chondum Tren Deeshan

Chandoom ta chondum tren deeshan
Neab ta nishaan lobmas na kuney
Prachome, saidan saadan bei tap reshan
Tim boozith lagi rewanae
Adha ho maali karnam dayya dyutnam darshunai
Saarini su deshaan paanai, paana naa kuney

Chandoom(tchhondoom) ta chondum(tcchondum) tren deeshan= I explored all the three worlds (sky, earth and the underworld) in search of my Lord Shiva; Neab ta nishaan lobmas na koonai=I found no clue; Prachome, saidan saadan bei tap reshan= I asked people both ordinary and awakened; Tim Boozith lagi rewanae= all of them responded with sheer ignorance; Ad ho maali karnam dyyaa ditnum darshunai= I persisted till the miracle happened that my Lord was gracious enough to present His glorious self before me; Saar nai so de shaan panai paan naa kunai= I drank deep the holy nectar and learnt to my surprise that He was omnipresent and omniscient and observed everything closely though hidden from the public view.

Lalla says: I explored sky, earth, and the underworld in search of my Lord Shiva, but I found no clue. I asked people both ordinary and awakened, but all of them responded with sheer ignorance. I persisted till the miracle happened that my Lord was gracious enough to present His glorious self before me. I drank deep the holy nectar and learnt to my surprise that He was omnipresent and omniscient and observed everything closely though hidden from the public view.

SM54. Chui Kuni Tai Choi Naa Kunai

Chui kuni tai choi naa kunay*2
vuchum ore yore naa kunay
Dai phal tao mool na kunay
Chhui chaaron tai gaarun na kunay

Chui kuni=He is somewhere; choi Naa kunai=yet invisible; Wuchum ore yore=searched everywhere; Naa kunai=invisible; Diiy phal=searched in fruits; mool Na kunai=searched in roots; Choi chaaron(tchhaarun) Tai gaarun Na kunay=searching you everywhere failed, you are in the core of heart.

O' infinite consciousness, even though your splendor is all pervading, yet you are invisible to the naked eye. I sought for you here, there, and everywhere, but got no trace of your existence anywhere. Oh! I saw you in the fruit of a tree, whose roots are too deep in the infinite. It is of no-avail to seek you in the exterior world, as you are seated within the core of my heart.

SM55. Dachinis Oberas Zayoon Zaanhaa

Dachinis oberas zayoon zaanhaa
Sadaaras zanha kadith wath
Meindis roogyas viedoot anha
Moodas zaanim na pranith kath

Dachinis= southern; oberas= clouds; zayoon zaanhaa= I might scatter; Samandaaras zanha kadith wath= I might drain out the sea; Meindis roogyas= incurable sick; vedoot anha = I might cure; anha=zanahaa; Meindis roogyas viedoot anha=I could learn to heal the sores of a leper; Moodas=fool; zaanim na pranith kath= I cannot convince. "I'm capable enough to divert winds to make them favourable and make a clean way to traverse through the fiercest seas. I can easily cure an ailing person even from an incurable disease but strangely enough despite all my advanced capabilities I'm unable to explain the truth to a fool."

I could learn to disperse the southern clouds, I could learn to drain out the sea, I could learn to cure the incurable sick, but I could never learn the art to convince a fool.

Elaborating it Lal Ded says: I might scatter the southern clouds, I might drain out the sea, I might cure the incurable sick, but I have failed in convincing a fool. So, I have a feeling of weakness and sadness, lurking in my mind. In this Vakh, Lal Ded is protesting with herself and her foolish mind, rather than rebuking others. It may be seen that once a certain habit has been formed it becomes a part of the reflex action. To make foolish mind to change its bad habit is not easy. I could never learn the art to convince a fool!

SM56. Dhama Dhama Mana Omkar Parnovum

Dhama dhama mana Omkar parnovum
Panai paran ta panai bozan
Suham padas aham golum
Tyali Lal bo vatses prakash sathan

Dhama Dhama=every moment; mana=with zeal, mind; omkar parnovum= recited the blissful word 'Omkar'; Panai paran=set forth sound waves, I was reading myself; ta panai bozan= sound energy levels would vibrate the drum of my ears only; Soham=I am He; Aham golloom= ego of "I" completely vanished, I cut off aham; Teli Lalla=thence, I Lalla; wachas=landed; prakash sasthan= abode of light;Bo vatses Prakesh Sathan= I reached state of illumination.

I, Lal, recited the wonderful and delightful word 'Omkar', with such a passion that it would set forth wave form or energy levels which would vibrate the drum of my ears only. With such zeal, it would set forth energy which in turn would send sweet sensations of the peculiar effect to the brain. Thus, the effect of ecstasy was felt. The entire ego of "I" completely vanished. Then, I saw the true form of consciousness with the cosmic radiation and lo! I am a realized soul I feel I have landed in Prakashasthan. Lal Ded has been a saint of distinction. She in her own lifetime attained the way of the supreme, 'paramagath' and entered the Abode of Light, '*Prakash Sathan*' of God

The most powerful mantra (bija-mantra) from first to last, which her guru, an able teacher, Sidh Srikanth, began, was the Vedic symbol Oum and Shaiva symbol Aham. Apparently, these are two different mantras, but in a synthesis connoting and denoting the same Reality of Shiva in supremacy and adaptation.

SM57. Damaa Dam Kormas Daman Haale

Damaa dam kormas daman haale
Prazlyome deep ta nanyaim zaath;
Andrium prakaash nebar chotum,
Gatti rotum ta karmas thaph.

Damaa dam kormas daman haale = slowly, slowly, did I stop my breath in the bellows-pipe (of the throat); Prazlyome deep= the flame of the Lamp; nanyaim zaath= shining steady and bright; Andrium Prakaash=inner light; nebar chotum (tchhotum)= I diffused the inner light, (and within, without, all was Light); Gatti rotum= in the darkness itself; karmas thaph= bright light revealed my true nature unto me.

Gently, I continued breathing at ease in complete rhythm of the letter 'OM'. I trained my mind to enter the essence of my spirit. Then, in the windless calm, the flame of the Lamp, shining steady and bright, revealed my true nature unto me. In the dark recesses of my soul, I seized upon Him and held Him fast. Then I diffused the inner light, and all was Light.

In the Vakh Lal Ded gives a beautiful expression of her constant exercise of breath. In perfect rhythm and proper timing and speed she indulged into the exercise for a long time. This she did under the guidance of her master. She didn't fault anywhere as the stability of her mind in complete unison was essential. The perfect concentration of mind with continuous exercise of breath made the internal spark of her soul glitter freely and revealed her all the secrets of awakening.

SM58. Dhaman Basti Ditto Dil

Dhaman basti dito dil
Dhamanas yeth dhamaan khaar
Shestaras sone gachee hasil
Vuni chai sul tai chandoon yaar

Daman basti=breathing; shestaras = iron; sone = gold; hasil= achieve; vooni= still; sul= too early; chandoon (tchhandun)= search; yaar= lord, God.

The practice of deep breathing, slowly and steadily, inhaling and exhaling, has an analogy. Just in the manner the Blacksmith works with his bellow, the iron in the blood, will gradually and progressively be converted into the golden coloured light, to mingle with the cosmic radiance. It will be of the same frequency and wavelength, as the celestial light. This is the essence of this Vakh and best to heed the doctrine.

SM59. Deshi Aayas Dash Dishi Teelith

Deshi aayas dash dishi chalith,
Chalith chotum shunya ta vaav,
Shivuy dyunthum shaayi -shaayi meelith
Shah ta-treh tropimas Shivay draav.

Deshi aayas=came home; Dash dishi chalith (tsalith), teelith= I roamed the ten directions; Chalith (tsalith) chotum shunya ta vaav= pierced the wind and the void; Shivuy dyunthum=I saw Shiva; shaayi -shaayi meelith = I closed the nine gates of the body and shut out the Thirty-six. The 36 tattva-s (literally) the categories or principles from Paramasiva to the earth, according to the Trika Saiva cosmology. (Through the ten directions I raced and came home, Fleeing, I pierced the void and the wind, and I found Shiva present everywhere). Shai ta-tre chatimas shivay draa = Shai ta-tre tropimus tu Shivuy drav; meaning closed the three and six and He appeared, Immanent!

After reaching home, Lalla says, "I roamed the ten directions and pierced the wind and the void. I closed the nine gates of the body and shut out the Thirty-six. Wherever I looked, I found the Lord Shiva present everywhere - within, without, and in the Void. I have seen Him in magnificence and tried to unhook Him away, from all worldly attachments, which the normal life is attached with. Yet His grace was free; free from all the six plus three attachments e.g. (1) Lust., (2) Greed, (3) Anger, (4) Conceit, (5) Attachment, (6) Pride; plus (i) Form (ii) Love and (iii) Passion.

SM60. Dihichi Lari Daari Bar Troprim

Dihichi lari daari bar troprim
Praan choor rotum ta dyutmas dhum
Hradyichi koothari andar gondum
Omki chobuka tulmas bum

Dihichi lari=physical body; daari=windows; bar=doors; troprim=closed; Praan choor rotum=took to meditation; ti dyutmas dhum=absorbed in thought; Hraidyichi koothari ander gondum= releasing the energy and increasing the bliss; Omki chobuk tulmas bum= recitation of the letter 'AUM' repeatedly.

We need to bolt the doors and shut the windows of the physical sheath of our body. The prana or the vital breath is hidden there. We need to put the fivefold prana under control, lest they should disturb the mental harmony.

After gaining full control over all the physical senses of the body, I closed the doors and windows of the house of my body. I switched over to meditation and was unmindful of external interferences. By releasing the energy levels produced by the recitation of the letter 'AUM', I saw all unifying spirit, mingled up with cosmic radiance. Shiva is AUM and AUM is Shiva. Meditation helps for the realization of Shiva state of mind, through japa, and Ajapa Gayatri.

SM61. Den Chezitai Razoon Aasi

Den chezi tai razan aasi
Bhutal gaganas kun vekaasai
Chendrie rahu, groohun maavasai
Shiv poozun gav cit atmasai

Den=light of the day; chezi tai= light of the day is quenched; razan aasi= When the light of the day is quenched in the darkness of the night; Bootal=the earth; gaganas=sky; Bhutal gaganas kun vekaasai= the earth extends to meet and dissolve in the ethereal sky; Chendrie=moon; rahu =the Demon of eclipse; groohun=eclipse; maavasai= on Amavasya all is blank and dark; Shiv poozun=the worship of Shiva; gav cit atmasai= The illumination of Cit-Atman is the true worship of Siva, the Supreme.

When the light of the day is quenched in the darkness of the night, the earth extends to meet and dissolve in the ethereal sky, and (on Amavasya*) all is blank and dark eclipse. But strange! Raahu, the Demon of eclipse, is swallowed by the New-born Moon. The illumination of Cit-Atman is the true worship of Siva, the Supreme. On the Amavasya of solar eclipse, Raahu is supposed, by popular tradition, to swallow the sun. But, says Lalla, that the seeker who treads the path has the experience of the manifested universe, the sun, and the sky and all the worlds, vanishing and becoming one with the unmanifest all-pervading Akshara. There, for the moment, it seems to be "dark, irretrievably dark" in the great Void; but soon it is lit up by the New-born Moon, the Paraa-Samvit, which is the illumination of the Higher Consciousness revealing the abode of the Supreme Siva. During her wandering in the space, she saw the moments of Sun set and setting of darkness on the globe, during a Solar eclipse. It appeared as if the entire mass of the globe is entering into the phase of ecstasy; when the earth is deprived of light or brilliance, the moment the Moon's nodes intersect the Earth's Orbit, or moon closes over the Sun's orbit on the day of Amavasya, the day when the Moon is in complete phase of darkness, or as per legends Rahu swallows the Sun and the Sun is eclipsed. She describes the moment of such a beautiful perception, as being in complete union with luminous light of the spirit and soul. This is the right moment of sitting in meditation, to observe the beaming countenance of the spirit or merging with divine grace of the Lord.

A story

When Rahu Swallows the Sun: The Eclipse According to One Hindu Myth

Rahu taking revenge on Surya (the Sun)!
The persistent battle between Rahu (really just the head of Rahu) and the Sun (Surya).

The myth to which Hindus refer is mentioned in the *Bhagavata Purana* (5.24, 8.9) and in the *Mahabharata* (1.19). It concerns *amrita*, the nectar of immortality, produced from Samudra manthana, the Churning of the Ocean of Milk. After the ocean is properly churned (in which Mount Mandera is used as a churning rod and Vasuki, the serpent king, is used as the pull rope!) coveted *amrita* is produced. Vishnu turns himself into Mohini, the only female *avatar* of Vishnu, an enchanting and erotic damsel, to distribute the *amrita* to the *devas* (gods), and to distract and keep it from the potentially robbing *asuras* (demi-gods). One *asura*, Rahu, sits with the gods and can imbibe the desirable *amrita*. He is spotted by Surya (the Sun) and Chandra (the Moon), who alert Vishnu. Lord Vishnu beheads Rahu with his *Sudarshan-chakra* (discus). Having drunk just a bit of the *amrita*, Rahu's head is made immortal while his body, called Ketu, not having come in contact with the immortalizing *amrita*, dies. The head of Rahu, then, remains and grudgingly attacks the Sun (and Ketu attacks the Moon) and is said to swallow it, and to cause the "eclipse"! Since Rahu has no body, he is unable to digest the sun and thus the sun is released, and the eclipse ends.

SM62. Dhobi Yeli Chavnas Dhobi Kani Pathie

Dhobi yeli chavnas dhobi kani pathie
Saz ta saban machnam yeichey
Saichi yeli firnam hani hani kachey
Ada lali me praavum param gath

Dhobi=washerman; yeli chavnas dhobi kani pathie=thrashed and kneaded on the washerman's stone; Saz ta saban machnam yeichey=Pasted and plastered with soap and clayey earth; Saichi yeli firnam hani hani kachey=Till the tailor's skilful scissors worked on my limbs; Ad lali me praavum param gath=Then, I Lalla, found my place in the Highest Abode!

Thrashed and kneaded on the washerman's stone,
Pasted and plastered with soap and clayey earth.
Till the tailor's skillful scissors worked on my limbs,
And I found my place in the Highest Abode!
"Now, after rendering me into a coarse cloth, I was put to a washerman, who vigorously dashed me on the washing stone. Then he threw me into a stony mortar, rubbed me with his feet, with all kinds of soapy mortar, then getting cleaned, I was dried up in the heat of the Sun. Still there was no end to my sufferings. I was further put to a tailor, for rendering me into a cloth to wear. Then the tailor cruelly worked his Scissors, on me and cut me with care and piece by piece. Then it is as such, I Lalla at last became an enlightened being after undergoing trials and troubles of life."

SM63. Dilkis Baagas Dour Kar Haesil

Dilkis baagas dour kar haesil
Adah deva pholie yemberzal baag
Mangnai umari hund haasil
Mout chhui pata pata Tehsildaar

Dilkis bagas dour kar hasil=the flowerbed of your heart; Adah deva pholie =may be thenit will blossom; yemberzal bagh=narcissus garden; Mangnai umari hund hasil=after death you will be asked for the results; Moat chui pata pata Tehsildar=death is after you like a tehsildar.

In this Vakh Lal Ded cautions to keep away dirt from the garden of your heart. Then, perhaps, Narcissus Garden will blossom. After death, you will be asked or the results of your life. Death is like a Tehsildar!

SM64. Diluk Khur-Khura Meh Mali Kustam Manuk Kotur Maray

Diluk khur-khura meh mali kustam manuk kotur maray
Neri lusum lookeh hunz lari ladan
Yeli paneh mohnew kadeth neenai panenay garay
Pateh pateh aasi lookeh saasa naeri aalvaan
Travith yenai manz madanas saavith dachineh laray

Diluk khur-khura meh mali =my heart beat; kustam =somebody; manuk kotur=pigeon hole of my heart; Neri lusum=my arms got weared; lookeh hunz lari ladan=helping others; Yeli paneh =when 'O' my body; mohnew =the people; kadeth neenai panenay garay=you are returned out from your house; Pateh pateh =afterwards, afterwards; aasi =will have; lookeh saasa =a thousand people; naeri aalvaan=waving their hands; Travith yenai =they will leave your body; manz madanas =set your body in the middle of the field; saavith dachineh laray=your own people will set you in a field laying you to sleep on your right side.

Make far from me proudness of heart, 'O' Father, -from the pigeonhole of my heart. My arm is wearied from making people's houses (i.e., helping others). When, 'O' my body you are returned out from your house. Afterwards, afterwards, a thousand people will come waving their hands. They will come and set you in a field, laying you to sleep on your right side.

SM65. Dhith Karith Raza Pherina

Dhith karith raza pherina
Nith karith trapina mann
Loob binaa zeev marina
Zeewant mari tai sui chui gyaan

Dhith karith= even if man is provided with all the kings' luxury; raza pherina= the mind of a person does not feel satisfied; Nith karith trapina Mann= it is one's attachment to the physical self; Loob binaa zeev marina=attachment that makes one lament the death and destruction of things; Zeewant Mari Tai Sui chui gyaan= noplace is in the world where a man may dwell, without being over powered by death. This is the essence of Truth.

The mind of a person does not feel satisfied, even, if he is provided with all the kings' luxury. It is one's attachment to the physical self that makes one mourn the death and destruction of things, which are doomed. All the things decay. Suffering is universal. The desire for transitory things leads to sufferings. To those seeking knowledge, the 'Lord' is eternal light. He is eternal righteousness; to those emotionally inclined He is eternal Love. In the end Lal-Ded says "No place is to find in the world where a man may dwell, without being overpowered by death. This is the essence of Truth. Anything whatever is brought into existence in this universe contains within itself the inherent germ of destruction. If the worldly pleasures allure the mind, people are trapped by greed even at the point of death."

SM66. Deev Vata Deever Vata

Deev vata deever vata
Pethu bon chhui ikavata
Pooz kas karak hatt bhata
Kar manas tui pavanas sangatha

Deev Vata= Idol is of stone; Diver Vata= temple is of stone; Petha= above (temple); Buna= below (idol); Chu Ikvatha= are one; Pooz Kas Karak=whom will you worship; Hout Batta=intelligent well read; Bhatta=conceited (big headed) Brahmin; Manas=mind; Pavanas=soul; Sangatha=union.

The above Vakh Lal Ded addresses to a Hoota Pandit. She says the Idol in the temple is made of stone and the temple itself is also made of stone. Above (temple) and below (idol) are one. Which of them will you worship O foolish Pandit? Here she wants to convey the message that Shiva transcends beyond the Shivalinga, and not to bind Shiva only in name within the icon of a stone. The Bhatta or Pundit should have an integral approach to Shiva, where Shiva and manifested Shakti are always in unison. Lal Ded seems to be always charmed with the name of Shiva. It is in the ecstasy of of joy to uphold unity within True worship must bind the vital air of the heart to the mind. "Manas the mind and Pavans-the fivefold Yogic breath." That is the call of spirituality. You make the union of mind with Soul. She is a strong critic of idolatry as a useless and even silly "work" and attaches the worshippers of stocks and stones to turn to Yogic doctrines and exercises for salvation.

Lal Ded was not a bigot but was much evolved soul as a Yogi should be. She was universal in her thoughts. Whatever she said about Murti Pooja should not be taken as an attack on any religious denomination. She wants to rise from that fundamental stage of Murti Pooja to the highest, termed as 'Para-the transcendental' as described in Pratyabijnya system of Kashmir Shaivism.

SM67. Doad Kyah Zaani Yas No Baney

Doad kyah zaani yas no baney
Gamkee jaama haa walith taney
Ghar ghar pheerus peyam kaney
Kanh ti dyunthum na pannai kaney

Dode kyah zaani yas no banai= only those who have suffered the troubles of life know their pinch; Gamkee jaama haa walith tanai= I wore the garments of sufferings all my life; Ghar ghar pheeras pyam kanai=I continued going door to door to convey my celestial message, I was not honoured everywhere, I was scorned at places and even frightened away by pelting stones at me; Kanh ti denunthum na pannai kanai= I persisted and continued with my noble mission. Sometimes I felt lonely as it seemed that nobody supported me.

What a suffering was it for Lal Ded! What bad treatment it was! It took people long time to recognize her greatness as a benefactor of the masses. Though she expresses sorrow over the attitude of these people towards her but knows fully well that their actions were not deliberate but only a result of their ignorance.

One who has not ever faced sadness and suffering of grief or sorrow, cannot feel the pain of the poverty-stricken multitudes, wearing the robes of anguish and sorrow, I wandered lonely, door to door, to express my anxiety in seeking His divine grace. I spoke in loud voice and cried but none came to my rescue. I shrieked, still no one came to my rescue, instead stones were hurled at me, as such, I was hurt, both in body and sentiments. Alas! "I have fallen on the thorns of life, and I bleed in suffering and pain."

The honour that was enjoyed by Lalleshwari in her later life and after her celestial flight is unprecedented in the history of Kashmir.

SM68. Doh Tara Duniyas Lol Borum

Doh tara duniyas lol borum
Patao zonum kenh nata kyah
Haavsa Lalli mei alimma porum
Pare pare karum ta porum na zaanh

Doh Tara=short time; duniyas=world; lol borum= fanciful longings, imaginary; Patao=ultimately; zonum=found; kenh nata kyah=the world is whirling and rocking due to greed, hatred, and ignorance of the people; Haavsa Lalli Mei alimma parum=I learnt 'love' is the essence of God; Par par karum ta porum na zaanh= I realized something out of nothing.

Lal Ded says that she had been attached with the glamour of the world for a brief period. But she at once got upset with its truth and senselessness. She realized that everything here including human existence was destined to come to an end. She says further that with great interest she had started to read books and literature of great authors and for a while she took great interest in learning all the knowledge contained in them but ultimately the truth revealed that everything that belonged to this world was temporary. This suddenly changed her heart. The worldly affairs disappointed her. It was an indication that she was an awakened soul. She says:

I entertained this world with all fanciful longings, but ultimately found it whirling and rocking due to greed, hatred, and ignorance of the people. Then I understood 'Love' is the real meaning of Gods heart, and it appeals to the deepest emotions of men and rouses in them a longing for Truth. I realized something out of nothing. At one time I gave it an understanding with the acquiring of knowledge the next moment I underwent deep study to seek temporal pleasure but now I confess that it failed to widen my understanding. O Lord! How weary and stale seems to me all the uses of this world. I can stand it no longer as my soul in full of discord and dismay.

SM69. Dokh Chein Travith Mokh Wuch Haras

Dokh chein travith mokh wuch haras
Teli deezi param saras manz thah
Chal zaanoon chui naar baav- saras
Chook zan kad tul shahmaras baal

Dokh= the troubles and anxieties; Chein Travith= Put it off; Mokh= Face; Wuch= See face to face; Haras= The Lord ; Teli:- In that situation; deezi=Jump in ; Param Sars= The vast expanse of universe, the world; Manz = Deep inside ;Thaah= Dive deep to see the lower world; Chal= Ingenuity; Zanoon= To know about; Chui = Have to undertake; Naar-Baav saras= Burning Vast expanse of universe; Chook= Blower, allegorical exhale and inhale of breath; Zan= As if ; Kad= Put off; Tul= Open the Lid or raise the vertebral column; Shah Marass= Legendry – serpent; Baal= Mountain allegorically vertebral column, to raise it to the extent to realize the awakening of kundalini.

Throw out the illusion and watch the grace of the lord. Submerge deep into the sea of bliss with a burning desire and willpower. This way all the physical energies with the powerful emotions will set free.
Lalleshwari followed Trika of Kashmir Shaivism which adopts Laya Yoga popularly known as Kundalini Yoga in Kashmir. She calls the Kundalini Shakti seated in the form of a serpent at the base of the spinal cord a Shah-Maar (Royal Serpent) the source of unlimited energy. This energy needs to be awakened and made to travel upward by sustained devotion. She calls upon the devotee to lift the massive lid, allegorically a big mountain off the container of the Shah-Maar (the dormant Kundalini Shakti) i.e., awaken it by the power of devotion. According to Kashmir Shaivism Lord Shiva is the principal deity controlling the universe. The lord has two aspects, Shiva, and Shakti though the two are the same, the two sides of a coin. Kundalini – The energy of depths.

On a scientific plane the brain is serially connected to neural networks which unify 'neural' vibrations which produce the spiritual consciousness of higher order. This is achieved through Meditation and deep exhale and inhale. As per Lal-Ded, 'Sadhak' releases a jet of air by exhale and inhale process which awakens the 'kundalini'. As such the knowledge of one truthful spirit is realized.

SM70. Dwaadashaanta Manddal Yas Diivas Thaji

Dwaadashaanta manddal yas diivas thaji
Naasikaa pavan dari anaahat rav.
Swayam kalpan anti chaji.
Paanay su deev; ta artsun kas?

Dwaadashaanta= a measure of twelve fingers, literally, here the distance found by measuring. The praana starts at the point of hrdaya and ends at dvaadashaanta, i.e., at twelve fingers from it; manddal= sphere, or locality; yas diivas thaji = as the abode of God; pavan=wind; Anaahatta rav= the eternal sound, self-created, the mystic syllable OM; Swayam kalpan anti tsaji= all vain imaginings flee from his mind, without effort, naturally; Paanay su Diiva; ta artsun kas? = He knows no God other than the Self, nor need he worship any other god.

He, who knows the Dvaadashaanta Manddala as the abode of God, can acquire the experience of developing the Supreme Consciousness of the mind. He can develop the crown of his head or sensors of brain or "Sahasrara".

He, who knows the constant Sound that is borne upon the prana rising from the heart to the nose, by breathing through the nostrils, can with proper care vibrates the mind, in such a manner that a frequency of Cosmic radiation is produced, which has an effect of landing, the seeker, to the thoughtless state of mind. It is a condition where all the vein imaginations flee from the mind and no other thought, except the concentrated thought "blissful state of the spirit," can penetrate inside the mind.

Naturally in this blissful state of mind Lal-Ded feels the pleasure of her merger with cosmic radiance. He who experiences this thoughtless state of mind is the magnificent person fit for worship. He knows no God other than the Self, nor need he worship any other god.

SM71. Dhami Dyunthum Shabnam Pyomut

Dhami dyunthum shabnum pyomutt
Dhami dyunthum pewan suur
Dhami dyunthum anigatti ratus
Dhami dyunthum dohus noor

Dhami= now; dyunthum=saw; Shabnum=dew; Pyomutt=formation; pewan=falling; suur=mixture of snow and rain; Anigatti=darkness; Ratus=night; Dohus=daytime; Noor=brightness

Now I saw dew formation; now I saw sleet and precipitation; now I saw darkness of night; now I saw day's sun bright. In this Vakh Lal Ded conveys about changing times. Nothing remains constant. Perhaps she hints towards Progress and realization of Divine powers, as nature is a manifestation of Divine.

It is impossible to reach God without change of mind, and those who cannot change their minds cannot change anything.

SM72. Dhami Aasis Lokutai Kuur

Dhami aasis lokutai kuur
Dhami sapnes zaam
Dhami chayes poffeh vargas tai
Dhami gayas poffeh nan
Doh yeli gai tai kaal aav kothan
Vaen chim vanan kostaan
Modur samsar tavnuk bazar
Praas chu ne kyazeh kanseh dwapaan

Dhami=just now; aasis=was Lokutai= small; kuur = girl; zaam= sister-in law; poff= father's sister; poffeh-nan= grandfathers' sister; doh= days; kaal= time; kothan= harden; vaen=now; chim vanan=they say, kostam=somebody; modur samsar= beautiful world; tavnuk bazar= deceitful things; kyazeh= why; dwapaan= questions.

Now I am a baby girl, now a sister-in law; as time rolls on, now I am an aunt to my brother's children, and now I become a grand aunt to my own brother's grandchildren; with passage of time, times hardened, and now I am called 'somebody.' Gorgeous and beautiful world, where deceitful things go on, Time does not tell, why! Time hath no stop and brings with it predictable quick and brief changes of life and things, resulting in man's feeling of utter insecurity.

The world is a dangerous place to live; not because of the people who are evil, but because of the people who don't do anything about it.

A separate Vakh:

SM 72A: *Doh yeli gai tai kaal aav kothan; Vani chim vanan kostaani.*
Modur samsaar taavnuk bazaar; Praas chhu na kyazeh kanseh daapaan.

I have passed the childhood, young and adult stages of my life. With the passage of time, the times have hardened, now I am being called as 'somebody' stranger. The world looks gorgeous and beautiful, but the deceitful things go on in this world and it is a dangerous place to live, time does not tell why it is so rather it brings with it changes of life and things resulting in a person's feeling of utter insecurity.

SM73. Dami Aasses Loukutai Kura-Jawan Kuur

Dhami aassses lokutai kuura
Dhami sapneyas jawaan kuur
Dhami aasses fearaan thoraan
Dhami sapneyas dazith soor

Dhami=now; Loukuti=small; Kura=girl; Sapnees=became; Jawaan=grown up; Kuur =girl; Aasis=was; Fehran Thoran =moving around; Dazith=in flames, ablaze; Soor =ashes.

Lal sees a continuous change. She says: Now I am a small girl; now I am seen as a grown-up girl; now I was moving around; now left as ash on ground. Learn from yesterday, live for today, hope for tomorrow. The important thing is not to stop questioning, where from I came.

SM74. Dami Deetham Gaej Dazwani

Dami deetham gaej dazvuni,
Dami dyunthum duh na ta nar,
Dami deethum pandavan henz maaji,
Dami dyunthum kraaji mas.

Dami=now; deunthum=saw; gaej=hearth; dazwani=ablaze; deh=smoke; na ta=neither nor; naar=fire; Pandavan henz moji=mother of Pandavas, (of Mahabharata); Kraji=potter's wife; mass=aunt.

Nothing in this world can last. It was but now I saw a hearth ablaze and now there is neither smoke nor fire it was but now I saw her as the Pandavas' mother and now she is merely a potter's aunt!
Everything changes. At one moment I saw the mother of the five Pandavas, at another moment I saw a potter's wife's aunt. The history of the Pandavas, and how their mother was reduced by misfortune to admit herself a potter's wife's aunt, is fully explained in the Mahabharata.

SM75. Dhami Deethum Nad Vahvani

Dhami deethum nad vahvani,
Dhami dyunthum sum na ta taar.
Dhami deethum thar pholwuni,
Dhami dyunthum gul nah tah khaar.

Dhami= just now; Nad=stream; deethum=to see; vahvani=flowing; sum=bank; taar=bridge; thar=bush; pholwuni= in bloom; gul=flower, rose; khar= thorn.

One moment I saw a little stream flowing, it was but now I saw it overflowing and flooded, another moment I saw neither a bridge nor its banks were seen. At one time I saw a bush blooming, at another time I saw neither a flower nor a thorn was seen! Look deep into nature, and then you will understand everything better.

SM76. Gaal Kadinam Bol Parinam

Gaal kadinam bol parinam
Dopnam tiy yas yuth ruchey,
Sahaz-kosmav puuz karinam,
Ba ami laney kas kya mochai

Gaal kadinam= they may abuse me; bol parinam =they may jeer at me; Dopnam tiy yas yuth rochai= they may say what pleases them; Sahaz-kosmav puuz karinam= they may worship me with flowers; Boh amlani kas kya mochai (mvotsey)= even these expressions of indifferent touches do not affect my mind.

Lal Ded says: Some people may abuse me or jeer at me, they may say what pleases them, and some may worship me with flowers. All these expressions of indifferent touches do not affect my mind. Since, I am a realized soul; I seem to be a stranger to myself with no duality in my mind. I am indifferent to blame or praise as I am concerned with my own self, and I do not bother what others have to say about me.

SM77. Gaatula Akh Vuchum Bwachi Suity Maran

Gaatula akh vuchum bwachi suity maran
Pan zan haraan pohni vaav laah
Neshidbodh akh vuchum vazas maaraan
Tana lall bha praraan tseyneyam na praah

Gaatula=wise man; Akh=one; Vuchum=saw; Bwachi=hunger; Suity Maran=dying of hunger; Pan=dead leaf; Zan Haraan=falling like dead; Pohni=winter season; Neshidbodh=a fool; Vuchum=saw; Vazas=cook; Maaraan=beating; Tana=since then; Praraan=waiting.

Lal Ded views life through every angle. This is her logical approach to understand the different sets and modules of life. Here Lal Ded portrays the poetic picture of two different approaches to life. This is in relation to 'food,' the daily need of the embodied souls. She explains, in the above Vakh as she views two approaches. She sees around her and is demoralized at the sight of inequality and injustice.

She has seen a wise man keeping hungry, nothing eating, therefore, is starving. The food is ready there for him, but he resists eating. He is getting pale, reduced to skeleton, withering, and falling like the leaves of autumn season, as do take place in the month of 'Poh' which corresponds to the month of November. Poh is the fall season in Kashmir. It is the season when the leaves get detached from the trees. Lal Ded considers him a *Gaatul* (a wise person).

She also noticed an utter fool, beating his cook for some fault in cooking his delicate dishes. What a contrast in human behavior!

This episode became an eye opening for Lal Ded. She weighed both the situations in the context of life standards and its impact on the life maintenance. Lal Ded gives a moderate way to both. To a man of learning, for want of food, who drops down dead like a winter leaf with slight wind, and a fool beating a cook. Since then, she looks for the day when false prestige will fade away from the minds of the people.

SM78. Gafilo Haquk Kadum Tul

Gafilo haquk kadum tul
Vuni chai sul tai chaandun yaar
Pur kar paida parvaaz tul
Vuni chai sul tai chaandun yaar

Gafilo=ignorant, regardless; haquk kadum tul=step forward first then desire; Vunie chai sul=it is never too late; chaandun (tchhaandun) yaar=make an earnest search for Him; Pur kar paida=have visionary feathers; parvaaz tul=soar high, think of Him; Vunie chai sul tai chaandun(tchhaandun) yaar=it is never too late to search for Him; God Shiva can be prayed any time.

To Lal Ded, God is one absolute Truth, Shiva, infinite and Omnipresent, all pervading. Lalleshwari is firm on Nirguna aspect of godhood, without any attributes, qualities, objectives or " personifications such as, God is gracious, merciful, just or great, as against its complementary Saguna counterpart, wherein visual or verbal images are used as catalysts of concentration on the focusing object, both as mental or material images so usually used by the followers of different religious sects in one form or the other. She tells the people to move in search of Him in the right direction. It is never late for any person to find Him. Have courage and determination. Any time is right to meditate and search for Him

SM79. Gagan Chei Bhutal Chei

Gagan chei bhutal chei,
Cheeie deyn pavan tai raath,
Arg chandun posh poen cheii
Soroi chei tai laagai kyah?

Gagan chei (tsei)= thou art the sky; bhuutal chei = thou art the earth; Cheeie deyn=thou are the day; pavan=wind; raath=night; Arg= sacrificial corn; chandun (tsandun)=sandal wood; posh=flower; poen=water; cheii =thou; Soroi cheei= Thou art all these and everything; laagai kyah= what may I, in worship, bring to Thee?

"O" Lord! Thou art the sky, and the earth,
You are the day air and the night.
Thou are the sacrificial corn, the sandal wood, flowers, and the water. Thou are all these and everything. What may I, in worship, bring to Thee?

SM80. Gaggan Paith Bhutal Shiv Yeli Dyunthum

Gaggan paith bhutal shiv yeli dyunthum
Ravas lobam na roznas shaaie
Sirikay prabhaav Shiv meh zoonum
Zal gav thalas sait meelith kyah

Gaggan paith=from the sky; bootlas=the earth; shiv yeli dyunthum= I experienced the whole universe as an embodiment of Supreme Shiva extended from the highest skies to the deepest extensions of underworld in such a huge form; Ravas labam na roznas shaaie= there seemed no place even for the Sun to show its face; Sirikay prabhaav Vishmy zonum= sun and whole universe as an embodiment of Supreme Shiva; Zal gav thalas sait meelith kyah= a superb spectacle of water and land mingled into one on its surface.

In my wanderings through the space, I see the beautiful Earth, as the creation of the Lord. I see His visionary glitter. I watch the reflections of the Sun rays coming from the Earth in all brilliant colours. The colours of the reflected rays are so beautiful that I find the rays of the Sun somewhat diminished in comparison to the reflected rays.

Since, Earth does not have any luminosity of its own, it is floating and revolving round its orbit, in the darkness of space, it is receiving light only from the Sun, rendering it beautiful. The beautiful Earth is thus, revealed to me through the light coming from the Sun. And since 3/4th of the Earth is under water, the land and water look mingled together, when seen from outer space. Lalla experiences a peculiar joy on seeing this charming phenomenon.

In this Vakh Lal Ded gives a depiction of her personal experience of her Lord's universal influence upon her ultimate awakening of self. She seems to have toured extensively and experienced Supreme Shiva as the manifestation of the whole universe in such a huge form as having extensions spread from the highest skies to the deepest underworld. She also gives a beautiful description of a strange spectacle experienced by her on the amalgamation of water and land on the surface of the earth with a few beams of sunlight making a beautiful illumination around. The depiction of Shiva in these lines suggests the essential spirit of Kashmir Shaivism that the universe is the manifestation of Supreme Shiva or Shaiva Darshan.

The Shaivas maintain that Shiva manifests himself as the universe through his cosmic energy Shakti, who is inseparable from Him. At the temporal level, these two cosmic principles, one transcendental and the other immanent, are represented by male and female principle. Shaiva's consider all females as manifestation of Shakthi.

SM81. Gaytrei Azappa Challa Aki Tajim

Gaytrei azappa challah aki tajim
Soo ham saatchi karmas thap
Ahmas loti pathi zathrei vaajim
Guru kath pajim chajim chaakh

Gayatri =The personified form of the Gayatri Mantra, a popular hymn from Vedic texts. She is also known as Savitri. The Gayatri is a universal prayer enshrined in the Vedas. Azapa = energy; Challah = by trick; Aki =by one; tajim= to know; Soo hum = Soo hum meditation has existed in India throughout the ages. It synchronizes the movements of breath with the mantra; Saatchi = of truth; karmas thap= To hold; Aham = ego; loti pathi = gently; zatheri = to clear the netting, especially of hair; vaajim= to work out; guru kath = masters orders; pajim= to obey; chajim = to tolerate; chaakh= complete surrender.

The observation of inhaling and exhaling through the nostrils and the Soo-Ham sounds, produced thereby was an innovation, which with due concentration of mind, helped me in the realization of celestial light. This was achieved only when I kept strong faith in the Guru's (Master's) direction, to watch and tune the rhythmic inhaling and exhaling; and thus, developed the technique of vibrating the mind by listening to the sounds of Soo-Ham without any interruption, for a definite period, a continuous wave form was released, and which enabled me to enter the thoughtless state of mind. To achieve such a state of mind and pleasure, I had to bear the reprimands of my Master to shun off the 'ego' or 'I-nesses with complete surrender, to His divine grace; So, I realized the highest conceivable state of Bliss of the human mind.

SM82. Gita Paraan Paraan Kouni Moodukh

Gita paraan paraan kouni moodukh
Gita paraan paraan kouni goi soor,
Gita paraan paraan zinddh keth roodukh,
Gita paraan paraan doud Mansoor

Here, to me it appears, Lal Ded advises that by reading Holy Scriptures one does not become God. She quotes an example of Mansoor**[7], who was the most controversial figure in the history of Islamic mysticism. He travelled widely, first to Baghdad, Mecca, and afterwards to Khuzestan, Khorasan, India, and Turkestan. When he returned to Baghdad, he had his bold preaching of union with God. So much so that he declared himself to be God. On this he was arrested and condemned to death. He was cruelly executed on (28 March 9I3) and later burnt He wrote several books and a considerable poetry. He passed into Muslim legend as the prototype of the intoxicated lover of God.

SM83. Gwarai Mole Tai Gwarai Maeji

Gwarai mole tai gwarai maeji
Gwarai divaan netran gaash
Yem chaeris maeris vaster laegiy
Chhui punyas bhagiy ta paapan naash

Gwarai=guru; mole=father; maejei=mother; diwan=gives; netran=eyes; gaash=light, awakening; yem chaeris moris vaster laegiy= to under-take service to fellowmen and poverty-stricken multitudes; chui punyas bhagiy paapan naash= It transforms the soul, as such the seeker is declared free from guilt, all sins, and punishments. Punyas bhagiy=a partner in return of good deeds. Paapan=sin, wickedness; Paapan naash=crusader of all sins committed by the disciple.

Lal-Ded strongly encourages all seekers of truth, to have close relations with the Guru. They must come together with the divine spirit of Guru with such passion, that they must take him as the personification of their parents. Guru changes the disciple's physical, mental, and spiritual powers. Thus, it is with the mild touch of the Guru that the mental "third eye" is awakened.

My Guru is sinless. He is humble, humane, and perfect. His holiness has directed me to under-take service to fellowmen and poverty-stricken people. It is the practical expression of Love. The actions which lead to Good Karma and bring peace are called Punya. Punya is the moral strength and transforms the soul, providing it with a source of energy to raise higher, as such the seeker is absolved of all the sins.

(Another version)

SM84. Guru Chu Ishwar, Gurui Maheshwar

Guru chu ishwar, gurui Maheshwar
Guru chuy saakhshatkar,
Guru chu mole tai guru chu maeji,
Guru devaan tran bhavanan tar

Guru=the supreme God for the disciple; chu Ishwar= is God; gurui Maheshwar=guru is Shiva; saakhshatkar = reality; mole =father; maeji=mother; devan=gives; tran bhavanan=three worlds; tar=bridge; guru is a bridge.

Guru is God,
Guru is reality,
Guru is father and mother,
Guru is a bridge to pass the three worlds.
Lal Ded was a great yogi. The yogi endowed with complete enlightenment sees through the eyes of spiritual knowledge, the entire universe in his/her own self and regards everything as the self and nothing else.

SM85. Gratta Chu Pheraan Zeari Zearey

Gratta chu pheraan zeari zearey
Vokui zaani gratuk chal
Grata yeli pheari ta zaivul neri
Gov vaati paanai gratai bal

Grratta chu pheran= the mill will turn; zeari zearey = Sure and steady; Vokui zaani=pivot of the wheel knows; gratuk chal=the tricks of the wheel; Grata yeli pheri=once the wheel is propelled; zavul neri=it will grind fine; Gov vati panai=the grain will automatically reach; gratai bal=destination.

The hand operated grinding wheel turns round and round; the central shaft round which it moves, feels the brunt of this movement; and once it turns it produces fine flour; the grain eventually reaches its destination.

When the mill is brought in motion sure and steady the mill will turn. Once you propel the wheel, we get fine floor. Mind is the pivot; it should know how best to turn the mill. Once it turns, it will grind fine, and grain will find its way to the mill. It means that man reaches his destination if he decides.

Lal Ded has woven a wonderful metaphor of a water-driven floor mill to establish the spiritual awakening of a devotee. The slow movement of water driven mill makes it grind a fine floor. The same is true of the seeker who tries to cross the stages of his development slowly and steadily. The floor is the outcome of his Sadhana. The slowly ground floor is of a seeker who can direct his mind slowly and steadily towards his realization of self and his mind towards his goals till the final stage of being one with his Lord is reached.

SM86. Guras Maal Pew Aamein Naatan

Guras maal pew aamein naatan
Beyan poshain swaad kyah aashiay
Yei haal gurus ta raah kya chaattan
Ath brahm kulis meo kya paiyei

Guras=master; maal pew=desired; aamein naatan= lamb's meat; Beyan poshain=other animals; swaad kyah aashiay=how would they taste; Yei haal gurus=if this is the attitude of master; raah kya chaattan=disciples are not to be blamed; Ath Brahm kulis meo kya paiyei= what type of spiritual fruit, this body's tree will produce.

Once 'Sed Mole', the famous guru of Lal-Ded, was enquired of as to what he would like to take as a special dish at Lunch. The Master replied '*Amme Natta,*' a preparation of lamb's meat. Lal-Ded listened to it with a restraint, and smile, obeying an impulse from within retorted silently. How cruel! Why lambs' meat only, why not to ask for tasting the flesh of other animals too. How poor! If this is the state of mind of the graceful master, what better can be expected of his disciples? How can the flesh of cruelly killed lamb bring forth the light of divinity in the Master and his disciples? What type of spiritual fruit, this body's tree will produce (on eating the poor lamb's meat). How can the Lord be grown in the digit of the moon or cerebrum of the brain by such wrong feed and cruelty?

SM87. Guru Kath Hridiyas Manz, Bag Ratam

Guru kath hridiyas manz, bag ratam
Gang zal naavam tan tai mann
So deh zeevan mukhti pravum
Yem bhyyii chollum poallum akh

Guru Kath=guru's sayings; hriadiyas manz=merged my heart; Gang zal= sacred waters of Ganga; Naavam=washed; tan tai man=heart and soul; zeevan mokhti= release my soul from the bondage of karma; pravoom=attained; Yem bhyyii chollum (tsolum)=the fear of death was removed; poallum akh=I came nearer to lord.

Ever since I have come close with my Guru, I have merged myself completely in him. I follow his rule with heart and soul. Having washed my mind and body with the sacred waters of Ganga, a strange realization of joy and ecstasy was realized by me and as such I was able to release my soul from the bondage of karma. I cut across the possibility of rebirth; as such I attained relief. With all my body intact, now I have become "Jeewan Mukhti". The birth of the birth less means the revelation of the mystery in the soul of man and thus I enjoy an endless and unbroken calm. As such the fear of death lurking within my mind was removed. So slowly and slowly I came nearer and nearer to the gracious light of the lord.

The 'Jeevan Mukhti', in his upward path towards union with God, receives light of illumination, in varying measures. The mystic illumination, in which the Absolute makes himself evident, is the divine essence of Lord. At this stage the aspirant becomes a perfect unit, to whom all resort for aid.

SM88. Guru Monui Lallishuri Guru

Gwrai monui Lalleshwari guru,
Gwrai vonduyo padan paan,
Tuith kya aasi yuth buthi horiyo,
Gwrai karyo paan arpan

Gwrai=teacher; monui Lalleshwari guru=Lal Ded acknowledged her Guru; vonduyo padan paan=she wanted to sacrifice herself at the feet of her guru; Tuith kya aasi yuth=what can there be; buthi horiyo=how can I repay you for the path you showed to me, how can I repay you for the knowledge you imparted to me; Guru karyo paan arpan= 'O' Guru, I want to sacrifice myself at your feet.

The Guru is the bestower of knowledge. In this vakh Lal Ded is all praise for her Guru. Lalleshwari was an awakened soul who had achieved all the stages of divine realization. She was quite knowledgeable and well-versed in the spiritual matters. Her preceptor (Guru) had guided her in every step till she achieved her goals. Her poetic compositions (Vakhs) are an ocean of knowledge and contain all guidance for spiritual growth. Lal Ded admits that all what she had achieved was due to her Guru for whom she had the highest regard. She wants to repay to her guru some gurudakshana for the knowledge he had imparted to her but finds nothing that can be equal to His teachings. She finally says that only to sacrifice at the feet of her guru would only be a befitting gurudakshana or my Guru. Lalleshwari was a great devotee of the divine word AUM (Pranava) and claims to have succeeded in her achievements by reciting and tuning her inner self to the sacred sound of the divine word. Her great sadhana bore the required fruits and she merged in her 'Chit-Jyoti', the luminous light of pure consciousness and got freed from the cycle of life and death rather dispelled the fear of death.

SM89. Gwar Shabdas Yus Yatchh Patchh Barey

Gwar Shabdas yus yatchh patchh barey
Gyan vagi ratey chet torgas
Yendri shomrith anand karey
Adha kus mari tai maaraan kas

Gwara shabdas=sacred words, yus=who so ever; yatchh patch bare=has faith; Gyan=true knowledge. Chet=consciousness; torgas=horse, controls the horse of his consciousness; Kus Mari=who dies; maaraan kas = never slain

He who trusts his master's word and controls the mind-(horse), with reins of wisdom, he shall not die, and he shall not be killed.

A true Guru is one who has removed pride from his heart. He preaches the truest of the true. He is Humble and contented. The Guru is sinless; he is above man's capacities. The candidate must merge himself with the Guru and be thus inspired with indestructible power and force. Those having faith in master's words, his true knowledge, and his towering personality, shape their lives towards attaining peace of mind. The Master becomes a connecting link between God and Man. He removes their hurdles and untwists the divine knowledge. He reveals the secrets of the organs of action and awareness. He makes the disciples to live in constant devotion and penance. The disciple who follows the rules and guidelines of the Master is enriched with a spiritual force and his vital powers soar higher and higher as such he never dies and is never slain. He holds his senses in control; it is he who enjoys the peace of mind.

SM90. Gwaran wonnum Kunui Vachun

Gwaran wonnum kunoi vachun
Nebra dopnam andar achun.
Suy gav Lali mey vakh ta vachun,
Tavai mey hyotum nahangai nachun.

Gwaran=guru, teacher; wonnum=told, directed; kunai=one; vachun=percept, become aware of something through the senses; Nebra doupanam andar achun(atchun)= to withdraw my Gaze from without to within; Suy gav Lali mey= Taking that to heart, I Lalla; Vakh ta vatsun=a phrase meaning ability to see, hear a song; Tavay mey hyotum=that is why I began; nahangai=naked; natsun or nachun=to wander, roam.

Lalla's Guru whispered into her ear one Gwar Shabad; "Draw within from without." He asked her to seek herself within her, not without. The magic worked. She at once by a reflex action withdrew from without. She merrily explored deep into the depths of her inner soul. She roamed about the depths of her soul in relation to her body and the super soul called Almighty Lord. The Vakh explicitly conveys that Lalla experienced instant spiritual transformation and was thrown into a state of ecstasy on receiving the Guru's word. The towering personality of the Guru assisted her in shaping her life towards divinity. She found peace with a wonderful heavenly awakening light around. She began to toss her head in energetic dance completely naked unaware of herself.

My Guru assisted me in shaping my life towards divinity. He directed me: "From without withdraw your gaze within and fix it on the innermost Self." I, Lalla, took to heart this one precept, and, therefore naked I began to dance. I found exceeding peace with a brilliant godly wakening light around. I began to toss my head in energetic dance completely naked unaware of myself.

Kashmiri phrase '*nahangai natchun*' apparently seems to be current rumor for common people like us. Unlike the English word 'Nude' equivalent to the English word 'naked' which is used in Kashmiri in multipurpose senses. (a) Without normal apparel; scantily dressed; sparsely appareled; Unmindful of dress worn by lady irrespective of the norms of the time. (b) Likewise, the Kashmiri word is double meaning equivalent to roaming about or dancing. (c) It has another meaning to me. The Sanskrit word NANGA means without any limb. ATMAN has no limb but is pure in spirit. It is both affirmative and intuitive, being the abode of ecstasy. It is Ananda.

Lal Ded has given highest importance to a guru in attaining spirituality. According to her a person who follows the advice of his guru with devotion attains merger with the Divine. After receiving the teachings from her guru, Lal Ded did not stop there. All around her were conflicts and chaos. Her people needed her guidance. She had a mission to perform.

SM91. Gwaras Precheome Sassi Latey

Gwaras precheome sassi latey
Yas nu kenh vanan tas kyah naav
Pritchhaan pritschaan thachis tu loosis,
Kenh nas nishi kyaahtaam draav.

Gwaras=teacher, guru; Precheome=asked, requested; Sass Lattai= thousand times; Yas Na Kenh Vanan= He that is nameless; Tas Kyah Naav= How shall the Nameless be defined? Pritchhaan pritchhaan=asked and asked; thachis ta luusas= got tired, weary, but all in vain; Kenh Nas Nishay= the Nameless Unknown; kyaahtaam draav= that nameless is the source of something that we see -this creation, universe.

Absolute truth can be learnt from the Guru. It needs firm faith in Gurus words.

Lalla says I requested my spiritual guide, a thousand times, with consciousness: "He that is nameless, how that nameless is named?" Since the curiosity to know is a worship of higher order, it implies a belief in the existence of higher power, without which there could be no worship. It was by gradual process of thought that Lal Ded wanted to become conscious of a new force, for establishing the identity of the Lord. As her soul was in anguish she asked and asked till she became tired, mute, and silent. Lo! The nameless non-existent and invisible became the source of her realization. This is the beginning of her awakening in spiritual bliss. That paved way to enter the realm of ecstasy and that resulted in the realization of 'something evolved out of nothing.' It was all puzzling but great and wonderful. The Guru directed her in seeing that **Nameless** within self.

The Vakh clearly state that when Lal Ded asked her master (Guru) a thousand times what the name of the nameless was and when she had exhausted enquiring repeatedly, she suddenly got awakened to the truth of her enquiry. The truth that was revealed to her was that the goal of man was only to be one with the universal void (Shunya). The truest truth of the universal Lord is His nothingness. The truth of the total realization of man is getting lost in this sea of nothingness and becoming an indivisible part of the whole.

SM92. Gyaan Marg Chaai Haak Vair

Gyaan marg chaai haak vair
dizeys shama-dama kreyi poni,
lam chakhr posh prani kreyi daar
khen-khen mvachiy vaarai chhen

Gyaan Marg=a divine and blissful garden; chaai=is; haak =haak (collard green) is a green vegetable very common in Kashmir, who eat it to their hears content; vair=a vegetable bed;Dizeys shama-dama=this is the approach of working with; 'Shama'=self-restraint; 'Dama'=continuence; kreeyi panni=well water(lit),here this green vegetable means to control self, ones actions, behaviour and deeds, lest some other animal enters and eats it. Here haak or green vegetable means actions and deeds of present life; Lam Chakhr =shakhti, kamandal; Lam Chakhr=the Yogic Mooladhara Chakra, situated at the base of spine; prani kreyi daar =actions, deeds; Kheyna-kheyna mwatsi vaaray cheyn = mere right thoughts won't do you any good to counter wrong action

The path of knowledge is like a kitchen garden, where a house holder grows the vegetables to meet his requirements. But this garden needs tobe irrigated regularly. This is the approach of working with 'Shama' i.e., self-restraint and 'Dama' i.e., continence.

Many complain about bad thoughts, effects of bad karma, etc. Lal Ded has an effective solution for these problems, one can let the thoughts come and go, if a bad thought appears then right action is needed to counter it. One needs right action to counter wrong action and mere right thoughts won't do you any good to counter wrong action. The pathway of Jnana is a kailyard; Fence it with self-restraint and pious deeds. Then let the goats of former karma browse in it and be fattened to be animals fit for sacrifice at the altar of the Goddess Shakthi.

(Goats of past actions and their fruits slain in sacrifice, leaving no karma behind), the kailyard of karma thus browsed away, you gain release.

SM93. Gyanaek Ambar Puurith Tane

Gyanaek ambar puurith tane
Yim pad Lali dapi tim hraidyei aankh;
Karaan pranavik liiye kor Lali
Chet jyoti kassee marnach shainkh

Gyanaek ambar= Clothed with the knowledge and wisdom; puurith tane =robes clad on body; Yim pad Lali dapi tim hreydi ankh= knowledge of truth engraved the vakhs that Lalla spoke; Kaarana Prnavaki layi kor Lalle = by means of the mystic syllable OM, Lalla merged; Chet jyoti kaosan maranun sheynkh= Lalla merged in her 'Cit-Jyoti', the luminous light of pure Consciousness.

Clothed with the knowledge and wisdom of truth engrave the vakhs that Lalla spoke. She says lock these in your memory and tune yourself with the recitation of sacred letter 'OM'. You will realize a situation where the soul shines forth in its purity. A pure awareness of self is realized. With the realization of the 'moments of illumination', immortality of higher order is attained.

SM94. Haa Manushi Kav Chuy Logmoot Parmas

Haa manushi kav chuy logmoot Parmas
Kya ze goy apzis pazyook broonth,
Dish boz vash karnookh par dharmas
Kow zan challie zen marnook kroonth.

Haa manushi='O' man; kav chuy logmoot Parmas=why are you fond of someone who is not your true love; Kya ze goy apzis=why have you taken false for true; pazyook broonth= mistaking falsehood for truth; Dish boz=understand and know; vash karnookh par dharmas = ignorance that binds you to the false; Kow zan challie= how can you overcome; marnook kroonth = the fear of life and death cycle.

Lal Ded puts a question to herself: "Ah me, you're drunk with the wine offered by some stranger and an enemy! How strange! You've selected falsehood for the truth. You acted as a fool and got lured to the glamour of this life and thereby stringed yourself to the unending wheel of birth and death."

She feels her personal consciousness has been behaving as if under the influence of a drink offered by someone who's not her love. She feels she has preferred falsehood for truth and cannot very strangely differentiate between the two. She laments further that she has been fooled into acting falsely against the reality and has thus been involved into the unending cycle of birth and death. She feels she has been caught by the illusion of this world.

Lalleshwari was a fully awakened soul who had come to this life with a mission of bringing home to the common man the futility of this existence. She wanted to get the man on the true path of existence to achieve the goals of life. She wanted the man to understand and know the ignorance that binds him to the false. She wanted the people to differentiate between falsehood and truth. The essential thing for a man to understand is that the human life is the only opportunity among millions of other life forms for working suitably for the absolute emancipation and proceeding nearer to our Lord.

SM95. Haa Manushi! Kya Ze Chukh Vothaan Seki Loor

Haa manushi! Kya ze chukh vothaan seki loor
Ami rakhi haa maali pakki na naav
Ye luuekhei narayanan karmani raekhee
Ti maali hekee na feerith kanh

Haa manushi= O man; Kya ze chukh vothaan= why do you twist; Seki loor= rope of sand; ami rakhi haa maali pakki na naav= You cannot tow your boat with it; YE luuekhei narayanan=what God has written; karmani raekhee= in karma's line, whatever is destined; ti maali hekee na feerith kanh=none can alter or reverse it.

So said Lal Ded.
O ye Ignorant man, why do you twist a rope of sand? With this you cannot tow the boat of your life. Whatever God has recorded "in your life-karma" Cannot be altered or reversed by anyone. God lays down reward or punishment not arbitrarily as one's 'fate', but according to one's karma. Ceremonial rites, pujas and yajnas and the like are 'rope of sand' and will not avail to change what God has ordered. The man must take the importance of karma into account. (The righteousness alone is the line that will ferry you across. The good deeds alone will change your destiny.)
However, if one is repentant of one's mistakes and does not repeat them then the prayers (japa) have the power of reducing the effect of karma to a large extent. The role of an umbrella (prayer) in the scorching sun is an example and karma being reduced to a pin prick instead of breaking a leg is another.

SM96. Haasa Bole Padinam Saasa

Haasa bole padinam saasa
Mei mani vaasaa khaid naa hai
Yudwai Shankar bakhchit aasaa
Mokris saasaa mal kya paiyee

Haasa bole padinam saasa, Mei mani vaasaa khaid naa ha = people living nearby ridiculed and taunted at me and called me names; Yudwai=if; Shankar bakhchit=devotee of Shankar, Shiva; aasaa=am mal=dirt; Mokris saasaa mal kya paiyee= I am like a mirror which does not lose its quality when rubbed with ashes.

In my forward march for the setting free of my soul, the people living nearby mocked and jeered at me and called me names with burning stinging words. As a true devotee of 'SHIVA', I would not feel any pain, nor would my sentiments get hurt. I am like a mirror, which does not lose its quality even when it is rubbed with ashes. God sees the righteous and keeps Him safe.

SM97. Hacivi Haarinji Pyatsuv Kaan Gom

Hachivi haarinji pyatsuv kaan gom
Abahak chaan pyom yath raazdhaana
Manz bhag bazaars kulfa ros vaan gom
Tirth ros paan gom kus maali zaaney

Hachivi=wooden; haarinji=bow; pyatsuv= a kind of grass; kaan gom =arrow; Abahak=unskilled; chaan=carpenter; pyom=got; yath=this; raazdhaana =palace; Manz bhag bazaars =in a busy bazaar; kuluph rous= without lock; vaan =shop; Tirth rous=without bathing in holy waters.

A wooden bow and rush grass for an arrow: A carpenter unskilled and a palace to build: A shop unlocked in a busy bazaar: A body uncleansed by waters holy am I, oh who can tell my plight?

Lal-Ded explains that without a proper Guide, it is very difficult to find the path of spirituality. She has an urge to learn about the mystic truth. She explains that she is like a wooden bow, with all potential energy, but without any effective arrow "a blade of grass." She is like a carpenter unskilled and a palace to build. She is like a shopkeeper in a busy street, who with his negligence keeps the shop unlocked in a busy bazaar. In her hopelessness she feels that she has been misled and misguided by none other than her own mind. Even though she has dived deep in the sacred springs for a celestial bath, yet she feels her mind and body uncleansed. She encourages the seeker of truth to look within for a change of heart.

A diligent study of Lalla Ded Vakhs reveals that she may have first tried her luck with a guru other than Siddha Srikanth. His prescription and spiritual discourses somehow failed to lead her far on the spiritual highway. It was in a vein of sheer dismay that she poured out 'Abakh chaan pyom yath razdanay'. Later a highly talented and reputed scholar yogi of the time, Sedha Mol of Srinagar was her guru. He taught her spiritual disciplines during the early years of her life.

SM98. Hai Gura Parameshwaraa

Hai gura Parameshwaraa
Bavtam tee chei chuy andrie veiud
Doshwii wopadaan kandi-puraa
Huh kav turoon ta haa kav tote

Hai gura=O Guru; Parameshwaraa =calling her Guru as God; Bavtam tee= tell me; chei chuy andrie veiud = you know the secret truth; Doshwii wopadaan= Both Praanas arise; kanda-puraa= from the navel region; Huh gao turoon= why is huh cold; haa gao tote = why is haah hot.

Lalla affirms the sutra of Guru Gitta that Guru is Parmeshwara-The True Divine Being. The blissful one is the Guru, to whom she addresses for bestowing her true knowledge, which is natural flow of the AUM –the seed of inner experience.

Lalla requests her Guru "O! Guru, you are as a god to me. Tell me, you know the secret truth. Both Praanas arise from 'Kandapura', the place of the navel region. Kindly tell me as to how the two components of breath in this body complex, "inhale" and "exhale", are cold and hot." Both the 'Ha-Ha and Hoo-Ha' are but 'Pranas' inhaling and Apana (exhaling) forces of life in the yogic processes. The short breath is cold, and the long breath is warm. Why so?

SM99. Ham Ham Karaan Gondum Ta Moroom

Ham ham karaan gondum ta moroom
Kaisar van vollum chattith nar
Yeli ho maali kaam kroodh lob moh golum
Teli ho maali labum und maidaan haal

Ham ham karan=with all my might, strength;gondum ta morum=gondum ta moroom=chained and kicked,refers to achieving success in capturing and killing the ferocious beast of my powerful emotions; Kaise=a lion, a beast; van vollunchattith nar = capturing the ferocious beast in the forest with all her might and dragging it to mere insignificance, the dense forest of my mind;yeli ho maali=when I;kaam,kroodh,lob,moh= pride, greed, lust, desirec;golum=controlled,killed;Teli ho maali=Then, I Lalla; labum lobum end maidaan-e-sar= I was able to realize my desired goals.

Mind can be controlled by patience and steady practice. Sadhana or meditation requires an alert nervous control and muscular coordination. Then only the feat of control of mind and judgement is achieved. It is like catching a lion in the jungle and dragging it by its mane and reducing it to mere insignificance. Achievement can be attained by killing the sinful instincts i.e., lust, anger, conceit, and greed within. Thus, by observing the discipline of control of mind my soul is freed from the weight which keeps it down and it rises to the top of the universe. Thus, I reached the abode of His lively presence and realized the 'Present' with the vision of His magnificent grace.

The Vakh clearly talks about the great passions like pride, greed, lust, desire etc. are responsible for all worldly woes. They blind all human reason giving rise to all conflict and trouble between individuals. These emotions stop spiritual progress as the mind every time keeps busy with one or the other emotional outburst. The mind gets no time to think on its purer thoughts. So, it's the first important function of a seeker in the spiritual field to rid his mind of these fiery emotions and keep it cool. Lal Ded had success over these most awful foes of spiritual progress. She beautifully compares them all to a wild beast of the forest. She says it was only after capturing and destroying the ferocious beast with all her might, that she was able to reach the goal.

SM100. Heh Nish Hah Draav Shah Kya Gavi

Heh nish hah draav shah kya gavi
Hehas ti hah-hus shah chi zaan
Ruh nish mur draav kya vuchui
Kya rood bakie kya gav faan

Heh=inhale; nish=from, nish also means near; hah=exhale; draav= came out; shah=breath; kya=what; gavi=means; hehas = inhale; hah-hus=exhale; chi=is; zaan=relation; ruh=soul, passion; mur or mor=body, birth; draav= come out; vuchui=seen, realized; kya=what; rood bakie= has remained; kya gav faan= what has perished, frozen.

Inhale gives rise to exhale and that is breath
The link between inhale and exhale is breath
When soul leaves the body, what is left behind
The dead defeated and demolished corpse

In this vakh Lalla lays emphasis on alternate nostril breathing, popularly known as Anulom Vilom, which is great for balancing and relaxing the nervous system. To focus attention on breath during asana. Inhale through the nose, and then open your mouth and exhale slowly, making a "HA" sound.

It is useful to exhale through the nostrils. The reason for this (aside from the nostrils being the way we are meant to breathe) is that during exhale breath is warm and would heat the tongue which then heats the rest of the system, when the aim of both these mouth techniques is cooling (the tongue in these acts as a heat exchanger), like a refrigerator. The connection between the inhale and exhale is the breath, the soul, the vital air (prana) rising from navel along pingla nadi is warm when exhaled from nose. The air gets warmed up by the heat glowing at the navel region. Lalla Ded asserts that Brahmand is the moon-region at the extreme end of sushmana nadi and is naturally cold. A cold current coming down the sushmana nadi cools the breath carried by Ida during the process of breathing in. When the soul (breath) comes out of the body-then only the physical dead corpse remains. And thus, nothing remains from the life of a person, the body gets destroyed and demolished.

SM101.   Hu Kus Ta Bo Kus Teliwan Che Kus

Hu kus ta bo kus teliwan che kus
Anoom batook ladoom daige
Shaah kitch kitch vaay mano
Brahman Brumus poonie chakoom
Brahma brumus tekis tekha
Hu Kheyie bhanga tu pur Jung-Tumaray Baba chalo

This vakh of Lal Ded has undergone a lot of corruption of words. However, picking up the threads, Lal Ded in this complex vakh speaks about the Trinity.

'Hu'- 'hu' is a Sanskrit word meaning that which is worshipped, honored, or adored.

*Line 1. Hu kus ta bo kus teliwan che kus (Brahma Vishnu, Shiva, - **Trinity**)*

*Line 2. Anoom batook ladoom daige ('Life' is conceived, and a perfect being enters in the womb of the mother in the form of **soul** to which, Lalla 'refers' in Kashmiri as 'Batook' a duck.)*

*Line 3. Shaah kitch kitch vaay mano (beginning of life comes about, and the soul or mind starts lively with the **inhale and exhale of breath**. Then by and by child grows in the womb)*

*Line 4. Brahman Brumus poonie chakoom (Brahman & Atman are the same thing. The fact that this doesn't easily make sense is the **illusion**.)*

Line 5. Brahma brumus tekis tekha (brum=illusion). Maya-The supernatural power used by gods and demons to produce illusions. Rig Veda does not suggest the word Maya as always good or always bad. Rig

Veda says there are two kinds of Maya: divine Maya and undivine Maya, the former being the foundation of truth, the latter of falsehood.

Line 6. Hu Kheyie bhanga tu pur Jung - Tumaray Baba chalo (life is maya) (leaving the body, the jīva atma, the soul has left the body to mingle with the **Parama -atama**, the main soul).

Bhanga has a nerve stimulant property. Bhang has been consumed in India for centuries. Effects of Bhanga include: An altered state of consciousness. The user may feel "high", very happy, ecstatic, relaxed, sociable, and uninhibited. Distorted perceptions of time and space. The user may feel more sensitive to things around them and may also experience a more vivid sense of taste, sight, smell and hearing. Apart from that, in Buddhism, bhanga a Pali term means "dissolution" or "breaking up." Bhanga is one of the 16 stages of knowledge through which the Buddhist passes during meditation until reaching **nirvana (heaven, paradise).**

Lal Ded in this complex vakh speaks about the Trinity, Soul, breathing process, Illusion, Brahman, and Atman being same. Every line of this six-line vakh carries volumes of meaning.

To recall, in one of Lal Deds vakhs she says that she has seen the Pralaya. Further to that —while in cosmos Lalla hears a conversation going on between three great cosmic figures.

Here Lal Ded uses the metaphor in a figurative expression.

Hu kus= Who is he? ***Brahma, the creator!*** comes the celestial reply.

Bu kus = Who am I? Divine answer comes-***Vishnu, the sustainer!***

Tele van Chu kus = Then, who are you? **Shiva, the destroyer!** A Heavenly voice retorts.
So, Hu Kus-Brahma; Bu kus-Vishnu; Chu kus- Shiva
Brahma, Vishnu, and Shiva -all the three work together in a never-ending pattern. Together, they represent Indian Trinity (Trimurti) and GOD. They are not separate Gods. They are an integral and inherent and intrinsic part of Nature.

Together they represent **Brahman** (Isvara), or in other words, the 3 most significant forms of Brahman are **Brahma, Vishnu**, and **Shiva**. Brahman is the Supreme Personality of Godhead.

Brahman supersedes the worldly distinction between being and non-being.

In Vedic cosmogonies, Brahman or Purusha or Devi are the terms used for the primary creator.

Brahma, Vishnu, Shiva = Trinity = Brahman

According to Bhagavat Gita, Brahman is identical with **atman** (the individual self) and created by Krishna, who calls it his "womb" and explains that the world sprung out of it. Brahman is the supreme controller. It manifests and controls the world. It creates **Maya or illusion.**

Brahman cannot be seen with the naked eye. It can only be experienced. Brahman is present everywhere. Sages of the past have experienced the Brahman and have become realized souls. Upanishad's praise and honour Brahman and say it is indestructible. Brahman cannot be burnt, made wet or blown away. It has neither shape nor color. It cannot be seen and cannot be smelt too. Brahman dwells in every living being according to Advaita.

Advaita - a Vedantic doctrine that identifies the individual **self (atman)** with the ground of reality (**brahman**).
The saying goes 'The Supreme Brahman alone is the truth, the universe is illusory', deceptive.

According to Advaita of Sankara, all **individual souls** are parts of the **Supreme Brahman**. After getting liberation from the human bodies, the individual souls become one with the Brahman. Death is meant only for the body and not for the **soul. The Soul is an immortal, illustrious and glorious bridge between human body and the God.**

We are born with human Soul, which originates from the God. Thus, -the **Ultimate Soul (Paramatma)** or the God is different from the **human being or human soul or (Jivatma)**. This duality of innate consciousness is the central theme of Vedas.

The personal self, which is subject to helplessness and sorrow, is Jivatma (the physical body). The other Self, which is free from every sorrow, is Antaratma, the indwelling Human Soul.
Dvaita Vedanta explains brahman as supreme of everything in the universe, and this world/universe is not illusionary but is the actual creation of Brahman. Therefore, there is an eternal (endless) distinction between absolute reality and individual self-reality.

Atman is the soul of man. The soul of man is one with and the same as Brahman. When Brahman within an individual is referred to, it is referred to as the Atman. Thus Atman = Brahman. The fact that this doesn't easily make sense is the illusion.

So, **Atman-Brahman** isn't a being, according to Hinduism. Atman-Brahman is the true reality of things, and it is everywhere and deep, deep inside of each person.

A person has an individual 'soul' (in Hinduism – the Jiva) that survives death, and it is the 'soul' that passes from one birth to another. The innermost part of the soul is the **atman.**

Lal-Ded is mystified as she wants to know; who is that? Who you are and who am I?" Then she herself answers that He; you, and I are permanent imperishable 'Self'. The delusion of "mine", "yours" and "His", is caused when one identifies the self with the perishable body. One should therefore separate oneself from the false sense of 'I'.

Here Lal Ded beautifully explains that it is by gradual process of evolution that 'Life' is conceived, and a perfect being enters in the womb of the mother in the form of soul to which, Lalla 'refers' in Kashmiri as 'Batook' a duck. It is at that very moment the beginning of life comes about, and the soul or mind starts lively with the inhale and exhale of breath. Then by and by child grows in the womb to its full growth then after the birth freedom of spirit is reached when God in him realizes itself.

Thus, God in the form of soul in the body develops to its full strength, and by and by the soul itself acquires the knowledge of nine gateways and develops ten powers. As such the body with its developed mind develops a character and inspiration of proceeding towards Him with all devotion and zeal. To gain God-consciousness of higher order, the body secretes a Hormone by intense concentration and meditation to which Lal-Ded calls 'Shashikal or Amrit. The celestial hormone is sprinkled in the Forehead in the space between the eyebrows. This makes us to feel cool and refreshing with the result, the mental "third eye", with penetrating vision appears in the space between two eyebrows, as a white scar.

It may also convey the meaning that things which appear between sky and earth are transient. Nothing is permanent on this earth. The things and persons whom we love passionately, all are decayable. The worldly things appear pleasurable due to moh-maya. A person never thinks of his/her own end under the impact of divine mesmerizing power called maya. Many spiritual saints and preachers tell in their sermons that don't run after money. Worldly things are illusion (moh-maya). God is truth. Human values like pity, mercy and love are divine virtues, but there is satanic power which leads us towards greed, sloth, gluttony, and treachery. The power which stops us to practice human virtues and keep us busy in all worldly activities is called Moh-Maya. Kabeer says, Maya is the most deceiving power and keep us busy in satanic activities so we should try to practice human virtue. All desires are illusions.

Many elderly people in Kashmir may be aware of one of the most popular cradle songs of Lal Ded told by grandmothers was, "Hukus Bukus Telli Waan Che Kus..." which was written during the time when Shaivism was at its peak in Kashmir. This lullaby without doubt across sections of the society in Kashmir topped the chart of lullabies. It is believed that since ages, the ones produced by the arrangement of words in this poem as well its rhythm has a calming effect for toddlers. Years later, it was realized that over the period, it got lost into translation and lately listened to correct one, which goes like this:

-Tse Kus Be Kus Teli Wan Su Kus

Who are you and who am I, then tell us who is the creator that permeates through both you and I.

-Moh Batuk Logum Deg

Each day I feed my senses/body with the food of worldly attachment and material love (Moh = attachment)

-Shwas Khich Khich Wang- Mayan

For when the breath that I take in reaches the point of complete purification (Swas = Breath).

-Bhruman Daras Poyun Chokum

Bhruman means between the eyebrows. So, as per Kashmir Shaivism and Sanatan philosophy we have a third eye in between eyebrows which is also called the main center in the human brain.

-Brahmish Tekis Takya Bane Tyuk

The brahm which I had, Brahm means confusion in Sanskrit, the brahm which I had that where is the God got clear and I got to know that it's within myself.

SM102. Hyath Karith Raaj Pheri-Naa

Hyath karith raaj pheri-naa
Dith karith trapti na man.
Luub veyna ziiv marina,
Ziivanatay mari tay suy chuy jnaan.

Raaj=empire, realm, kingdom; Dith karith=to give away; trapti=satisfaction, happiness; Na=nor; man=body, mind; Luub=desire; Veyna=without, except; Ziivanatay mari=to die while alive.

You will not know peace of mind if you a kingdom gain. Nor will you gain content or rest if you give it away. Only the man, free from desire, will never die. Only he has true knowledge that, though alive, is as one dead, dead to all desire.

SM103.   Haii Hung Naad Zan Wazaan

Haii hung naad zan wazaan
Gumband wazaan, doo doo dith
Sozan ishara saetein bozaan
Kozan na bozaan damam dith

Hung naad=beating o drums, trumpets; zan wazaan=as I am beating, producing sound; Gumband wazaan=as I there is an echo in a dome, as If some decision is pending raising alarms in the dome; celestial waves are heard; Sozan ishara saetein bozaa=the blessed quickly understand this; Kozan na bozaan damam dith=the rude have no effect of such perceptive.

In this Vakh Lal Ded laments about the ignorant masses that do not pay any heed to realize truth.

Lal Ded was once passing through a thick forest. She was touched by the calm, peaceful and soundless environment of the forest. The chirping of the birds, the blowing of the breeze and the jungle lore produced by the swinging cones and needle like leaves of the conifer trees, producing celestial music. There was an echo of delighted melodies. It appears as if the nature is making its best effort to make people realize the divine truth. In the sweet melody of jungle lore, the wise and blessed one listens to such music, only through the vibrations of the celestial waves. So, it is a place where man and nature nestle together in a state of glory to realize the truth. But such tunes and soft touches produce no effect to the ignorant, even when the drums are beaten before them.

SM104. Ho'nd Maarrtyan Ya Kath

Ho'nd maarrtyan ya kath
Lalli nalavath tsali'nah zanh.

Hond= a lamb; maarrtyan= kill; kath= a sheep; nalavath=a stone, a pebble; tsali nah zanh= never miss.

(Whether they kill a ram or sheep, Lalla will never miss her shingle").

Once on a festive occasion while filling a pitcher at the riverbank, she was asked by her girlfriends what the festivity and merriment at her home was all about. Lalla replied in a Vakh.
She said, "Whether they slaughter a ram or a lamb, Lalla will never miss her shingle".
(They may kill a big lamb, or a small one Lalla will have the large pebble on her plate)

SM105.   Kaalan Kaal Zole Udwiiy Chei Gole

Kaalan kaal zole udwiiy chei gole,
Vandev grah vaa vendev vanvaas.
Zaanith sarv gath prabhu anmole.
Yothuy zaanak tuithei aas.

Kaalan Kaal zole= desires break the bonds of time; udwiiy chei gole= should you destroy vain thoughts; Vandev grah vaa vendev vanvaas= should we live the life of a householder, or should we realize the Lord; Zaanith sarv gath Prabhu anmole= realisating the magnificence of the Lord makes one potentially divine; Yothuy zaanak tuithei aas= whatever you know, realize, the true consciousness is to realize the "self."

Lalla says by cutting down the ego and pride, the desires break the bonds of time. Then one acquires a consciousness that gives carriage and assurance. Then each soul becomes potentially divine. Then, one may live at home or in jungles, a house holder's life or in a hermitage. It has no significance to the seeker of Truth. The realization, of the glory of the Lord, makes one divine. Every individual sacrifice made, helps to realize the true consciousness to realize the "self."

SM106.   Kaamas Saitee Priyei No Barem

Kaams saitee priyei no barem
Kroodas ditum pyavoon faish
Loobas mohas charan chatim
Traishna chajim gyas khosh

Kamas saitee= desire for lust; priyei no barem= I nourished not; Kaams saitee priyei no barem=I did not nourish the desire for lust; Kroodas dyutum pavnun faish=I cleansed my mind of all kinds of anger; Loobas mohas charean Chatith= I cut the feet (roots) of all worldly desire and attachment; Charan=feet and legs; Trashna chajim (tsajim)= I freed myself of all thirst for the worldly attractions; gayas khush=became satisfied eternally.

In this Vakh Lal Ded says that she exercised control on five passions, Kama (lust), Krodh (anger), Loobh (desire) Mooh (attachment) and Ahankaar (false pride). These are the basic requirement for all spiritual development. This way she freed herself of all thirst for the worldly attractions and satisfied herself eternally. The great yogini had a super soul. She achieved all the goals of spiritual awakening and hence there was nothing that had remained unachieved for her. Lal-Ded encourages the seeker to give up animal desires like lust, rash cravings, and selfish desires. It is not by Kama (Desires), not by off-springs, not by wealth, not by sacrifice that immortality is gained. It is gained by renunciation, sacrifice, solitude, and purity. Physical discipline is essential.

SM107. Kaayas Ander Roodum Achit

Kaayas ander roodum achit
Nayayas thavnam chopari shaaiiy
Paaiiy kenh loboom no maaiiy chas karith
Zaayas na aayas logum naav

Kaayas= in the body; ander= inside; zaayas= born; aayas logum naav= as soon I was born, I was given a name.

What gives me pleasure and grace is to see the Lord. I see Him in the infinite corners of my body without getting absorbed in my body stream. Yet He is invisible and beyond recognition and reach. That is the cause of impatience in me. Even though I am conscious of His existence, yet He is beyond my reach. That is a mystery here abides. There is something which I must know, for I am like a child who does not reason and has no care. No sooner I was born, I was given a name indifferent from Him, that makes me feel indifferent and is the cause of impatience in me.

SM108. Kaayas Bal Choi Maayas Zaagun

Kaayas bal choi maayas zaagun
Praans bal choi shabd swroop
Aayas bal choi tat videe zanoon
Gyanas bal choi aad ant taani

Kaayas= body; bal= strength; zaagun= to watch, recognize; Aay =long life; videe = intellect; gyanas=spiritual knowledge, consciousness.

The complex human body is a great wonder. The four behaviors are:
The physical
The emotional
The intellectual and
The spiritual.
All of them work together so quickly, that man fails to recognize their fine distinction. The emotional and intellectual structures eventually result in developing the spiritual consciousness. Thus, the physical body acquires a feat, to go nearer and nearer to Lord's grace. Further, she says, by concentrating and listening to the sounds produced in the nostrils, during the process of exhale and inhale, the sounds of 'soo' and 'hum' is produced, Lal-Ded calls it 'Shabad swroop' or incarnation of the sacred letter "OM". By acquiring control over breathings one can know the act of gaining longevity in the life span of one's life.

SM109. Kachul Ta Maval Kath Kuit Chhui

Kachul ta maval kath kuit chhui
Tote kuit chhui shaant sobhaav
Krai hund aagur vati kyut chhui
Ant kyut chhui gwar sundh naav

Kachul= a small brass pot for keeping vermelon, Sindoor; maval=flower; kath kuit choie=what for are these things; Tote kuit chuie shaant sobhav=you need virtuous acts; Krai hund aagur=the constant practice Ant kyut=in the end; chhui gwar sundh naav=Guru's name is required to gain entrance in the heavenly abode.

It is by constant repetition of virtuous acts that one becomes upright. This constant practice transforms the soul, providing it with energy to rise higher.

The Lord's grace is gained neither by superior race or tribe, nor by higher position or riches. Only the dignified principles and manners help one entering the heavenly abode. It is by constant repetition of virtuous acts that one becomes virtuous. This constant practice transforms the soul providing it with a source of energy to rise higher. In the end with the grace of Guru one can find a real self within. The Guru is sinless and is above man's capacity. The Guru is responsible for one's increasing his force and energy. That is why in the end Guru's name is required to gain entrance in the heavenly abode.

> **SM110. Kalamie Parum Ti Kalamie Sorum**
>
> Kalamie parum ti kalamie sorum
> Kalimie kachum panuni paan
> Kalami heni heni mouen tourum
> Adeh Lal vaachis lamakan

La –Makan is a typical Islamic conception.
Tu Ae Aseer-e-Makan! La Makan Se Door Nahin
Woh Jalwagah Tere Khakdan Se Door Nahin-. Ilama Iqbal
'O' Prisoner of Space! You are not far from the Placeless Realm— That Audience Hall is not far away from your planet.

Whether Lal Ded has used the word La Makan or not is a different issue. To me it appears the word has got corrupted during oral communication of the Vakh, as Lal Ded has mostly used the word Prakashasthan which conveys transcendence of Shiva who has the essential attribute especially of Shakti.

As per the concept the creator and the created are the two separate polarities and the twain do not meet. God is at the highest pedestal and after creation leaves the world alone to its own fate. In sharp contrast to this Kashmir Shaivism holds the view that shiva as the absolute reality is both transcendental and immanent.

SM111. Kaman Sanna Neindar Tai Kamsana Woodie

Kaman sanna neindar tai kamsana woodie
Kaman nish bodh bawaan
Kamsaana loal naar dadee
Kamsaana saas tai kamsana sone
Kamsana marnas broonthie moodie
Timai aasai saas tai sapdee sone

Kaman sanna neindar= who are the people who get a sound sleep; kamsana woodie= who are the people who enjoy wakefulness; Kaman nish bodh bawaan= who are the blessed one, with intellect; Kamsaana loal naar dadee= who are the people blessed with Love; Kamsaana saas tai kamsana sone= who are the people who have turned from dust to Gold; Yem Sana marnas broonthie moodie = those who die to the self and lower self to all the evil elements; Timai aasai saas tai sapdee sone=they are the base people who became gold.

Who are the people who sleep a sound sleep and who are the people who enjoy wakefulness to realize bliss? Who are the people with intellect and wisdom grown to find Absolute as the eternal beauty? Who are the blessed one with whom beauty leads to Love and Love to Bliss? Then further she says who are the people who have turned from dust to Gold.

"Those blessed one's who die to the self by a process of mortification and their lower self is purged of all the evil elements so that the outward and inward purification go together. It is then that absolute becomes conscious of itself in all its diverse aspects.

"In discharge of ordinary duties of life, a seeker of 'Truth' never fails to strive for self-improvement. There is thorough genuineness in him. He does not find himself in any situation in which he is not the master of himself, such a seeker turns from dust to Gold."

SM112. Kandeev Grah Teez Kandan Vaanas

Kandeev grah teez kandan vaanas
Yuthui chook te tethuie aas
Manas dheer rath sapdak suwas
Kyah chui malun soor ta saas

Kandeev=some people; grah=homes; teez kandan=renounce homes; vaanas=go to woods to live as hermits; Yuthui chook te tethuie aas=be satisfied with whatsoever you do; Kyah chui maloon soor ta saas= why rub the skin with ashes to make one's presence feel.

Some persons renounce their homes and go to woods to live as hermits. They try to make their minds devoid of all earthly desires. One can learn the gospel of Truth even by staying at home and the realization of His awareness will automatically come forth. Also, there is no need of rubbing the skin with ashes to make one's presence feel. A seeker is satisfied with whatever God does or God will be satisfied with whatsoever he does. "Our whole work in this life is to heal the eye of the mind by which we see the God. Contentment is a great virtue. Absorption in God is the supreme goal of Human attainment. It is the blending of light of Soul with the light of God.

SM113. Kandyav geh te'zy kandyav vanvaas

Kandyav geh te'zy kandyav vanvaas,
Veyphoal, mann na rattith ta vaas.
Deyn-raath ganzarith panun shwaas,
Yuthuy chukh ta tyuthui aas

Geh te'zy=go to; kandyav vanvaas= hermitage; Veyphoal=restless; man=mind; na rattith ta vaas= knows no rest; Deyn-raath=day and night; gaenzarith=watch, measure; panun=your; shwaas=breath; Yuthuy chukh=as you are; tyuthuy aas = stay where you are.

Some people leave their home, and some people leave their hermitage, but the restless mind knows no rest. Then count and watch your breath, day, and night, and stay where you are.

SM114.   Kando Karakh Kandi Kandey

Kando karakh kandi kandey
Kando karakh kandi velaas
Bhoogie meethiy ditam yath kandey
Yath kandi rozi na soor tai saas

Kandev=body, people; karakh kanday kanday= you will be asking to fulfi the demands of this body, saying my body, my body; kandee = sweet candies; velaas= adore, love; kandee velaas=you will be asking for sweetmeats for your body; bhoogie=good foods; meethe=sweets; ditim =give; yeth =this; rozi no= will not have; soor=ashes; saas=existence; yeth kandi=this body; rozi ni soor tai saas= It has to burn into ashes without leaving even a trace. The ashes will mix with the dust, and you will lose your existence.

[Here it is a personification, calling a person who is in flesh or in material form] Love not your body such, or don't admire your body thus, and make it attractive]. Lal Ded was a great poet; mark the alliteration of words in this vakh- the consonant 'k' 'kando karakh kandi kanday.'

Lalla says: "Some people are so much conceited that they look to this body as something unshakable and strong. They nurture their bodies with all sweet and delicious things. One cannot imagine a better or a more interesting life than this. However, delicious, and tasty food one feeds this body, it meets its decay even its ashes are mixed with dust. Hence, one loses its existence. The wise understand this, through the blessings of the Lord.

SM115. Kanptha Chetan Gamnas

Kanptha chetan gamnas
Kaachi lajnas katham yaro
Sui deev choi poor ta manas
Sui deev guppaan-labakh soroi

Kanptha=shivering, trembling; chetan=mind; gamnas=full of sorrows; Kaachi lajnas=cut me to pieces.

From the core of my heart, I loved my Lord. But He cut me piece by piece. I suffer with the indecision of mind. I need solitude, a place, a time to be with Him. I am passing through frustration, O' Mind. Lalla has faith. She will see His benign grace and will also make her way for her admission into the realm of eternal life-immortality!

SM116. Karmook Kul No Choi Banith Gachoon

Karmook kul no choi banith gachun
Wanit gachoon kya chui paaie
Kashfook phal chui meelith gachun
Wallith rozun kus chui nyaye

Karmook= action; kul= tree; wallith = remain covered;

Here Lal-Ded urges the people to conquer unholy desires. She says one should resist temptations of every kind. She wants to adore the Lord not by outward observations but by internal purity and goodness. She exhorts people to live in the world of nature with intense feelings and emotions. She says man has capacity to go beyond his Karma "the accumulated result of action". So long as the soul is fettered by the bonds of Karma, it is bound up with the soul when the soul departs it carries with it the accumulated force of Karma. The end of this life is to gain liberation from the chains of the body and merge with his pure existence.

Lal-Ded is strict in observing austerities as such exhort the seeker to live nude and unadorned, even without any possession of property. "The life of a seeker is plain and yet not unattractive. It is simple yet full of grace. It is easy and yet methodical." 'Truth' is the beginning and end of his existence.

SM117.   Karum Zu Kaaran Tre Kombith

Karum zu kaaran tre kombith[**1]
Yava labakh paraluukas annkh
Voth khas surya-manndal tso'mbith,
Tavay tsaliy maranun sheynkh.

Karum=Karma; zu kaaran= karmas two, Good and bad; tre=three; kombith= by practising kumbhaka yoga; Karum zu kaaran tre kombith=give up the karmas two and causes three;Yava labakh paraluukas annkh = you will be honored in the world to come; Yava labakh paraluukas ankh=and you will find an insight into the higher world; Voth khas=arise and ascend; Surya-manndal tso'mbith= cut through the Sun's orbit, Surya-maddala, through which the soul has to pass on its way to the Supreme,arise and ascend and tear through the sun's orb; Tavay tsaliy maranun sheynkh= Thus will you overcome the fear of death.

There are two types of actions performed by the persons of vision and stature; first the action that leads to immortality, second the action that binds one to life and death cycle. Then further, the frontier of human mind knows no barriers. Here Lalla says do away with two types of karmas good and bad, and the three causes- the three mala-s, impurities, that bring pleasure and pain from karma. You will be honored in the world to come. Arise, ascend, and cut through the Sun's orbit, the Surya-maddala, through which the soul must pass on its way to the Supreme. This way you will overcome the fear of death by practicing kumbhaka yoga.'

SM118.   Kath Ha Vanai Kath Ha Vanai

Kath ha vanai kath ha vanai
Kath meoan lavi laal
Manz maidanas neinder payee
Domb heth chali shaal

Kath = a tale, a story; ha vanai = let me tell you; meoan = mine; lavi = cost; laal = a diamond, a precious thing, her wisdom, here Lal Ded tries to prevail upon the masses to understand the importance of her words; Manz = in the middle of; maidanas = ground; neinder = asleep, dead, numbness, lifeless; payee = be a victim of; Domb = viscera, the intestines, the bowels; heth chali = will carry away; shaal = Shaal is the Kashmiri name for a jackal (Canis aurcus), Shal is found in all villages and in waste lands . They come out during night and howl. Their tail is long, and skin is sometimes used as fur.

It seems Lal Ded has used Shaal in her different vakhs with different connotations depending upon the circumstances. Mark the repetition of word 'kath' that Lal Ded has used in this Vakh. She wants to convey to her devotees the words of wisdom by saying that her words are valuable than the precious jewels; and the inspiration of giving of a free-thinking worship in the name of Siva. And to forget Him in the lifetime, the consequences can be destructive; as Siva is the symbol of the eternal process of destruction and creation; and Kala (Time, Destroyer). He is at the same time instinct with love. Siva maintains the equilibrium between Life and Death. When the dead body is left on the ground, it is vulnerable to wild creatures, who can gladly run away with the viscera leaving the skeleton there unattended. Only good deeds pay in future life. Lal Ded found the Supreme Light in her own soul. She realized that the Supreme Self (God) and-her own soul was one.

SM119. Katha Boozam Ta Katha Karem

Katha boozam ta katha karem
Kathai karam charayee sath
Shaaster kini katha boozam
Kathai basayem satach vath

Katha boozam ta katha karam= I indulged in wide-ranging spiritual discourses both giving away and hearing them; Kathayi karam charayee(tchharai) sath= whatever I've learnt and achieved is because of these celestial associations; Shaster kini katha Boozam= I attended numerous spiritual discourses of great souls besides delving deep into the authentic religious scriptures; Kathai basaim satach vath= I was guided in my achievements through spiritualways.

Lal Ded says:
I listened to religious discourses. I gave expression to pious thoughts which inculcated in me, purity, patience, and universal love. I listened to the religious discourses through sacred books and that inspiration reassured me of my faith in the self. Listening to pious thoughts and sermons has been a success which is required to be turned into realization. She admits that all her knowledge and awakening was due to her association with both scriptures and celestial association.

SM120. Kavo Chook Tsetaan Anine Vachh

Kavo chook tsetaan anine vachh
Trukai chhukh ta anderi atchh
Shiv chui ati tai kun mo gatchh
Sahaj kathi myani karto patchh

Anine vachh= beat your chest like a blind man; Kava chookh tsetaan anine vachh= Why do you beat your chest like the blind; Trook hiiy chook = If you are wise; anderi ach= look within; shiv chui ate=Lord is there in the corner of your heart; kun mo gach=no need to go anywhere; sahaz kathi=easy talk; maiani=mine; karto pach =believe it.

Why do you feel around like the blind? The gifted and clever as you are look within and watch for the moments of enlightenment. Seize the reality and become one with the Lord seated in the corners of the heart. It is then you will have a deep vision. Live with intense feelings and emotions. Keep faith in my simple tale of truth, for every individual is equipped with a force of energy which enables him to attain spiritual perfection.

What is the cause of your distemper? Why do you fumble thus like the blind? If you are wise, enter within. And see the Lord Himself is there. You need not search Him here and there. Pray, doubt not what I say to you. Absolute truth is everlasting self, existent and infinite. It produces effects without action. It accomplishes its end without being conscious.

SM121. Kenchan Dithitum Torai Aalav, Kenchav Rachie

Kenchan dithitum torai aalav
Kenchav rachie naalie Wyeth
Kenchan mus chet achhi laji taalav
Kenchan papit gai haalav kheth

Kenchan=to some; dithitum torai aalav=to some people you ngave a divine call; Kenchav rachie naalie Wyeth= Wyeth is the other name of river Jhelum. Some have been going to sacred places, rivers to attain divinity; mus chet=having tasted the mystic nectar; aach lagi taalav=keep on searching with their eyes wide open; Kenchan papit gai haalav kheth=(haalav =locusts); (khet=having eaten); some worked hard and were ready to reap the harvest, but their ego gave them a slip, in the end they failed.

Some people are so great and have done so much good things that God himself calls them to the heaven; Some people are so unable and uncapable that they do not achieve anything in life like a man not able to quench his thirst even if he tries to collect the whole water from the River Jhelum (Wyeth). Some people earn so much wealth that makes them arrogant, they forget the fear of God, become luxurious and finally meet a disastrous end. They have drunk wine and lift their eyes upwards; Some people work hard but due to their ill fate do not get anything at the end. They raise crops and when it ripens the locusts come and destroy it.

Lal Ded had a rich vocabulary. She had command on the use of words. In this Vakh she uses the repetition of word 'kenchan', which means to a few. To me, it means, Lal Ded refers to some people who have a divine inkling, a spiritual call to follow that path. There are people who in spite of going to religious rivers or sacred places fail to attain His Lords grace. Some even after imbibing a delightful drink repeatedly look to above but fail as they have malice in their hearts. They think that they have achieved the goal, and everything belongs to them. Here she gives a metaphor, just as somebody has worked very hard in a field which is ready to harvest, but then, the field is attacked by a swarm of locusts and nothing is left out, similarly, one must tread very carefully when one is near achievement of his goal to spirituality.

(Another version)

SM122.	Kenchan Dithitum Ore Aalav …Khev Totie

Kenchan dithitum or aalav
Kenchan dithum yuut khev totie
Kenchan dithum yuut na ti tout kya
Kenchan papit gai haalav kheth

Ore aalav = a call from there, you have given the blessings; yuut khev totie= in hot haste; yuut na ti tout kya= neither here nor there; pipit=ripened; haalav=locusts; kheth= eaten.

God has given to some (blessing) here and there (i.e., in both the worlds), and He has given to some nothing either here or there.

SM123.   Kenchan ranei chhai sahaz boonie, nerav nebar shuhul karav

Kenchan ranei chhai sahaz boonie,
nearav nebar shuhul karav.
Kenchan ranei chhai bar peth hunie,
nerav nebar tah zang khenav.
Kenchan rani chhai adal tah vadal.
Khenchan rani chhai zadal tshai.

Kenchan (kentsan)=to some; ranei = wife; shihij = shady, boonie= a chinar tree; nerav nebar= on going out; shuhul karav= to cool ourselves; bar=door; peth=at; huni=dog; zang=leg; kheyiwo=bite; adal tah wadal= in confusion; zadal = bad; tshai = thatch.

Lal Ded says:
Some people have wives like a shady Chinar tree, they enjoy the coolness in that shade of Chinar. Some have wives just like the watch dog at the door, when they go out, they get their legs bitten. Some have wives always in confusion, and some have wives like bad thatch upon the roof.

SM124. Kenchan Mali Dithuth Yeti Kya Tatai

Kenchan mali dithuth yeti kya tatai
Kenchan mali yeti na ti tati kya
Kenhan bakshut che lal trotei
Kenchan gash manz gottoi gav

Kenchan mali dithuth =to some you gave plenty; yeti kya tatai=here as well as there; yeti na ti tati kya=some did neither get here nor there i.e., after death; Kenhan bakshut che=to some you gave; lal trotei=plenty of jewels and diamonds; Kenchan gash manz= some did not get in the bright day light; gottoi gav=remained ignorant.

Lal Ded has been a poet of spiritual thinking and her usage of words in her vakh has been phenomenal. Mark the alliteration of words 'Kenchan' in this vakh. As a follower of Shivaism, exploring and exercising the spiritual gifting is a vital and exciting part of one's spiritual journey. The spiritual gifts God has given has to be realized and seen. "There are different kinds of gifts, but the same Spirit distributes them. There are different kinds of service, but the same Lord."

In this vakh she reiterates that some devotees are bestowed with bounties here as well as in the next world; and some neither here nor there; to some He bestows and donates precious diamonds and jewels, comforts of life; while some remain ignorant and unaware of the bliss and ecstasy of the God.

SM125. Kenchan Ditith Gulal Yechie

Kenchan ditith gulal yechie
Kenchan zonuth na dinas vaar
Kenchan chunith nael brahmahachi
Baghwan chaen gatchhi namaskar

Kenchan(kentchan)=to some; ditith=awarded, gave, bestowed; Gulal Yechie= Infinite existence, Pure delight, Magnificence; zonuth na dinas vaar= were not found fit for such a favor; Kenchan chunith(tchhunith) nael=some you made them face the outrageous fortunes; brahmhachie= Misfortunes; Baghwan=O blessed one, God, Lord; chain gatchhi Namaskar= I salute thee and to your wondrous pastime. To some you gave many poppies (i.e., Sons); And some you haltered (with a daughter) for murdering a Brahman (in some former existence). O Bhagawan, I adore your greatness.

Some people have Lord's kindness. They have blessed them with pure joy and complete truth with magnificence and splendor. There are others who were not found fit for such a favor. With some other misfortunes have made them face the disgraceful fortunes, as such they bear the lashes of time and bear the oppressor's wrong. O, Lord! How weary and sour your affairs are; I salute thee and to your wondrous pastime.

SM126.   Kenchas Pyath Kyah Chui Nachun

Kenchas pyath kya chui nachun
Mwatchi kenh na ta natchun traav
Poat pheerith chui totui atchun
Koat chui gaachun pakun traav

Kenchas peth= on what; nachun (natchun)=dance, delightful; traav= to give up; poat feerith= in the end; oauti aachun= to meet death; koat chui gaachun= don't get astray.

Why do you dance over this nothingness, you too will contract to nothingness, so abandon this dance, and on return you have to go back to nothingness, so bear this thought in your mind?

Lal Ded hints to her devotees as to what makes them so delightful and enjoyable; as nothing in the material world remains, and therefore, one should contain himself. Having finished all the amusing, in the end one must meet death. Hence, it is better not to get astray but to pray to your lord with devotion. There is a deep symbolism in this, the philosophic import we should be careful not to misinterpret, for it shows us the god of destruction as one and the same with the creative principle, the act of death as a source of generative power.

In some literature the last line of the vakh changes like:
"Yogai vatchun thaav."

SM127. Kenh Chiy Nenderi Hatte Vudiy

Kenh chiy nenderi hatte vudiy,
Keanchan vudeyn nesar peyiy,
Kenh chiy sanan karith aputi,
Kenh chiy gaeh bazith akrai,

Kenh=some; nenderi hatte wodee= though asleep are yet awake; Kenchan=some; wodien=awake; Nesar paiye=fall asleep; sanan karith= despite baths, despite ablutions; aputi=unclean; greh bazith= despite householders' day to day life; akrai= untouched. Some people though asleep are yet awake. (Some people though awake are yet asleep; Despite washing and cleaning their bodies some people are still unclean, some, by their actions, are untouched.)

"Every individual is equipped with a force of energy which would enable him to attain spiritual perfection in the moments of illumination. It is God's revelation of Himself. It is His joy that assumes all forms".

Some though asleep are yet awake; some though awake are yet asleep; some others, who have washed and cleansed their bodies to make themselves feel clean and pure, suffer with doubt and uncertainty. There are others who live a house-holders active life, practicing the good with devotion and zeal. It transforms their soul providing it with a source of energy to rise to beyond pleasure and pain. They remain detached with the fruit of their actions; as such they realize a state of no mind.

SM128. Kenh-Chan Ranei Chai Sahaz Boonie

Kenh-chan ranei chai sahaz boonie
Nerav nebar shuhul karav
Kenh-chan ranei chai bur peth hunie
Nerav nebar zang khenav
Kenchan ranie chai adal ti badal
Kenchan ranie chai zadal chaay

Kenh=some; Ranie=wives; Sahaz Boonie=shadow giving Chinar tree; shuhul karav=enjoy the coolness in the shade of Chinar; bur peth hunie=watch dog; zang khenav=bite a leg; adal ti badal=some people have wives who give halfhearted relief; zadal chaay(tchhaay)=temporary shadow of tree which have less leaves.

Some people are lucky to have good wives, they are like shade trees, like a Chinar. There are some who are unlucky as their wives are just like watch dogs, their wives are crooked and change colours like chameleon. Some people have wives who give halfhearted relief like the temporary shadow of trees like a thatch hut.

SM129. Kheth Ti Moodhee Na Kheth Ti Moodhee

Kheth ti moodee na kheth ti moodhee
Naahkiiy gondnakh kroodhan naar
Yim ha maali handi wopal haakas peth roudhie
Tim ho maali adha moodhee na zanh

Khait= having eaten; moodee= to die; naahkiiy= unnecessarily; kroodan=anger, sinful; naar= fire, burn; handi wopal-hakas= dandelion and other vegetable mostly used by saints.

Those, who eat, drink, and make merry and even go for fasting die in the end. They burn inside with the developed sinful instincts of anger in them, till the death lays its icy hands on them. Blessed are those, who live a life of simplicity, moderation, restraint, and heavenly sympathy. They attain perfection, the bliss of consciousness and immortality.

SM130.   Khaith Gandith Shami Naa Manas

Khaith gandith shami naa manas
Braanth emove trav timai giiy khasit
Shaster boozith chui yama bhiiy kroorie
So na poz tai dhanya lasith

Khaith=having tasted; gandith=having worn fine dresses, jwellery; shami naa manas = bring man no lasting peace; Braanth emove trav=those who gave up hope; tima giiy khasit= unafraid of Death's terrors, ascend; Shaster Boozith= having listened to Holy Scriptures; chui Yama bhiiy kroorie= the fear that the death is cruel; So na poz tai dhanya lasith = that is all absurd and should not be believed in.

The enjoyment of tasting yummy foods and wearing of rich garments, bring no lasting peace to the mind. They who give up false hopes and don't put trust in the things of the world, Ascend, unafraid of Death's terrors. The fear that the death is cruel and horrible, as depicted in the Holy Scriptures, is all ridiculous and should not be believed in. Blessed are those who have lived a contented life, with moderation and heavenly sympathy. They have not to settle account with the death, for they lived for Truth, honour, and conscience.

SM131. Khyana Khyana Karaan Kun No Vaatakh

Khyana khyana karaan kun no vaatakh
Na khyan ghachakh ahankaari:
Somui khai maali somui rozakh
Somi khyana muchran barnyan taari.

Khyana khyana karan =by overeating; Kun no vaatakh = you get nowhere; Na khyan=by fasting; ghachakh (gatchhakh)=you get; ahankari=vanity, pride; Somai khai maali=be moderate; somoi aasakh =live a modest life; Somai khaina muchran (mutsaranai)=by modest eating, open; muchran barnain taeri=the gates of heaven be wide open.

For Lal Ded, food is essentially for survival of the physical, but not the ultimate end. The ultimate is bliss, known as Ananda. The wisdom of a person is in laying emphasis on the soul-searching attitude to life, instead of giving importance to the food, or the sensuous life. Lal Ded understands the pulse of the common man, who is more particular to satisfy the base desires of the senses, instead of balancing it with ultimate search for Shiva.

Be moderate in food and drink and live a moderate life. By over feeding, you will become a glutton. You will be unable to reach your goal. By penance and fasting, you get pride. Therefore, you should eat and drink with moderation. This will bring moderation in your behavior too. The gates of Heaven will surely be thrown open wide for you.

SM132. Kol Ta Mol Kath Kuit Choei

Kol ta mol kath kuit choei
Tote kuit chui shaant subhav
Krai hund aagur vati kuit choei
Annt kuit choei guru sund naav

Kol=clan; Mol=riches; kath kuit choei=what for; Tote kuit chui= dignified manners help enter the heavenly abode; shaant subhav= Peace, calm and dignified manners; Krai hund aagur vati kuit choei= constant practice transforms the soul with energy to rise higher and thence to heaven; Annt kuit choei= in the end; guru sund naav= Guru's name is required to gain entrance in the heavenly abode.

The Lord's grace is gained neither by superior clan nor by riches. Peace, calm and dignified manners help enter the heavenly abode. It is by constant repetition of good acts that one becomes virtuous. This constant practice transforms the soul providing it with a source of energy to rise higher and thence to heaven. In the end with the grace of Master one can find a real self within. The Guru is responsible for elevating one's character and increasing his force and energy. That is why in the end Guru's name is required to gain entrance in the heavenly abode.

SM133. Kosoom Bagas Heut Mai Achoon

Kosoom bagas heut mai achoon
Pachee mun ta achoon praav
Swaroop darshun chooi tatooi achoon
Kot chooi gachoon pakoon traav

Kosoom= blissful, immortal; Bagas= garden; achoon= enter; pachee mun= if your heart feels; achoon=enter; Swaroo darshun= to see the face of Lord.

I have entered the universe of immortal bliss. It is a situation where a person and nature nestle together, in the state of glory and uplifting grace. Now I have entered in the garden of ecstatic bliss with all my free will, as such I am enjoying the pleasures of immortality. O, the sages of the universe arise awake and stop not till you gain entrance into such a state of divine melody.

SM134. Kriya Karem Dharm Karum

Kriya karem dharm karum
Tirthan novum panun kaai
Papan sombrith basum korum
Tati kus ose ta yeti kam aai

Kraiyaa Karam dharm Karoom=after performing all the religious rites and dharma; Tirthan= pilgrimages; navum panun kaay=washed my sins; Paapan Sombrith=all my sins together, instincts of sin; basum koroom=burnt to ashes; Tati kus ose Ta yeti kam aaiiy= every man has the inborn potentiality to rise and reach the divine stature.

After going through all the necessary religious rites and tasks, I cleansed my body at the springs of holy places and pilgrimages to wash off all my sins. This way I was able to burn all the instincts of sin in me. For God realization, I set fire to all I had. I was intoxicated with the awareness of divinity. My path to the self-realization was illumined. As such, the belief, that the 'truth' travels over the earth secretly and it finds nest amongst the people of outstanding vision was established. And, that every man has the inborn potential to rise and reach the divine stature, if he strives for it was certain.

Lalleshwari says she performed all religious ceremonies, visited various pilgrimage spots to wash away her sins but ultimately understood that the Lord is present everywhere and there's no need to travel long distances as the Lord's grace can be obtained at any place with proper consolidation of spirit. She clearly indicates that the foremost duty of man is to get detached from the worldly desire and the pleasures. All ceremonies in religion, visiting holy places and sacred temples and other houses of God are of secondary importance compared to the purification of inner self and development of love for God and his people. How would these ceremonial activities help them who're engaged actively in the affairs of the world and the pleasures of sense, and their hearts are deeply submerged in the murky waters of existence! Their sins cannot be washed away by the holiest of the holy waters and they should not expect any advancement of their spirit with the performance of grand ceremonies and congregations in the name of God.

SM135. Kunirey Bozakh Kuni No Rozakh

Kunirey bozakh kuni no rozakh
Kuniran karnam hanya kaar
Kunai aasith dhoen hund jung gome
Sui bay-rang gome rang karith

Kunirey=oneness, unity of existence; bozakh= recognizes; haaniakaar=high regard, love; Kunai aasith= though He is One; Dhon hund=two, duality; Jung gome= caught in the War; Soi=although, though; bairang= He has neither colour nor form; gome karith rang=yet his wondrous forms, multiplicity.

Lal-Ded recognizes only one God who is everlasting self-existent, and Omniscient. He is the sole object of esteem love and worship. He moves, He moves not, He is far, and He is near. He is within and He is without. Would you understand what Oneness is? It has turned me into nothingness.

Lal-Ded encourages the people to worship and love the One Soul within, and not countless Gods. Whosoever worships another deity than this self, thinking He is one and I am another he suffers with ignorance and delusion? She expresses the restlessness of mind to grasp the true Nature of reality. Though He is One, Alone, and All, yet I am caught in the War of Two.

She attempts to solve the doubts of duality. It is to live in infinity as only infinite is everlasting. This duality makes her feel proud with the ego of 'I'-ness. Though He has neither colour nor form, yet I am caught in His wondrous forms.

SM136. Kus Bub Tai Kousi Mougi

Kus bub tai kousi mougi
Kamu logie baazi bhut
Kol gazak, kanh no bub kanh no mougi
Zaanith kav lagith baazi bhut

Kus= who; bub=father; mougi= mother; kamu= who; baazi bhut= a cheater; kol= dumb; gazak= to become; kanh no= none; zaanith= knowing.

Lal Ded was a great mystic. She had a glorious past life with rich Karmas. In her Vakh she makes assertions of her personal divine attributes saying, when the time of death comes, then who is father and who is mother! Who has played jugglery with you; when the time of death comes, you won't be able to speak a word, you will be dumb; neither your own father nor your own mother can help you; knowing this all, why still your deceit people by your treachery? Like a great soul she cautions the people to simply have the grace of Lord and enjoy the choicest blessings of the Lord to achieve the highest goals of liberation with very little effort. Lal Ded has a purpose. She wants people to proceed on celestial path and own rightful experience in their way of spiritual development.

SM137.   Kus Marri Tai Kasu Maaran

Kus marri ta kasu maaran
Mari kus ta maran kas
Yus Har Har travith ghar ghar kari
Adha sui marri tai maaran tas

Kus marri=who dies; kasu maaran =who is slain; Yus=the one, he; Har Har travith=forsakes God; Ghar Ghar karay=gets involved in worldly affairs; Adha sui marri tai maaran tas= it's he who dies and who is slain.

Who will die and who will be killed,
who will kill and for whom will be killed,
one who is always worried about the worldly things and forgets the name of Lord,
he would certainly die and be killed for sure.
Lal Ded puts a question: Who dies and who is slain? Then she replies, he who forsakes God's Name, and gets involved in worldly cares. It's he who dies. It's he who is slain. Lal Ded believed that a person must distinguish between his gross body and subtle one. Those who view their bodies as distinct from their mind are infact sages and not ordinary human beings. She suggested that one should believe in monoism (non-duality) so that he will never be alone (without God). She herself merged with the God and lost herself forever.

SM138.   Kusoo Dengi Tai Kusoo Zaagi

Kusoo dengi tai kusoo zaagi
Kusoo sarwater telyee?
Kusoo haras poozi laagi?
Kus param pad meelee?

Kusoo dengi= who dozes off? Kusoo zaagi=who is alert; Kusoo sarwater telyee=which lake constantly oozeth away; Kusoo Haras poozi laagi=what should be offered in worship to God? Kus Param pad meelee= what best should one gain.

In this big complex of our body, what is that that is dormant and what is that that is wakeful; What type of vibrations are being emitted? What is the blessed thing that one should offer to the Lord to fascinate His grace? What is the inspiring goal for which one should crave?

SM139.   Kyaah Kara Paantsan Dahan Ta Kahan

Kyah kara paantsan dahan ta kaahan, *4
Vakhshun yath leji yim karith gai.
Saari samhan aksi razi lamhan,
Ada kyaazi raavihey kahan gaav

Kyah Kara=how to control; Paantsan= the Five (Bhuta-s); dahan= the ten (Indriya-s); ta kaahan= Eleventh, their lord the mind; Vakhshun yath leyji= Scraped this pot; yim karith gay= and went away; Saari samhan= had all assembled; aksi razi lamhan=pulled one rope; Ada kyaazi raavihey kahan gaav= why should the Eleventh have lost the cow? (Why should the soul have gone astray?)

Lal Ded is conscious of the damaging effect caused by the impure instincts in the body. She is showing us how to control the mind. The Five (Bhuta-s), the ten (Indriya-s), and the Eleventh, their lord the mind; they all lick cooking kettles and go away. If we gather and pull the same rope, in the same direction, then, how can a single cow Elude eleven of us? That is why should the Eleventh have lost the cow? Why should the soul have gone astray?

Here Lal Ded wants to convey "What should I do with the five, the ten and the eleven? These all worn out my vessel again and again and left it powerless of following the purpose of my life. Would that all of them unite and together pull the rope and take me across!" She further says -- had these instincts and senses and their respective organs in the body along with their master 'the mind' joined together in good faith, to pull on the boat of this existence, why should all the eleven pulling on together have lost the cow, i.e., the essential spirit of the body.

'Eleven people desperately looking for a lost cow' is a very popular Kashmir proverb and Lalleshwari has used it appropriately in case of a desperate search of eleven human capacities for the search of their lost grace of the Lord. All human consciousness is stopped in the first instance by these five instincts followed by the senses and the mind. Once the seeker can keep them under control a fast spiritual development follows.

SM140. Kyah Bodhukh Moh Bhav Sodur Daarie

Kyah bodhukh moh bhav sodur daarie
Soth lohrith payee tim pankh.
Yem vath karnay kaal chola daarie,
Kow zan kaasi marnean shainkh.

Kyah bodhukh= Why have you sunk; moh bhav= illusory pleasures of the world; sodur daarie =in the sea; Soth lohrith= you pulled down the high-banked road which could have led you safe across; Yem vath karnay kaal chola daarie= dense darkness surrounds you now, and, at the appointed time, Yama's apparitors prepare to drag your body bleeding to death; Kow zan kaasi= who can chase away; marnean shainkh= your fear of death?

There are many desires of man. These illusive pleasures have overwhelmed the persons with greed and vanity. How is it, you have put off the path of morality. Please search for the truth and guard it. In this affair there is a marvelous simplicity. Now, the time bound, pitch darkness of death is ready to lay its icy hands and the very thought of death may force out the live sensations and fill the desolate heart with paralyzing awe. To liberate the soul from the captivity and to conquer the fear of death should be the ideal, to achieve the eternal truth.

SM141. Kyah Kara Kangri Pan Chein Karinyam

Kyah kara kangri pan chein karinyam
Ami kaani kundli gondham naar
Kaapi iheiem kaapi kadhan
Kyah kara chas challan

Kangar= Fire Pot, interwoven with thin twigs; pan-cheni= Half burnt leaves of Chinar and other trees, used for warming the fire pot; kaani= The thin fine twigs of trees; kundli= The earthen fire pot, symbolically Kundalini which is awakened with intense concentration and meditation of mind at the base of the spine; with its release, a transcendental state, (When the body consciousness in merged with the absolute reality) is realized; gundnam naar= Felt release of intense heat; kaapi eheim= I could get hold on its outer frame (Kope Kashmiri) twigs with which it is enveloped.(Physical body); kaapi kadhan = I wish I could (Kope Kashmiri) remove its outer insulation and expose the kundalini open for its realization; kya kar chass challan= There is no alternative than to bear with its pain, on its release with Fortitude, to enjoy the perpetual bliss.

Here Lal-Ded in her sadhana wanted to acquire capabilities to know all the feats of sadhana as she wanted to awaken the kundalini which brings new awareness, beyond thought and emotions.

Here she refers to the despondency in her failure to realize the release of kundalini allegorically by referring to Kangri Kashmiri (earthen fire pot, interwoven with fine thin twigs). The half-burnt leaves, burnt in the fire, pot gives intense heat for a moment then it is reduced to ashes. So, she weeps for the joy as such she feels having lost the vitality for realizing the truth. She in her attempt to realize and release the kundalini, has burnt all her vital energies by burning all the elements of air within with severe exercise of inhale and exhale as such she feels an urge to catch hold, of this vital energy kundalini and make it easily perceptible and released. She wishes she could bear the brunt of its heat like the fire in the earthen fire pot and wants to feel its sensation and effect. She wants to observe and experience the brunt of the heat of kundalini released for that she requires the courage of the moth to burn in the Flame, and such she laments for her courage, and determination, which she is bearing to conquer the grosser self for the realization of Truth.

SM142. Kokalee Sath Kol Gachan Paatali

Kokalee sath kol gachan paatali [*3]
Akali zal mal varshun pean
Mammas takee tai mas' kay pyallee
Brahman ta chraelli ekwat khen
Maaji ha karan korein draali
Zanam nish sari wasit pean.

Kokalee= evil, bad times, kalyug; *sath*= seven; *kol*= river, streams; *zal mal varshun*= acid rain; *mammas*= flesh, meat; *mas*= wine; *pyallee*= cups; *chraelli*= mischevious people; *ekwat*= together; *khen dine; maaj*= mother; *korein*= daughters; *draali*= middleman; *zaman*= by birth; *sari*= all; *wasit pean*= perilous fall.

Here again Lal-Ded speaks of the coming events when torture, brutality, barbarity, humiliation, treachery, and degradation of character will be the order of the day with the result that their past seven generations will suffer a perilous fall from heaven. The people will witness an untimely fall of polluted rains. Brahmins will dine with mischievous people, across the table and will devour meat dishes along with the drinks of wine. This will be their favourite pastime. The mothers with their daughters will move together to sell their chastity. So, beauty will have better commerce. As such the very purpose of man's birth will suffer perilous fall.

SM143. Kus Push Tai Kus Poshaanee

Kus push tai kus poshaanee
Kam kosam, lagizes puuze
Kav sari goadd deezyas zaldaani,
Kav sanna manter shankar swaatma vuze.

Kus push= who is the florist; kus poshaanee= who the flower-girl; Kam kosam lagizes puuze =which flowers should He be worshipped with; Kav goadd deezyas zalchi daani= in what water should He be bathed? Kav sanna manter= with what mantra; Shankara=Lord Shankara; swaatma vuze= with what mantra should we awaken Shankara.

Who gathers the rose buds? Who wreaths the garlands? With which flowers the Lord should be worshipped with? With what type of sacred water, the Lord should be bathed with? O! With what divine mantra should Lord 'SHANKARA' be awakened, both in body and in spirit?

SM144. Kush Posh Tel Diiph Zal Naa Gatshe

Kush posh tel diiph zal naa gatshe
Sadbhaava gwara kath yus mani heye,
Shambhuhas swari neyth panani yatshe,
Suy dapize sahaza kriyi.

Kushgrass, posh, tel, diiph, zal, naa gatshe= things like Kusha, flowers, Dweep Jyoti or water for the worship of the Lord; Sadbhaava gwara kath yus mani heye= one who follows carefully the precepts of his Guru, master; Shambhuhas swari neyth panani yatshe= One who meditates unceasingly on the holy name of Shiva with full dedication; Suy dapize sahaza akriyi, na zeyye=there is no worship that would surpass him as his is the truest worship of the Lord.

Lal Ded says one who follows the directions of the Guru with truest devotion does not need any worship of the Lord. She says Guru is the ultimate Lord for a sincere disciple. The seeker does not need any of the objects for worship like flowers, milk, water, Kusha grass or Dveep Jyoti as for him the only essential thing is the truest devotion of his Guru because it's only Guru who can make him progress far ahead in his sadhana. The seeker does not need the sesame seed; Flowers and water if he is of honest faith, and accepts his Guru's word, On Siva meditates constantly.

SM145. Kyah Bodhukh Moh Bhav Sodur Daarie

Kyah bodhukh moh bhav sodur daarie
Soth lohrith payee tim pankh.
Yem vath karnay kaal chola daarie,
Kow zan kaasi marnean shainkh.

Kyah bodhukh= Why have you sunk; moh bhav= illusory pleasures of the world; sodur daarie =in the sea; Soth lohrith= you pulled down the high-banked road which could have led you safe across; Yem vath karnay kaal chola daarie= dense darkness surrounds you now, and, at the appointed time, Yama's apparitors prepare to drag your body bleeding to death; Kow zan kaasi= who can chase away; marnean shainkh= your fear of death?

There are many desires of man. These illusive pleasures have overwhelmed the persons with greed and vanity. How is it, you have put off the path of morality. Please search for the truth and guard it. In this affair there is a marvelous simplicity. Now, the time bound, pitch darkness of death is ready to lay its icy hands and the very thought of death may force out the live sensations and fill the desolate heart with paralyzing awe. To liberate the soul from the captivity and to conquer the fear of death should be the ideal, to achieve the eternal truth.

SM146. La Illah Il-Lalah Sahi Korum

La illah il-lalah sahi korum
Vohi korum panun paan
Vojood travith mujood rotum
Teli meh muluem la-makaan

La illah il-lalah= there is absolutely no deity worthy of worship except Allah, The Meaning of La Ilaha Illa Allah (None has the right to be worshipped but Allah); sahi korum= rightly educated; vohi korum = blazed as red hot coal; panun paan =my body; Vojood travith =leaving the source; mujood rotum= clasping and holding the present; Teli meh muluem =then I realized; la-makaan= the ultimate and the final goal.

Rightly educating there is absolutely no deity worthy of worship except Allah.
Lal Ded blazed her body as red-hot coal.
leaving the source, clasping the present
Then I realized the ultimate and the final goal.
Whether Lal Ded has used the word La Makan or not is a different issue. To me it appears the word has got corrupted during oral communication of the vakh, as Lal Ded has mostly used the word Prakash asthan which conveys transcendence of Shiva who has the essential attribute especially of Shakti. As per the concept the creator and the created are the two separate polarities and the twain do not meet. God is at the highest pedestal and after creation leaves the world alone to its own fate. In sharp contrast to this Kashmir Shaivism holds the view that Shiva as the absolute reality is both transcendental and immanent.

SM147. Leka Ta Thoka Paith Sheri Hetcham

Leka ta thoka paith sheri hetcham
Nenda sapnam patt bronh taam
Lal chhas kal zanh no chenim
Ada yeli sapnis vyepi kyah

Leka =abuse; thoka=spit; shairi haicham (hetcham)=on my head; Nenda=back bite; Lal chas=I am Lalla; kall zanh no cheinim = full of conviction and faith.

Abuses and spits I wore like a crown, behind my back and in my presence, I tolerated all the abuses, but I am Lalla, I never deflected from my goal, my being suffused with God, where is the room for the ill which people spoke of me.

Lal Ded says, "I remember, once, I lay in utter surrender to His magnificent grace. The crooked people, spit at me, even hurled abuses at me. They planned to kill my soul by uttering all non-sense. I felt condemned for all times to come. But all that I bore with joy and grace. As I am Lalla, full of conviction and faith. I did not lose my patience, and I lived, absorbed in the bliss of consciousness. My limited understanding widened. I set aflame, my mind. And, when it was all empty of love, it finally led me to His awareness. O Lord! How shall I thank you, for the realization of the merger of imperfection into perfection?"

SM148.   Lal Bo Draayas Kapsi Poshie Sachie

Lal bo draayas kapsi poshie sachie
Kade tai doonie karnam echay gath
Tuy yeli kharnas zawiji tuye
Vovurni vana gayam alaanzhie lath

Lal Bo draayas = I, Lal, set out; kapsi poshie sachie = hoping to bloom like a cotton flower; Kade tai doonie=ginner and carder; karnam echay gath=But was beaten and trampled by ginner and carder; Tuy yeli kharnam= Shredded and spun; zawiji tuye=I was spun into fine a yarn; Wowuri waana= weaver on his loom; gyam alaanzhie lath=and hung and hit by the weaver on his loom.

Here Lal Ded gives narration of her life's sufferings. Hoping to bloom like a cotton flower, I, Lalla, set forth in the colorful world. But soon the cleaner and the carder came and gave me hard knocks and blows. Spun into a yarn by a woman spinner on her spinning wheel, I was helplessly hung upon a loom, and given more knocks from the weaver's broom. Now turned into cloth, I was dashed and dashed by the washerman on the washing-stone. Then into a large mortar made of stone, he threw me, and with his grimy feet, rubbed me with fuller's earth and soap. The tailor now worked his scissors on me, and cut me with care, piece by piece. Thus, was it that I, Lalla, at last entered the High Estate of God.

SM149. Lal Bo Draayas Lolarey

Lal bo draayas lolarey
Chandaan lusum dyann keho raath
Vuchhum Pandit panani garey
Suy mai rotus nechhuthar ta sath

Lal Bo draayas lolarey = I Lalla travelled along way for your love; Chandaan(tchhaandaan) lusum= set forth in search of Him for days and nights; Vochoom pandit panananai garai= I saw the Pandit (Shiva) in my own home; Soi mai rotus nechhuthar Ta saat=that was the most perfect and auspicious moment of life.

I Lalla travelled a long way in search of Him. I wandered for days and nights. I finally gave up the search and turned back. I saw the Pandit in my own home. Then lo! That was the most auspicious moment of my life. I mingled up with my spirit. This was the memorable moment of my life.

Passionate with longing in mine eyes searching wide and seeking nights and days, Lo I behold the truthful one, the wise. I saw the Pandit in my own home, I saw God in my own home. Here in mine own house to fill my gaze. (Translation by R.C. Temple)

Driven by love, I Lal, rushed out, and searched till the end of night and day, But the Pandit (Shiva) I found within myself, and that for me was the perfect moment, auspicious my stars!

I found the all-knowing self within in the sanctuary of my own heart. (Translation by Jiya Lal Kaul).

SM150.   Lal Buh Lusis Chaaran Ta Gaaraan

Lal buh lusis chaaran ta gaaraan
Hal mai kormas rasniiy shatiee
Wuchhun hyotmas ta taier deenthmas baran
Mei ti kal ganaiyee zogmas tatee

Lal=I Lalla; Buh looses=struggled beyond my strength; chaaran ta gaaraan =in search of; Hal mai kormas=I found a solution; rasniiy shattee = I remained vigilant, lest I may miss the chance of seeing Him; Voochun hui-tmas= I tried hundreds of ways to seek Him; ta taier deenthmas baran = finding His doors bolted and barred; Mei ti kal ganaiyee=I firmly resolved; zogmas tatee= fixing my gaze upon His door I stood just.

"As a seeker of Shiva, I went every quarter searching and waiting for Him. I, Lalla, wandered and sought for Him, and even beyond my strength I struggled. Finding His doors bolted and barred I remained vigilant, lest I may miss the chance of seeing Him. I tried many ways to seek His presence. To my bad luck, I found all the entrances bolted. Still then I stood just there with longing and love, fixing my gaze upon His door. In silence I watched the moment, when the Lord would grant me the favor, so that unheard becomes heard and unknown becomes the known."

Lal Ded was all wakeful to recognize the projection of her mind, within her own spirit-Atman. She could observe the attainment of Shiva. That was her sole purpose.

SM151. Lalith-Lalith Vaday Boh Vay

Lalith-lalith vaday boh vay
Cheta muhach peyiy maiy
Roziy no pata looh-laengarac chhay
Niz-swarup kyah mothuy hai

La'lith-la'lith=after taking rest, to make someone to lull to sleep; vaday=weep; boh=I; Tseyta=mind, self; mAy =maya; looh-laengarac=an iron chain, an anchor with which life's boat is kept stationary, family; Niz-swarup=soul, the real self; mothuy hai= why forgotten.

I will weep and weep for you, O Mind, My Soul! The world hath caught you in its spell. Though you cling to them with the anchor of steel, not even the shadow of the things you love will go with you when you are dead. Why then have you forgotten your own true Self?

SM152. Lal Boh Chaayas Somana Baag Baras

Lal boh chaayas somana baag baras,
Vuchum shivas shakhti miilith ta waah!
Tati liiy karmas amritsaras,
Zindiiy maras ta mai kari kyah.

Lal Bo=I, Lalla; chaayas=entered; somana= my own mind; baag Baras= the garden-gate; Vuchum=saw; Shivas Shakht=Shiva and Shakhti; miilith ta waah= sealed in one, in this endless state of bliss; Tati=there itself; liiy karmas amritsaras = I merged in the Lake of Immortal Bliss; Zindiiy=while alive; maras ta=I die; mai Kari kyah= what can the world do unto me?

In the Vakh Lal Ded is referring to the worldly class who conceal deeper into worldliness. To stir these people up Lal Ded has addressed this Vakh to them.

With affection and zeal, I, Lalla, entered by the garden-gate of my own mind. I happened to see Siva with Shakti sealed in one. Shiva, the Lord, in all His splendor, mingled up with His all-pervading spirit the 'Shakti.' There itself I merged in the Lake of Immortal Bliss. Now the life and death have no meaning for me. I am mingled up with the infinite matter of the universe. I am unchained from the wheel of birth and death.

Individual soul is in fact an essential part of the universal soul (Param-Shiva) left apart with a purpose. It is an opportunity provided to man to work for his awakening and return to his original abode. Lalleshwari tells us about her own experience with her Lord. She finally got admittance into the chambers of her Lord suggesting her personal awakening and being one with her Lord. She found her Lord nowhere else but inside her own loving heart. She says that there was no need to hang around as the ultimate truth could be experienced inside one's own capable heart.

Lalleshwari says she dived deep into this sea of eternity and became eternal free from the pains of birth of death. She achieved eternal freedom from all worldly affairs which she calls death for the world and the consequent eternal life in the company of her Lord. On achieving such stage of complete freedom of self she became one with her lord just as a tiny drop of water merges into the vast ocean and becomes one with its vastness.

SM153. Lal Bo Draayas Dooray Dooray

Lal bo draayas dooray dooray
Kuloof thavith vachas
Yus none neri so, phat krray
Khuin deiton Yechas

Lal= Lal Ded; Bo= I; Draayas= Wandered; Dooray= Far and wide; Kuloof= Lock; Thavith= Kept; Vachas= Breast, bosom; Yus= Who so ever; None-Neri= Reveals; Su= He; Phat= Falls; Krray= Well; Khuin= to be eaten; Deiton= Be given; Yechas= Ghosts

With my breast locked, I, Lalla, wandered far and wide. With the bliss of lord's grace, my limited understanding widened. Observing complete silence, I did not reveal my identity to anybody. For, who so ever, reveals the Mystic truth, for worldly gains, meets a serious fall and becomes a feed for the Ghosts. The Vakh means "I, Lalla went too far in my spiritual achievements but at every stage I guarded my secrets closely. Those who want others know and make a show of their achievements are liable to lose them fast. They come to a great loss so they should be given to a ghost for a meal."

SM154. Lal Bo Draayas Shiv Gaarney

Lal bo draayas shiv gaarney
Vuchhum shiv ta Shakti akaei shaiye
Shakti vuchhum peth sahsaaras
Maaraan gayas tamee graaiiy
Bo paeri Shivas ta Shiv sandis garas
Bo Lall maras ta mai kari kyah

Lal Bo=I, Lalla; draayas=left my abode; Shiv gaarnay=wandered in search of Shiv, that is wandered to conquer all misery; Voochoom=I saw; Shiv Ta Shakhti akei shy= I saw the most glorious Sun kindled, in the form of 'Shiva' mingled up with his spirit, 'Shakhti'; Shakhti woocham=I saw Shakhti; paith sahsraras= seated in the digit of the moon or Sahasrara; Maaraan gyas = I could not contain myself with the joy; Tami graaiiy= began to dance hand in hand with my love; Bo pariiy Shivas=I salute Shiva; Ta Shiv sandis garas =and the abode of Shiva; Bo Lal maras ta mai Kari kyah= I Lalla, am happy to die in the passion of Lord.

Sahasrara [sa-has-rara] *The Sahasrara chakra is also known as "the bridge to the cosmos."*

The highest chakra, the sahasrara chakra is in the cranium (skull) at the top of the head. It is also known as the crown chakra, the thousand-petaled lotus, or the "seat" or "throne" of God. At the center, all the rays of the brain radiate outward so that the soul is finally united with God. The rays keep the physical body nourished with energy.

Sahasrara or the crown chakra is considered the seventh primary chakra in yoga traditions, and it means "thousand-petalled". These are arranged in 20 layers, each with approximately 50 petals. It is usually represented by the color violet.

This wheel, of pranic energy is said to be the center of one's spiritual connection to the divine and yogic teachings assert that it gives us the ability to experience a connection with God. The sahasrara chakra represents the soul in its aspect of Perfect Being. It is the seat of liberation for enlightened beings. As the goal of yoga practices is samadhi or the superconscious union of the ego with the divine self, the crown chakra is the point at which the soul dissolves ego consciousness. The union may be experienced as merging with a calm inner light. In the light, one can expand one's consciousness to infinity. The soul lets go of its delusion of being separate from the light and thus becomes the universe.

In spirituality, the third eye often symbolizes a state of enlightenment. The third eye is often associated with religious visions, the ability to observe chakras and auras, precognition, and out-of-body experiences.

Lalla says: I left my abode and wandered to conquer all misery and to awaken new Sun. My joy knew no bounds when I saw the most glorious Sun kindled, in the form of 'Shiva' mingled up with his spirit, Shakhtee. I saw Shakhtee, seated in the digit of the moon or Sahasrara of the Lord, glowing Golden coloured waves in all directions. I could not contain myself with the joy and began to dance hand in hand with my love, I cried and cried, "I salute thee and to thy abode" and began to toss my head in sprightly dance completely unaware of my state. The passion of Lord set fire to all in me and now I am happy to live and happy to die.

SM155.   Lal Mai Dopukh Look Haand Krainee

Lal mai dopukh look haand karinee
Tawai chajim manach shainkh
Maag novoom naar cholloom
Kraihnel kosoom manai sheinkh

Lal mai dopukh=to me Lal, I was told; look haand krainee= called me by derogatory names and even uttered curses; Tawai chajim manach shainkh=a stigma, I won't be able to wash off those dirty stains from my face; Maag novoom= I had to bathe in the ice cold water; naar cholloom= for the Lord had set fire to all in me; Kraiy hanz kasoom manas sheinkh= I was declared guilt free of all the religious rites and traditional doubts.

People close by, called me by derogatory names and even uttered curses. I believe, I won't be able to wash off those dirty stains from my face. They intended to kill my soul by uttering absurdities. But it had no effect on me, as I had killed all the evil in me. Ever since all the doubts about me and my affairs vanished off. I am fused completely with the Lord's graciousness. To attain this height, I had to bathe in the ice-cold water, when air was biting, and passion of Love for the Lord had set fire to all in me. Thus, I was declared guilt free of all the religious rites and traditional doubts. As such, I enjoyed the murmur of my prayers.

SM156. Lalli Gwar Brahmand Peth Kani Vuchum

Lalli guvr brahmand peth kani vuchhum
Sheshikal vuchhum paadani tal
Gyanik amrit prakrath barem
Loobie morum andh-vandh taani

Lalli guru brahmand peth kani Vuchum= I Lalla, saw my master (guru) sitting elegantly on the crown of my head; Sheshikal wachem paadani taani= the overflowing nectar of the mystic moon (Sheshkal) overflowed my whole body; Gyanik Amrit prakrath baram= my whole being was filled with the ultimate awakening of all the secrets of my Lord's world; Loobie morum andewand taaney=I got freed from the desire of the world especially the ego.

I, Lalla, while in meditation completely absorbed in HIS divine spell, felt the presence of my Guru (Master) at the top of the brain or Sahasrara in "vibration form", which helped me in the profusely gushing out of the Hormones or Shashikal, which trickled down to the body and covered the entire essential cells of the body from head to foot, with the result the intelligent faculty for the realization of His divine spirit was revealed and that resulted in the mass conversion of the entire State of the body, into vibration ENERGY form and thus synchronization with the Lord's vibrations was achieved and whole environment round me turned celestial. It is, as such, I have been able to kill the evil instinct of geed in me for good.

SM157. Lattan Hund Maaz Laaryom Vattan

Lattan hund maaz laaryom vattan
Akee haavem akichi vath
Yim yim bozan tim kona mattan
Lali booz shatan kunie kath

Latan hund maaz= soles of my feet; laryom vatan = soles of my feet wore off on the roads; Akie haavem= He was all and everywhere; akchi vath=He showed me one way, I had nowhere to go nowhere in search of Him; Yem yem bozan=whoever learn of it; tim kona matan= will they not wonder; Lali booz shatan= Lala listened, with patience; koonie kath=only one thing that is truth.

The soles of my feet wore off on the roads while I wandered in search of Him. I chanced to see His presence, with the guidance of my Master (Guru). Then lo! On a sudden, I saw that He was all and everywhere, I had nowhere to go in search of Him. This was the Truth of a hundred truths. Whoever learns of it, will they not wonder? Those who will hear all this will go mad, after Him.
I found the sum and substance of all discourses; He is the truth out of a hundred truths.

SM158. Lolaki Naar Lolli Lallenovum

Lolaki naar Lalli lolli lallenowum
Marnai moyas ta roozes na zarai
Rang raech zaachaie kya na rang howum
Bo dapun cholum kya sanna karai

Lolaki naar= In my extreme ecstasy of love; lolli nowoom= I took my Lord, my love in my arms and shook Him to and fro; Marniiy moyas= I was dead before my natural death; ta roozas Na zariiy= I lost my individual self completely in the process and became one with my Lord; Rang reach zaachaie ya na rang gvoom= there was not a single trace left of my person with its caste, creed and colour as I had attained the newest colour of my Lord; Bo dapoon chaloom kya sanna kariiy= all traces of my personal identity along with all egos had vanished and I am basking in the glory of my achievement.

The beautiful alliteration and the way this Vakh are narrated are marvelous. I rocked my 'Love' in the cradle of my lap. I am overpowered by his beauty. My feelings were ignorant and selfish. I have become conscious about the nature of time without end. I vanished, without losing my breath. I felt as if I am reduced to nothingness. I mingled with the nothingness of Cosmos. I adorned Him with the colours of my liking and of Lotus in bloom. Tears of joy softened my mind. Thus, I am free from the sinful instincts of conceit. As such, I am lost in wonder, love, and praise. In the totality all duality has gone.

SM159.   Loluki Vokhla Vaalinj Pishim

Loluki vokhla vaalinj pishim
Kokal chajim ta ruzas rasa
Buzam ta zajim paanas cheshim
Kav zan tav saeet mara kina lassa
Buoy na moyus ti buoy na mareh
Yeli achev denshi ti kanav bozeh

Lole ki =love; wok lay=mortar; vaalinj=heart; pishim= ground; Lole ki wok lay vaalinj pishim= I took out my heart (considered to be the source of all fine emotion besides its logical function in the body) ground it in the mortar of my love and thus got rid of all my animal passions and felt relieved; kokal=evil;chasim(tsajim)=removed;roozes rasay= I sat serene and unperturbed; Buzem te zaijem paanas chaishem= I roasted it and burned it before eating (indicating her intense dedication in order to rid of all the evil passions); Kave zane tave seit mare kine lassay= Now I sit in peace but still apprehensive whether I would die or live.

In the mortar of love, I ground my heart, I parched and burnt and ate it out. Thus, all my evil thoughts removed, and I got peace. I sat serene and unperturbed. I roasted and burnt and consumed it myself, yet still I doubt if I can know whether I shall die or live (and find release from birth and death). With the passage of time Lal Ded became one with God and an embodiment of love.

In this Vakh Lal-Ded shows the depth of the dedication and devotion towards her Lord. In a brilliant poetic creation, she has expressed her deepest feelings and love for her Lord. The success may escape for ages, but true devotees continue waiting for some miracle to happen. She says one must encourage love inside oneself. Lal Ded lays emphasis in this Vakh and says that she took out her heart, ground it in the mortar of the love for her Lord and then after roasting and burning it, she chewed it, indicating again her intense dedication to rid herself of all the evil passions of the body.

SM160. Loob Maarun Sahaz Vyatsaarun

Loob maarun sahaz vyatsaarun
Dro'g zaanun kalpan traav.
Nishi chuy tay duur mo gaarun.
Shuunyas shuunyaah miilith gav.

Loob marun=killing of desire; sahaz vyatsaarun=meditating on realization of self; drog zaanun=hard to achieve, expensive affair; kalpan traav=give up vain thoughts; nishi chuy= Your Lord is so close to you; duur mo gaarun=seek not afar; shuunyas=void; shuunyaah miilith gav=merges with the void, (the stilled mind merges in pure consciousness).

Realization is rare indeed: Seek not afar; it is near, by you. First slay Desire, and then still the mind, giving up vain imaginings; then meditate on the Self within, And lo! The void merges in the Void.

Lalleshwari had attained the highest goals of spirituality. She says that concentration on the Lord's name and meditating on one's real self is the key to get rid of the worldly desire. She had a clear imagination that achieving the status of being one with the Lord was not so hard for everyone who wanted to reach there. The main hurdle in the achievement of spiritual goals is one's own incapacity. Lalleshwari has a clear message for a simple devotee -- -- your Lord is nearer to you than everything else! Never imagine Him to be far from away! Just keep under control the fiery body emotions. There is no need to seek Him anywhere else. He is there inside your loving heart. The individual soul is an essential part of the supreme. Once it achieves the essential realization of self, it takes a swift flight to meet the Lord and become one with Him. Atma becomes one with Paramatma. Shunya merges with the absolute. Human being loses its personal identity and becomes one with the Lord. All duality between the ordinary soul and the supreme soul is finished. Lalleshwari had attained this experience and there was nothing further unattainable for her.

SM161. Laachari Bichaari Pravad Karoom

Laachari bichaari pravad karoom
Nadir chiv tai haieve maa
Pheerith dubara jan kya wonum
Pran ta ruhoon haieve maa

Laachari=poverty driven; Bichaari= shortage stricken; Pheerith Dubara=refers again; Jan=good; Wonum=said.

Lal Ded felt elevated on listening to the poverty-stricken Boat lady's note as such she again refers that this world of fancy does not last long nor has any potency like the stem of Lotus (Nadir) and she exhorts the people to go for purchase of Ruhoon, Garlic allegorically the soul and its salvation with the exercise of 'Praan' the exhale and inhale of breath, to acquire self-discipline which begins with the mind first. The spiritual knowledge cannot be acquired by mere exercise of will. It requires the exercise of mind too. It is an existence which flows eternally with peace tranquility, freshness purity and bliss.

SM162.   Larah Lazam Manz Maidaanas

Larah lazam manz maidaanas
Aind aind karmas takiya ta gah
Swa rozi yetti tai bo gacha paanas
Vounya gao wanas phalave dith

Larah lazam= built a beautiful house; manz maidaanas= in the centre of a ground; Aind aind karmas=all around decorated; takiya ta gah=pillows and dazzling luminous lights; Swa rozi yetti ta= it is like a mirage, that will remain here; Bo gacha paanas= I shall leave this beautiful house without any care; Vounya=shopkeeper; wanas=shop; phalave dith=closed the shop.

Childhood passes into youth and youth into age without asking for it. The worldly attractions are hard. We forget the ultimate end of this life and go on enjoying this sequential existence. We collect worldly possessions least caring about its truth. Our body gets most of our attention decorating it and ignoring the soul which keeps it going. Upon death the soul takes flight to an unknown destination the body remains of no use and is disposed of immediately. Lal Ded says:

I built a beautiful house in the centre of a ground. I decorated it with the pillow shaped blocks of supports with dazzling luminous lights. I built it to look like a lotus with the hope that it would ever and ever bloom. But ah! I am conscious this feeling of triumph and happiness will disappear one day, as whatever is created or? Built will be dissolved. It is like a mirage. It will vanish like a nightmare. So, who will enjoy its beauty that delights the sight? Only the gracious Lord! He only will enjoy its magnificence. I shall leave this beautiful house without any care, the way the shopkeeper closes his shop with no hope to return, for nobody knows the moment when this life will cease to be or will meet its end.

In this beautiful Vakh Lal Ded describes the uselessness of the charm of life and its attractions. She weaves a beautiful metaphor saying she had constructed a beautiful house (suggestive of the human body) and decorated it tastefully with nice furnishings and gadgets (suggestive of maintaining a beautiful body structure with nice garments etc) but soon she left for an undisclosed destination never to return (suggesting sudden death in the peak of health and youth). This is truly the hard reality of life. It is a strange dreamlike situation. We come and pass different stages of life from infancy to youth and then to age followed by death. Change is the destiny of this life. We experience these changes unnoticeably.

> **SM163. Lazz Kaase Sheet Niwaree**
>
> Lazz kaase sheet niwaree
> Trin zal karaan aahaar.
> Ye kami updesh karoi ho batta,
> Acheetan vattas scheetan kath deion ahaar.

Lazz kaase= covers your shame; sheet niwaree = saves from cold; Trin zal=grass and water; karee aahaar= food and drink; ye kami updesh= who counseled you; karoi ho Batta= O Brahmin; Acheetan vattas= lifeless stone; cheetan=living; kath=sheep; deion ahaar=sacrifice.

Revelation comes to Lalla, her symbols and allegories can be cryptic, and yet the frankness of her Vakh moves us deeply, viscerally. She celebrates resolution in the quest, contrasting physical agony with spiritual flight and dwelling on the obdurate landscapes that the questor must negotiate. Lalla's poetry is fortified by a palpable, first-hand experience of illumination; it conveys a freedom from the mortal freight of fear and vacillation. She cherishes these, while attacking the parasitic forms of organised religion that have attached themselves to the spiritual quest and choked it: arid scholarship, soulless ritualism, fetishized austerity and animal sacrifice. Her ways of excelling these obstacles can seem revolutionary as in this Vakh where she confronts the priest with the brutal fee demanded by his idolatry. Lal Ded says that the innocent sheep gives us wool to make our garments and cover our body from cold. The sheep feeds on mere water and grass. O intelligent Brahmin! Who has directed you to slaughter a living sheep as a sacrifice unto a lifeless stone in a temple to please the God?

SM164. Maarith Panch Boot Tim Phal Handi

Maarith panch boot tim phal handi**2
Cheetan daana vakhur khait
Yudwiiy zaanakh param- pad chandi
Hihooiiee khosh khowoor koot na khait

Maarith=sacrifice; panch boot= Five Bhuutas; phal handi=thus fed; Cheetan daana vakhur khait= offer these fatted rams as sacrifice unto the Lord; Yudwiiy zaanakh=if you will know; Param- pad Chandi= the abode of the Supreme; Hihooiiee Khosh khowoor=left handed practices in which some grains of rice, flowers are offered along with meat and wine; koot na khait=wines, hymns recited in His name, till then He does not eat,.

After killing the five invisible sinful instincts, which had become powerful like fattened rams, on the feed of your sinful instincts, by bearing self-restraint and discrimination of self. For this purpose, meditation proves to be very useful. Meditation alone gives one an understanding of one's inner realm. One should try firmly to fix the mind. With will power gained, sinful instincts automatically, are starved. They lose their strength and then die. The religious ceremonies and rites will cease to have any meaning and the conception of right and left will become misnomer. Thus, evil instincts will be barred at the entrance to the body.

SM165. Madh Pyome Sendi Zallookyoot

Madh pyome sendi zallook yoot
Rangan leilimie kam ta keeuch
Kaeet khyem manush mamas ki nali
Soi bo lall taai gow me kya

Madh=wine; pyome sendi zallookyoot= often I drank that wine with the water of River Sindh; Rangan leiloom kam ta keeuch= how often I have changed the forms and colours, while acting on the stage of this world; Kaeet khyem manush mamas ki nali= how often I saw the cruelty in the man, eating up the flesh of his fellow being; Soi bo Lal taai gow me kya= yet I am the same Lalla still.

"O! River Sind! How often I have come to wander lonely on your banks, to converse with you, about the love that touches the human heart. How often I drank the blissful water and experienced the intoxication of the type of spiritual bliss. O! How often I have changed the forms and colours, while acting on the stage of this world, regardless of my existence. O! How often I saw the cruelty in the man, eating up the flesh of his fellow being. O' There is still much suffering in store, for the people, much of their blood will be squeezed out by the hands of greed? Since, I have renounced the attachments of the world, I am the same Lalla. I feel the impulse of intoxication of the water of Sind conveying to me more of a moral good than that of evil exploitation."

Eating the human flesh is a part of sixty-four main Tantric Sadhana. The idea is to get rid of vritti's (habits of the mind) such as attachments to one's body, etc. Lalla laments eating of human flesh that causes sufferings. She wants to get rid of habits of mind.

SM166. Manai Dengi Tai Akul Zaagi

Manai dengi tai akul zaagi, **3
Daid sarpaanch indrai sarwater teelee,
So vechaar ponie puuzi haras laagai,
Param pad chentan shiva meelee.

Mana = mind; Dengi = is sleeping; Akul = mind is in the wake ful state when it is tuned to the Lord in meditation; Daidsar= always.

It is the mind that dozes off. When the mind in the body is absorbed in worldly actions, it is asleep for the divine impulses. It becomes inactive to the cosmic impulses. It is the Akula that is (ever alert), when the mind is absorbed in meditation and turns within, it becomes sensitive to all the cosmic radiations. The mighty senses are the lake constantly oozing out, constantly filled again. The constant awareness of the Self is worship befitting the Lord, and Siva hood the supreme station man should gain. The five senses in the body are always emanating five different frequencies or wave forms. The sense organs are always tempted by their desires.

SM167. Mannas Gonn Chhui Chanchal Aasun

Mannas gonn chhui chanchal aasun
Cheetas gonn chhui gachun doore
Zeewas gonn chhui bochhi traish aasun
Aatmas gonn chhui na aasoon leef

Manas=mind; gonn=quality, character; zeewas gonn chhui bochi traish aasun=living body needs nutrition, food, and water; aatms gone choi na aasoon leef=soul can release the super consciousness.

The mind is a stream of thoughts. When the intelligence of man is not firm and focused the mind functions to alter one's purpose; so, he never finds himself in a situation in which he could keep his balance. As it is the flow of thoughts, that constitutes, the mind, so indecision is one of its chief qualities.

Lal Ded says that nothing in this world is permanent. Everything is momentary. The emotional attachment of thoughts and desires dry up and wither away like petals when the fruit emerges out. Likewise, the forgetfulness is one of the chief qualities of the intellect or mind. The physical body requires to be fed by natural foods which give it enough power to maintain its strength. Hence, the hunger and thirst are the chief requirements of the living body.

The last of all, there, is one reality that is the 'soul'. The soul is free from all doubt, perversity, and indefiniteness. The soul is universal, supreme, universal spirit which embraces everything. The soul of which we are in search is not the object of knowledge but the basis of knowledge of all finite objects. The individual soul possesses the highest potentiality which can release the super consciousness.

SM168. Mandachi Hanz Hankal Kar Cheneim

Mandachi hanz hankal kar cheneim
Yeli hedoon gailoon assone traave
Orook jaama kar sanna dazyam
Yeli andrim khaarook rozyam wara

Mandachi=shame; hankal=chain; Mandachi hanz hankal= bonds of shame; kar=when; cheneim =break; Yeli=when; hedoon gailoon= jibes and jeers; assone=laughter; traave=give up, when I feel indifferent to the jeers that I face from people! Orook jaama=body frame, jaama=dress; kar sanna dazyam= when the frame of my body will burn; Andrim=inside; khaarook=desire, when shall I reject the robes of all worldly dignity? When the desires of the world stop troubling me!

Peace and harmony live in a core place in Lal-Ded's teachings. She says, when can I break the bonds of shame and shyness within me? It is only when I am indifferent to jeers of wrong, mockings, tauntings and the things which weigh heavily upon my Mind". Spiritual uplift for being one with the Lord was Lal Ded's one truest purpose of all life. Her expression of personal celestial experience at places is simply an indicator to the path of piety and awakening. When will the frame of my body burn? It is the moment when the impurities within me are burnt, conceit and desire cease to have its effect, it is then the spirit within me is freed from bondages of karma. Truth is the beginning and end of existence.

SM169. Manas Graaiye Chaje Pazikooe Ann Khoyome

Manas graaiye chaje pazikooe ann khoyome
Tawakooi bal gome karmas kriiy
Aagura vatith amrit zal chome
Shiv liiye man gome barmas praiiye

Manas= mind; graaiye chaje= free of blemish, mark; pazikooe= rightful, correct; ann=food; khyome= eaten; Aagura vatith= God realization; amrit-zal= nectar; chome= drank.

"By feeding myself with the rightly earned food, doubts about my willpower and strength of mind vanished. Strange, invisible lines of forces developed within my mind, which guided me to the path of God realization. Thus, I reached to the source, where Nectar 'Amrit Jal' was flowing. I quenched my thirst with the sacred water. Lo! It has enlightened my knowledge and understanding. Thus, imperfection merged with the perfection, and I found myself fused with His grace. "

> **SM170.   Manas Saethi Manai Gandoom**
>
> Manas saethi manai gandoom
> Cheetas ratoom chopaer vagh
> Prakrach saaietee porush no vollum
> Sreh mai karome labam vath

Manas saethi manai gandoom= with serious hard work I was successful in controlling my mind; Cheetas ratoom chopaer vagh= I remained on guard from all sides to avoid all incoming negative worldly influences affecting my conscience; Prakrach saaietee porush no vollum= I did not allow any irrelevant thought to gain entrance in my mind; Sreh mai karome labam vat= I developed deepest devotion for my Lord and found the ultimate way towards the goals.

Human mind is very indecisive and liable to quick influences from everywhere as thoughts go on shifting very fast from one to another. It's very hard to control the vacillating mind. Yoga and meditation help to keep mind under control. Lalleshwari indicates her personal experience in this regard. After she achieved considerable success in controlling her mind, she guarded herself from all digressions. Her devotion and Sadhana led her to her goals.

In this Vakh she says:

With the concentration of mind, when I was absorbed in knowing the true nature of His divine grace and kept strict vigil over the vacillations of my consciousness, I had to struggle for it. I did not allow any irrelevant thought to gain entrance in my mind. I tuned my mind with the energy levels of the sacred letter AUM; with the result the resonance of the order of celestial wavelength was restored. Thus, a condition of thoughtless state, was created and established, within my mind, I plunged into the ocean of divinity, and thus, purified. I merged into the bliss of God-Consciousness.

SM171.   Mandas Dudur Tai Vadris Sukray

Mandas dudur tai vodrus sukray
Sukray karakh marakh na zaanh
Sukray travith karak kukaray
Vokuray gachi balakh na zaanh

Mandas=mand budhi; feeble minded body , Ahmak; Dudur= illness, disease, sickness rot,decay; tai= to cross limit ; Vadris= a sick person should be thankful, to prevent, avoid ; Sukray= to thank, be thankful; karak= behave, act, work; marak= to die; na zaanh=never ever; travith= give up, surrender; karak= will do; kukaray=bad deeds, bad actions; vokuray= dented; injured; gachi= become, get, develop; balakh= recover, mend, improve; na-zaanh= never, on no occasion;

A decaying body, a sick body.
Remain thankful to Lord.
Being thankful to Him, you remain alive.
Being ungrateful, and doing bad deeds
You get dented with injuries to your body which never mend.
Surrender to absolute reality of Lord Shiva

SM172. Mansai Maan Bhav-Saras

Mansai maan bhav-saras
Choori koop naires naara chokh
Laikh log tai bo na kunnay
Tooli tooli tai tool na kenh

Mansai maan= mind of man; bhavsaras = Ocean; Naara chokh= destructive fire.

O Blessed seeker: Naara. Ocean and the mind of man are both alike. Under the ocean's bottom lies the destructive fire, and in the breast of man lies rage, the fire of wrath. The flames of anger and the abusive words can bring more harm which needs to be controlled. Human Mind has the large capacity for emotions and feeling. It can embrace the entire universe. It is the universal and all-pervading spirit which embraces everything. Besides the emotions, there are animal instincts in human beings, which are desire ridden, passionate and selfish. Their intellectual bias is limited. They engage themselves in quarreling and fighting. They speak words which can cause violent anger and raging the wrath. The flame of hot words can burst into destructive fire. So, upon this hot and distemper sprinkle cool patience. Even though these hot abusive words are pinching and explosive, do not give due thought to it.

SM173. Marookh Maar Paanch Bhoot

Marookh maar paanch bhoot
Kaam, krodh, loob, moh
Nata kaan barith maarnai paan.
Manuy kheyn dikh, sovechar shram,
Vishay tihund kya -keoth doar zaan.

Marookh=slay; maar=kill; paanch bhoot=five demons; Kaam, krodh, loob, moh= Lust, Anger, Greed, and attachment; Nata kaan barith=or, aiming their arrows at you; maarnai paan=they will shoot you dead; Manuy kheyn dikh= feed them; sovechar shram= feed them on self-restraint and unfairness of the Self; Vishay tihund kya -keoth doar zaan= thus starved, these demons will become powerless and weak.

Lal Ded says: Needed desire is called 'Kama'. The sensual passion should be shunned. She tells an aspirant of yoga to kill the invisible instincts of lust, anger, greed, attachment, and conceit, which have gain admission in the body complex. These, may otherwise, turn into missiles and weapons, sufficient to kill one's personality and one's link with Shiva.

Take care; feed them on self-restraint and discrimination of self. With firm mind get going in the moderate form to make your dream come true. With your will power the sinful instincts will be starved. They lose their strength and die. Desire obstructs the growth of devotion and desire cannot co-exist with Sadhana.

SM174.   Methya Kapat Asath Trovum

Methya kapat asath trovum
Manas korum suy updesh
Zanas andhar keewal zonum
Annas khyainas kus chum doosh

Methya=I; kapatt= fraud; asath=untruth; trovum =renounced; Manas Karoom=to my mind; soi updesh =that I taught; Zanas ander=knowing the fellow men; keewal zonum= to see the One in all my fellowmen; Annas khainas= accepting the food offered to me; kus chum doosh=w hy to discriminate between man and man.

I renounced fraud, untruth, and deceit. I taught my mind to see the One in all my fellowmen. I didn't maintain any distinction between man and man. I didn't see any shyness in associating with any of them or taking their foods. I found Him only one of its kind and spread all through. I accepted the food offered to me with love by my fellow men.

Lal Ded was very liberal in her associations with all kinds of people. She was revered equally by the people of all faith as to her all faiths were equally authentic ways of God. She taught them the ultimate way of living, extending all love and compassion to everyone high and low, rich, and poor and doing everything in the Lord's name.

SM175. Muuda Kraiy Chy Na Daarun Ta Paaroon

Muuda kraiy chy na daarun ta paaroon
Muuda kraiy chy na dharein kaah
Muuda kraiy chy na paanch agen daaroon
Muuda kraiy chy na deh sandaroon
Muuda kraiy chy na rachin kaay
Sahaz gaaroon chui updesh

Mooda=fool; kraiy=action; chy na daarun ta paaroon=observing fasts and wearing rich robes; Na dharein kaah=to observes fasts on the auspicious dates; Na paanch agen daaroon=to burns incense and sacred fires; Na deh sandaroon= looks for bodily comforts; rachin(ratchhin) kaay=eat delicious foods; Sahaz gaaroon chui updesh= In study of the Self alone is right action and right counsel for you.

O fool, right action does not lie in observing fasts and ceremonial rites. O fool, right action does not lie in providing for bodily comfort and ease. In study of the Self alone is right action and right counsel for you.

Here Lalla cautions- that he is a fool who seeks Truth by wearing rich and ceremonial robes. He is a fool, who observes fasts on the auspicious dates. He is a fool, who burns incense and sacred fires, as a ceremonial rite. He is a fool, who looks for bodily comforts and ease to realize the truth. He is a fool, who uses foreign aid to adorn himself for when the body is unadorned, it is adorned the most. To seek truth in the real sense is the direction that 'I' LALLA direct you to follow. Absolute Truth is indestructible, eternal, self-existent and infinite. So, truth means the realization of one's being.

SM176. Mudas Gyaanach Kath No Wanizay

Mudas gyaanach kath no wanizay
Kharas gor dina raavi doh.
Yus yuth kare su tyuth swaray
Krerey kari-zyina panun paan.

Mudas=fools; gyaanach kath no wanizay= Impart no truth; Kharas=donkey; gor= molasses; raavi doah=waste of time.

It is no use to explain the spiritual thoughts about God realization, to an ignorant person. The ignorant would never appreciate the spiritual state of experience. All that would go in vain like feeding an ass with brown raw sugar. It depends upon the inclinations of a person. The thought is responsible for the action. It is no use for a Guru to waste his energy in such spiritual communications, for which any listener is hard to find. We should in no way put ourselves in the well of ignorance. Action (Karma) is followed by its result. With this thing in mind, we need to develop the spiritual path of life.

(Another version-here last two line change)

SM177. Mudas Gyaanach Kath No Vanizey -Seki Shaathas

Mudas gyaanach kath no vanizey
Kharas gode dina raavi doh
Seki shaathas byol no vavizey
Kom yaajen raavi teel

Mudas=to a fool; gyaanach kath= mysterious or cryptic truth; no wanizay=do not tell, Mudas gyaanach kath no vanizey= Impart not mysterious or cryptic truth to fools; Kharas=to an ass; gode dina=feeding molasses; Kharas gode dina raavi doah= Nor on molasses feed an ass; Seki shaathas=sandy beds; byol=seed; no vavizey= Do not sow; Seki shaathas phal novavizey= Do not sow seed in sandy beds;raavi=waste; kom yaajen =cakes of bran; teel=oil, Nor waste your oil on cakes of bran.

Tell not truth and godly knowledge to fools,
Nor waste your day feeding molasses, to a donkey,
Do not sow seeds in sandy soil,
Nor waste your oil in making the cakes out of husk.

In another version:
Mudas gyaanach kath no vanizey; Kharas gode dina raavi doh
Yus yuth kari su tyuth swaray; Krei karizina panun paan.

Do not impart truth and godly knowledge to the fools, nor waste your day in feeding molasses to the ass, action is followed by results. A person will get the results as per his actions, don't waste your energy in such spiritual communications for which any listener is hard to find. Do not put yourself in the well of ignorance.

SM178. Moodas Pranvoon Chuie Moi Waal Chaidoon

Moodas pranvoon chuie moi waal chaidoon
Moodas pranvoon chuie mori deon koh
Moodas pranvoon chuie samander pooran
Moodas pranvoon raavi doh

Moodas= a fool; pranvoon= make understand; chuie=is moi-waal= a hair follicle; chaidoon= drill a hole; koh= a mountain; samander= a sea; pooran= to fill; raavi doh= waste a day.

O blessed one- It is very difficult to bring an understanding in a fool. As to counsel a fool is like piercing through the fine filaments of a hair. As to counsel a fool is like filling the sea with pebbles. As to counsel a fool result in wasting the day's labour.

SM179. Mun Choor Maroon Gandun Neshkal

Mun choor maroon gandun neshkal
Pend vattith thaav hee
Deeva putra suo wani paanaiiy vendo
Soi dapzai sahza kriiy

Mun choor maroon= difficult to control one's mind; gandun neshkal=difficult to reduce it to insignificance; Pend vattith thaav hee=control your mind, make your mind to behave as flexible as a lumped mass of cooked rice; Deeva putra =O, the sons of sages; suo wani paanaiiy vendo= His hands though unseen, will direct your mind to righteousness and Truth.

It is very difficult to control one's mind and to reduce it to insignificance. Make your mind to behave as flexible as a lumped mass of cooked rice, but under control. Lalla says: O, the sons of sages! His hands though unseen, will direct your mind to righteousness and Truth. Have faith in yourself and in His divine grace that is the exercise or SADHNA in the right direction. This will lead you to His awareness.

By proper effort, an individual gets such a strength and virtue, that "not even God can change into defeat the victory of a man who has overpowered himself" that is the exercise or SADHNA in the right direction.

SM180.   Muudh Zanith Ta Pashith Laag

Muudh zanith ta pashith laag
Zore, ta kole, shur, wadwoon, zad-roop aas,
Yus yee dapi tas tiy boz
Soi chui tattva vedas abhyaas.

Muudh zenith= be as a fool; ta pashith laag = though you are wise; Zore, ta kole=deaf and dumb; shur, wadwoon= be as a playful kid with childlike manners; zad-roop aas=be as innocent and unaware; Yus yee dapi=whatever anyone tells you; TAS tiy boz= patiently bear with all you meet, politely talk to everyone; Soi chui tattva Vedas abhyaas= this practice surely will lead youto the realization of the Truth.

Though you are wise, be as a fool; though you can see, be as one blind. Though you can hear, be as one deaf. Patiently bear with all you meet, and politely talk to everyone. Be as a playful kid with childlike manners. With cool patience bear with all you meet. Talk politely with everyone you meet. This practice surely will lead you to the realization of the Truth.

[Note. At some places the first line reads as muudh zaa'niith pa'shith ta ko'r]

SM181. Mal wondi Zolum

Mal woandi zolum
Chander go'l tay mo'tuy cheyth.
Tseyth go'l tay keynhti na kune.
Gay bhoor bhwaah swaah veysarzith keyth.

Mal vwandi zolum= I cleared my mind of all worldly dross; Chander go'l Tay mo'tuy cheyth=

The sun sets, the moon begins to shine (Praanaa the sun moving upwards, Apaana the moon moving downwards); the moon sets the mind alone is left; the mind dissolved, nothing remains; Earth, atmosphere, and sky (Bhuuh, Bhuvah, Svah.) depart. And in the Supreme are absorbed.

SM182. Mal Vonda Zolum, Jigar (Kam) Morum

Mal vonda zolum,
Jigar (kam) morum
Teli Lalla nav draam
Yeli dael traevmas tatti

Mal Vonda zolum=I freed myself of all the emotional outbursts, I burnt the foulness of my soul; Jigar (kam) morum=I killed my desires, I killed my passions;Teli Lalla nav draam= then, I achieved all my purpose and came to be known Lalla, my name as Lal spread afar; Yeli Dael travimas tattie=I spread the edge of my garments and just there in utter surrender to Him, I achieved all my purpose only when I devoted myself wholly to my Lord.

Lalla Ded says that she surrendered herself entirety to His grace. Human ignorance results from three limitations of consciousness. These are the three impurities known as maya, karma and anava. Maya and karma need to be consumed and removed in the glowing fire of yoga. Anava mal as such cannot be removed through any form of Yoga. It needs Shiva's grace.

These three limitations are also known as the 'malas' or "impurities," which obscure consciousness and prevent a person from realizing one's true nature. When alive, the powers of the human being become restricted within the individual mental processes, senses, and actions, all of which reinforce a sense of separateness between self and others and between self and the true self, Shiva.

Lal Ded reflects upon the power of each of the three 'malas' to block spiritual realization. The 'malas' are spots or smudges on the mirror of identity; they prevent the self from seeing the self within. She says: When my mind like dust from a mirror got removed from all impurities; the knowledge came to me that He was everything and I nothing.

SM183. Mann Posh Tai Yach Pushaani

Mann posh tai yach pushaani
Bhavaki kosam lagizes poozai,
Shisharas goad deezyas zalchi daani,
Chopi manter Shanker su atme-woozai.

Manai push= Mind is the florist; yach pushanee = Devotion the flower-girl; Bhavaki kosam= flowers of faith; lagizas poozai= He should be worshipped with; Shisharas goadd= the glittering dew drops collected from the top of the beautiful petals of roses; deezyas zalchi daani= is the only sacred offering, with which the Lord should be bathed with;In one version it is Shivas goad dizeys ashwaaney, tchepi mantar Shanker vuzey; Shiva is to be given a bath of tears of devotion. Mantras are to be recited in silence so that He can be awakned from within.

Chopi manter= Silence is the mantra; su atme-woozai= that awakens Him. And, in the deep stillness of the mind, He wakes up in the inmost Self.

Mind is the florist and gathers the rose buds and the faith is the consort (flower girl), who wreathes the garlands to offer unto His divine grace. He should be worshipped with the flowers of faith. He should be bathed with the glittering dew drops collected from the top of the beautiful petals of roses. Silence is the mantra that awakens Him. In short, the silence is the language of truth; give it an understanding but no tongue. And, in the deep stillness of the mind, He wakes up in the inmost Self.

SM184. Maryam Na Kunh Ta Mara Na Kansi

Maryam na kunh ta mara na kansi
Mara nech ta lasa nech

Maryam na kunh= I mourn for none; mara na kansi= none mourns for me; Mara nech=happy to die; lasa nech=happy to live.

Alike for me is life and death; Happy to live, happy to die, I mourn for none, none mourns for me. Lalla reminds us of Raza hams: Royal swan who is supposed to sing melodiously at the point of his death. Drawing an analogy - You were as intelligent as the Royal Swan. How is it? You have turned mute now. O! Someone has robbed you of something within. How is it? All the organs of body have ceased to function. The brain itself has ceased to respond to the impulses of mind. Now nothing can be swallowed, so choking has come about. Ah! The essence of life 'the soul' has gone off unnoticed. Like the grinding stone mill stopping and the grains choked and the miller running away with the grains unnoticed.

Thus Lal-Ded explains when the end of life comes about the soul departs along with the accumulated fruit of action (Karma) and is drawn to such a state which is suitable to it.

Lal Ded passed away, leaving a shadow behind. It is a matter of surprise that no monument to this saintly figure has been erected to mark the place where her body was cremated or laid to rest.

SM185. Mayas Hu Na Prakash Kunay

Mayas hu na prakash kunay
Lai hu na tirth kanh
Dhayas hu na bandav kunay
Bayas hu na sukhai kanh

Mayas=love, affection; Prakash=light; Lai Hu= like the love of the Supreme; Tirth Kanh= no pilgrimage; Dhayas Hu= like the Lord Himself; Bandav Kunay= no relative; Bayas Hu= like the fear of God; Na Sukhai Kanh= no comfort.

Lal says-There is no light greater in warmth than the love and affection of the 'Lord'. There is no light like the knowledge of ultimate 'truth', no pilgrimage, like the one of the loves of the Supreme. She says there is no pilgrimage-worth the name than the place where one sits to seek His gracious presence. It is the seat of emotions and feeling. It is a place where one gets blissful intoxication; it is a place where one does not have impure thoughts. Further she says no relative like the Lord Himself, and no comfort like the fear of God.

SM186. Mokris Zan Mal Chollum Manas

Mokris zan mal chollum manas
Ad mai labam zanas zaan,
Suh yeli dyunthum nish paanas
Sorui suy tai bo no kenh

Mokris=foulness; zan mal chollum=foulness got cleared; manas =mind; Ad mai labam zanas zaan= then recognition of Him came to me unmistakable and clear; Suh yeli deunthum=when I saw Him; nishi paanas =near me; Sorui suy=He was all; Bo no kenh = I was not.

Foulness from my mind was cleared as ashes from a mirror, and then recognition of Him came to me unmistakable and clear. And when I saw Him close by me, He was all and I was not, and there was nothing else.

Foulness when got cleaned from my mind, then I recognized Him close by me, He was all, and I was nothing.

SM187.   Na Pyaayas Na Zaayas

Na pyaayas na zaayas
Na khaiyam haund na shoonth
Na chhes shen pata
Na chhes saadhan broonth

Na zaayas= never born; na pyaayas= never given birth to a child; Na khaiyam=never ate dandelion leaves, a vegetable used in Kashmir in early days; na shoonth=no ginger; Na ches shein pata =not after six sinfulinstincts e.g., lust, anger, greed, envy, conceit and attachments; Na chhes saadhan broonth= not gone farther in my awareness of God realization than to those 'saints'.

I was never born, and I have never given birth to any offspring. It is the immortal soul which has gained entrance to my body complex. I never underwent any pain on account of childbirth. I never took any ginger or any special medicinal infusion of herbs for restoration of my health: I am neither given to six sinful? Instincts e.g., lust, anger, greed, envy, conceit, and attachments. Nor I have gone farther in my awareness of God realization than to those 'saints' who have had realization of truth and are enjoying eternal and immortal life.

SM188. Na Rozie Vandha Tai Na Retkoului

Na rozie vandha tai na retkolui,
Na boze shravnun peth kastoor,
Na rozie khushi tai na rozie maatam,
Na vazie sahilas saaz santoor

Na rozie vandhi tai= neither winter will stay; na retkoluy, =nor summer will last; Na boze =not heard; shravnun=month of July-August; peth kastoor= Kostur; A Kashmiri name for - Tickell's Thrush is prevalent to the Indian subcontinent and has a discontinuous breeding range from Pakistan through Kashmir to Nepal and western Bhutan. It is a common summer visitor in Nepal and is known to breed in that country just across the border from Zhangmu which is in the southern part of Tibet; Na rozie khushie tai na rozie matam= Neither will there be happiness, nor mourning for ever; Na vazie sahilas saaz santoo= Nor will there be music and entertainment forever.

Neither will winter last long nor will summer, the bird Kasturi will not hear you during the rainy season of Shravan, neither will happiness last long nor will sorrow, the musical instruments for celebrations will not play for ever.

Lal Ded says: "Things change; seasons change. And friends leave. Life doesn't stop for anybody. Everyone thinks of changing the world, but no one thinks of changing himself."

Nothing lasts forever, neither winter nor summer.

Nor will there be the incessant singing of Kastoor, a migratory bird to Kashmir. The bird Kasturi will not be heard during the rainy season of Shravan.

Neither will there be happiness, nor mourning for ever.

Nor will there be music and entertainment forever.

Kasturi; A Kashmiri name for - Tickell's Thrush is prevalent to the Indian subcontinent and has a discontinuous breeding range from Pakistan through Kashmir to Nepal and western Bhutan. It is a common summer visitor in Nepal and is known to breed in that country just across the border from Zhangmu which is in the southern part of Tibet. Kostur is common in open forest in the Himalayas and migrates seasonally into peninsular India. Males of this small thrush have uniform blue-grey upperparts, and a whitish belly and vent. Adults have yellow beak and legs while it may be darker in juveniles. There is a yellow eye-ring which is thinner and fainter than the Indian black bird which is usually bigger in size. Females and young birds have browner upperparts. Thrushes are omnivorous, eating a wide range of insects, earthworms, and berries. They nest in bushes or similar. They do not form flocks but loose groups of two to five spread across tens of meters have been spotted in bird sanctuary. A story tells about the sacred Song of the Hermit Thrush; of how the elusive bird got its song and why it only sings to a few lucky people.

Another version:
Nai rozi vandeh tii nai retkoli.
Nai boli Shravan pati kastoor.
Nai rozi Shravan Nai kastoori.
Nai vazi dohai yi saaz santoor.

SM189. Na Lal Zaayas Na Lal Pyaayas

Na Lall zaayas na lall pyaayas,
Na Lalli khyaw woppal-haakh ti handh,
Na Lall saneyas lukk handhies nyaayas,
Tavay Lall chhas bu haraan.

Na lall zaayas =no birth; na lall pyaayas = no labour, motherhood, kinship, maternity; na lalli khyaw woppal-haakh =neither Lal ate red spinach; ti handh = nor dandelion; na lall saneyas =neither I Lal measured, considered, meddled, gossiped, interfered; lukk handhies nyaayas= public problems, civic glitches; tavay lall = that is why I Lal; chhas bu haraa = am surprised, astonished.

Lal says:
No birth, no maternity
No red spinach, no dandelion
No gossip no civic glitches
That is why I, Lal am astonished.
Upset and astonished, Lal Ded in this vakh says that she knows not what birth or maternity is; she has neither tasted red- spinach nor dandelion, a vegetable rich in vitamins and given to the women during and after delivery; She has never gossiped on any civic glitch or anomaly about anybody, and yet there is a murmur going around.

SM190. Naar Gachi Chaalun Ta Aar Gachi Galoon

Naar gachi chaalun ta aar gachi gaalun
Odhur gachi kadun vopal haakas ti handaiy
Hadh gachi ratun ta madh gachi vaalun
Veih gachi chaalun ada achak grandey
Shoob gachi kaanchien loob gachi maarun
Paan gachi naavun amie Senday

Naar gachi(gatchhi) chaalunta (tsaalun)= one should tolerate the strong fire of all anger; aar gachi galoon= kill all pity for the worldly trouble; Odoor=moisture; gachi(gatchhi) kadoon=should be removed; vopal hakas ti handaiy= moisture of 'vopal-haakh' and hund wild vegetable cooked and eaten on some sacred occasions);Hade gachi ratoon ta mad gachi waloo=mind should be tuned and kept under control; Veih gachi chaaloon ada achak grandey= Celestial excellence should be favored instead of the worldly glamour;Shoob gachi kaanchien= One can reach a higher stage of realization; loob gachi maroo= worldly desires and sensual pleasures should be made ineffective by controlling them strictly;paan=self,body; gachi naavun=must clean;Paan gachi naavun amie senda= one should thus be able to take a deep dive in the egoless and selfless clean waters of the Indus (Senday) of divinity and reach higher stages of realization.

Lal-Ded is regarded as a teacher of Morals. She has a firm belief in higher values of life, she is conscious that in her teachings she is expressing the will of the Lord. She says:

One must be calm even when one is angry by distemper. Let you be cruel but not unnatural. Take away all the Moisture from the dry leaves of vegetables like 'Hand' and 'Wopalhaak.' (Kashmiri names of vegetables- a tradition of drying the green vegetables to be used in harsh winter due to scarcity of food items). Acquire control over your senses and the pride to keep these within limits. Bear with the temptations which seize a man unawares. Keep holiness as an aim to sanctify every pursuit. These are steppingstones on the road to holiness. It is simple, graceful, easy, and methodical. Thus, seekers mind and body become pure as flame from smoke.

SM191.   Naath Naa Paan Naa Paraznovoom

Naath! naa paan, na per, praznovoom,
Sadaa budhum akui deh.
Chei bu! Bu chei! muel na zonum,
Chei kus ta bo kus chum sandeh.

Naath=the supreme Lord Shiva; paan naa paraznovoom= I did not know who I was; Sadaa boodam akoi deh= I knew only this body of mine always; Chei Bo=Thou and me; Bo Chei= I am Thou; mull naa Zonoom= I did not know; Chei kus=who are thou; Bo kus=Who am I; chum sandeh=that is the doubt.

Lord, I did not know who I was, or Thou, the Supreme Lord of all. I knew only this body of mine always. I was nursing and caring for my body alone. I had no idea about His being seated within the core of my heart. The relation between Thou and me, That Thou art I and I am Thou and both are one, I did not know.

But now I know, to ask: 'who art Thou, who am I?' is doubt of doubts.

SM192.   Nabad Boaras Attagand Dyol Gome

Nabad boaras attagand dyol gome
Deh kaan hol gom heka kow hee
Gwar sund vanun raavan tyol pyome
Pahali ros khyol gome heka kiho

Nabad Boaras=candy pots; Attagand dyole gome=sling around going loose; Deh Kaan Hol Gom= backbone has bent due to heavy load; Heka Kow Hee= how to carry the load under stress; Gwara Sund Vanun Ravoon Teul Pyome= Master warns to renounce the worldly attachments; Pahali Ros Khyol Gome= a shepherdless flock; Heka Kiho= I cannot bear the suffering of my 'Soul.'

The sling of my candy load has gone loose, (and it galls my back). While bearing with the sweet worldly attachments, like carrying the sweet candy pots, on the back and the sling round has gone loose the backbone has suffered a bend with the heavy load. So, I am at a loss to understand, as to how I shall carry the load under such heavy stress. A depressing feeling of impotence and loneliness tortured my mind. The master's warning, to give up the worldly attachments, to defeat my spirit, sounds painful. I feel, as if I have lost my will and strength of mind. I am like a shepherd less flock depressed and desolated and now I cannot show my face to my Master, for I cannot bear the suffering of my soul in agony.

In its totality, Lalleshwari describes the worldly life and its attractions that keep a person engaged absolutely throughout life. She compares worldly engagements with a heavy backload of sweet candies though its slings loosened and the heavy impact of the load affecting heavily on her deeply bent her back. The comparison is worth understanding as the sweet candies indicates the worldly comforts and the loosening of the slings and the impact of the heavy load on her back indicates the fear of imminent end of worldly existence. Now she is heavily tortured in the situation and unable to make a choice, whether to carry on with the world or leave it to seek her Lord. She is awakened to the truth of the worldly existence such that she falls into delusion. Now she gets a reprimand from her Guru to immediately shun all worldly affairs and engage herself in the pursuit of her Lord, but she's repeatedly tortured by her indecision as she on one hand wishes to follow her master's biddings but on the other is unable to leave the world because attachments of the world are too hard to escape. Her condition is also compared to a flock without a shepherd. The beautiful epithet 'Rawan'e Tyol Pyom' is very right in the context.

SM193. Nabisthans Chai Prakrath Zalvani

Nabisthans chai prakrath zalvani
Hindi's tam yati pran vatagat
Brahmandas pyath chai nad vohvani
Ha-ha tava turun ha-ha tava tot

Nabisthans= The navel-region, technically called kand-pura, is the sun-region where heat glows incessantly.

In this vakh Lalla Ded explains the whole process of pranayama. The navel-region (Nabisthans), technically called kand-pura, is the sun-region where heat glows continually. The vital air (prana) rising from navel along pingla nadi is warm when exhaled from nose. The air gets warmed up by the heat glowing at the navel region. Lalla Ded asserts that Brahmand is the moon-region at the extreme end of sushmana nadi and is naturally cold. A cold current coming down the sushmana nadi cools the breath carried by Ida during the process of breathing in.

SM194. Nabisthans Chet Zal Wani

Nabisthans chet zal wani
Brahmasthaanas shishroon moakh,
Brahmandas chiiy nad behwani,
Tawi hoo gav turoon ta haah gav tote.

Nabisthans= Gut, Abdomen; Chet = Brain (in the abdomen); Zalwani = Warm; Brahmasthaanas= Cerebrum, large brain; Shishroon= Cold; Mokh= Face; Brahmandas= Cerebellum; Nad= Sublime tube in hinder brain; Bahwani= Flow of hormones (released from Ductless glands) of the brain; Tawi=that is why; Hoo gav turoon = the cold air that we breathe in; Haah gav tote= the exhaled air is hot. [At the navel region is the Place of the Sun, where Prakriti glows as hot as fire; from here hot breath rises to the throat. At the crown of the head is the Place of the Moon, from here cool nectar down the naaddi-s flows, thus haah is hot, and huh is cold.]

The master (Guru) was happy over the originality and creativity of Lal Ded. He in his heart of heart attributed it to the idea that "the younger people show more powerful activity in the memory related areas of the brain than the elderly does". The Guru strongly urged Lalla to condition her brain and the body for experiencing the state of ecstasy.

Then she explains, "The abdomen or the Gut has a brain of its own just like the larger brain in the head. This system sends and receives impulses, records experience and responds to emotions, the nerves in the lining of the abdomen are highly inter-connected and have direct influence on things like the speed of digestion, the movement and contractions of the different muscles and the secretion of various juices in the abdomen."

The brain in the Gut plays a major role in the human happiness and misery. In fact, nearly every substance that helps run and control the brain has turned up in the Gut. That is why she says that the brain in the Gut is very sensitive so it should be kept warm.

Secondly the neurons in the cerebrum the brain proper is to remain cool. The Neurons in the sense organs of the brain are required to create necessary impulse for the emission of the celestial waveband, which is required to synchronize with the waveband which the Almighty Lord is emitting and is spread up in the universe as a thin tenuous web-like thing to acquire the mingling with the Lord and His grace. Thirdly the hormones released by the Ductless glands produce an important role in the realization of ecstasy and spiritual bliss. The air in the breath plays an important role in bringing chemical combination in the internal metabolic activity of the cells in the brain and other parts of the body. That is why Hoo the 'inhale' and Haa the 'exhale' is cold and hot, respectively.

SM195.   Nafsui Myon Chhui Husituiy

Nafsui myon chhui husituiy
Ami hasti mongnam gari gari bal
Lachheh manz saseh manz akhah lustui
Nah tah hetinam sari tal.

Nafsui =soul, gluttony, lust; Myeon=mine; Chhui=is Husituiy=elephant; Aami=that; Hasti= elephant; Munganam=asked; Garih garih=again and again; BAL=food, power; Lachhih=one hundred thousand; Manzah=out of; Saseh= thousand; Akhah=only one; Lustui=survived; Nah tah=otherwise; Hetinam=took; Sari=all; Tal=under, crushed.

My soul is like that of an elephant, and that elephant asked me every hour for food.
Out of a lakh and out of a thousand but one is saved; if it hadn't been so, the elephant had crushed all under his feet.
In its totality Lal Ded says: One's craving lusts. Have control on desires. Have control on hunger.

SM196.   Nafus Dituth Orai Meenith

Nafus dituth oari meenith
Gachkhai cheenith karakh neh fout
Dum deev hakas lal zan zeeneth
Nateh chui kul nafus za-eika- tul-moat

Nafus=desire; dituth=provided; meenith=measured; Gachkhai cheenith=if you realize; fout=demise; Dum deev hakas=patiently get your share; Lal zan zeeneth=you will reach the goal; Nateh=otherwise; chui kul nafuz za-eika- tul-moat=desires may kill you.

The God provided measured desires to everyone, if you realize it correctly, you will not die, patiently and honestly get you share, you will reach your destination, otherwise the desires may kill you.

SM197. Nath Buvno Rannie Mangay

Nath buvno rannie mangay
Meh ravnun raj karem kya
Yi goam leekhith ti ma harbum
Harbum harbum ti harbum kya

Nath = God, Shiva; buvno =universe, worlds; Meh = to me; Ravnun raj= Ravan's rule; karem kya= how will it affect me; Yi goam leekhith = whatever has been destined, fate; ti ma harbum =that is the will of God Shiva; Harbum harbum ti harbum kya= Shiva, Shiva, Shiva only

God the universal, demand anything.
Ravan's rule, regulations affectless for me
Whatever in fate has been written, that is destined by God
Shiva, Shiva, Shiva hermit by himself, and bountiful for others.
Lalla regards the world as an array of traps for the unwary, so long as the self remains amnesiac towards its true nature. On realizing that the world is the playful expression of the Divine, and that the Divine and the self are one, anguish and alienation fall away from the consciousness, to be replaced by the joyful recognition that all dualisms are deceptive. Ravana is described as a devout follower of the god Shiva. His devotion to Lord Shiva earned him the respect of the God. When he ruled, he had proceeded on a series of campaigns conquering humans, celestials, and demons. He was a tyrant of mighty power who was holding the gods at ransom. Finally, he was punished by Lord Shiva to whom he had prayed for a boon. The fact that the writing is being done with a finger suggests that it is the hand of God tracing the words in the fate of mankind. Once you have done something you will regret, there is no way to erase what has been written because it is also engraved in your own memory. Life only moves in one direction.

SM198. Nav Trapraviith Deh Shomrawith

Nav trapraviith deh shomrawith
Kahim ratith kunuei zaan
Dubari choong yuth na gachi bramak
Ad kati labak param daam

Nav trapraviith=nine gateways with which the soul is equipped with; deh shomrawith=the advanced soul possesses ten powers - five relate to five senses, and five other powers known as (i) bodily power (ii) mind power (iii) speech power (iv) power of respiration (v) power of being in possession of allotted span of life; kahim ratith kunuei zaan= the eleventh power is power of karma; dubari choong= an idiom meaning to work long hours without rest, working late into the night and beginning again early in the morning,double minded, confused;bramak=tempted, allured; ad kati=then; labak param daam= to attain the divine perfection.

The philosophy of Lal Ded teaches us how to conquer the self for the realization of Truth. Here she refers to Nine Gateways with which the soul can acquire the knowledge, to free itself from the bondages of body.

The first gate way is that form of knowledge with which the soul recognizes an object through the process of sense organs; the knowledge formed on some verbal evidence of 0mniniscient; the knowledge in the form of recognition of particular occurrence; the knowledge of what is in other sacred thoughts; the knowledge of final merging with the impulse of the Lord; the knowledge about soul and its existences; the knowledge of Bondages of the soul; the knowledge of the power of the soul which is capable of destroying all its bondages which imprisons it; the knowledge of freedom of soul from all actions.

Further Lal-Ded says: The advanced soul possesses ten powers - Five relate to five senses, and five other powers known as (1) Bodily Power (2) Mind power (3) Speech Power (4) Power of respiration (5) Power of being in possession of allotted span of life. The eleventh power is power of Karma viz.the accumulated force of actions performed by a person. The influx of karma is by virtue of certain powers through which the soul draws in matters.... from without, through the functional activity of mind, speech, and body. So, karma or effect of actions good or bad flows into the soul and impedes its progress. It enters through sense organs through emotions namely anger, conceit, greed, and too much attachment to material objects, through the agency of mind or speech.

Lal-Ded thus strongly urges the seeker to shake off all the karma matter which prevents the unfolding of right vision. So, the soul which has acquired right knowledge begins to put into practice the rules of right conduct. Karma matter is bound up with the soul. When soul departs, it carries with it the accumulated force of karma and is drawn to such a state which is suitable to it. Every chained soul is under the influence of Karma. So, Lal-Ded advises the seeker to understand the power of all these forces, to attain the divine perfection. When the soul is freed from the bondage of karma and has transcended the possibility of rebirth, it attains liberation. Therefore, the karma is the key to the puzzle of life. Punya karma is the moral strength and paap is moral weakness.

SM199.   Niyam Karooth Garbaa

Niyam karooth garbaa
Chaitas karba payee
Marn broonthi marba
Marith martaba hari

Niyam karooth= you vowed; garbaa = In your mother's womb, A common belief that a child resolves thus in his mother's womb, In your mother's womb you vowed not to be born again; Chaitas karba payee= When will you recall the vow; Marn broonthi= And die, even while alive (to all desire, and be released from birth and death); marba=die, And die, even while alive (to all desire, and be released from birth and death):Marith martaba hari= Great honor will be yours in this life and greater honor after death.

How is it you have forgotten the promise, you gave to the Lord when you were in the mother's womb. You had described yourself immortal by doing deeds of goodness. When will you remember it? Please try to face life heroically, by facing fearful odds. Then you will look glorious great honours and appreciations will be showered, even after your death. Great honor will be yours in this life and greater honor after death.

It's said everyone makes a solemn pledge in his mother's womb not to be born again and work for complete liberation from the recurring cycle of birth and death. But you've forgotten to fulfil it. When will you recollect it to make your present life a success? Perhaps the lure of the world is so enchanting that almost none fulfils the promise. Lalleshwari wants to awaken man to the same pledge. She says it will not only add to his honour in this life but also make him glorious after his actual death especially because he will in the first instance get freed from the vicious cycle of birth and death and add to his glory by coming nearer to the Lord.

SM200.   Omui Chu Voth Path Omui Chui Sorun

Omui chu voth path omui chui sorun
Omui chu opdesh apoor zaan
Omui paroon Omui sorun
Omsii saet kar zaenee zaan

Omui chu voth path=Om is a great source of energy; omui chui sorun=Om must be recited; Omui chu opdesh=Om is some advice; apoor zaan=pronounce it correctly; Omui paroon=Om must be reverberated with continuous rhyme and rhythm; Omui sorun=Om be recited with dedication silently; Omsii saet kar zaenee zaan=Having passionate zeal with Om one achieves the recognition of consciousness in body as well as in spirit.

Lal Ded has used OM in many of her vakhs. Om (also spelled Aum) is a Hindu sacred sound that is considered the greatest of all mantras. The syllable Om is composed of the three sounds a-u-m (in Sanskrit, the vowels a and u combine to become o) and the symbol's threefold nature is central to its meaning. It represents several important triads:
- The three worlds - earth, atmosphere, and heaven
- The three major Hindu gods - Brahma, Vishnu, and Siva
- The three sacred Vedic scriptures - Rg, Yajur, and Sama

Thus, Om mystically embodies the essence of the entire universe. This meaning is further deepened by the Indian philosophical belief that God first created sound and the universe arose from it. As the most sacred sound, Om is the root of the universe and everything that exists, and it continues to hold everything together. Here Lal Ded advises, the Seeker or Saadak that since the letter 'OM' is a source of great ENERGY, it must be recited in a manner so that the effect or "frequency" of the exact order is set free. It must be taken as the directive or the order, to pronounce the letter correctly with proper pause, and proper pitch. It must be reverberated with continuous rhyme and rhythm, with the passionate zeal, so that a continuous energy level or wave form is released, so that one achieves the cognizance of the letter, both in body and in spirit.

SM201. Omai Akui Achhur Porum

Omai akui achhur porum
Sui ha maali rotum wondas manz
Sui ha maali kani peth garum ta churum
Aises saas te sapnis soen

Omei= OM; akui Achhur= single letter; porum=read; Sui ha maali rotum= I, Lalla got absorbed in its Bliss; wondas manz=focused it on my mind, bossom; Sui ha Maali kani peth garum ta Churum = literary (engraved and adorned on the stone), i.e. I made arduous effort to give the letter proper pitch; Aases saas=ash, I was base, Iwas knowing nothing; ta sapnis soen = I have transformed into pure Gold.

I chanted the unique divine word "Om" repeatedly and saved it lovingly in my heart. I shaped and grasped it with my persistent dedication and love, I was just ash and by its divine grace got transformed into gold.

I, Lalla got absorbed in the Bliss of ecstasy, by rhythmic recitation of single letter 'OM' with concentration of mind. I made arduous effort to give the letter proper pitch and loudness with the result vital effect was set free, which resulted in the attainment of enlightenment that is from ashes I have transformed into pure Gold.

SM202. Omkaar Ye'li Layi O'num

Omkaar Ye'li Layi o'num
Vuhay ko'rum panun paan.
Shu-vt travith sath-marg ro'tum,
Teyli lal bo'h va'tsas prakaashasthan.

Omkaar= supreme word (aum); ye'li layi o'num = When I became one with the Supreme Word OM; Vuhay ko'rum= blazed as red-hot coal; panun paan=my body; Shu-vt travith= I gave up the Path of the Six; sath-marg ro'tum=took straight path; Teyli Lal bo'h va'tsas Prakaashasthan= I reached the Abode of Light.

When I became one with the Supreme Word (Aum), my body blazed as red-hot coal. Such blazing is an actual experience. It does not mean burning out impurity or selfhood). Then I gave up the Path of the Six i.e., six paths according to Trika Darshana, viz Varna, mantra, pada, kalaa tatva and bhuvana). I then took myself to the straight true Path. This easy path which requires rigorous Sadhana led me to the Abode of Light.

SM203.   Omuy Aadi Tai Omuy Sorum

Omuy aadi tai omuy sorum
Omuy thurum panun paan
Anitya travith nitya bhosum
Tavay provum parmsathan

Omuy aadi=the syllable 'om' is the beginning; omuy sorum=i meditate on 'om'; Omuy thurum panun paan=I made myself with 'OM'; Anitya travith=having left the perishable (body); Nitya bhosum =I behold the imperishable (God); Tavay provum Parmsathan=by doing that I attained the supreme abode.

The continuous recitation of the letter 'OM' produces blissful ecstasy in its wake. Since, the 'OM' letter is a source of Energy; I found that I have become the embodiment of the sacred letter. Since, 1 am completely absorbed with this situation now, I have clear perception of the visionary gleam, for all times to come. That is how I have reached to the top of my glory and am permanently absorbed in the state of enlightenment or visionary gleam.

SM204.   Ora Ti Paanai Yora Ti Paanai, Poat Waannai

Ora ti paanai yora ti paanai
Poat waannai rozei na zaanh
Paanai gupt ta paanai gyani
Paanai paanas mood na zanh

Ora=that side; paanai=self; yora=this side; poat waanai=last one; rozei na zaanh=never be gupt=hidden.

Lalla says:

Lord is the eternal beauty. I find no difference in Him and me. I feel His graciousness as such I feel natural affection for Him. The purpose of His creation is to manifest beauty that leads to love and happiness. As such, all duality melts and the Lover and the beloved become one. God is conceived as everlasting beauty and manifests itself. The passion for beauty is a means to link the soul to God, so the soul will establish contact with the eternal spirit. This can be realized only through direct experience. And the Lord declares to him. "This is my word of promise that he who loves me shall not perish". The faith that is required is to form a conviction that knowledge of the self alone, can give the supreme peace". The 'soul' when it once seizes the reality, loses itself in its meditation and enjoyment, and takes bright spiritual form.

SM205.   Ora Ti Panai Yora Ti Panai, Paanai Paanas

Ore ti panai yore ti panai
Paanai paanas choo na melaan
Pratham achais na mullai daaniiy
Soy ha, maali chei aashchar zaan

Ore ti panai yore Tai panai = as the blessed Lord is seated in me, so I find no difference in Him and me; Ore ti panai yore ti panai means He is there and He is here, He is sought after and He is the seeker; Paanai paanas choo na melaan=yet the two do not meet; Pratham achais na mullai daaniiy=there is not even hairline difference between the two; Soy ha, maali chei aashchar zaan=this knowledge is the wonder of wonders.

The Lord puts in the person, a spiritual substance –the 'soul,' which is neither separate from God nor joined to the man's body. The seeker receives this enlightenment in proportion to his capacities, strength, and resolution. His simplicity and His Magnificence touch me the most. It is not so easy to mingle with His grace. The Human soul draws nearer to the divine grace only by thought of God's power, wisdom and by constant remembrance of Him with a devoted heart. The wonder is that no foreign body, even a smallest grain can be contained within our body, yet He, with all His magnificence is seated within the core of our heart.

SM206.   Ore Ti Yorie Yore Ti Orie

Ore ti yorie yore ti orie
Yeth doderis kya sanna shoob zanoon
Gindoon chui pannai hur te morai
Apzis huris hanch thavakh

Doderis = Decayed body; gindun = lively play; hur= the place at which the child is born; mor = Body; apzis = False belief; huris = the floor at which the child is born; hanch = Intentional false statement.

The supreme soul though unborn and undying becomes manifest in human personification for rooting out of the forces of ignorance and selfishness.

Lal Ded says: The Lord is spread up in the entire universe. He, as well is in my heart's core. He does not lose His nature. So, there is no charm in adoring this decayed body. As the entrapped soul must gain liberation from captivity, it is a lively play for the soul to come into this world as a human being. So, it lives in the heart's core. It is free from sin, free from old age, death, or rebirth. It repeatedly exists even when all the experiences are suspended. It lives in the world but as a stranger. It lives all hardships of flesh, yet it lives not after flesh. Its existence is on earth, but its citizenship is in heaven. It is a mistaken belief that the soul in man is born and dies. Simply, it is transformation of soul from one state to another. There is no birth and no death. It is an optical illusion, and its expectancy might be called miraculous. So, the nature is a living thing to which all souls are tuned.

SM207. Omkar Shreer Kewal Zonum

Omkar shreer kewal zonum
Shabad supersh, rang, roop, ras gandith
Atma swroop so paania zonum
Param tut doorum sheras peth

Since, I have become the embodiment of the spirit of the letter 'OM', mixed up with the inexhaustible spirit of the sacred sound, touch, colour, form and taste of the divine radiance. I have realized the essence of the realization, with the bliss of ecstasy and exultation, with the result the celestial ENERGY released found a straight path, to the mind, for bringing enlightenment and merger with the perfect and supreme light.

SM208.   Paanai Aasakh Ti Paanai Kaasakh

Paanai aasakh ti paanai kaasakh
Panas nish labak sadoor
Zindaiy marakh ti marith labakh
Ad deshakh shiv sund mukh

Paanai aasakh be you yourself; ti paanai kaasakh=you the remover, eliminator; Panas nish =within yourself; labak sadoor= you will find duel influence; Sador =faithful; Sador is a dual influence—at times you can be extremely happy, expressive, full of fun, and good natured; yet at other times you find it almost an impossibility to give to others, being controlled by self-pity, moods, and depression. Zindaiy marakh =a living thing dies; ti marith labakh= after death you will find; Ad deshakh =then you will see; shiv sund mukh=face of Shiva.

In this Vakh Lal Ded says that you are Shiva. Shiva is the universe, and that Shiva is consciousness, also known as Chit. The universe is made from Shiva's awareness, and we are here due to Shiva's will. The universe is created by Shiva extending his will and restored to tranquility by withdrawing it. Human beings have a spirit, in Scripture, only believers are said to be spiritually alive, while unbelievers are spiritually dead. The spiritual is pivotal to the life of the believer. The spirit is the element in humanity that gives us the ability to have an intimate relationship with God. Whenever the word spirit is used, it refers to the immaterial part of humanity that "connects" with God, who Himself is spirit. Shaivism provided relationship between God, nature, and man. It also provided the philosophy of Shiv-Shakti and Nara (man), which forms the main philosophy of all Shaivic philosophies. In this vakh Lalla speaks a philosophy of salvation.

SM209. Paanai Aasakh Ta Paanai Kaasakh

Paanai aasakh ta paanai kaasakh
Panas nish labak sadoor
Zindiiy marakh ta marith labak
Ad deshakh Shiv sund mokh.

Paanai = self, himself; aasakh =heaven, sky, divine instinct; ta paanai kaasakh=self can attain spiritual perfection; Panas nish labak sadoor= one becomes one with His grace; zindiiy=while alive; marakh=die; Zindiiy marakh ta marith labak=one shouldknow how to die better; ad=then; deshak=will see; mokh=face; Ad deshakh Shiv sund mokh=then only one comes nearer the lord.

Every human being has a potential, a divine instinct in him, which enables him to attain spiritual perfection, as such unheard becomes heard and unknown becomes the known. One becomes one with His grace. It is His joy that assumes all forms. If you know how to die better, it is by facing fearful odds. Then only one comes nearer and nearer the Lord. When one comes near light of the Lord he is transformed into the Potential soul of the Lord. As such, he becomes calm, grand, and peaceful. Then only immortality of higher order will touch his feet. It is as such one can see Him in person with all His grandeur and grace.

Another Version:
Paanai aasakh ta paanai kaasakh, Adah choen dinai marfatukh sadoor.

Diye yodh kasak sui yodh aasakh, Yodh naav thaavanai en aleem bazati alsadur

SM210. Paanas Laagith Roovuk Meei Cheii

Paanas laagith roovuk meei cheii,
Meei chei chaandaan loosum doah.
Paanas manz yeli deeunthuk meei cheei
Meei chai ta paanas ditum choh.

Paanas laagith roovuk meei cheii= O Lord! You continued to be with me but still evaded me your holy presence; Mei chei chaandaan= I went on looking for you; loosum doah=in your search I spent all my life, here and there till my life began to wane away; Paanas manz yeli deeunthuk mei cheei=amazing! I experienced your presence in the deep recesses of my own heart; Mai chai ta paanas ditum choh= It was such an ecstasy that I forgot myself completely when I understood that the duality had vanished.

What a nice poetic description has been given by Lal Ded in this vakh! It is an expression of gratitude to Shiva. It is an expression of real supreme grace. The discovery is within for Lal Ded. In an ecstatic mood, Lal Ded sees Shiva in the nerve cell of her own being. Her purpose of life has been solved. "Chhandaan" is for soul searching process and "Dyuntthuk" refers to the mystic transparency, where the worldly experience and spiritual awareness meet. Mark the poetic flow of sublime of words and see how they built an artistic medium to convey the philosophical truth.

Thou were absorbed in Thine Own Self, hidden from me; I passed whole days in seeking Thee out. My joy knew no bounds, when I saw Him, as my own spirit, then I tried to mingle up in His magnificence by practicing meditation, with the result, the energy levels of celestial grace were released, which resulted in my final absorption in His celestial waves.

Lal Ded has repeatedly used the word 'meei cheei' in this Vakh. By doing this she has been repeatedly dramatizing the event with various connotations. She says that her Lord continued to be with her all the time and still she couldn't get even a single clue about Him. She went on seeking Him till the dusk of her life. She in the end realized that her Lord was nowhere else but inside her own pure heart. It was the real revolution of herself as the truth had dawned upon her. This awakening of self is the greatest mystery of this world. The Lord is always eager to see his devotee nearest to Him, rather being one with Him but the distance is always there because the human beings mostly keep glued with the affairs of the world and do not hear the call of their Lord.

SM211.   Panchav Nishi Paanch Ravim

Panchav nishi panch ravim
Emov choorav karham yerwaninaav
Lagh kath shaatas vaat kath ghatas
Manz dariyavas lajmach naav

Panchav nishi panch ravim= five invisible instincts and five senses; emov choorav(tsoorav) karham yerwaninaav = five invisible instincts (anger, envy, greed, pride, and attachment) have caused damaging effect; lagh kath shaatas waat kath ghatas= laments how to reach the riverbank, compares herself to the boat under the influence of torrents in the river; manz dariyavas lajmach naav= she feels that her life's boat is stuck up during the river.

Lal-Ded is aware of the harmful effect caused the five unseen instincts lurking in the body (Like: anger, envy; greed, pride, and attachment). Since these impure instincts are likely to slow down the power of knowledge and intelligence, they have an evil effect on physical and spiritual aspect of life, as such five senses in the body lose their sensitivity and become easy prey to moral weaknesses. She understands that emancipation (liberation) can only be attained through suppression of lower elements by the higher spirit. Morality is necessary to shape man's nature and the path to liberation is through inner conversion. So, she laments over the influence of bad instincts and feels desolated and expresses her inability to suppress the lower elements and the rude self which she compares herself to the boat which has gone out of control by the power of fast-moving water in the river. She feels that her life's boat is stuck up during the river; as such she has lost the courage, to conquer her disgusting self for the realization of truth.

SM212.   Pannai Aav Paanas Saetee

Pannai aav paanas saetee
Paanai karoon panun vechaar
Pannai panun paan nechnovun
Paanai gupun panun paan

Pannai aav paanas saetee=The moment the inception of life comes to an embryo in the mother's womb , the Lord gains entrance in that body as a conscious substance capable of development; Paanai karoon panun vechaar=after birth the secrets of mystic truth gave the realization about infinite existence and absolute truth; Pannai panun paan nechnovun=His graciousness gifted him with the vision to penetrate in every direction; Paanai gupun panun paan=His blessings preferred invisiblity to keep the sanctity of his grace.

The Lord has gained entrance in this body complex as a conscious substance capable of development, in the form of soul, the moment the inception of life comes about in the mother's womb. His fate revealed the secrets of Mystic truth which gave me the realization of my infinite existence, absolute truth, and pure delight. His graciousness gifted me with the vision which made my faculty of vision, penetrating. His providence preferred invisibility to keep the sanctity of his grace.

SM213. Par Ta Paan Yemi Somui Mone

Par ta paan yemi somui mone,
Yemi hivui mone deyn kyoha raath,
Yemi advai mann saopun,
Tami dyunthui su -Gurunaath.

Pur ta paan yemy somuy mon=he who sees no difference in the spirit, either of one'e own self or of another being, is a realized soul; Ye'my hyuuh mon deyn kyoha raath= he who regards alike both day and night; Ye'mysay adway man saopun= he whose mind is free from duality; Tamiy dyuu'thuy sura-gurunaath= he alone hath seen the God of gods, Shiva.

He who regards himself and others alike, He who regards alike both day and night, He whose mind is free from duality - He alone hath seen the God of gods. The absolute awareness is in seeing Shiva. He who sees no difference in the spirit, either of one's own self or of another being, is a realized soul. he who sees that are all equal in the eyes of divine and thinks that joy and sorrow are but the phases of life, is approaching towards the realm of Shiva. He, who becomes free from the limits of self and from dualism, gets spiritual strength in seeing the effulgence of Shiva. That is the state of merging with the god. Shiva is essence. That truth is known as svara guru natha. Shiva is sound Aum, of the guru mantra.

SM214. Paraan Paraan Zev Taal Phojim

Paraan paraan zev taal phojim
Chei yugei krai tajim na zanh
Sumran phiraan neth ta ongajh gajim
Manachi duiee maali chajim na zanh

Paraan paran=reading and learning; Zev=tongue; Taal=palate; phojim=worn out;My tongue and palate got worn out while reading the sacred scriptures; Chei yugei krai tajim na zanh=I could not perform the desired worship of my Lord properly; Sumran phiraan=doing Sadhna to get desired results, telling beads; neth ta ongajh gajim= worn thin my fingers and thumb; Sumran phiraan neth ta ongajh gajim=my thumb and fingers got worn out while doing sadhana and telling beads continuously;Manachi=of mind; duiee= uncertainty, unsureness, doubt; chajim Na zanh= have not been able to put off the instinct; Manachi duiee maali chajim na zanh=but I am not able to dismiss doubt, uncertainty and attachments from my mind.

Lal Ded in this Vakh admits:
My tongue bruised with my continuous reading the sacred scriptures. I read them aloud. I could not perform the desired worship worthy of my Lord. My thumb and fingers got worn out with continuous telling of rosary beads, but I remained still attached with the worldly affairs and could not dismiss the duality from my mind.

Lal-Ded had shattered her patience and had worn out her palate and tongue. She had an admission in her looks that she had neither been able to learn the desired Feat, nor had acquired the desired end of her Sadhna, so that she could become one with the Lord and experience oneness with Him. She had worn thin her fingers and thumb with the tiresome job of telling beads, even then, she had not been able to put off the instinct of duality and conceit from her mind.

The description is an assessment of people who spend a lot of time and money in doing formal worships in temples as well as their homes. They read aloud the Holy Scriptures, arrange formal worships, visit holy places, and take dips in the holy waters at pilgrimage spots and engage themselves in holy Mantras but unfortunately experience no change of heart. All this becomes merely a routine. For spiritual development purity of mind and detachment from the temptations of the world are required.

SM215.　　Paras Ha Mali Parum Ti Panas Vonum

Paras' ha mali parum ti panas vonum
Vana kas Lali chum meh panas rah
Vai goam dilas meh kya korum
Kunui aasith sorum neh zanh

Paras' ha mali parum=I read and repeated; panas vonum =I questioned myself; Vana kas=to whom to ask; Lali chum meh panas rah=I, Lalla, am to be blamed; Vai goam dilas=she laments; meh kya korum=alas! What I did; Kunui aasith=being only one; sorum neh zanh=I never cared for Him.

Lalla laments that knowing His existence she never cared much. Her wailing and lamentation echo and reverberates her mind every time. Lala does not blame anybody for this. She feels dejected that knowing His oneness she could have done more than what she did.

SM216.   Parith Ti Boozith Brahmin Cheitan

Parith ti boozith brahmin cheitan
Aager khatan tihandi veeid saeti
Patanich san diith thavan Mattan
Mohit mann gachi ahankari

Parith=after reading sacred scriptures; Boozith=after listening to sacred scriptures; Brahmin=the so called Brahmin; cheitan(tchhetan)=become impure, immoral; Aager= source, truth, wisdom; khatan=disappear; tihandi veeid saeti= due to the wrong interpretations of the divine Gospel; Patanich san diith thavan Mattan =valuables stolen in north of Kashmir (Pattan in North Kashmir) will be hidden in South of Kashmir,(Mattan, a place in South of Kashmir; Mohit man gachi ahankari= mind will be in conflict and confusion.

In the coming future, the so called Bramins will read and listen to the sacred scriptures in the manner that it will spoil the essence of Truth. The people with faith will turn immoral on listening to it. Truth and wisdom will disappear due to the wrong interpretations of the sacred Books. The people will be deceptive and cunning. They will steal away valuable goods at Pattan (Place in north Kashmir) and hide these at Mattan (place in South of Kashmir). People in general will see no sin in harming even their own relatives. They will have an amazing skill in exploiting the fears and weaknesses of common man. They will desire greed, arrogance, and conceit, as such; their mind will be in a terrible state of conflict and confusion. By gradual process the people will lose their character and insincerity in their thoughts will be the order of the day.

SM217. Parun Svalab Paaloun Dvarlab

Parun svalab paaloun dvurlab
Sahaz gaarun sukshim tu krooth
Abhyasik ganiraiyy shastra motthum
Chetan anand nishchy goam

Parun svalab=it is easy to read scriptures; paaloun dvurlab= difficult to practice, it is difficult to understand the message of the Shastras into ordinary practice; Sahaj=natural, it denotes both the nature of human being and the means for realizing it. Sahaz resides at the very core of Lall Ded's message; Chetan anand= ultimate bliss of awareness.

Lal Ded says: "I tried to make every effort to put that into practice, what the Shastras have taught me." She made every possible effort to get the glimpse of Sukshama, which is fine excellence (transcendence). She did decide to be conscious of her actions, which eventually made her to realize Chetan Ananda or the ultimate bliss of awareness.

"It is easy to read but difficult to practice. To seek truth is harder as it is wearing a veil in Mysticism. One can achieve truth by indulging in continuous exercise of meditation and concentration with dedication. I forgot all the studies of the sacred books and thus bliss of super consciousness was realized. I acquired that knowledge which shines by its own luster that is beyond all books, beyond all creeds and beyond all the varieties of the world. I had realization of Lord within my-self as such infinite existence, absolute truth and pure delight-was realized.

By improving the quality of thoughts and by giving proper directions to thoughts, a state of bliss of mind is achieved.

SM218.   Parun Polum Apuruy Porum

Parun polum apuruy porum
Kesara vana volum rattith shaal,
Paras prounum ta paanas polum,
Ada gom moluum ta zinim haal.

Parun= to read; polum= to practice; apuruy=which was not taught; po'rum =learnt; Kesara=a lion; vana =from forest dwelling; volum=got; shaal= jackal; polum=acted; Ada gom=then.

I practiced what I read and learnt what was not taught. From its jungle residence, I brought the lion down as I am jackal would; (From pleasures of the world I pulled my mind away). I practiced what I preached and scored the aim and objective.

This Vakh of Lal Ded has a great lesson for humanity. She says that to study a variety of scriptures and associating with great souls does not do the entire job. The main concern is to keep under control all animal passions and the desire of the world. In an allegory she gives an example that unless the wild ferocious animal instincts of the human passion are tamed and made to behave like a simple harmless creature there cannot be any substantial development. Even if we are equipped with the highest spiritual philosophy and theories of religion, we cannot achieve our desired goals. Hence, it is important that we distance ourselves from the world and keep all human instincts and fiery emotions under control. (L-1 above is reported as *"Na kuni chondum na kuni chondum)*

SM219.   Patnaech San Dith Thavan Mattan

Patnaech san dith thavan mattan
Loob boch bolan gyanaki geet
Phaet phaet neraan tim kati watan
Truk ha mali chook paer kad path

Patnaech= Pattan (Town in North of Kashmir); san dith= steal away, booty; thavan=keep, hide; Mattan= (town in South of Kashmir); Loob boch bolan= their greed will make them speak; gyanaki geet= speak thoughts clouded by insincerity and inaccuracy; Fati Fati nairan tim kati watan= how weary will this world appear and real world will be harsher; Truk ha mali chook=if you are wise; paer kad path= keep watch over the coming events.

In future times the intelligent and cunning people will steal away valuable things at one place and will hide them far at different place. Here Lal Ded gives example of two towns; Theft and loot at Pattan (Town in North of Kashmir) will be kept at a hiding place at Mattan, (town in South of Kashmir). Their greed will make them speak thoughts clouded by insincerity and inaccuracy. False show and false appearances will make them lose their entire good faculty. O God! How weary, will this world appear than the real world? Life will be indecent and undisciplined, drinking and gambling will be rife. False show and appearances will be the order of the day.

Lalleshwari reprimands those who in the name of religion and spirituality deceive both themselves and others equally. These so-called mystics or showmen with their certain magical power perform some miraculous feats to impress people and gain popularity. They do so only to satisfy their greed for money. They simply sell their mystic knowledge if they've any and can never be of any benefit for the masses.

SM220. Pawan Poorith Yus Ani Vagi

Pawan poorith yus ani vagi
Tas bhawina spursh na bochi na traish
Tee yas karun antah tagai,
Samsaras sui zaivi neich.

Pawan poorith yus ani vagi = He who can direct his praana aright; *Tas bhawina spursh na bochi na traish* = is not troubled by hunger or thirst; *Tee karun yas antah tagai* = And he who can do this unto the end; *Samsaras sui zaivi neich* = is born fortunate in this world.

He who develops full control over the sense of breathing and lives with the power of his mind can vibrate the senses of his body in perfect harmony with the vibration of the sacred letter 'OM'. This in turn synchronizes with the nature's celestial wave form. Thus, the spiritual awareness of the higher order is restored. In this state of consciousness, one is not affected by hunger, thirst, or sense of touch. No stimulation of any sort can ever distract one away from the spiritual ecstasy so experienced. Such blessed ones attain a state of ecstatic compassion and are born fortunate. They achieve undying order. So, they are liberated Souls.

SM221. Pawan Ta Praan Somui Dyunthum

Pawan ta praan somui dyunthum
Meelith rooduym sheri khor tani
Deh yeli mothum ad kya motsum
Na kuni pawn tai na kuni praan

Pawan ta praan somooie duenthoom= I feel the breath (Pranayama) and the spirit of the body mixed;Meelith roodum Sheri khor tani= I had virtually forgotten my existence as my body from top to toe had reduced to a single element; Deh yeli mothoom ad kya motum=on full awakening the seeker forgets all the interests of the body and the worldly existence as a whole and gets merged with the Supreme Shiva leaving no traces of any individual existence; Na kuni pawn tai na kuni praan=on full awakening, there is no inhalation or exhalation of breath as the self has lost its individual identity.

(Weightlessness in space)
In her wanderings through the space, she experiences the state of weightlessness. She describes its nature, "thus I feel the air and the spirit of the body mixed as one unit whole." Since there is no trace of air in the space and at the same time, she is a living creature, she is aware of her spirit and feels both, air and spirit mingled up together. Since she is in the state of weightlessness, she feels "floating like a gas ball from head to foot" what is precisely conveyed by Lalla's words "SHERI, KOHOOR, TAANI" implying head to foot and experience with which present day astronauts are quite familiar. Since, there is no weight of the body in the space, as such she has forgotten the entire feeling of body weight and she has become a body of floating Mass. In this sensitive state what has remained is neither the air nor the spirit. So, she experiences the blissful state of glory.

On achieving mastery in Pranayama, the seeker does not find any difference between the normal respiration and the practice of

Pranayama. His normal respiration becomes a controlled process, and the body does not require the normal breathing. The whole body is reduced to nothingness (naught). The body shrinks, head and the feet almost union into one. There is no inhalation or exhalation of breath as the self has lost its individual identity. All the interests of the body and the worldly existence as a whole and gets merged with the Supreme Shiva leaving no traces of any individual existence. This is the stage of higher consciousness where the human soul becomes one with the universal Lord and there remains nothing for him to achieve further.

SM222. Poorak Kumbak Reechak Karome

Poorak kumbak reechak karome
Pavanas travam paithkani vath
Anaahats basam karoom
Kainh nai motum soi cham kath

I practised the feat of controlling the sense of breathing for when the breath moves, the mind moves, with the steady breath, the mind emits steady vibrations, and with the result the fickleness of the mind vanishes. So, I landed into the state of ecstasy and became one with the energy levels of the sacred letter. It resulted in the release of divine hormones which brought about mass conversion of the body form into the celestial wave form which resulted in the ending of the body into nothingness. Reduced to nothingness I, Lalla, mingled with the nothingness of the Cosmos. So, it became possible for me to vanish and appear again and again. This is the tale of my journey for the realization of the Soul.

SM223. Pota Zooni Vathith Mot Bolnovum

Pota zooni vathith mot bolnovum
Dag lalanavam dayi sanzi prahe.
Lal lal karaan lalla vozanovum,
Miilith tas mun shrochyom deh.

Pota zooni= in the last watch of the moonlit night; vathith=rise, get up; mot bolnovum= Complaining with my naughty mind; Dag=pain; Lalanaovam=soothed; Dayisannzi=of God; prahe=love, I soothed my pain with the love of God; Lali Lali karaan="O Lalla, Lalla";Lal Vozanovum = gently, gently, accosting myself, I woke my Love, my Lord and Master; Miilith tas= In whom absorbed; shrotsyom dahe =my mind was cleansed ;

Lalla Ded is a firm believer in herself. She was a proud Shaiva-bhakti who as a self-recognized soul harbored a consciousness of unity with Shiva even when she engaged herself in normal chores and responsibilities of world and life.

In this Vakh Lalla enacts the theatre of her devotion in different rolls; she desires, she demands, she laments; she can be prickly and irritable with the Divine yet throw herself at Its mercy and sing of bold passion. Lalla Ded had Shiva as her personal god. She served Him as a servant, made friends with Him and loved Him intensely. In strong and powerful moments of love she sang out her love-Lorn song to awaken her beloved within her frame for unity and complete purity. Sings Lalla--

SM224. Praanas Saetee Lye Yeli Karem

Praanas saetee lye yeli karem
Dyaanas thaavnam na roznas shaaie
Kaayas ander sorui vuchhum
Paayas powum kadamas graaie

Praanas saitee lye yeli Karoom= When I succeeded in mastering the movement of Praana; Dyaanas thaavnam na roznas shaaie= there remained no need for any other kind of meditation; Kaayas ander soroi vochhum= I experienced everything inside the recesses of my heart; Paayas pawoom kadamas graaie= It was a complete revolution of self as I had awakened to all divine mysteries.

In the state of weightlessness, in the space, "I had no course other than to keep myself mingled up with the spirit of my body. No room was left for me to go for insight or 'Dyana' or enter the state of spiritual ecstasy. I observed the essence of spiritual benevolence within. I have started experimenting on the nature of the blissful state of my spirit and performed various activities.

Lalleshwari says when she mastered the exercise of Pranayama there was a complete revolution of herself and with it there remained no requirement for any further form of meditation or kriya as she had experienced the supreme Lord face to face inside her holy person. She in fact lost consciousness of her personal self by experiencing all the contours of the cosmos inside her own person. Thus, she got awakened to all the divine secrets and there remained nothing unrealized for her.

SM225. Pranvuni Lookan Chuk Pranaan

Pranvuni lookan chuk pranavan
Panas chui ni gachaan kanan
Yeth paeth puej chai nata kinan
Panas na pooshan pakmondi ti kan

Pranvuni=you are the life giver; lookan chuk pranavan= give life to the people; Panas chui ni gachaan kanan= you yourself are unmindful of it; Yeth paeth puej chai nata kinan; Panas na pooshan pakmondi ti kan

This Vakh may have different interpretations. One elucidation may be that Shiva as erotic brings life into the world, and He himself is unmindful of it. A comparison is made with a butcher who sells meat and at the end of the day he is not left with even the feet or ear of the sheep. [needs further clarification]

SM226. Prath Tirthan Gatchhaan Sanyasii

Prath tirthan gatchhaan sanyasii,
Gwaraan swadarshan myul.
chetha parith mo nishpath aas,
Denshakh duure dramun nyuul.

Prath = to every; tiirthan = pilgrimage, shrine; gatshaan = goes; saniyasy = a saint; denshakh = to see; duure = far off, from a distance; dramun = grass; nyuul = green.

The pilgrim sannyasin goes from shrine to shrine, seeking to meet Him who abides within himself.
Knowing the truth, O soul, be not misled; It is distance that makes the turf look green.

SM227.   Praan Ta Rohoon Kunooi Zonoom

Praan ta rohoon kunooi zonoom
Pranas buzith lab na sadh
Prans boozith kenh ti naa khaizai
Twai labam sooham saadh

Praan= Onion, allegorically exhale and inhale; Rohoon= Garlic allegorically 'soul' which realises the salvation; Saadh= A person who has attained liberation is called 'Saadh' or Sidha. A sidha is a person, without cast, unaffected by smell, without sense; of taste feeling, hunger, pain or sorrow, joy, or old age, enjoying unbroken calm. During moment of illumination, one must keep complete fast, for attaining; spiritual vision, as such the Sadhak enjoys, infinite existence absolute truth and pure delight.

Lal-Ded says that she has realized the oneness of breath and soul with unbroken calm. It is a deep unspeakable and inexpressible vision. It is observed in the moments of illumination. In such a situation the seeker is not affected by the sense of hunger and thirst as all the senses of the body are tuned to the Lord's divine wave form.

All the pure and clean information is in the soul which manifests itself when worrying and distressing elements are killed. When the soul in freed from the weight which keeps it down, it rises to the top of the universe, as such liberation can only be attained, through suppression of lower elements by the higher spirits.

With the practice of meditation and concentration, an act which coordinate one with the divine scheme of things a force or energy is released which enables the seeker to attain the spiritual perfection, by burning the elements of air in the body, with the process of exhale and inhale, as such one attains the thoughtless state of mind, and the soul seizes the reality.

SM228. Raajas Boj Yemi Kartal Tuji

Raajas boj yemi kartal tuji
Swargas boj chhiy taph tai dhaan.
Sahazas boj yem gwar -kath paaeji
Paap-pwani boj chhui pananui paan.

Raajas=a king; boj=gains, admire, praise; yemi kartal tuji= who wields the sword; Swargas=paradise; boj choy=is gained; taph tai daan= penance and alms; Sahazas boj=the self within; yem gwar kath paaeji= Follow the Guru's word; Paap-pwani boj chui= of his own virtue and his sin; pananui paan= man himself reaps the fruits.

A king is kingly, when he shows courage and his sword to maintain law and order. The ruler must be respectful and the ruled Loyal. Paradise is gained by penance and alms giving. The truth is gained by following the directions of the master, with devotion, and zeal. The virtue and sin are the outcome of one's own actions.

SM229.   Raaza-Hams Aasith Loguth Koloiye

Raaza-hams aasith loguth koloiye
Kus tam chollie kyaahtaam haith
Gratta gav bandh tai gratan huith golloi
Gratta vole cholie phal phol heath

Raaza-hams= royal swan; aasith=you were once; loguth koloiye= now turned mute; Kus tam chollie= someone has run off with; kyaahtaam haith= something of thine; Gratta gav bandh tai= the millstone stopped; gratan huith golloi= the grain channel was choked with grain.

Gratta vole cholie phal phol heath= away ran the miller with the grain.

Raza hams: Royal swan who is supposed to sing melodiously at the point of its death. Royal swan is also a symbol of a Parmahamsa, God in human form having all human qualities and God awareness. Lalla says: Thou were a royal swan once, now turned mute at seeing something that has struck Lalla dumb. Lalla has seen, but she cannot describe what she has seen. Has she had a glimpse of Vishvarupa, the Cosmic Form, its indescribable splendor and awe, so that she, who was vocal till now, cannot speak? That something has taken away her powers of speech. Someone, it seems, has run off with something of thine. When the millstone stopped, the grain channel was choked with grain, and the miller running away with the grains unnoticed. Thus Lal-Ded explains when the end of life comes; the soul departs along with the accumulated fruit of action (Karma) and is drawn to such a state which is suitable to it.

SM230. Rangas Manz Chuie Byon Byon Labun

Rangas manz chuie byon byon labun
Chaalakh hai ta barakh sokh
Chakh reish ta vaeri gaalakh
Ad deshak Shiv sund mokh

Rangas manz chuie= He is in limitless colours and forms, lit., rangas manz, on the stage of the world where the play is going on; byon byon= countless; labun= Seek Him out; Chaalakh(tsaalakh) hai ta= Patiently suffer whatever your lot; barakh sokh= and happy be; Chakh(tsakh) reish ta vaeri= Anger, hate and enmity; gaalakh= destroy; Ad deshak= all this done; Shiv sund mokh= Behold thy God.

This world is a stage, and the people are the actors, to produce the dramatic effect fashioned in real life, then the spirit is held with such a joy that it warms us like the sun. This intoxicates joy. This bright and firm faith comes over us more and more frequently. All that we must do is to control our senses and mind and kill the sinful instincts of anger hate and enmity. All this done we observe a great stunning light inside like the sun in the sky and visible to the aspirants' eyes. Then one rejoices with a childlike joy.

SM231.   Rav Matt Thali Thali Tapeetan

Rav mat thali thali tapeetan
Tapeetan uttam uttam deesh
Varun matt luk garh acheetan
Shiv chui krooth tai chain updesh

Rav=the sun; thali thali tapeetan =will shine on alike; Tapeetan=give heat; uttam uttam deesh=only to holy lands; Varun=God of water; math look garh Acheetan=will rain not visit all homes alike; Shiv chui krooth=Siva is hard to reach; tai chain updesh=then heed the doctrine this teaches you.

The Lord does not observe any discrimination. The Lord does not believe in high and low, poor, and rich. Lalla explains this by saying as follows:

'The sun shines in the universe alike. Does it radiate light and heat waves on the prosperous countries only? Does not the cool wind enter the houses of all, both high and low equally? I am at a loss to understand how this discrimination has been stuffed into man's brain.

SM232. Ravan Manz Ravun Ravoom

Ravan manz ravun ravoom
Ravith athi aayas bhava sarai
Assan, ta, gindan sahez provum
Dapnai karum panas sarai

Ravan manz ravun ravoom=it appeared I was losing my anchors, and chains within my search for my Lord; Ravith athi aayas bhava sarai= soon what seemed to be a losing battle, I began reestablishing my identity within this losing game. I began establishing in a bigger way; Assan, ta, gindan sahez provum= I had achieved my cherished goal of being one with my Lord; Dapnai karum panas sarai= I had not to ask for it at all but just try becoming worthy and once I became eligible, I got it.

Lalla, during her visit in the space felt the heavenly state of joy. She found herself lost, both in body and spirit. After losing the universal consciousness, she found herself merging with cosmic radiations. With all this glory and adventure her spirit was filled with pleasure. She fluttered and danced in the sea of Bliss. Without asking for any desire, she realized the Goal of her life. Then she plunged into the ocean of divine grace. Thus purified, merged into Him. Lal Ded says that in deep meditation I lost my ego, I realized myself free from birth and death and I attained field of pure subtle, in a playful way.

(Another version)

SM233. Raavnas Manz Raavun Rovum, Raavnas Kenh Ne...

Raavnas manz raavun rouvum
Raavnas kenh ne sawaeliye
Shaaster poulum, shester goulum,
Kohche soun goum khaeliye....

Raavnas=to lose, misplace; manz =in; raavun =Ravan (Ram's rival), king of Lanka, a Shiv bhakth; Rouvum=lost; Raavnas kenh ne sawaeliye=Ravan not questioned for his misdeeds; Shaaster= scriptures, the holy books; poulum =educated, read, reared; shester =iron; goulum,=liquified, melted; Kohche soun goum khaeliye= This line has a duel meaning; kohche means a lap; kohche also means a mountain; soun means gold, soun also means deep; goum khaeliye= has exhausted.

Misplaced Raven
Ravana not questioned.
Scriptures sifted; iron dissolved.
Mounds of gold vanished.
A Shiva. devotee king Ravana of Lanka takes away Sita by evil design; nonentity questions him; scriptures sifted, and hard work done; the gold Lanka gets burnt tunneled and hollowed due to evil desire and plan of Ravana.
According to Hindu mythology Ravana was born to a great sage Vishrava and his wife, princess Kaikesi. He was born in the Devagana, as his grandfather, the sage Pulastya, was one of the ten Prajapatis or mind-born sons of Brahma and one of the Saptarishi or the Seven Great Sages during the age of Manu. Ravan's siblings include Vibhishana, Kumbhakarna and Ahiravana and a stepbrother Kubera. The Kingdom of Lanka was an idyllic city, created by the celestial architect Vishwakarma himself and was the home of Kubera, the treasurer of the gods. It is said that Kuber, the

treasurer of devas once ruled Lanka and hence Lanka was famed as sone ki Lanka. The popular saying that 'even the dust of Lanka was gold' is that Lanka was called Swarna Lanka or golden Lanka due to abundance of gold in Lanka.

When Ravana demanded Lanka wholly from Kubera, he threatened to take it by force. Although Ravana took Lanka, he had been a benevolent and effective ruler. Lanka flourished under his rule and Ravana had proceeded on a series of campaigns conquering humans, celestials, and demons.

Lanka is the name given in Hindu mythology to the island fortress capital of the legendary demon king Ravana in the epics of the Ramayana. The fortress was situated on a plateau between three mountain peaks known as the Trikuta Mountains. The ancient city of Lankapura is thought to have been burnt down by Hanuman. After its king, Ravana, was killed by Rama with the help of his brother Vibhishana, the latter was crowned king of Lankapura.

Valmiki's Ramayana paints Ravana as a tyrant of mighty power who was holding the gods at ransom, and he continues to be treated as a wretch in India even today. In the classic text, he is found kidnapping Rama's wife Sita, to claim vengeance on Rama and his brother Lakshmana for having cut off the nose of his sister Surpanakha.

Ravana is described as a devout follower of the god Shiva, a great scholar, a capable ruler, and a maestro of a veena, known as the Ravanhattha.

The story goes that Ravana to please his mother had decided to bring the mountain Kailash to Sri Lanka. As he lifted the mountain, God Shiva was angered by his arrogance and pushed it back down, trapping Ravana. The King of Lanka had torn off one of his own arms and made a musical instrument, ripping out sinews to form the strings. He used the newly invented ravanhattha to sing the praises of Shiva, creating music of such beauty that Shiva wept and forgave him. Ravan's devotion to Lord Shiva earned him the respect of the God. So much so that he built his devotee a temple. This is the only time when a temple is dedicated to the one who prayed and not the one being prayed to. All the same Ravana was killed, and his golden Lanka burnt by prince Rama for kidnapping his wife Sita.

The soul and the spirit are the two primary immaterial parts that Scripture attribute to humanity. However, in Scripture, only believers are said to be spiritually alive, while unbelievers are spiritually dead. Human beings have a sinful nature, and our souls are tainted with sin.

Another Version:

SM233A

Raavan manz raavun rovum
Raavit athi aayas bhava sarai
Assan ta gindaan sahez provum
Dapnai korum paanas sarai

First it appeared to me if I was losing my chains and anchors while searching for my Lord, it seemed like a losing battle. Soon I began re-establishing my identity with smiles and playful mood, I achieved my cherished goal of being one with my Lord, I had not asked for it, but my efforts became worthy and once I became eligible, I attained my goal of merging into Him.

SM234. Rozani Aayas Gachoon Gachoom

Rozani aayas gachoon gachoom
Pakoon gachom waav look paal
Kehnas paith nachoon gachoom
Achoon gachoom sookhsham prakash

I was born to live in this world to spread up in the path of God realization. My aim is the abandonment of self-hood and to lead a life of truth. This is attainable here upon this earth. In the end I would like to leave for heavenly abode for absorption. I can use a force of energy which would enable me to attain spiritual perfection. It makes me hum a Song. I toss my head in sprightly dance to mingle with His grace." I wish I could attain the "moments of illumination".

SM235. Rut Ta Krut Soruy Pazyam

Rut ta krut soruy pazyam
Kanan na bozan, achan na bhav,
Oruk dapun yeli vonda vuzaim
Rattan deep prazlyome varzani waaw.

Rut ta krut=well or ill; soruy pazyam = whatever befalls; Kanan na bozan= my ears will not hear; achan na bhav= my eyes will not see; Oruk dapun= when the inner voice calls; Vonda vuzaim = when the voice calls from within the inmost mind; Rattan deep Prazlyome= the lamp of faith burns bright; varzani waaw= even in the wind.

Good or bad whatever comes, let it come. My ears will not hear. My eyes will not see. But, when the voice calls from within the innermost mind, the lamp of faith, burns steady and bright even in the stormy wind. This is the most glorious heavenly light of human happiness.

SM236.   Sabur Chui Zuer Marech Ti Noonie

Sabur chui zuer marech ti noonie
Kheneh chui tyoth ti kheyus kus
Sabur ha mali chui sona-soound tourei
Moul chhus thod ti hayes kus

Sabur =patience; chui =is zuer =cumin seeds; marech =black pepper; noonie=table salt; Kheneh chui tyoth=bitter to taste if taken in large quantities; ti kheus kus=who will eat; Saboor ha mali chui sona-soound tourei=patience is a gold bowl; Moul chhus thod ti hayes kus=precious to buy.

In this Vakh Lal Ded is beautifully explaining the word saboor, i.e., patience. Here she gives metaphors of patience with condiments and gold vessels. First, she compares patience with black pepper and cumin seeds and salt. They add to the flavors and taste of foods, but these are all temporary enjoyments. Great works are performed not by strength but by preservance. Secondly, Lal Ded compares patience with a gold bowl which is precious to buy but good to look at. It is hard to find a man who will volunteer to die, then to find those who are willing to bear pain with patience. She believes that a trusting approach and a patient attitude go hand in hand. She says when you let go and learn to trust God, it releases joy in your life. And when you trust God, you're able to be more patient. Patience is not just about waiting for something... it's about how you wait, or your attitude while waiting.

SM237. Sahazas Sham Ta Dam No Gachay

Sahazas sham ta dam no gachay
Yechi no praavakh mukhtee dwar:
Salilas noon zan meelith gachay,
Toti chuy dorlabh sahaza vechaar.

Sahazas=self-realized, God conscious ness; sham=self-control; Dam=the celibacy or continence;sham ta dam= breath control in yoga practices; gachay= to obtain; Yechi no=not by desire; praavakh=gain; Mukhtee =salvation, Salvation is the inner renunciation of the 'Ego'.; dwar= gate, door, mukhtee dwar=the door of salvation; Salilas=water; noon=salt; zan meelith gachay= get mixed, when salt and water mix they become one; Toti=yet, still; chuy=it is; dorlabh=hard, tough; sahaza vechaar= true knowledge of the Self, sahaza vechaar is spontaneous thought which is directed towards Shiva.

Truth is not attained only through 'Shama' (self-control) and Dama (the celibacy). A seeker may undergo the strict discipline of 'Shama and 'Dama,' which gives the spiritual strength. Lalla Ded must have undergone 'sham' and 'dam' the breath practices in higher levels of Yoga. Having hardened herself through strong practices of yoga she calmed down her Chita (mind). She cleansed the mind from impurities of distraction, gloom, and despair. Lal Ded conveys that Shiva (Sahaj) does not need sham and dam for identity with Him. He needs to be attained through Iccha which is sure path to spiritual fulfillment. To get hold of God awareness one need not go for any breath control. Mere desire or wishing will not lead one to the portals of Salvation. God is everlasting beauty. The passion for beauty is a means to link the soul to God. It is like mixing of salt with water; even if the seeker realizes such absorption even then it is difficult to realize the true knowledge of the Self.

Lal Ded says: Sahaza vechaar is true knowledge of the Self. Sahaza vechaar is spontaneous thought which is directed towards Shiva. It is verily, the timeless approach filled with the Spanda/vibrations. To have Divine grace, the aspirant needs to know the thought vibrations within. When Sahaza vechaar of 'AUM' develops, all the channels leading to that eternal are opened without any delay. The difference between time and space are seen no more. Constant practice is required for realizing Sahaza vechaar.

SM238. Sahib Chu Behith Paane Vaanas

Sahib chu behith paane vaanas
Saeri mangan kenh-cha di
Rote na kansi hund raechh na vaanas
Yi che gachi ti paanai ni

Sahib=the supreme God; chu behith (bihith)= is supervising; paane= himself; vaanas=shop; saeri=everybody; mangan=demanding; kenh cha di=all the aspirants are demanding something as per their liking; rote na kansi hund raechh na vaanas=there is not even a watch over the shop; Yi che gachi=whatever you like to buy; paanai ni= it is to be earned by your own effort.

The Super- Lord is supervising His shop with personal care. All the aspirants are eager to take away wares of their liking. Whatever, you would elect to buy, does not admit of any intermediary; It is to be earned by your own effort, since the shop is devoid of any hinderance and even a watch is not kept over it." This is the acme of Lalla's message. Man has been exhorted to seek his own self front within, without any external aids. Self-effort is precursor of self- education finally culminating in self-consciousness - Shiva - as she calls it.

As long as the silvery bellows of the Vitasta maintain their rejuvenating rhythm, as long as the virgin snow on the Himalayan heights retains its unblemished splendor and stature, the exquisite 'Vakhs' of Lalleshwari soaked to the full in the inherent values of Kashmiri culture and human understanding will go on, unimpeded of course, in providing dignity to man to recognize his own self and not to run after deluding shadows; since the culture of a land never dies, the message of Lalla portraying meaningfully the humanistic attitudes ingrained in our culture, will never grow stale. Its fragrance and flavour are evergreen.

SM239. Sidh Maali Sidho Sedh Kathan Kan Thav

Sidh maali sidho sedh kathan kan thav
Che doh barith kaal soran kya
"Balko" tohi ketho dhen raath barev
Kaal aav kuthaan kariv kya

Sidh maali sidho= Lalla in her rare discourse, with her master known as 'Sidh Mole' says, O Sidh; sedh kathan kan thav=listen, you have attained liberation, your mind shines in purity; Che(tsea) doh barith kaal soran kya= time is passing and it is difficult to keep pace with it; "Balko" tohi keth dhen raath baro= she urges the children that life is short lived; Kall aao kuthan kariv kya= not to waste their time and make good use of time.

Lal Ded in one of her rare discourses, with, her teacher 'Saidh Mole' says, O Sidh! Since you have attained liberation and your mind shines out in its purity and wisdom, please take me under your fold. I am helpless and I am burning in the love of the Lord, to dissolve in the sea of Bliss. The time is running, and it is difficult to keep pace with it. The life is short lived and then she urges the children, who were watching her meeting with the Guru nearby, not to waste their time unnecessarily. They should try to make better use of time available as hard times are following and there is no way to rescue. thus, she conversed heart to heart with her master. This eased her mute pain.

SM240.   Samsar Hav Mali Yaarivu Jungul

Samsar hav mali yaarivu jungul
Lari kelam ti beyi badboo
Ghara karun hav mali pyatha pyon sangur
Nerakh nangur ta darog govai

Samsar (sansar)=the universe; hav mali=is like; yaarivu=pine, fir trees; jungul =forest; lari=you get, attach, award, attribute; kelam= coal tar,a byproduct from petroleum obtained during refining of petroleum, the pitch, tar, coaltar; ti beyi=and also; budboo= bad smell, reek, stench, stink; gareh karun=to run a home, domestic life; peth=over, on, a happening; sangar=hardship, adversity, difficulty; nerakh=to come out; nangur= a waste;

Universe a pine forest
Deceitful and reek
lifespan and hardships
Waste if not utilized.

The world is a forest of pine trees, you will get stained with tar and receive bad odour, to run a household is as cumbersome as a mountain coming crashing down on you, you are likely to be rendered poor and proved a liar.

In this vakh Lal Ded makes a judgement in the life span of humans and hardships; between the universe full of beautiful, lush green forests; with the coal tar, a petroleum byproduct, with a stinky smell.

SM241. Samsar Niyiam Taev Tachhi

Samsar niyiam taev tachhi
Mudan kechay taavan aai
Gyaan mudra chaii gyanain kichi
Su yuog kali kinie parzani aayae

Samsar =the universe; niyiam= a mortar; taev=griddle, a frying pan; tachhi=hot; mudan=a duffer; kechay taavan aai= a blemish, a flaw, a defect, a curse; gyaan=knowledge; mudra= A mudrā is a spiritual gesture; chaii gyanain kichi= is for knowledgeable, conversant persons; su yuog= that period; parzani aayae= may be recognized.

Universe a hot griddle
ignorant vexatious and cursed.
knowledge familiarized.
inaudibly received

SM242.   Samsaaras Aayas Tapasii

Samsaaras aayas tapasii
Bodh prakash lobum sahaz
Maryam na kanh mar na kansii
Mara nech lasa ta nech

Samsaaras=in the world; aayas=was born, came; tapsii =meditation; samsaras aayas tapasii=I tapasvin came into the world; Bodh prakash= divine light of consciouenss; lobum sahaz=attained state of Shivahood; Maryam na kanh marna kansi= she is liberated as liberation while living, for me life and death are alike, I mourn for none, none mourns for me; mara nech=happy to die; lasa nech=happy to live.

Lal Ded in essence was a Shaiva-Yogini par-excellence and a born saint. She was clear in saying that she was born in the world for meditation, a known yogic practice of wide acceptance. It was through intense meditation that she attained the divine light of consciousness' (Bodh Prakash), a state of Shiva (Shiva hood), She was liberated while living (jeevan-mukhut) as a perennial state of Shiva-consciousness which is beyond the condition of rotation of life and death. She lived broadly and fully with the power of her soul. So, she was happy to live and happy to die, as there was nobody to mourn for her, and she mourned for none.

Lalla was a Tapasvin, and life did not appear upsetting to her. She wanted to open her heart before all people so that they could see how she wished their welfare. Tears of happy gratitude softened her mind. For her, life and death were alike. She was happy to live and happy to die. She expressed that she mourned for none, and none mourned for her.

In this Vakh Lalleshwari gives a clear expression of her superior self. She says she came into this life, a fully realized soul. She had attained the superior spiritual understanding. She had enough awakened and was fully equipped with all worthy karmas. She could reach the highest stages of spiritual development because of the choicest blessings of the Lord and past superior karma. Now, though an ordinary human being she was already lifted above the ordinary existence free from the fear of life and death.

SM243. Samsaras Manz Bagh Kath Shayei Rozay

Samsaras manz bagh kath shayei rozay
Roz param shiv shambus agoor
Lola manz bagh bei lului-navun
Gigras manz bagh karus goor goor

Samsaras manz bagh =in this universe; kath shayei rozay=with what hope; Roz =remain, be; param shiv shambus agoor=the supreme lord Shiva who is hermit by himself and bountiful for others; Lola manz bagh = with full devotion and love; bei lului-navun= let the lap be cradle for Him; Gigras manz bagh =in the heart; karus goor goor = lull him in the silence of your lap.

In the universe be hopeful
Dedicate yourself to Parum Shiva
Bestow and lull him, let the lap be cradle.
In the heart of hearts, you will feel stillness.
In Shaiva-Yoga Shambavopaya is the highest practice. In it all mental activities cease and mind glitters without a stir of thought. The seeker with his mind calmed and stilled turns inwards. Inward light shines and flashes. With regular practice such a state is to be prolonged. It results in going beyond the time-space limitations. The seeker with highly intuitive qualities gets a feel of his Shiva-like powers and ultimately cognizes himself as Shiva.

SM244. Sani Khota Soun Chui Mann Kui Samandar

Sani khota soun chui mann kui samandar
Woath laiy khaar mukhta haar,
Sati chi razi lum sati chi vati pakh,
Ada mali labakh bhavsar taar

Sani khota soun chui = deepest among the deep; munn koi samandar= mind is deeper than the sea; Woath laiy= jump into; khaar mukhta haar= bring out the diamond necklace; Sati chui razi lum = be on the truth; sati chui vati pakh= veracity followed; Ada mali labakh= then only you find; bhavsar taar=salvation, deliverance.

Of all the oceans, mind is the deepest. Jupm into the depth of your mind through sadhna and devotion, you will get pearls and necklaces in the form of knowledge and consciousness. Hold the rope of truth and follow the path of truth, then you will get eternal peace and reach your destination of God.

Deepest is the mind.
Dive into it and get the essence.
Follow truth, veracity is the track.
Salvation may follow.
The Mind can do wonders. Believe in yourself! Have faith in your abilities! Without a humble but reasonable confidence in your own powers you cannot be successful.

SM245. Saras Saetee Sodaa Korum

Saras saetee sodaa korum
Haras koroom goed seeva
Sheras peth kani nachaan dyunthum
Gachaan dyunthum aayam pach

Saras saetee sodaa karum= I made a clear agreement of convenience with my lord; *Haras karoom gode seewan*= doing all proper form of worship,took time to see my devotion culminate into fulfillment; *Sheras peth kani nachaan (natsaan) deunthum*= Ultimately my Lord was happy with me and to my astonishment I saw Him dancing with joy on my very head; *Gachaan deunthum aayam pach*=I was convinced my devotion had borne fruit that my Lord had appeared before me, the situation that's wished for by all devotees and very few are able to achieve.

Lalla says: I have set up a close relationship with the lord 'my love.' I washed Him with the tears of my joy to see Him the most beautiful. I offered all my senses unto His Service. Lo! I see His benign grace in the form of infinite consciousness or energy levels concentrated at the top of the brain, whirling round, and round. O! I am tuned up with His celestial waves and observe the glorious phenomenon of His creation. O! Good fortune I have just lived through a magnificent moment, maybe the best moment of my life for wherever I look I see my own self as the incarnation of the Lord.

Lalleshwari brings home to the seeker that with selfless devotion and complete surrender can one achieve all the heights of enlightenment for himself. And another fact that comes to light here is that human being is already invested with full divine emancipation, but the infinite energy is dormant inside him for want of awakening of his energies with appropriate sadhana and the devotion of the Lord.

SM246. Sehni Hund Shikar Vaskav Zaani

Sehni hund shikar vaskav zaani
Haenth kav zaani potrai doad
Shamhuk soz lesh kav zani
Maechh kav zaani pomprin gath

Sehni=lioness; shikar=prey; vaskav=lamb; kav zaani=does not know; Sehni hund shikar vaskav zaani=The lamb knows how a lioness catches her prey, cruelty; Haent=barren woman; kav zani=has not experienced; potri doad=value of a child; Haenth kav zaani potrai doad=a barren woman cannot experience value of a child, as she has not undergone labour pain and womanhood; Shumihuk soz=movement of candle flame; leish kav zani=wood which gives clouds of smoke; shamhuk soz lesh kav zani=the burning wood which gives clouds of smoke and odour cannot be compared with the wavy movement of candle flame; Maech kav zani=compares a fly; pompri gath=movement of butterflies. Maechh kav zaani pomprin gath=the house fly which gives annoying buzz, does not know lovable movement of a butterfly.

Lal Ded tries to make us understand the reality of life by giving some comparisons like-

The prey of a lioness, a cruel act; a barren woman not undergone labour pain and womanhood being indifferent to a child; burning of a candle with wavy flame in comparison to the burning of wood which produces clouds of smoke and odour; lovable flight of a butterfly and annoying buzz of a fly. In totality there is more pain and evil than goodness.

SM247.   Sheel Ta Maan Chhui Kranjli Poonie

Sheel ta maan chui kranjli poonie
Mochhi yemi rote malliiy yudh waaw
Hastis yus mas waal gaandy
Tee yes tagay soi ada nihal

Sheel ta maan= name and fame of a person; chui kranjli poonie=is as temporary as water in a colander (sieve); Mochi=fist; yami rot=whoever can hold it; malliiy yudh waaw=whoever has power to stop the storm and hold it; Hastis=elephant; yus mas Waal gaandy=whoever can tie an elephant with a hair of his head; Tee yes tagay soi ada nihal= to such rare men, all heights are possible.

Lalleshwari has used the best possible metaphors to explain her faint view about this transitory life. She explains how to keep under control the desire of the world. One who's successful in understanding its truth and works for his liberation in all stress and strain of worldly temptations is the true winner. The name and fame of a person is as temporary as water in a colander. One should not be influenced by the temporary emotions of name and fame. They do not last. Whoever can hold a storm in his fist or tie an elephant with a hair of his head, it is he, whose name and fame lasts. Lalla urges us to arm against the evil and attain a life of higher quality. "Watch the men who can cure the evils. Cultivate their friendship with love and regard. The sages who experience such a faculty have power to stop the storm and hold it in their fists or even more so can tie down an elephant with a fiber of hair. To such rare men, all heights are attainable. They see a world in a grain of sand."

The action is also compared to a trainer who controls a wild elephant with a frail rope like a single strand of hair which's impossible. One who follows the real purpose of life and gets awakened to its truth and its Lord is the real warrior as his work gets him the everlasting benefit of getting freed from the cycle of birth and death and being one with the Lord. The trap of the world and the attached pleasures of sense coil him in such a web of ignorance that all indications of the temporariness of this life fall flat on him till the end comes and he is taken to an unknown destination never to return. He is forced to leave back everything, power, money and riches, family and children and go alone at the mercy of the Lord which is the ultimate truth. He is accounted for his deeds, good and bad and sent for another term of life according to the merits of his karma.

SM248. Shevan Chattith Shashikal Vuzum

Shevan chattith shashikal vuzum
Prakrat hu'zum pavana saeti.
Lolaki naara vaolinj buzam,
Shankar lobum tamiy saeti.

Shevan (she-six, van-forest) chattith (tsatith)= Cutting my way through Six Forests, i.e. (kaama, krodha lobha, moha, mad and ahankaara); shashikal vuzum= I came upon the Digit of the Moon (Sahasraara =top of the head). By means of the practice of praanaapaana, (by controlling my vital airs...);Shevan chattith shashikal vuzum= I cut the path of my development through six forests (conquering all inborn human instincts) and achieved the height of Sahasrara on the top of my head; Prakrat hu'zum pavana saeti= through systematic exercise of breath; Lolaki naara vaolinj buzam= I roasted my heart in the heat of my love for my Lord Shiva; Shankar lobum tamiy saeti= for me and I experienced Supreme Shiva face to face.

After gaining full control, over the five senses and the mind I cut through my way to the top of the brain called Digit of the moon, (Sahasrara =top of the head). By means of intense concentration of mind and vigorous breathing exercises, the practice of praanaapaana, (by controlling my vital airs...), I felt the world of matter shrank for me. Then with my hard labour of love, I found my God.

The Secretion of Shashikal or Celestial Hormone had resulted in the mass conversion of the state of the body form into the vibrational form of Energy. Thus, world of matter had ceased for Lal Ded. Consuming herself with such Yogic exercises, in the fire of love, she had found her Lord "Shankara" and thus, was able to release her soul from the bondages of the body. She had found herself as a realized soul.

SM249. Shiliyaz Hunz Dutma Bazum

Shiliyaz hunz dutma bazum
Sombar muethuk posh aasan peth
Manas andar vabchar karum
Vuchum ti deunthum sheel kani peth

Shiliyaz – a soft stone; Hunz = whose; Dutma = uttam, (dutam aasan) meditation; Bazum = to offer prayers; somber = balanced; muethuk = sweet; Posh = flower; posh = flower; aasan = remains; peth = upon, on; manas – in the mind; andar = inside; vabchar = thought, assumed; karum = did think; vuchum ti deunthum= looked and saw, observed; sheel kani peth = upon the sloppy stone

Sitting on a stone meditating and offering prayers
Balanced and honied.
Meditating on a flower bed; understood for a while and saw him again on a stone.
Lalla says, I prayed to God and saw Shiva sitting on a stone, He was in a dutam aasan, meditating and offering prayers. He was somber, balanced and honied.

SM250. Shishiras Vuth Kus Ratte

Shishiras vuth kus ratte
Kus bavke ratti vaav
Yus pantsh yindray cheaylith chatte
Suy ratte gatti rav

Shishiras=frost; vuth=drip; kus=who; ratte =hold, bring to hault; Kus=who; bavke=handful; ratti=hold; vaav =storm, strong wind; Yus=who.

Who can stop the drip in the frost? Who can hold wind in the palm of his hand? Who can see the sun in the darkness of night? He, who holds his senses under control, can in the dark catch hold of the sun.

SM251. Shiv Chui Zawiul Zaal Wahraavith

Shiv chui zawiul zaal wahraavith
Karan zan chui manz kranzan kath
Zinda nai wuchan ad kathi marith
Paan manz paan kad vechaarith kath

Shiv Chui=Shiva is with; *Zawiul*=fine; *zaal*=net; *wahraavith*=spread out; *Karan zan manz kranzan* = as if He spread throughout (something), skeleton, pervades; *travith kath*=giving a divine message; *Zinda nai wuchan*= if you while living can't not see Him; *ad kathi marith*=then, how can you when dead; *Paan manz paan kad*= sift the true self from the self; *vechaarith kath*= Think deeply over the whole process.

Like a weak web Siva spreads Himself, Penetrating all frames of all things. If while alive, you cannot see Him, how can you see Him after death? Think deep and separate the true Self from the self. Shiva permeates with the mankind. If thou whilst living can't see Him, how can thou when dead. The mankind is always receiving the waves from the Cosmos. Among them the almighty Lord is also sending forward His own divine wave forms (energy). They are like a thin weak web. The divine energy penetrates both living and nonliving matter. Only the mind in the human body is conscious of its presence. The human body has an ability to tune the divine frequency by releasing the energy of that order. This unity and harmony of Cosmos can tune one's mind to divine frequencies till there is life in the body. After death such tendency dies with the disappearing of the spirit. The whole process to sift the true self from the self needs consideration.

Lal Ded puts no value on anything done without the saving belief in Yogic doctrine and practice, one of the results of which is the destruction of the fruits of all work, good or bad. The aspirant should try to attain perfection in this life. He only requires faith and firmness.

SM252.   Shiv Chhui Thali Thali Rozaan

Shiv chhui thali thali rozaan.
Mo zaan hyond ta musalmaan,
Trukkai chhukh ta panun paan parzaan,
Soi chhai sahibas zaani zaan.

Thali thali =to look over in detail and admire some loved one; wuchhan=sees; Shiv chuy thali thali wuchhan=Shiva is witness to all, Shiva is everywhere, she confirms this realization in this Vakh; Trukai=gifted, talented; Soy chay=that is; zaniy zan = true acquaintance.

Lal Ded lived a universal mind. She saw Shiva in every embodied soul. She felt Shaivite radiance both in animate beings and lifeless manifestations. Her way of vision was not limited to the personification of the Divinity, but her way was to feel Shiva's tenderness in every molecule of manifestation. It is said Lal Ded is a living AUM.

Shiva spreads through every place and thing; Do not differentiate between Hindu and Musalman, if you are truly sensible and intelligent, recognize your own self; it will help you achieve the eternal truth of acquaintance with God.

The most important object of Lal Ded's mission was to take away the confusion caused among the masses by the preaching of zealots. Having realized the Absolute Truth, all religions to her were merely paths leading to the same goal.

Lal Ded stressed for communal harmony. During her times many sufi saints came to Kashmir. They were highly influenced by the preaching's of Lal Ded and the prevalent faith of Kashmir. With the passage of time several Hindu and Muslim saints were produced by Kashmir. With the result a Rishi cult prevailed in Kashmir that made the lives of its inhabitants to incline towards peace and brotherhood. The saints were revered by both Hindus and Muslims. Lal Ded laid the foundation of communal harmony in Kashmir. Since then, the valley began to be called as Raeshvaer, as it had been an abode of Rishis and Suffis. In the past valley has stood as an epitome of multi-cultural and multi religious ethos. Lal Ded was a visionary for composite culture of Kashmir. That is why she is revered by all till date irrespective of caste, creed, or religion.

SM253. Shiv Gur Tay Keshav Palns

Shiv gur tay keshav palns
Brahma parihainas wolsais
Yogi yoge kali parzainas
Kus dev ashwaar paith chadyas

Shiv gur= Siva is the horse; Keshav palnas = Vishnu the saddle; Brahma parihainas wolsais = Brahma becomes the stirrups; Yogi=it is the yogi; Yoge kali = knowledge of yoga; parzainas =knows; Yogi yoge kali parzainas= The yogi through his yoga will come to know; Kus=which; Dev=god; ashwaar=horse; paith chadyas=can mount Kus dev ashwaar paith chadyas=Which God will dare to mount this horse.(Siva is the horse; Vishnu the saddle; Brahma the stirrups.)

Yogis of great activity and doings can see with Yogic feats and with celestial eyes which god can mount the horse. To such a blessed spirit, 'Shiva', the Lord Destroyer acts as the horse for riding, 'Vishnov', the Lord preserver holds the saddles and 'Brahma', the Lord creator holds the stirrups. He is the only glorious and dignified one who enjoys the eternal bliss.

SM254.   Shiv Shiv Karaan Hamsa-Gath So'rith

Shiv shiv karaan hamsa-gath so'rith
Ruuzith veywahari deyn kyoha raath
Laagi-rost yus man karith
Tasi netyh prasan suura-guruunaath.

Shiv Shiv karaan= constantly invoking the name of Siva; hamsa-gath so'rith= meditating on the way of the Swan; Ruuzith veywahari=engaged in worldly attachment; deyn kyoha raath =day and night; Laagi-rost yus man karith =with devotion; Tasi netyh prasan Suura-Guruunaath= wins the favor of the God.

By constantly invoking the name of Siva and Meditating on the Way of the Swan (a Mystic name for "Soham" i.e.,' I am He '), is sometimes used to denote Parmasiva. From time attachment is set free to such a one when one feels is busily engaged in the affairs of the world, both day and night, wins the favor of the Gods.

SM255. Shiv Shiv Karan Shiv No Toshay

Shiv Shiv karan shiv no toshay
Gev kand zalik menish su aasay
Gabdev dehas deh dour aasay
Gevnay dehas dukh dour kassay

Shiv = Lord Shiva; toshay = mirthful, joyful, ecstatic; gev = ghee; kand = big cone shaped sugar crystals; zalik =burnt; menish = near me; su = He; aasay = will be with me; Dehas = soul; Deh dour aasay = away from the soul; Gevnay = without singing; dukh = misery, gloom, depression; kassay = remove, eradicate.

We Hindus believe in the *super soul* from which other souls are born in the form of lives. After the completion of the life cycle of human beings or return to the super soul, we merge with it, depending upon the deeds and merits we have accumulated in our lifetime. Lord Shiva is the Supersoul and prevails over everything and is everywhere. In other words, He is the source of all divine powers, all living and non-living beings. The universe is created by Shiva in His own image for He is Unlimited Consciousness and consciousness alone exists. In the Shaiva philosophy, it is the power of will which makes Him both innate and superior and form and space do not limit Him. He leads the individual to a state of Eternal Bliss.

SM256. Shiv Ta Shakhti Katyoo Deenthim

Shiv ta Shakhti katyoo deenthim
Timove ratam kaayas jaai
Daayas dharsie sanun myuthum
Teelith roozas travith lar

Shiv=Lord Shiva; Shakhti=His spirit 'Shakhti'; katyoo=where; deenthim=saw; Timove=they; ratam kaayas jaai= seated in the core of my heart; Daayas dharsie= sensational vision; sanun meethum=deep cheer; Teelith roozas=having wandered carefree; travith lar= I lie on the couch.

I saw the Lord and His spirit 'Shakti,' mingled up together, seated in the core of my heart. This amazing dream gave me bliss. I felt overjoyed. I felt intoxicated with the glories of the Lord. I felt unaware of the physical state of my body. My limited understanding got widened. After wanderings when I lie on the couch, in meditative mood, I enjoy the flashes, of the bliss, of solitude.

SM257.   Shiv Vaa Keshava Vaa Zin Vaa

Shiv vaa keshava vaa zin vaa
Kamalajanaath naamadhaarin yuh,
Mey abali kaastan Bhava raoz,
Su vaa su vaa su vaa suh.

Shiv vaa=Shiva; Keshava=Shiva's other name; Zin vaa = Buddha; Kamalajanaath=the Lotus born Brahma; Mey abali kaastan bhavaraoz= May He remove from me the sickness of the world; Su vaa su vaa su vaa suh= It maybe He or He or He.

Lalla calls Lord by several names: Shiva or Keshva or Budha. In later Sanskrit literature "zin vaa" is used for the Buddha. Or Brahma, the lotus-born Lord, whatever name He bear, May He remove from me the sickness of the world! It maybe He or He or He, for He is one though called variously.

SM258.   Sirius Hu Na Prakash Kunay

Sirius hu na prakash kunay
Gangeh hu na tirth kanh
Bois hu na bandav kunay
Zani hu na sukh kanh

Sirius hu = Like sun; na = not; Prakash = light; kunay =anywhere, any place; Gangeh hu = like Ganges; tirth = pilgrimage; kanh= like, bois= brother; hu = like; bandav= relative; kunay= anywhere; Zani hu= like wife, zani means wife; such= comfort

Lal Ded's Vakhs reveal a quarrel. Once, Lal Ded's husband approached her teacher, Sedha Mol, requesting him to help make Lal Ded return home. The teacher agreed and the discussions that took place included an interesting explanation.
Lal's Husband says:
No light equals the light of the sun, no pilgrimage is there like the one To the Ganga No relative excels a brother, and No comfort is there like that of a wife!

SM259. Shran Ti Dyan Kya Sana Kari

Shran ti dyan kya sana kari
Chetas rath trakary vag
Manas ti pavanas milvan kari
Sehazas manz kar tirth sanan

Shran= to bathe; ti dyan= to meditate; kya sana kari= of what use; Chetas =consciousness (chit); rath trakary vag=keep your consciousness balanced; Manas = mind; ti pavanas = breath; milvan kari = to unite; Sehazas = Sahaj- natural, it denotes both the nature of human being and the means for realizing it; manz = within, inside; kar tirth sanan = take a dip, bathe there in.

Just bathing and meditation is not enough to attain Ultimate Reality. Chit - Shiva is the universe and that Shiva is consciousness, also known as Chit. According to Vedanta, Brahman (chit) is the Ultimate Reality, while Kashmir Shaivism calls this Ultimate Reality as Parmasiva. The act of Pranayam – which involves breathing in and breathing out methodically; to breathe during yoga, one must focus attention on breath during asana. Inhale through your nose (heh), then open your mouth and exhale slowly, making a "HA" sound.

Bathing and meditation are not enough, keep consciousness balanced; that will unite your mind through pranayama; this is natural means for realizing chit.

The renowned sages have explained yoga as 'not only the realization of God, but an entire consecration and change of the inner and outer life till it is fit to manifest a divine consciousness and become a part of divine work. Yoga is a comprehensive name for all shades of spiritual practices that were/are acted out by seekers at various hermitages presided over by rishis (seers).

SM260.   Shuunyuk Maedaan Kodum Paanas

Shuunyuk maedaan kodum paanas,
Mea Lalli roozum na boadh na hosh.
Vey zay sapnas paanai paanas,
Adha kami heli phoal Lalli pamposh!

Shuunyk maedaan= vastness of the Void, empty space; The Shunya =void is to be understood and realized within. Lal Ded did it. She says:" All the intellect vanished away. All the body consciousness was gone. It then enlightened me." The men with virtue seek refuge in the wisdom of sages.(To feel the vibration of SOHAM-I am that Shiva);koddum=travelled; paani paanas=I, me, myself; Mai =me; Lalli=Lalla; roozam Na= leaving behind; Bodh Na hosh= no reason and sense; Veyzay Sapdas= Then came upon me, (lit. I became a confidante of my Self); paani paanas= the secret of the Self; Ada kami= unexpectedly; hilli= (hyal in Kashmiri is a dirty ground, covered with litter, mud, dirt used as manure, also, hil is an aquatic weed growing in Dal Lake); pholli =bloom; Lalli Pamposh= In mud the lotus bloomed for me, (symbolic: What was valueless (my body or myself) became precious and a thing of beauty and joy).

I travelled far beyond in the space, leaving behind me reason and sense. Then, came upon the secret of the Self; All on a sudden, I experienced a feeling of strange delight. I suddenly lost the entire intelligence, in the bliss of ecstasy. I started realizing my own true spirit rising to the heights of spiritual kindness.
Lalla says: "I travelled alone extensively the higher reaches of my Lord's influence. I crisscrossed alone the whole field of shunya (nothingness). The sights and scenes were so enchanting that I lost my conscience. But soon I was awakened to the delicate mysteries and secrets of my inner self. Thus, I Lalla with such a humble background was ushered into the crowning glory of celestial emancipation. Thus, I Lalla flowered like a lotus from the marsh."

Shunya is a broader concept of the Supreme Lord. It is not anyway comparable to nothingness in its ordinary sense, because it holds in its purview the whole cosmos as an influence of the Lord. Lalleshwari was a highly awakened soul who had achieved all the goals of divinity. In the ecstasy of her achievement, she says she toured the extensive fields of Shunya, the Lord's influence during her celestial journey so much so that she lost all the consciousness of her body sensations but soon upon gaining the awakening of her real self she gained the greatest satisfaction. The achievement is beautifully compared by Lalleshwari to the lovely blossom of a lotus field on the muddy surface of wet lowland which indicates her down to earth background and her subsequent achievement high up into the skies.

SM261. Shunikie Maidaan Waar Waar Pakzai

Shunikie maidaan waar waar pakzai
Tati chei badi badi dob tai naar
Amee naar andi andi neerzai
Tati chui dorlab sahaz vechaar

Shunikie= empty space, Shunikie maidaan= wanderings through the space; waar waar=slowly and steadily; tati chei=there are badi badi=big and bigge; dob=pits; naar=deep clefts; dob tai naar= black holes; andi andi neerzai= avoid dangerous routes and move ahead with care.

Lal Ded in her wanderings through the space had observed big black holes and deep fissures[**8]. She cautions all the spiritual saints daring to undertake such an adventure, to travel through the space that they must avoid dangerous routes and move ahead with care. The black holes are objects in the space, which are so dense and gravitationally strong that neither matter nor light can escape them. However, energy is released, as matter plunges into the hole's deep gravity well.

SM262.   Shurah Ta Dah Yus Sumrith Khaarai

Shurah ta dah yus sumrith khaarai
Dwadshant ander gumnohee
Trei sumrith kenh matras prarai
Soi dapzai sahaza kriiy

Shurah ta dah yus sumrith khaarai= One who's able to concentrate systematically on the recitation of AUM with controlled breath; Dwadshant Ander gumnohee= from Dwadashant Mandala to the nose in calm and composed manner; Trei sumrith kenh matras prarai= in sequence and rapid succession of sixteen and ten respectively with a little pause in between the two sequences and a little intermediate pause after every third sequence with suspended breath; Soi dapzai sahaza kriiy=he has achieved a great divine purpose.

"There is no limit to the power of mind. This power can be intensified by concentration and meditation. By repeating the sacred letter or 'Shabad Swroop', in calm composed manner, in sequence and rapid succession of sixteen and ten times respectively, with a proper pause in between while doing breathe exercises. The energy levels emitted by murmuring or reciting the sacred letter, synchronizes with the celestial wave form, present in the environment round. The energy levels on reaching the sensors of the brain, called Sahasrara, set it in resonance and thus synchronize with the celestial wave form in the Cosmos. Thus, one merges with cosmic radiance." That is the exercise or Sadhana or a step in the Spiritual ladder.

SM263. Shai Aases Ta Shai Chhas

Shai aases ta shai chhas
Lal bo pannay panas chhas
Neerith gachaan teelith yivaan
Lal bo paanai Daiyee chhas

Shaiy aasas = I was already an awakened soul in my past life Shaiy in kashmiri also means hope ; ta shy chas=I continue to be an awakened soul; Lal bo pannay panus chas=I Lal, I'm already one with my Lord and acquainted with all the secrets of nature; Neerith gachaan(gatchhaan) teelith evaan= I've the capacity to traverse at my will all the echelons of my Lord's influence and the universe as a whole and returning instantly to my current position; Neerith gachaan teelith yivaan=I transform myself into vibrational (energy)form and through it I travel beyond cosmos and then come back to my physical body form. Lal bo paanai Daiyee chhas= lo! I am the incarnation of the Lord. I'm a divine spirit in the garb of a human being.

I was born with all intellect and wisdom. I became the incarnation of his divine grace. This was achieved only by meditation. Now I have acquired the feat of travelling far beyond in the void, to the infinite and return to my physical body form again. Ah! I have acquired the feat of merging with His celestial magnificence to become one in all and all in one. So, I am a realized Soul and a saint par excellence; Ah! I have achieved the Godhood.

Lal Ded has been quite kind about keeping the ordinary man well informed even about her deepest secrets not usually shared by the spiritually advanced people among the ordinary. She claims to be already a highly awakened soul both in her past and present life. She says she has come with enough awakening and continues to be so. She says she has the capacity achieved through her spiritual advancement to travel at her will the whole of her Lord's influences or the universe created by Him and return. She also claims to be become one with the universal spirit (Supreme -Shiva) which is the goal of all spiritual seekers.

SM264. Sinhki Salali Yudvai Mul Kasak

Sinhki salali yudvai mul kasak
Aasak aana khota prazulvun sheena khota proun
Panai marak panai lasakh
Lagakh oun zor kol ta revan
Shoos saetan yeli kathan rasakh
Shiv chui panai thu parchun

Salali=patience; rasakh; yudvai = if;mul = impurity; kasak =shun, throw up, give away; aasak = will be; khota = than; prazulvun= bright, shining; sheena = snow; proun = fair minded; panai = yourself; marak = die, perish; lasak=survive, last; lagakh = pretend; oun = blind; zor = deaf; kol = dumb;revan = lame of one leg;shoos = trachea, part of lung; saetan = with; yeli = when; kathan = talks,discussions; parchun = introduction, recognize, identify.

Patiently shun impurities; Be a luminary; Judge yourself to Mar or make yourself. Be calm, meditate and recognize Shiva. He is the universe, and that Shiva is consciousness; The universe is made from Shiva's awareness, and we are here due to Shiva's will. The universe is created by Shiva extending his will and restored to tranquility by withdrawing it.

SM265. Soi Kul No Dodha Saet Sagizey

Soi kul no dodha saet sagizey
Sarpeni thoolan dezi no faah
Yus yuth kari su tuth swari
Kreri karizina panun paan

Soi= Stinging nettle, (Scientific name Urtica dioica); kul=herb; dude=milk; saet sagzay=irrigate; sarpeni=snake; thoolan=eggs; dezi no faah=desist from hatching; yus=who so ever; yuth kari=whatever he does; su=he; tuth sori=has to reap; kreri=to go into the well, don't go into mess; panun paanyourself.

In this Vakh Lal Ded cautions us by giving two examples; One, not to irrigate the stinging nettle with milk, as it is inherent in the herb to sting. Secondly, we should refrain from hatching snake eggs. Snakes also bite. One must reap the harvest of one's actions, good as well as bad. As you sow, so shall you reap? Good for good and bad for bad. Therefore, it is no use to go deep into the chaos of the world.

SM266. Soi Mata Roopi Payee Diyay

Soi mata roopi payee diyay,
Soi buriya roopi karaan veshash,
Sui maya roopi ani ti subeh heyiyay,
Shiv chui kruth ta cheen updesh

Soi mata roopi= that very woman acts as a mother; payee diyay = suckles a baby; soi buriya roopi = that very woman acts as a wife; karaan veshash = lingers in love; sui maya roopi = as maayaa; aniti subeh heyiyay = as maayaa she takes one's life in the end; Shiv is kruth = Shiv is hard to reach; ta cheen updesh = then heed to the doctrine.

As mother a woman suckles a baby,
As wife she lingers romantically in love,
As maya she takes one's life in the end-
And yet in all these forms a woman she is.
Siva indeed is hard to reach; Then heed the doctrine this teaches you. The obvious doctrine this teaches us is that our true self is the spirit, which is all pervading like the stone in earth which has assumed various forms, shapes, and sizes.

SM267. Soman Gaaroon Manz Yeth Kanday

Soman gaaroon manz yeth kanday
Yeth kandi dapaan swroop naav
Loob moh chali shoob yi kanday
Yeth kandi teez tai sori prakash

Manz yeth kanday= in this body; gaarun= seek; loob=greed; moh=illusion; chali=removed; shoob=happiness; teez= radiance; soar prakash= glory will surround

Should you, in this body, seek? The Supreme Self that dwells within. Greed and illusion soon removed. A radiance of glory will surround this very body of yours

Please search for that supreme self within your body. Drink the nectar of Love within yourself, for this body is the incarnation of 'His' living presence that is why it is called 'His Sroop' or 'His form'. Shun off, your greed and attachment to the false. Then this body will light up with divine radiance.

SM268. Sootas Ta Saatas Pachas Na Rumas

Sootas ta saatas pachas na rumas
Somas mai Lalli chav panunui Vakh
Andrim gatkaar ratith vollum
Chatith ditmas tatee chaakh

Sootas ti saatas=I did not wait for a moment, or even for an auspiscios occasion; pachas na rumas=did not wait for a fortnight or less; somas mai chav panonui Vakh= Whatever I experienced I converted into my poetic expression (Vakh).andrim gatkar=it was an internal storm; rattith wollum=I grabbed it and controlled it; Chatith ditmas=(Chatith or tsatith) I did not allow it to overpower me; tatee chaakh= I succeeded in transforming it into my compositions.

Lal-Ded says that she did not let herself remain idle even for a moment. She resorted to repeating and concentrating on the Lord's name and as such remained active with her spirit chained too supreme. She vigorously followed the path laid down by Her Master. It is there that she observed the "enlightenment". She gave vent to her blissfulness in sweet, simple, and melodious tone.

Thus, the darkness lurking inside was rendered into the moments of illumination. She realized in her a liberated soul with an eradication of mind. She had acquired the confidence that there is nothing higher than the Lord.

Lalleshwari gave expression to her personal experience in her Vakhs. She gave a clear insight of her spiritual advancement and the stages of her development that she had reached in her vakhs. She had a mission to perform. She had a responsibility for her people whom she wanted to educate and put on the right direction. Being a master artist and a genius poet, she converted all her experience into her poetic compositions and the response that her orations received was equally tremendous. Her Vakhs were instantly preserved by the masses in their memory and sang them as a word of the Lord.

SM269. Swargas Feeras Bergas Bergas

Swargas feeras bergas bergas
Torgas khasit maarim chay
Andh no lobum chaanis vargas
Bu kas Lal mea kya naav"

Sorgas=heaven; pheeras=wandered; bargas bargas= all objects in nature, another meaning of berg is a leaf; torgas=celestial horse; khasit=riding; maarim chay (tchhaai)=rejoiced wandering in nature; andh=end; no=not; lobum=to find; chanis=your; vargas =boundary, vastness; bu kus lal=who am i lalla; mei=me, i; kya=what; naav=name

Lalleshwari gives a vivid expression to her personal experience of ultimate awakening of self and realization of the secrets of the Lord. In her ecstasy of achievement, she claims to have toured the whole expanse of her Lord's influences suggesting her ultimate realization of all her desired spiritual goals.

During her wanderings in the space, she had a chance to pass through the heavens. Riding a celestial space craft, she felt as if all objects in nature rejoiced in her happiness. She found no end to the Lord's glory. She found no end to his vastness. His grace was felt in its totality at all places of her travel. She says that His state of presence was felt by her at every place with spiritual delight. Then, she found herself completely lost. She was utterly in Love with the "Lord."

The tour was so absorbing for her that she forgot everything about herself, so much so, that there was no trace of her individual self-found anywhere. In fact, she had attained the highest stages of awakening and had thus become one with her Lord. On reaching this stage there remains no significance of the body. The individual soul becomes one with the universal Lord which is the ultimate ecstasy and freedom from the cycle of life and death. In fact, the symbols like heavens, horse etc is just for an ordinary man to gather the extent of the grace of the Lord otherwise this is all a wider experience of the inner self of a seeker. The mind of an advanced devotee serves as a guide to go deep into the deepest recesses of heart and experience all the complicated secrets of the Lord there only.

SM270. Sorgus Mazun Kya Chui Basuni

Sorgus mazun kya chui basuni
Narkas vasun aasun doosh
Chak resh nasun shiv meh aastoo
Paanai aasun kasun baid

Sorgus mazun kya chui basuni=why live-in heavens? Narkas vasun=to go to hell; aasun doosh=is sin; Chak resh nasun shiv meh aastoo=not to be a tarnished rishi, a blemished sage; be like Shiva; Paanai aasun kasun baid=you yourself remove differences, variances

Why proud in heaven?
Why sinned in hell?
Be not a smeared rishi, be pure like Shiva.
Yourself eliminate your rows.
If you look after goodness and truth, heaven will take care of you.
Find the vices within you. Look for goodness in others, for beauty in the world, and for possibilities in yourself.

SM271. Swarg Jamma Praavith Alakh Prowum

Swarg jamma praavith alakh prowum
Dag lall navoom dai sanz prayei
Pot zooni vothit mote wuz nowum
Chain ta: maali kulis peth nesar payii

Sowarag jamma praavith=aAfter wearing celestial robes; alakh praovoom= I attained freedom from the worldly attachments; Dag lall navoom diiye sanzi prayei= I respected the devotion of my lord in my heart like a shooting pain; Pot zooni vothit mote vooz novoom= I got up very early in the morning to wake up my Lord in my imagination and continued being absorbed with Him all day without a wink of distraction; Chain (tsain) ta: maali kulis peth nesar payii= Dear seeker, just follow what I say. You busy yourself with the worldly pleasures as if enjoying deep sleep on the branch of a tree with nice air blowing to and fro least caring about the danger to your life.

Lal Ded says: after wearing heavenly robes and wanderings in the wilderness, I have renounced the attraction of this world. My false ego dissolved. I am now waiting and lamenting in search of my Lord in whose love I am bearing all pain. In the early hours of the morning in the last phase of moon lit night, I awakened my love, I felt I am running carelessly with heedless steps on, I feel as if I am sleeping on the branch of a tree where a little carelessness will result in my fall and bring an end to my life.

SM272. Sarafas Nish Kahvacha Kharoon

Sarafas nish kahvacha kharoon
Rachi rachi toulun choni maa haar
Chowoohmi bazara phaa loge*6
Panchami sapdak kundan kaar
Shat-wuhmi bazara moloom sapdee
Panai graak tai paanai sowarn kaar

Sarafas=gold smith; kahvacha=a stone used by gold smiths to test purity of gold; Rachi rachi= small quantities;toulun=to weigh; choni=less measure; haar=necklace; choni maa haar=to check purity of necklace; Chowoohmi bazara=first stage of spirituality; Panchami=25th stage of spirituality; kundan kaar=achieve divine bliss; Shat-wuhmi bazara=26th stage, highest stage of spirituality; moloom sapdee= will realize; Panai graak=yourself a customer; paanai sowarn kaar=yourself a goldsmith.

When the Lord blesses the 'Seeker' with the mystic truths, under the guidance of the 'Teacher' or 'Guru', the divine bliss is automatically generated in the sensors or digit of the Moon or so called Sahasrara of the brain. It is a stage at which the golden light is realized, with the full confidence. The guidance of the Teacher or Guru is a must.

After gaining full confidence the Pupil will submit himself, with all devotion and zeal to the Guru or Teacher, for testing his feat. The Teacher or Guru with all his perfection in the art will try and test each step of the discipline of the Pupil, for twenty-four days. If the Pupil stands the test firmly and comes out successful, as declared by the Master, then it is the most auspicious day of the Pupil's achievements. On the 25th day, the Master will honour the Pupil, in the convocation of gracious saints, for having gained mastery in the art of Mystic Truths. Now the realization of golden coloured light will be stabilized. On the 26th Day, automatic realization of ecstasy of the order of divine realization will be set forth, and the duality or ego of any sort even between the Pupil and the Master will be vanished. Grasping each other firmly, they sink in each other's embrace, two bodies and one soul, with a profound feeling of immortal bliss and thus, ideal mingling and realization of the soul is realized.

SM273. Sat Sangye Paviter Doroom

Sat sangye paviter doroom
Navi shar roozas traprith baar
Dash dashami dwar parznovum
Eekaadashi chandramas karoom lye
Dwadash mandlas deh shamroovum
Treyodash trivinee navam kaay
Chaturdash choddah bawan shom navim
Pooran panch dash chandraman karoom vodai
Akdoh boogith paan sandoorum
Sat lye gachit kalpun trov
Sori sombrith ehaii karam potlain pooz

Lal Ded gives the description of the stages of her personal spiritual development. She was fortunate to have her Guru who was very competent and highly awakened and guided her through various stages of her development. She was a highly enlightened soul with enough clear conscience who had come to this life with the purpose of her ultimate personal awakening, probably the last leg of her achievements.

In the booming environment of cosmic radiance, I got my mind and body cleansed. With the new keenness and dedication, I sat down, to become one with Super Consciousness, to merge with the Supreme Void or with the knowledge of Truth. Lo! I recognized the gateway of His divine grace, on the 10th day of my penance; and on the 11th day of my Sadhna, I had a glimpse of the full rotundity of the Moon, with all its beautiful shine and glamour; On the 12th day I observed the force of the sum total of energies of my body concentrated as a pencil of light; in the digit of the moon or sensor or SAHASRARA; On the 13th day, there was a sudden release of HORMONES, or SHASHIKAL, in abundance, from the cells of the sensors and the ductless glands of the brain. Thus, I got a peep into the celestial bliss; and enjoyed the celestial bath in the sacred waters of ETERNITY. So, I got my body and mind cleansed. On the 14th day of my strange exercise, with the gushing out of hormones I observed the pleasure of the mass conversion of my body form into the mysterious vibrational form or energy levels and thus, I travelled in the wave form to see the picturesque scenery of the fourteen different galaxies of the universe (beyond the void).

On the 15th day my joy knew no bounds, when I observed the rise of full moon, with its full rotundity and celestial shine on the back portion of my head.

On the 16th day, I observed complete rest and remained at ease, filled with divine intoxication. Thus, I experienced the joy of the thoughtless state of mind. It is a condition, where all the imaginations flee from the mind and no other thought, except the concentrated thought, of the blissful state of the spirit, can gain access to the mind.

Thus, under such environment I undertook deep meditation and thanked the Lord through the spell of prayers and felt the pleasure of my watching the liberation of my Soul and its merger with the cosmic radiance. It is an indescribable and ineffable vision; so "unheard" has become the "heard" and "unknown" has become the "known."

SM274.   Sone Drav Dehion Ta Mal Gose Wathit

Sone drav dehion ta mal gose wathit
Yeli mai anel ditus taav
Kater zan gayas lole weglith
Ithpath kathkosh gole ta nish rav drav
Lal bu ruzus teli sheleth
Yeli chetas pev bu tus naav

Sone=gold; dehion=black soot; mal= dirt; wathit=removed; taav= heat; rav=sun; kathkosh gole= frozen ice starts melting.

The flame, golden colored, shining steady and bright, got illuminated and converged into the pencil of light and got merged with the cosmic radiations. Lo! the black carbon soot has vanished off and then firmly resolved I continued, the practice of breathing with full faith and devotion, the temperature of the body has started receding and celestial hormones, from the ductless glands of the brain and sensors, have started trickling down and the body temperature has started coming to normal, in the manner, the ice starts melting, absorbing the latent heat, from the warmth of sun rays; keeping the temperature constant till the entire ice melts into water at 0°C.

When I learn that He is in me, then I got enlightenment when I came to know about this.

SM275. Sone Thaav Thaij Tai Hosh Thav Phokas

Sone thaav thaij tai hosh thav phokas
Lolki naar sorus vechaar
Soi ras sartali waawat paiyee
Adha sone sapdee kundan kaar
Chet chai eernai gyan dokurai
Pati kanas kuneei taar

Sone=gold; thaav=keep; thaj=crucible storing pot; hosh thav phookas=careful about breath; wawat= a chemical used by the goldsmith to extract pure gold acting as catalyst; sartal=copper etc. impurity in the gold; kundan kar=pure gold; chet=consciousness; eernai=anvil; gyan=knowledge; dokurai=hammer; pati=then; kanas=extract; kuneei taar=single wire.(In this Vakh Lal-Ded has mentioned the names of the tools which are still used by goldsmiths.)

The composition of this vakh of Lal Ded is the supreme example of high-class poetic skill. She uses fine metaphoric presentation of a comparison between a seeker performing his exercise of breath control (Pranayama) for the purity of his inner self with that of a goldsmith trying to extract the purest form of gold.

The seeker is advised by Lal Ded to use the fine intellect, to avoid any disturbance of thoughts. This, she is comparing with the working of a goldsmith, who with his skill extracts pure gold mixed up with other impurities. Here she is referring symbolically to the various tools, which goldsmith uses, for the extraction of pure gold out of the impurities and converts it finally into a thin, fine wire of pure gold.

The moment celestial light has started emerging out, as a thin ray of Golden coloured light breathing exercise should be kept on in complete harmony with the release of energy levels in the environment of complete surrender, devotion, and zeal. The environmental situation so conceived will work us a catalyst, for bringing early changeover of energy levels released by the vibrations of the mind into cosmic radiations. Then the brilliant celestial light, devoid of any carbon soot starts emerging out from the sensors of the brain cells.

The energy thus generated, will make the brain cells, to undergo a change in the internal metabolism, by virtue of which some sort of nuclear fusion takes place in the elements of the cells, to produce a ray of light of celestial waves, in the direction of cosmos. Hence, the energy released by the mind completely synchronizes with the divine cosmic energy, which the almighty God is always emanating and spreading over the entire universe.

SM276. Taeer Slilas Khot Tiiy Taeeray

Taeer slilas khot tiiy taeeray
Ham trai giiye byon abyon vemersha
Cheetan rav baati sab samaiye
Shiv miiy charachar zag pashaa

Salalilas = Water formation; Ham Trai giiye=ice formation, three forms i.e., water, snow, and ice; byan= maayaa (multiplicity); byanaabyan= vidyaa (unity in multiplicity); abyan= Shakti (unity).

The intense cold freezes water into other solid forms e.g., ice, icicles; snow and hailstorm. Water as a liquid has disappeared by the intense cold and converted into solid state. It is the essence of Lords revelation of Him. It is His joy that assumes all forms that we observe. It is difficult to imagine the reality that soul or Atman is the universal supreme and all-pervading spirit which embraces everything in this broad universe in all forms of creation. It stimulates the mind. And when the sun of pure Consciousness shines, the world of living and lifeless things, the universe and whatever exists, are, in the Supreme, seen as one.

SM277. Tala Chhui Zyus Ta Petha Chhukh Nachaan

Tala chhui zyus ta petha chhukh nachaan
Vanta maali mann kith pachan chhui
Sorui sombrith yati chuy motsaan
Vanta maali ann khit rochaan chhuy

Tala=under, beneath; chhui=have; zyus=ditch; petha=over, above; chhukh nachaan (natchaan) =carefree dancing; sorui sombrith yati chhui motsaan= you've to leave everything behind, all your possessions, whatever you've collected here when you go; Vanta maali ann khit rochaan (rotsaan) chhuy= I'm at a loss to understand how you still enjoy your life and cherish your food and drink.

There is a deep ditch under, and you are dancing overhead. What makes you dance over this endless deep well? All the riches you are amassing, nothing of it will go with you. Since you are conscious of the miserable end, I wonder as to how do you like your feed!

SM278.   Tana Mana Gayas Bo Tas Kunui

Tana mana gayas bo tas kunui**5
Boozam satuk gantaa vazaan
Tat jaayei dhaarnaai dhaarna dichem
Aakash ta prakash karoom sara

Tana mana gayas= I turned my heart and soul; Bo Tas kunuai=towards Him; Boozam=heard; Satuk gantaa= Bell of Truth; wazaan=ringing; Tat jaayei=at that place; dhaarnaai dhaarna dichem= in dhaarna, fixed in thought; Aakash=sky; prakash=light; Karoom sara=I soared high in the sky and explored.

Lalla says: I turned to Him heart and soul. He listened to the warm murmur of my prayers. I did this in the calm and silent environment. Lo! I heard the ringing of the Bells of Truth. The bells of holiness were booming the whole environment round me. There, in meditation, I fixed my thought. My heart rejoiced with pleasure and bliss. I got absorbed in the flashes of truth. I got thrilled and realized the depths of my joy. I was in the sky and far beyond in the regions of light.

In this Vakh Lal Ded conveys a fact about her ultimate success in her personal awakening and becoming one with her Lord. She says she dedicated herself heart and soul to seek the Lord. She progressed rapidly and heard the bells of truth ringing as a clear message from above. She at once took the clue and concentrated on it till, she was able to rise far above the mortal world into the higher reaches of immortality.

SM279. Tanthur Gali Tai Manthur Mochai

Tanthur gali tai manther mochai.*5
Manther gol tai mwotui chet
Chet gol tai kenh ti na kuney
Shuunyas shuunyaah milith gav

Tanthur=holy tantric books; gali ta=has died, gone, Tanthur gali= Holy books will disappear; manther mochai (mwatchey)= only the mantra sound remains, mystic formula will remain Manther gol=mantra departs; tay=and; motoi cheit= consciousness is left behind, naught but mind was left; Cheit gol tay= when consciousness itself is gone, when mind disappeared; kenh ti na kunnai= nothing was left anywhere; Shuunyas shunnyaah miilith gav= void became merged within the void, void merges with void.

For seeking truth, the blessed saints resorted to various feats, for acquiring that state of consciousness. Let go the sacred tantra rites and holy books go; only the mantra sound remains. With the incoming of new knowledge tantra lost utility. Followed by Mantras, the Mantras which were words selected, to produce sounds and prayers by the old sages for the performance of sacrificial rites and ceremonies, the Vedas and other sacred books which are transmitting truth through Mantras are regarded as divine revelations. When the mantra sound departs, only the consciousness is left behind. Then when consciousness itself is gone, there is nothing left behind. The void merges in the Void "shunya goes to shunya".
{Translation by Greirson}
In search of truth, the saints resorted to various feats. One such method was to meditate with the recitations of strange utterances or words of incantations, spells and charms and hymns of devils

and demons, which are called Tantras. That knowledge was called Tantric (Science) or Kriya.

With the incoming of new knowledge, it lost it utility. Followed by Mantras, the Mantras which were words selected, to produce sounds and prayers in set forms by the old sages for the performance of sacrificial rites and ceremonies, the Vedas and other sacred books which are transmitting truth through Mantras are regarded as divine revelations for they contain high sentiments.

With the evolution of new thoughts and knowledge of spiritual science these Mantras also lost its effectual use due to wrong recitation and loss of morality of the people. Then the awareness of Mantras and the actual text fell into forgetfulness. With the intense practice of Meditation and thought, the concept of Mantras also faded away and the sages experienced oneness with the universe. Since meditation produces physiological changes, like reduced oxygen consumption, blood level and respiratory rate, the body feels deeply relaxed, and the mind remains alert. This relaxation counteracts with states of fear, anger, and anxiety. The candidate observes the ways of those saints that are virtuous. As such they briskly follow the path laid by the high sages. That is the path which leads to happiness. It is there that the enlightened soul dwells in the sweet blissfulness.

Yantra: meaning 'device' or 'instrument', is usually geometric representation designed to identify the mind of a worshipper with his or her chosen deity. A yantra is the outward form of deity, while a mantra is the deity's subtle form. In essence the mantra is the deity and when a yantra is inscribed with its bija-mantras and empowered by consecration the deity is installed within the yantra. When a yantra is consecrated by auspicious rites it brings prosperity and peace and removes all wicked and malicious influences from the worshipper's family. Yantras can be used for magical purposes and when employed in destructive rituals the yantra becomes more of a prison than a place for the deity.

SM280. Tatav Prakash Anath So Wani Paaniiye

Tatav prakash anath so wani paaniiye
Vend saraswoti ganga yemen
Sangam ta yaman bend soi naad zan
Soi dapzai sahzaa kriiye

Please defer irrelevant thinking. Think only of the Lord and His glory. He, with all His love, will encourage the spark of love within. This will result in releasing the celestial waves in the Cosmos. Lala gives an example. The manner, rivers Ganges, Yamuna and Sarsowti join in confluence, they lose their identity and thus become one in all. Like that the vibrations merge with celestial waves in the Cosmos. So, try to merge with infinite and render yourself into celestial vibrational wave form. That is the real form of worship.

SM281. Tember Paiyes Kuv No Chagin

Tember paiyes kuv no chagin
Mus rus ku awhana gen gose
Shanten hunz kray tuli muli vaagin
Andrim gah yeli neber peous

Tember= a spark of awakening; kuv no chagin= should tolerate its impact; mus rus=without a holy drink; awhana gen gose= lead astray; Shanten hunz kray vaagin= reduces the value of the saadna of respected but calm awakened souls; Andrim gah yeli neber peous= internal celestial luminescence should not show out but remain hidden inside.

Lal Ded says: One who experiences a spark of awakening should tolerate its impact. It is said that yogis earn great mental equilibrium along with realization of self. They have their emotions in perfect control and for them there is no reason to speak high. They laugh mysteriously in the face of all such and other emotional provocations. These great masters are the masters of their senses to the extent that they maintain no difference of taste, smell or touch as their life is far above the ordinary. These yogis achieve liberation from the cycle of birth and death by becoming one with the Lord. They are the winners of their death too as they have the capability to leave their mortal coil at their will. It is in the same context that Lalleshwari cautions the seekers to earn great mental balance along with the achievement of goals as the divine journey must be traversed with great caution and care as there is always danger of a sudden downfall from any stage of eminence whatsoever.

> **SM282.   Tim Chi Na Manush Tim Che Reshi**
>
> Tim chi na manush tim che reshi
> Yiman deh manna nishi gav
> Badith ta budith byak kya rachhi
> Futimitis baanas pyayi gev

Tim chi na manush=those persons are not normal human beings; tim che reshi=they are eminent shining souls; yiman deh manna nishi gav=they are the people with the power of karma, their mind in the body lose all sense of pleasure pain and grief; badith=when you grow; budith=in old age; byak kya=some other person; rachhi=take care of, nurture; it means that spiritual path and sadhana has to be initiated in the young age, the body has no capacity to undertake such a thorough exercise in old age; futimitis=cracked; baanas=pot; pyayi gev=contain ghee; means it is like a cracked pot which can't contain ghee forever, as it will leak the moment the ghee melts.

Karma has an attachment to the body. As such, the mind in the body loses all sense of humour, and visual pleasures of pain and grief. Therefore, such souls shine in eternal wisdom and infinite delight. The souls of such eminent persons have capacity to destroy the effects of past Karmas too. To acquire such a power; these aspirants are required to initiate the spiritual path in the early childhood itself. Otherwise, the body loses the capacity to undertake such a thorough exercise at the old age. It is, like the manner, the cracked pot with developed leakages cannot contain ghee, as it will leak the moment it melts. Similarly, one cannot widen one's faculty of wisdom in old age. As such the feat of Sadhna must be practiced at the young age.

SM283. Tori Ti Panai, Yori Ti Panai

Tori ti panai, yori ti panai,
Panai panus chui na maylaan,
Athem aches mula daani,
Sui ha maali chay aasar zaan

Tori ti panai, =Therefrom yourself; *yori ti panai*=yourself from this side; *Panai panus*=self and myself; *chui na maylaan,* =never meets; *Athem aches mula dhari*= the eighth, Muladhara chakra location is the base or root of the spine between the genitals and the anus. In male, its location is in the perineum, midway between the anus and penis. In the female, its location is near the cervix, where the vagina meets the uterus; *Sui ha maali chay* = that only is; *aasar zaan*= limitless acquittance

Shiva is the creator, and He is the destroyer too, and the two actions never compromise and shall never meet. Muladhara is a Sanskrit word "Müla" means the root, base, or bottom, which is the Kundalini, and "adhara" means support; it literally means "Root Place or Root Support." The organs associated with Muladhara are Blood, Foot, Vertebral column, Tooth, Bone, Skeleton, Leg.
Muladhara chakra location is the base or root of the spine between the genitals and the anus. In male, its location is in the perineum, midway between the anus and penis. In the female, its location is near the cervix, where the vagina meets the uterus.
Animals also have chakras; the main difference between man and an animal is that animals' topmost chakra is Muladhara and for the man, the bottom chakra is Muladhara. Muladhara chakra is transitional, where the animal reaches the top of its existence and where human existence begins. That is why; this chakra has animal instincts and functions. The basic quality of this chakra is innocence based on every good character. This innocence is visible

and expressed in babies and small children. It represents the action without motive or desire for gross personal gain. This innocence is apparent by the inborn child wisdom. A baby knows fundamental aspects of nature by instinct; it knows how to show discomfort by crying, or how to suck to obtain food. This chakra makes us struggle for basic family needs such as looking a job, earning money, and acquiring home. This chakra brings us health, prosperity, security, and dynamic presence which one should realize.

SM284. Treshi Bochhi Mo Kreshi–Naavun

Traishi bochi mo kreshi–naavun
Yaani chepi taani sandarrun deh
Frath choun daarun ta paarun
Kar vopkarun soi chiiy krai

Treshi=thirst; bochi=hunger; mo kreshi–naavun= let not your body suffer from; Yaani chepi(tchepi)= whenever it feels hungry; taani sandarroon deh= feed it that time; Frath choun daroon ta paroon= suspend your fastings and religious robes; Kar upkaroon=do good; soi chiiy kraiye = therein your duty lies.

Do not let your body suffer with hunger and thirst; feed it when it feels the urge. Do not let doubt creep into your mind. Put off your fasting's and religious robes. No outstanding achievement is possible, without helping the cause of miserable and suffering people that is the only way to achieve Godhood. Suppress your base impressions; there lies your duty and penance. Right action is the way to the true knowledge, for it purifies the mind.

SM285. Trei Nengi Sara Asari-Saras

Trei nengi sara asari-saras,
Aki nengi saras arshas jaay.
Harmokh konsar akh sum saras,
Sati neyngi saras shoonia kaar.

Trei nengi=three times; Sara=the lake; asari-saras= flowed its shore; Trei nengi sara asari-saras= Thrice the lake overflowed its banks, I remember; Aki nengi=once; Saras arshas jaay= waters and the sky did meet; Aki nengi saras arshas jaay= once the lake did rise to the sky; Harmokh= Haramukh is a mountain in the north of Kashmir; Konsar=a lake called Kausarnag in the south of Kashmir; akh sum saras= Haramukh to Kaunsarnag in one vast sheet; Harmokh konsar akh sum saras= One lake it was from the Harmukh to the Kaunsar; Sati neyngi=seven times; saras Shoonia kaar=seven times I saw the lake vanishing in the void, Sati neyngi saras shoonia kaar= and seven times the void swallowed the lake.

During her wanderings in the space, she says, "I have seen three times Earth near the Poles, where water appeared to be at its brim. At one time I have seen at the Equator, where water appeared to have risen to the great heights than at the Poles." Since, the two Poles are the two extremities of the Earth, she named the two extremities as Harmukh and Konsar as these names must have been known as the two tops (boundaries) of the Kashmir Valley. Since she was moving into the Orbit, she must have been going round the globe, through the phases of light and darkness off and on, as such, she has witnessed seven times globe entering the phase of darkness or nothingness, where nothing could be seen from a distance.

SM286. Tulkatur Shishar- Gaanth Sheen Sharanita Mani

Tulkatur shishar- gaanth sheen sharanita mani
Byone beyone sanpani paanch
Vemarashaa poori yeli khotui rav
Samit eman akoi gav

Tulkatur = the ice cover; shishar- gaanth=icicle; sheen=snow; sharanita =snowstorm; mani=icebergs; Byone beyone=separate; sanpani paanch=appear five forms of water in solid state; yeli khotui rav=with sunrise; Samit eman akoi gav=all these melts with sun rise and change into water form; Lal Ded is speaking of only one God.

The ice cover, icicle, snow, snowstorm, and icebergs are different solid states of water. These apparently appear five forms of water in solid state, but, is one - 'water'. So, Lal-Ded intends to give us an understanding that the universe is like ice, icicle, snow, and the Lord is the water. With one sun rise all solid forms melt into one 'water.' She is speaking of oneness of God, and attributes to Him unity of essence, and unity of acts. There is only one God without any second and all the manifestations appearing to be diverse and countless are centered in that oneness only.

SM287.   Tyoth Modur Ta Myuuth Zahar

Tyoth modur ta myuuth zahar
Yas yuth zonukh jatan bhaav
Yem yeich karie kal ta kahar
Su tat shehar vaatith pew

Tyoth=bitter; modur=sweet; ta muith zhar= what is sweet at first is poison in the end; Yas yoith zonook jatan bhaav= everyone is given the choice; Yemi yeich karie kal ta kahar= all depends on the effort put in, and the tireless firm will; So, tat shehar=he, to that city; watet pew=arrives the city of his choice.

Every man has the innate potentiality to rise and reach the divine stature if he strives for it.

What is bitter at first is sweet in the end, what is sweet at first is poison in the end. (To everyone is given the choice) It all depends on the effort put in, and the unflagging determined will; there is no fun in chasing a mirage, for, whoever, strives must soon arrive at the city of his choice.

Lal Ded pinpoints a remarkable fact of life. She says whatever tastes bitter in life is sweet and whatever tastes sweet is in fact the bitter poison.

Lal Ded pinpoints a remarkable fact of life. All the glamour of the world seems sweet and enjoyable, but it is not so. All the charm and thrill in this life results into attachment to this transitory life which is destined to end miserably. Everybody falls into this trap never to get freed. This is the strange but bitter fact of life that we go on ignoring its essential purpose life after life and never fulfil its real purpose.

SM288.   Vakh, Maanas, Kwal, Akwal Naa Ate

Vakh, maanas, kwal, akwal naa ate,
Tshwapi, mudri ati na praviish.
Rozaan shiv-shakt na ate,
Motiyay kenh ta suy vopadish.

Vakh= utterences; Mannas-mind; Kwal= kulachar, that is the teaching in the Tantric system; akwal=akulachar that is monoistic way of the Agamas cannot fathom that secret; mudras=the body postures; ati no praviish=do not penetrate that top secret (rahasya)-mystic happenings; Rozaan Shiv Shakti na ate=Shiva and Shakhti the two universal principles described in Puranas do not live there.

The top secret (rahasya) is not known by mere utterances of the Mantra, as the mind is engrossed with fluctuations. For the purposes of realization, there is need of complete silence and coolness of mind. Shiva and Shakti, the two universal main beliefs described in Puranas do not live there. These are pure vibrations of AUM. Vows of silence and mystic mudra-s cannot gain you admittance here. Lal Ded teaches us that Divine does not possess any form. It is pure consciousness to be addressed by different ways. Lal Ded emphasis on one Vedic truth: 'Divinity is one.'

SM289. Vadneh Saeti Gaash Ho Mare

Vadneh saeti gaash ho mare
Vadneh vadneh mealee na zanh
Mann kar saaf tai zeri aki mealee
Yimav shaleh tungav nearee kyah

Vadneh saeti =weeping; gaash ho mari=you lose sight; Vadneh vadneh meeli na zaanh=weeping leads you nowhere; Man, kar saaf tai =have a clean mind; zeri aki meeli= with slight effort; Yemav shaleh tungav by your howling like a jaclal; neri kya =you achieve nothing.

Crying and weeping lead us nowhere; with a clean mind and effort things may be achieved, otherwise howling like a jackal is waste of energy. According to scriptures, Karma moves in two directions. If we act virtuously, the seed we plant will result in happiness. If we act non-virtuously, suffering results. If karma exists, the world changes. There will always be karma to be taken care of.

There is a variation in the second line- Vadneh *madun* meeli na zanh; here 'madun' means the Lord or Shiva. By weeping we can't reach the God.

SM290A

Pouen Chavan saeth tun no shruchi (water sprinkling does not purify body)

Khen travun saeth Dai no tothi (fasting does not lead to attaining god)

Munn kar saaf zeri aki meli (pure heart and little effort helps)

Yimav shaleh tungev neri kya (shedding crocodile tears does not help)

SM290. Vakh Sedhee Chuie Dith Mokhas Beethim

Vakh sedhee chuie dith mokhas beethim
Sokhas labum na roznas jaay
Dokhas ander nender meetham
Bodh yeli zeethem meethem kath

Vakh sedhe= whatever I say is readily fulfilled; dith mokhus beethim= I'm unable to contain my joy; sokhas=pleasure, happiness; labum na=did not find;roznas jaaye=no place to keep;dokhas=in distress;dokhas ander=when in distress;nender meetham= even in my extreme worldly distress or pain I'm comfortable; Bodh yeli zeethem= my personal knowledge became ripe, gained experience;meethem kath= all my talk displays extreme depth of wisdom and knowledge.

Having gained the awareness of God consciousness, high state of peace was observed by me. My word became a letter of faith with the people. Whatever I pronounced was readily realized and came out true. The defeat turned into victory, despair into joy, and sorrows into smiles. I felt happy over the new situation. There was large gathering of people around me. But, with the incoming of more people my concentration got disturbed. I felt horrified. So, liked to be under the spell of meditation, wherein I was unaware about all external happenings. Then I suddenly felt my intellect and wisdom had grown to such a stature, that I began to express, the voices that speak celestial truth, all this appeared to me like one grand sweet song. Lalleshwari expresses here her personal experience to make the ordinary beings understand the excellence of the achievements upon coming nearer to the blessings of the Lord. She says the worldly joy and sorrow are quite temporary happenings in the ordinary life. These things do not disturb the peace of awakened souls. They treat them alike as they've achieved a status far above ordinary thing. They're far above worldly affairs. All wealth and riches, relations, brothers, and family are no more of any concern to them.

Though she gave vent to her feelings openly for the benefit of the common man she had lost all interest in the matters of the world. In the circumstance her wisdom and knowledge had grown vast. Her sayings were equipped with great knowledge and experience. She gained strange interest among her listeners. Her popularity increased manifold. Her word became the word of God. Whatever she spoke was the sweetest utterance ever spoken by a human being. There was no limit to her spiritual excellence. She had the realization of self which was truly her highest aspiration to be fulfilled.

SM291. Wathoo Rannya Archoon Sakhar

Wathoo rannya archoon sakhar
Athas kaith alpal wakhoor haith
Yudwiiy zannakh parampad akhshar
Hai shikhar khai shashikhar haith

In the totality of this Vakh Lal Ded tells: 'O Blessed Ladies: "Come up and sit in meditation with full devotion and zeal. Have the experience of spiritual consciousness. This will coordinate your organs of action in the divine scheme of things. Stand up with all the materials of worship in hand to realize self which continually exists even when all experiences are suspended. Try to release the force of energy which would enable you to attain spiritual perfection. The Lord is attained neither by learning nor by genius or knowledge of books. It is attained in moments of illumination in Meditation.

SM292. Waawech Graaya Paanas vuchhim

Wawach graaya paanas vuchim
Paanas duenthum souri rang vas
Dyanas ander dham dham meelas
Gonan traevem muchrith baar

Wawach graaya=a transformation; *paanas wuchum*= upon achieving the full realization of self; *Paanas deunthum*= I experienced; *suri rang vas*= my body interiors too changed into a colourless pattern, a strange transformation of body hues from normal to silver white; *Dyana sander*= I took recourse to deep meditation; *Dam dam meelas*= I became unconscious of all external surroundings; *Gunan trowoom muchrith baar*= I gradually fell into fits of ecstasy, a state of elated bliss with all the gates of myself open to all goodness.

When the mundane is transformed into ethereal and the ordinary into special that is full realization and is truly an extra-ordinary achievement. This is the goal of all spiritual seekers when the Lord's grace is bestowed with a big bang.

Lalla describes a return journey: "On my return journey to the place of my dwelling, from my wanderings in the space, I had to pass through the vagaries of atmosphere and its wind pressure with the result that I was turned into light dark colour in appearance. Further due to friction and other radiations, there was a danger of temperature rise, my survival became almost difficult. I took recourse to deep meditation, wherein I became unconscious of all external surroundings. In this search I utilised all my faculties, which I had acquired during my wanderings in the space for my safe arrival at the place of my home."

Upon achieving full realization of the truth about her Lord, Lalleshwari experienced a strange sense of weightlessness of body. It indicates her awakening of the universal truth and being one with the Supreme Lord.

SM293. Wuchaan Bu Chas Saras Andar

Wuchaan bu chas saersey andhar
Wuchum prazlaan saersey manz
Boozith ti roozith wooch haras
Garah chui tasunduy bo kuese lall

Wuchaan=I see; bu chas saersey andar= I see my Lord in everything around; Wuchum prazlaan saersey manz= there is not a single thing without His dazzling presence; Boozith ti roozith wooch Haras= you can concentrate on His divine grace and experience His presence as the whole universe is the abode of the Lord; Garah chui tasunduy Bo Kuese Lal= with Him only the ultimate truth and everything else trivial without any standing, who am I Lal.

Lo! I am blessed with heavenly eyes; I see Him omnipresent; I see Him shining everywhere. Ah! I listen to His celestial talk; so, with all His grandeur and glamour He is in my presence. I am the incarnation of His spirit.

Oh! I am lost, in wonder, love and praise; now where is Lall? So, Lalla is realizing the highest state of bliss and ecstasy, where she has absorbed and has become one with the Lord. She experiences oneness with 'Him'.

She experiences the generously glaring Lord Shiva everywhere and not a single object without His gracious presence. Strangely enough Lalleshwari was nowhere seen as her existence had reduced to nothingness. This is a situation that's experienced by the awakened souls.

SM294. Yas Na Kenh Kaan Tai Chonoi Yas Toroi

Yas na kenh kaan tai chonoi yas toroi
Su kus shoor veer yudus neeray
Andra niiy gali tas vehnooi beoloi
Shy nai aasi tai krai kati vepai

Lal-Ded inspires into the world a new spirit. Her confidence is the highest rule of good life. So, she proclaims the Royally of her mind. To attain such a status a person of faith and willpower is required to realize the celestial vibrations of mind. Lal-Ded explains, just as a warrior without any arms and skill cannot go to fight a battle, similarly a person who has no vigour in his blood cannot coordinate his actions in the divine scheme of things. An individual must practice virtue and self-restraint. Without realization of self the life has no aim, no purpose, and no support.

SM295. Yath Saras Sirini Phole Na Vechee

Yath saras sirini phole na vechee,
Tat sari sakli pooieni chein.
Mrag, sragaal, gannddi, zalhasti,
Zain naa zain ta tatee pain.

Yath saras= the lake; sirini phole na vechee= too small even for a mustard seed; Tat sari sakali pooieni chein= all living beings come to quench their thirst; Mrag=deer; sragaal=jackal; ganndi=rhinoceros; zalhasti=sea elephants; Zain naa zain ta tatee pain= in this struggle for survival, the powerful ones survive, and others die.

Lal Ded says: Affectionately will they drink water from the very lake that is too overflowing to contain even a mustard seed anymore? Deer, Jackal, rhinoceros, sea-elephant arise like waves of rhythm and splash, in the ocean of space and time, to share pleasure and, pain, merriment and grief, for a while in transition and then, wither away and fall back into the same lake.

Lalla says: The human body cannot bear inside any foreign body as little as the smallest rice particle. The wonder is how the germs, parasites, bacteria, other living microbes, and virus of different forms enter our body. Here Lalla compares the shapes of these microbes to the shape of deer's, jackals, rhinoceros, and other infinite number of water microbes. She is amazed to say how they find their way inside our blood stream to quench their thirst.

Thus, a fight goes on with our blood corpuscles. In this struggle for survival, the strong ones survive, and others die. Same way, in this world some are born and some die. This goes on without our knowledge. So, the cycle of life and death continues both inside our body stream and outside in the external environment. The purpose of creation is to manifest the beauty of 'God'. The passion for beauty is a means to link the soul to 'God'.

*The corpuscles in the blood stream are urged to conquer unholy microbes and unholy instincts which give rise to unholy desires and unholy passions. The body and soul of man possess an innate potentiality to kill all such undesired elements to attain a nobler life. The purpose of creation is to manifest the beauty of 'God'.

The clear bright sun, projects forth warmth bearing light to sustain biological life and causes phenomenal, natural changes in the atmosphere, hydraulic cycles as well as physio-chemical actions and reactions, continental drifts, and storage of energy in various forms, known or unknown. All of these are for the uniform benefit of life on earth without any distinctions or discriminations of any kind what-so-ever. Almighty Lord Shiva is Omnipresent, Omniscient and exists in the very electric charge in the nucleus of even the smallest atoms of matter.

SM296. Yav Taeer Chali Tim Ambar Heta

Yav taeer chali tim ambar heta
Yav bochi chali tee ahaar ann
Cheta soper vechaaras pettaa,
Chentan ye deh van-kaavan

Yav taeer chali= ward off cold, bear cold; Tim ambar heta= wear only such clothes; Yav bochi chali=to satisfy your hunger; tee Ahaar ann =eat only that food; Cheta soper vechaaras pettaa= devote yourself to the knowledge of the Supreme Self; Chentan ye deh= Consider this body; van-kaavan = to be food for the forest ravens.

O blessed one-You should wear clothing, as will keep you away from the cold. You should eat food, only to put off your hunger. O, Mind grow your consciousness that will give you poise and assurance. Bear restraint and caution; consider your body nothing more than a potential meal for the forest birds.

SM297. Yehiie Shiila Chyii Piitthas Ta Pattas

Yehiie shiila chyii piitthas ta pattas
Yehiie shilla chyii prathuoon deesh
Yehiie shilla chyii shoobwanis gratas
Yehiie shilla chyii kaasan beid

Yehiie shiila chyii=this very stone; piitthas ta pattas =the same stone makes a pavement and seat; Yehiie shilla chyii prathuoon deesh= the countries, cities and towns have come up with this stone; Yehiie shilla chyii shoobwanis gratas=the same stone for a grinding mill; Yehiie shilla chyii kaasan beid= this very stone is used in Making an 'Idol'.

The earth is a big rock of stone. The countries, cities and towns have come up with this stone. This very stone is making and shaping the beautiful stony grinding mill. This very stone is used in making an 'Idol'.

SM298. Yi Kyah Aasith Yi Kyuth Rang Gome

Yi kyah aasith yi kyuth rang gome
Sang gome chatith hud hud nai digyii
Saarani padan koonoi vakhun pyome
Lalli mei traag gome lagi kami shaathyii

Yi kyah aasith yi kyuth rang gome=What was I in my childhood and young age, what have I become now in my old age; hud-hud=hoopoe in English and satut in Kashmiri; The hoopoe also includes kingfishers, bee-eaters, and rollers. Hoopoe were seen frequently in Kashmir. The diet of the hoopoe is mostly composed of insects, although small reptiles, frogs, and plant matter such as seeds and berries are sometimes taken as well. It is a solitary scavenger which typically feeds on the ground. More rarely they will feed in the air, where their strong and rounded wings make them fast and maneuverable, in pursuit of numerous swarming insects.

More commonly their hunting style is to step over relatively open ground and periodically pause to probe the ground with the full length of their bill. Earthworms, Insect larvae, pupae and mole crickets are detected by the bill and either extracted or dug out with the strong feet. Hoopoes will also feed on insects on the surface, probe into piles of leaves, and even use the bill to lever large stones and flake off bark. Common diet items include crickets, locusts, beetles, earwigs, cicadas, ant lions, bugs, and ants.

I weep at the suffering of my soul. My knowledge is difficult to understand, and my heart is empty of love. My love is insignificant. My colourful face has gone colourless. I am lost in the yearning of my 'Love.' I have turned like a rock, which cannot be cut even by the sharp cuts of the bird's beaks. My speeches or Vakhs, which appear like grand sweet songs render similar meanings and explanations, have lost that inspiring love, which could make my eyes aglow. I do not know to which bank of the lake my life's boat will be anchored. I wish I could tear my heart out and trample it with my own feet.

SM299. Yi Yi Karum Kara Pyatrum Paanas

Yi yi karum kara pyatrum paanas
Arzun barzun beyyis kyut.
Antih laagi-roust pusharun swaatmas,
Ada yuuri gatsha ta tuury chum hyout.

Arzun Barzun=fruit of labour, wages; beyyis kyut=for others; Antih=at the time of death, to get some money after doing some work to offer to God; yuuri gatsha=wherever I go; tuury chum=here and after; hyout=good.

I must suffer the consequence of whatever I do, even if I work for others' gain. But if, with mind from attachment free, I dedicate all works to God, it will be well for me wherever I am, here and hereafter. In this Vakh Lal Ded says: Something is there for us to know, a certain mystery here abides, it cannot all be meaningless.

A man should do his karma without any selfish motto. A man should sincerely work and leave the results on Him. In Upanishads it is recommended to be away from frauds and deceit and do good karma. Sadhaks pray to God that nobody should interfere in their sadhana. They want to be away from frauds and deceptions.

SM300.   Ye Kyah Aasith Ye Kyuth Rang Gome

Ye kyah aasith ye kyuth rang gome,
Bay rang ka'rith gome lage kath shathay.
Tabe raz'dane abakh chhaan pyom,
Jaan gome zonum pananui paan.

Ye kyah aasith=what was I, a child, my colour; ye kyuth rang gome=what has become of me, my old age, faded colour; Bay rang ka'rith gome= my youth has faded; lage kath shathay=I have grown old not knowing what will happen to me; razdane=palace; abakh chaan pyom=an unskilled carpenter worked to build the palace; Jaan gome zonum=good thing about me is; pan'nuy paan= I've realized the essence of myself.

Lal Ded experiences a revolution of self that she has experienced, both internal and external! Lal Ded finds a change of body shape from youth to old age is a normal feature. Though she finds it disturbing but realizes that these are signals of coming end of this life. Most of us commonly ignore all such signals though only a few, quite a negligible number give them some belief and act properly. The life serves no purpose if lived ordinarily from birth to death with its active involvement in the affairs of the world. Raising a family, collecting material possessions, and struggling to earn a living are not the essential purpose of self-realization. Lalleshwari is sarcastic about her present condition of self. On one hand she regrets the horrible change of her body shape from youth to age but on the other she's happy with her realization that something worthwhile has been done. She makes a fitting comparison between the changes of her body shape from youth to age to an unskilled carpenter working on a palace for its renovation. He works on the palace of her youth and damages its structure and outer facade so much so that it looks only a damaged version of the original. The description further suggests that the strange changes that a body experiences with time are signals that predict its end without a purpose if at all the real purpose is not followed.

SM301. Yem Ho Tundhey Bar Tal Zagan

Yem ho tundhey bar tal zagan
Tas panun sharbat panay chaavey
Yus beun beun pather kunai mangan
Yus su tothi ti sui ada kya chaavay

Yem ho =those who; tundhey bar tal=at your doorstep; zagan= fixing the gaze; guard, observe; Tas=to him; panun sharbat panay chaavey=will face his own trial, destiny, as you sow so shall you reap; Yus beun beun = he who differentiates and discriminates; pather kunai mangan= acts and demands; Yus su tothi =on whom He is pleased; ti sui ada kya chaavay=then he need not worry.

Those Stupid and jealous fixing and gazing upon your doorsteps.
They will be punished by the Lord Shiva Himself
Those who differently dramatize and demand.
Those, upon whom the Lord is merciful, He showers His blessings upon them, what else the man desires.
Those who commit all sorts of evil deeds, claiming karma doesn't exist, they erroneously maintain that since everything is empty, committing evil isn't wrong. Such persons fall into a hell of endless darkness with no hope of release. Those who are wise hold no such conception. Treat those who are good with goodness and treat those who are not good with goodness. Thus, goodness is attained." Good people bring out the good in other people.

> **SM302.   Yemai Shei Chei Timay Shei Mei**
>
> Yemai shei chei timay shei mei**6
> Shyam gallaa bein tothas chuie,
> Yohie binnaa beid chei tai mei
> Chei shein swami bo shein mooshes.

Yemai shei chei= O Lord thou art in possession of five senses and the mind; timay shei mei=I have the same six senses; Yemai shei chei timay shei mei=the six You have, I have too; Shyam gallaa=thou have a blue throat; bein tothas chuie= this is the difference; Shyam gallaa bein tothas chuie= Blue-throated One, estranged from you I suffer! Yohie binnaa beid=there is surely the difference; Yohie binnaa beid chei tai mei=The only difference between You and me; chei tai mei = between you and me; Chei shein Swami= Thou art the master of the Six; Bo shein +mooches= By the Six I have been robbed, Chei shein swami bo shein mooches=You are master of the six, while I enslaved!

Lalla says: 'Lord SHIVA', thou art in control of five senses and the mind, like those you have blessed me with such senses and organs too. You have a Dark Blue throat which I have not. The main difference between you and me is that you have complete control over your five senses and the mind and possess all the six divine virtues, but I am entrapped by all the six invisible sinful instincts and thus have little control over the senses and the mind.

The senses and the emotions are the worst enemies of all spiritual development. They keep a person glued all his life to the affairs of the world and never give him an occasion to think beyond and work for its real purpose. Lalleshwari as a great master gives an ironic comparison of the capacities of herself and her Lord. She claims to possess six things as her Lord, but unfortunately, she's controlled by her five emotions and the mind while Lord Shiva enjoys the mastery of his six great powers that make Him the universal Lord (powerful sovereign, omnipotent, omniscient, all inclusive, all pervasive and eternal). Lalleshwari has also conveyed the ultimate truth of the suffering humanity. Man has become an eternal slave to certain human capacities and other demands of body which act forcefully all the time thus distancing him from the real path.

SM303.   Yemi Lodui Chone Kaamani Dushaar

Yemi lodui chone kaamani dushaar
Chapnas tas kenh kuni shaiye
Yes gov lolas ta manas hishar
Tas kyah kari fakeer ta dhaye

Yeme=one whosoever; lodooye= equipped with arms; chuine, Kamaani Dushar = Bow and Sharp tipped arrow; Chapnas tas= seek any shelter; kenh kuni= anywhere; yes, gov lolas= who is blessed with Love; ta manas hishar= absorbs his mind with the light; kya kari=what will; fakeer ta dhaye=saint and God.

One who is equipped with arms and ammunition e.g. (bow and arrow), to strike at his enemy, with will and strength of mind, there is no need for him to seek any shelter anywhere. For, he is out to face his enemy with all his will and skill. Similarly, one who is blessed with endless Love absorbs his mind with the light of the Lord and drinks the nectar of His making. He conquers unholy desires and resists temptations of every sort. There is nothing that can keep one away from self-realization. The realization of Truth requires cultivation of love and self-control.

SM304. Yemi Kar Khamas Taleh Kin Zaagi

Yemi kar khamas taleh kin zaagi
Tas gayie ratas ti kamas chenh
Rababukh shud yeli yorum seenas
Kabab kini deechmas pananui naat

Yemi = whosoever; khamas = kacha, unripe; taleh kin = from below, underside, beneath; zaagi = prey, watch keenly; tas = to him; gayie ratas ti kamas chenh = blood separation; Rababukh shud = tal, tune; yeli = when; yorum senas = applied to my chest, body; kabab kini = instead of lamb's meat from which kabab is made; deechmas = gave; panani naat = my own flesh.

Note on eating of human flesh: that eating the human flesh is a part of sixty-four main Tantric Sadhana. The idea is to get rid of vritti's (habits of the mind) such as attachments to one's body, etc. I have no practical experience with such eating but see Sri Ramakrishna the great master by Swami Saradananda, translated by Swami Jagadananda. Sri Ramakrishna Math, Mayapore, Madras.

SM305.   Ye'my Luub Manmath Mad Tsuur Morun

Ye'my luub manmath mad tsuur morun
Vata-naash maerith ta logun daas.
Tamiy sahaza ishwar gorun,
Tamiy soruy vyendun saas.

Who slays the highway robbers three, Greed, Lust and Pride, and yet, in utter humility, serves his fellow-men-- He truly seeks out the Lord, disregarding as worthless ashes all other things?

SM306. Yihay Maaira-Ruup Pay Diye

Yihay maaira-ruup pay diye
Yihay bariya roop kar dasheeshas
Yihay maya roop ananta zuvyai
Shiv chui krooth tai chean updesh

In this Vakh Lalla explains different forms in which a woman appears. As mother a woman suckles a baby, as wife she dallies passionately in love, as maayaa she takes one's life in the end- and yet in all these forms a woman she. Siva indeed is hard to reach; then heed the doctrine this teaches you.

SM307. Yot Ba Gayas Tati Os Sui

Yot ba gayas tati os sui
Tati dyunthum mole sui
Kanan chuanith vole sui
Su va su va su va su

Yot Ba Gayas= wherever I went; Tati Ose Soi=His grace was there; Tati Duethum Mole Soi= I saw Him as the father of the universe; Kanan=in His ears; Chuanith (tsanith) vole soi= rings in His ears; Su va Su va Su va Su= it is He! It is He; it is He!

Lal Ded says: Wherever I went I saw His grace. I saw Him as the father of the universe showing paternal affection all around. O! I saw the Lord, both in body and spirit, with beautiful rings in His ears. I have seen Him in his physical state, with magnificent grace and observed waves of joy mounting higher and higher within me and I began to cry with joy-

It is He.
It is He.
It is He; Alone.
If He, is He, who am I?

SM308. Yus Hav Mali Haidyam Gelyam Maskhara Karyam

Yus hav mali haidyam geylam maskhara karyam
Sui hav mali manas kharyam na zanh
Shiv panunui yeli anugrah karyam
Lukan hund hedun mea karyam kyah

Yus ha mali=whosoever; Haidyam geylam maskhar karyam=mocks, jeers, slanders; Soi=he; manas kharem na zanh=will not be disliked; Shiv=Lord Shiva; panoon=My Lord; yeli=when; angurah=blessings; karem=have His blessings; look hund=peoples; haidoon=mocks; mei karem kya=these indifferent taunts have no effect on me.

In spiritual realm, Lal Ded advocated for tolerance as a purifying water for enabling a person to come closer to God. She said that if a person washes all his dirt with the purifying water of tolerance he will shine like a mirror and spotless like snow. Then, he will be able to control his birth and death. He will also be able to control his all-sense organs once he merriments in conversation with the supreme God. He will realize that he is himself Shiva and there is no need to make enquiries about God.

Even today the examples of the tolerance of Lal Ded are quoted in Kashmiri household. If a lady is referred as Lal Ded, it means that she is having enough patience and tolerance in domestic and social matters. Lal Ded says:

One who mocks, jeers or hurls slanders at me, with burning stinging words, even then he is not being disliked by me. When the 'Lord SHIVA' showers His blessings and grace on me, these expressions of indifferent touches of people can bring no harm to me.

SM309. Yi yi Karum Suy Archun

Yi yi karum korum suy artchun
Yi rasini vetchorum tii mantar
Yihay lagamo dehhas partchun
Suy Parma Shivun tanthar

Yi yi karum= whatever (karma) work I did; suy archun= became worship of the God; Yi rasini vetchorum= whatever word I uttered; thi mantar= that became a mantra (prayer); Yihay lagamo dhahas partsun= this body of mine experienced became the Sadhana; Suy=that; Parasivun tanthar = Saiva Tantra illumining my path to Paramaśiva. Suy Parasivun tanthar=that became a charm a Samadhi, an amulet.

Lalla says: Whatever work I did become worship of the Lord; whatever word I uttered became a mantra; whatever this body of mine experienced became the Sadhana of Saiva Tantra illumining my path to Parmasiva.

Lalla fills her teachings with many truths that are common to all religious philosophy. There are in it many touches of Vaishnavism, the great rival of Saivism. In the following Vakh Lal Ded says that whatever she did became worship of Lord.

SM310. Zagtas Ander Kaetyah Paalim

Zagtas ander kaetyah paalim
Saaree chaandaan dai sanz wath
Shen manz akis daya zaenim
Maanim ta zaanim Ishewar gath

Zagtas=universe; ander katyah paalim= I met and pampered numberless people in this God's world; Saaree chaandaan (tchaandaan) dai sanz wath= All of them wished to achieve exclusive spiritual advancement. Shen manz akis daya zainem= only a few possessed true fellow feelings; Manin=recognized; zaanim Ishewar Gath= I'm truly amazed at the strange ways of the God.

Lalleshwari had come to this life with a mission of showing people the spiritual path. Among those who followed her she observed lots of people inclined to seek the grace of the Lord but only a few held some sympathy for the suffering humanity. She was wonder struck to observe that lots of people claimed to be the lovers of God but did not love or have sympathy for their brethren.

Lalla says: "O Lord! Having come into this world, I want to know as to how many people you have bestowed your grace. How many people are there who are absorbed in knowing the true nature of your magnificence? I have observed the failure of five senses and the mind to plunge into the ocean of your divine grace. Out of these six, only mind was gracious enough to tune me to thy magnificence. Thus, I saw that all actions, whether within or without, are performed by the will of your divine grace." The essence of body is consciousness.

SM311. Zal Ho Mali Lusui Na Pakaan Pakaan

Zal ho mali lusui na pakaan pakaan
Siri lusui na dolgaan Sumerav
Chandrama lusui na maraan ti zevaan
Manush lusui na karaan nendya

Zal = water; lusui= is not tired of; pakaan=moving, flowing; siri=the sun; dolgaan=melting the snow; Sumerav= The mountain peaks of Sumerav; Chandrama or tsandram =the moon; maraan=to die; zevaan= to be born; manush =the man; karaan=doing; nendya=speaking ill.

Water is not tired of flowing; the sun is not tired of melting snow on the peaks of Sumerav mountain; the moon is not tired of waning and waxing; likewise, the man is not tired of speaking ill of others.
 Lal Ded believed it is the human nature to speak ill of others. The easiest thing in life is to criticize. People can't change their nature, for them Lal Ded has spoken the above Vakh.

(Another version)

SM312. Kus Ha Mali Lusie Na Pakan Pakan

Kus ha mali lusie na pakan pakan
Kus ha mali lusie na dulgan samrav
Kus ha mali lusie neh maran ti zevaan
Kus ha mali lusie neh karan neindeh

SM313. Zal Paeth Pakun Thakun Loukan

Zal paeth pakun thakun loukan
Naaras achun maras dabun
Aakash gumunuv vufun aasun
Kaput baasun aasun chet

SM314. Zal Thamuno Hutva Turnavano

Zal thamuno hutva turnavano
Uurda gamano par-varzeyt carit
Kaattha deni dwad shramanaavano
Anti sakalo kapatth careyth.

To stop a running stream, to cool a raging fire, to roam the skies on sandalled feet, to milk a wooden cow - All this is fraud and jugglery.

SM315. Zanam Pravith Karam Sovoom

Zanam pravith karam sovoom
Dharam pollum soi cham sath
Netran ander praiyam daroom
Choroom ta monnum yohie akh

Zanam pravith=when I came to this world; karam sovoom=I adopted karma by doing householders activities; Dharam pollum=I kept mission of divinity with me; soi cham sath= that gave me satisfaction; Netran ander=within my eyes; praiyam=love; Netran ander praiyam daroom=my eyes bloomed with the love for my beloved God; Choroom=choose, select; monnum=agreed, decided; yohie ahkh=this only one God; Choroom ta monnum yohie akh=I choosed Him for a lasting association and have confidence in Him alone.

"Since, I was born, despite house holders' active life, I kept no attachment with the material world and cultivated intense desire to fulfill the mission of divinity, my eyes bloomed with prime perfection with the fountain of Love, which ensured in me, the lasting allegiance and confidence in Him alone."

> **SM316. Zanam Pravith Vebhov No Chondoom**
>
> Zanam pravith vebhov no chondoom
> Looban bhoogan baram na priiy
> Somuy ahaar saithaa zonum,
> Chollum dokh waaw polum dai.

Zanam=in life; pravith= I sought; vebhov no chondoom = neither wealth nor power, Zanam pravith vebhov no chondoom= having taken birth, I searched not enhancement; Looban bhoogan baram na priiy = nor ran after the pleasures of sense, Desires and enjoyments I like not; Somuy Ahaar saithaa zonum= moderate in food and drink, I considered moderate food enough; Chollum dokh waaw polum Dai= I lived a controlled life, and loved my God, I bore pain and poverty and worshipped god.

On getting the human form I didn't choose any unnecessary worldly addictions. All my efforts were to keep all the desires away and be engaged with Dharma or righteousness. Ever since I was born, I sought neither wealth nor power. I never ran after the pleasures of sense. I adopted moderate food and drink. I lived a controlled life and loved my God.

SM317. Zanuni Zaayaay Ruty Tay Kutiy

Zanuni zaayaay ruty tay kutiy
Karith vodrus buhu kalish
Pheerith dwar bazneh vati tutui
Shiv chui krooth tai chaenupdesh

Plump and comely were they born, causing their mother's womb great pain; yet to the womb they come again. Siva indeed is hard to reach; Pray, heed the doctrine this teaches you.

SM318. Zaanahaa Naaddi-Dal Mana Ra'ttith

Zaanahaa naaddi-dal mana rattith*101
Chatith vatith kutith kalaish
Zaanaha ada ras ta rasayan gattith,
Shiva chuy krooth ta chein updesh.

Zaanahaa=if I knew; naaddi= the tubes through which the vital airs circulate of which the principal ones are ten, dashi naadi vaav, the vital airs of ten naaddi-s; dal mana ra'ttith =control my naadis;Tsattith=to cut bonds; vattith kuttith kaliish=to bind, to serve and to pull the bonds of desire; Zaanaha ada astah rasaayan gattith = I should have known how to compound the Elixir of Life; Shivachuy kruutth=Shiva is harsh; ta tsen vopadiish=this is the message.

Lalla Ded initially was not introduced to the yogic practices. It was her Shiva-guru who introduced such practices to her. Over a period, she came to realize their vital role and efficacy in attaining identity with Shiva. Through practices (abhyas) of controlling her fickle mind she learnt perfect art of yoga for spiritual destination of unity with Shiva.

Lalla says: I wish I could have such a hold on my mind that it could gain control over the functions of the main junctions of the nervous system. I wish I could know its operations, i.e., cut, twist the nerve fibers at the main junctions of nerves.

She further says: I wish If I knew how to control my naaddi-s, (the capillaries, and tubes), as to, how to sever them from the pull of desire, how to bind them to the inner Self, and how to cut the bonds of sorrow, I should have known how to amalgam the Elixir of Life. Siva indeed is hard to reach; then heed the doctrine this teaches you. Nadies are the ethereal nerves that move prana and have the full understanding and power to control all its movement for the advancement of my spirit. According to her understanding and realization of supreme Lord leads to highest happiness of consciousness.

SM319. Zain Mali Zaino, Angan Angan

Zain mali zaino, angan angan
Chet chai zainin tum kas kanai
Rayas kanai, rai kya dichnam
Khasun gur ti vasun naav
Khasit gayas bu tas kunai
Tati labum kutur muter mamnei
Tami dichum gaav toor
Sui pyoem jaggaras
Jaggar lagim kanmpnay
Kaan lagim yernai
Satuk nai tu mraituk
Bun ju meon kul taruk

Zain Mali Zaino=to attain, to conquer; Angan Angan= control over the sense organs; Chet=consciousness; Chai Zainin=have to win; Khasun=to ride; Gur=horse, a stead; Vasun Naav =boat to sail, ferry; Khasit Gayas Bu Tas Kunai= to enjoy, the thrill and joy of heavens; Tati =there; Labum=found, saw; Kutur Muter Mamnei=Lord in the company of saints and liberated souls; Tami Dichum=they gave; Gaav Toor= bowl of celestial Nectar; Sui =that; Pyoem Jaggaras=drank to my fill;

Lalleshwari composed her philosophy in the language of the people; she expressed her spiritual and mystic experiences in Kashmiri. Her songs became popular, and the people committed to their heart and passed on from generation to generation.

In totality, the meaning of this vakh is that -
To attain, a pure awareness free from all thoughts O! Seeker of Truth! You will realize a situation where all conflicts disappear and the soul shines onwards in its purity, cleanliness, and becomes

all knowing, all seeing, and all wise. The easiest way to attain endless calm is to get complete control over the sense organs and realize pure consciousness and awareness of self. It is attained in moments of enlightenment. Only the Almighty God father has blessed me with all this joy and comfort.

The gracious Lord has blessed me with steed, which carried me with infinite speed, to galaxies and beyond to the place where Lord is seated up in the company of enlightened Souls. There He made me sit in a boat like structure, to enjoy, the ecstasy and merriment of heavens. The boat ferried me across the heavens to see its grandeur and grace.

There I found the realized Souls of saint's par-excellence, rendered into small glistening insignificant particles. The great saints blessed me with a bowl of celestial Nectar, which I drank to my fill. My body felt marvellous with all glory and shine. I observed the essence of spiritual kindness within and started watching the blissful state of my spirit. The blessed saints watched my energetic dance on my entry into gardens of heaven. Now, it is alike for me to live a life of Godhood or to merge with His infinite grace. I am happy to live and happy to die.

Since I am a realized Soul, His grace is calling in me that I should bring salvation to the entire set up round me and turn myself into a guiding star, shining steady and bright. Oh Joy! I have achieved the liberation of my Soul and now I bear the power to cancel my imprisonment. Ah! Now I am shining like a star, with my physical body intact. So, I have now become the brightest star or my clan.

SM320. Zuv yeli dangi Aun kati rochie

Zuv yeli dangi Aun kati rochie
Renimachi neymach dolnai kaichie
Chum yeli chonie, chonie aadeh mochie
Teli mali khochinie paninie bachie

Zuv yeli = when the physical body with soul ; dangi =deteriorates; Aun kati rochie = foods detest; Renimachi = cooked; neymach = fragilities, frailties; Renimachi neymach = cooked dishes for which man has weaknesses; dolnai kaichie= remain untouched and untasted; Chum = flesh of the body, shrinking skin; yeli = when; chonie =decrease, drop, fall off; chonie aadeh mochie = only skeleton remains; Teli mali =then; khochinie= scared; paninie bachi =your own kith and kin; Teli mali khochinie paninie bachi = then your own kith and kin will be scared of you.

Body deteriorates, foods detested.
Cooked delicacies untouched and untasted.
Shriveled skin and skeleton left.
Scares kinfolk.
Here Lal Ded admonishes and cautions, that when the human body deteriorates, foods are reviled and the weakness of foods that one had are eschewed; the skin withers leaving only the bones; the person gathers a dreadful look and scares his own family members.

Miscellaneous and Relevant

1) Lal Ded Spiritualism and Mysticism

The experience of mystical union or direct unity with ultimate reality reported by 'mystics' is called mysticism. It is the belief that direct knowledge of God, spiritual truth, or ultimate reality can be attained through subjective experience (such as intuition or insight). The belief that union with or absorption into the Deity or the absolute, or the spiritual apprehension of knowledge inaccessible to the intellect, may be attained through observation and self-surrender. Belief characterized by self-delusion or dreamy confusion of thought, especially when based on the assumption of occult qualities or mysterious agencies. Until recently mysticism was hated for being some vague and unscientific discipline and not a part of human nature. Albert Einstein after many centuries from Newton revived mysticism by his many celebrated utterances. He said of mysticism: "The most beautiful experience we can have been the mysterious. It is the fundamental emotion which stands at the cradle of true art and true science." Mysticism is, therefore, a search for the unknown. It involves dreaming about nature's mysteries. The scientist dreams, the seer also dreams. Indeed, in the post-Einstein period, mysticism has acquired a new dimension and the philosophy of science has moved on towards a non-mechanist view of the world by the scientists. Prof. Ilya Prigogine, who won a Noble Prize in Physics in 1977 on thermodynamics of natural systems has done ample work on describing this change in the philosophy of science. His book, "Order Out of Chaos", is worth reading. Here Alvin Toffler in his foreword says that "we are becoming more and more conscious of the fact that on all levels, from elementary particles to cosmology, randomness and irreversibility play an ever-increasing role. Science is rediscovering time". Prigogine himself speaks of mysticism:

"Today the balance is strongly shifting towards a revival of mysticism, be it in the press media or even in science itself, especially among cosmologists. It has even been suggested that certain physicists and popularizers of science that mysterious relationships exist between parapsychology and quantum physics." Prigogine talks of profound change in the scientific concept of nature. Indeed, he seems to endorse the view of Tagore who during his discourse with Einstein on the meaning of Reality said that "even if absolute truth could exist, it would be inaccessible to the human mind". Einstein had emphasized that "science had to be independent of the existence of any observer".

Thus, we find new and very perceptive books being well-received by the scientific community which provide a thematic approach to science, a theme to provide a bridge for human understanding. Gerald Holton's book "Thematic Origin of Scientific Thought from Kepler to Einstein" is a profound contribution in this direction.

With a new emphasis on mysticism, and a thematic approach to science, the world is witnessing a new dialogue between mysticism practiced by seers like Lal Ded that produces pure consciousness in human beings and the new science of philosophy. Lal Ded's vakhs are full of mysticism of nature. Human being is a part of nature. Thus, by practicing Omkar, Lal Ded says, one can bridge the gap between self and cosmic consciousness and may be rightly called as "the science of spiritualism." Lal Ded also calls for achieving pure consciousness by the practice of yoga. After all she feels that yoga is the realization of God from within. Thus, Lal Ded has shown close nexus between mysticism and observing reality in the universe. She has urged scientists to combine scientific search with search for spirituality and pure consciousness. Science and spiritualism of Vedanta are seen as one and inter-dependent entities.

Loob maarun sahaz vyatsaarun, Dro'g zaanun kalpan traav.
Nishi chuy tay duur mo gaarun, Shuunyas shuunyaah miilith gav.

In the above vakh she says: "Realization is rare; indeed, seek not afar; it is near, by you. First slay Desire, and then still the mind, giving up vain imaginings; then meditate on the Self within, And lo! The void merges in the Void. Lal Ded had attained the highest goals of spirituality. She says that concentration on the Lord's name and meditating on one's real self is the key to get rid of the worldly desire. She had a clear imagination that achieving the status of being one with the Lord was not so hard for everyone who wanted to reach there. The main hurdle in the achievement of spiritual goals is one's own incapacity. Lal Ded has a clear message for a simple devotee ---- your Lord is nearer to you than everything else! Never imagine Him to be far from away! Just keep under control the fiery body emotions. There is no need to seek Him anywhere else. He is there inside your loving heart. The individual soul is an essential part of the supreme. Once it achieves the essential realization of self, it takes a swift flight to meet the Lord and become one with Him. Atma becomes one with Paramatma. Shunya merges with the absolute. Human being loses its personal identity and becomes one with the Lord. All duality between the ordinary soul and the supreme soul is finished. Lal Ded had attained this experience and there was nothing further unattainable for her.

Lal Ded was once passing through a thick forest. She was touched by the calm, peaceful and soundless environment of the forest. The chirping of the birds, the blowing of the breeze and the jungle lore produced by the swinging cones and needle like leaves of the conifer trees, producing celestial music. There was an echo of delighted melodies. It appears as if the nature is making its best effort to make people realize the divine truth. In the sweet melody of jungle lore, the wise and blessed one listens to such music, only through the vibrations of the celestial waves. So, it is a place where man and nature nestle together in a state of glory to realize the truth. But such tunes and soft touches produce no effect to the ignorant, even when the drums are beaten before them.

2) Lal Ded and six great signs of spiritualism

Lallishwari's Vakhs are an expression of high thought & spiritual truth, precise apt & sweet. Some of these saying or vakhs have been collected & published by Dr. Grierson, Dr. Barnett, Sir Richard Temple, Pt. Anand Kaul Bamzai, and Prof. Jai Lal Koul.

Lalla has six great signs of spiritual advancement.
1. Constant devotional attachment to Shiva.
2. Full attainment of Vakh siddhi.
3. Attainment of controlling power over all the five elements.
4. She had acquired the capacity to accomplish the desired end.
5. She had acquired the knowledge of all e.g., what is it by knowing of which everything can be known.

Now the experiences of her travels to space, as per her Vakhs can be explained as she travelled to the 'hyperspace,' after converting her whole mass of the body into electromagnetic wave form as an energy particle. Normally time, length of an object and mass are all absolute quantities and cannot change by any other means. Einstein's explains.

"That when particles travel with extra ordinary speed through space.

i) Clocks in higher speed go slow.
ii) The length of an object contract at higher speed
iii) Mass of an object increases at higher speed.

These strange looking phenomena were experimentally confirmed. In this theory called theory of relativity he derived a famous formula known as mass-energy formula $E=mc^2$, where

E-Energy,

m-mass,

C-Velocity of light, which is 3x100000, 3 Lacs kilometer per second.

As per this realization when one gram of mass of a material 'is converted into energy it yield 2.5 x 10 raise to power 7 (seven) kilowatt hours of electric energy. This formula is the basis of energy in nuclear reactors and in our Sun & stars.

The Einstein in this theory showed that

1. light rays bend coming from star while passing by the Sun.

2. He also showed space round a massive star is curved so that any object which enters the space moves in a curved path.

Planets, mercury, earth, mars, and Venus which are nearby to Sun move in a more eccentric path than Pluto which is at largest distance from the sun.

3. He also showed major axis of elliptical orbit, which our earth is tracing round the Sun is rotating, which was believed to be stationery. In this theory Einstein showed how light spends some energy while escaping from the gravitation of its own source, that is he explained the gravitational shifts of light in the space. These details have been given as to know how Lal Ded must have experienced when she travelled in the space as the energy particle with the velocity of light.

Assas kuni sapdas saitha
Nazdeekh asith gayas door

3) Lal Ded and the concept of Shunya (Nothingness)

Lal Ded has been the originator of the concept of Shunya (Nothingness) in Kashmiri poetry. According to some of her vakhs, a slippage to Shunya is a union with Supreme Shiva that resides in every particle of this universe. Lal Ded said,

> *Gwaras precheome sassi latey; Yas nu kenh vanan tas kyah naav.*
> *Pritschaan pritschaan thachis tu loosis, Kenh nas nishi kyaahtaam draav*

I asked my guru thousand times, what is the name of the nameless, having got exhausted and tired of asking, but eventually something was visible out of nothing, nameless is the source of something that we see (His creation of this universe). Lal Ded believed that the limitless and supreme Shiva is the destroyer of darkness leading to emergence of light. Lal Ded vastly advocated that Shiva is the essential Supreme ruler of Shunya (Nothingness).

"Shunya" or a "zero point" is where the mind become still, and you become the observer. This way you are not the ripple of the waves, but stillness in the depths of the ocean. Shunya is a deep, meditative state of consciousness where the 'separate' self-identity softens into stillness. This state of being is so pure and clear that it is often referred to as a state of 'zero'. In Shunya, the greater aspect of 'Self', or the 'higher self', is available and the experience of oneness is realized. The characteristics of Shunya are inbuilt. The features of Shunya are graceful, soulful, neutral, sensual, accepting, and allowing. There is no judgment, expectation, opinion, pushing, or intellectualism. It is a pure form of love. In this state of consciousness, the Infinite is in charge and what happens is limitless.

The Masters of Kundalini Yoga, say that the highest state of consciousness is called 'Shunya', where the ego is brought to complete stillness. A power exists there. We do not hassle or try to act. With folded hands of devotion, Infinity acts for us. In that state of "zero," if we can focus our mental projection on a clear intention, which acknowledges our higher self and the Creator within us, it will be so.

Shunya, nothing, or no-thing. There is no miracle. The mind is infinite when it concentrates the magnetic energy of the psyche. There are only two things: energy and matter. Any composition, permutation of any energy into matter and matter into energy, can be caused by a disciplined mental concentration. That mental concentration is in you, it is not outside.

Lal Ded thinks dissolution of 'self' (Aham) essential for Realization. According to her, Sadhak has to reach that mental attitude where there is no difference between 'Him' and 'self'. She says one who considers his own self and others alike ends the distinction between 'I' and 'you', who treats days and nights alike, who is above sorrows and pleasures, can only realize God in his own self. According to her, differentiation between the human soul and Divine-self was Zero. Lal Ded is the first woman mystic to preach medieval mysticism in

Kashmiri poetry. She used metaphors, riddles and other mediums for her expression.

4) Lal Ded and Aum (Om) Emphasis

Lal Ded, the 14th century woman saint and poetess of Kashmir was fully conscious of the word OM. In many of her Vakhs she has emphatically used OM, AUM or Omkar. In fact, many Vakhs begin with OM which have been passed down as a way of expressing the essence and foundation of universe at a fundamental level.

Lal Ded has said

Akui Omkar yus naabi darey, komboi brahmandas sum garey,

akh sui mantar yus chetas karey, tas saas mantar kyah zan karey.

A person who meditates on the single syllable "OM" or "AUM", with yoga connects the lower most aspect of his self with the uppermost aspect, remembering all the time one sacred syllable, OM, for him all other thousand syllables are meaningless.

Om is spoken at the beginning and the end of Hindu mantras, prayers, and meditations and is frequently used in Buddhist and Jain rituals as well. Lal Ded has used OM in many of her vakhs. Om is used in the practice of Yoga and is related to techniques of auditory meditation. From the 6th century, the written symbol of Om was used to mark the beginning of a text in a manuscript or an inscription. Om Parvat, a sacred peak at 6191m in the Indian Himalayas, is revered for its snow deposition pattern that resembles 'Om'. The syllable 'OM' or 'AUM' is discussed in several the Upanishads, which are the texts of philosophical speculation.

With its threefold nature, special shape and unique sound, Om lends itself to a variety of detailed symbolic understandings. The symbol of AUM consists of three curves (curves 1, 2, and 3), one semicircle (curve 4), and a dot (5).

The upper curve 1 denotes the state of deep sleep (sushupti) or the unconscious state. This is a state where the sleeper desires nothing nor beholds any dream.

The large lower curve 2 symbolizes the waking state (jagrat), in this state the consciousness is turned outwards through the gates of the senses. The larger size signifies that this is the most common ('majority') state of the human consciousness.

The middle curve 3 (which lies between deep sleep and the waking state) signifies the dream state (swapna). In this state the consciousness of the individual is turned inwards, and the dreaming self-beholds an enthralling view of the world behind the lids of the eyes.

These are the three states of an individual's consciousness, and since Indian mystic thought believes the entire manifested reality to spring from this consciousness, these three curves therefore represent the entire physical phenomenon.

The dot signifies the fourth state of consciousness, known in Sanskrit as turiya. In this state the consciousness looks neither outwards nor inwards, nor the two together. It signifies the coming to rest of all differentiated, relative existence This utterly quiet, peaceful, and blissful state is the aim of all spiritual activity. This Absolute (non-relative) state illuminates the other three states.

Finally, the semi-circle symbolizes Maya and separates the dot from the other three curves. Thus, it is the illusion of Maya that prevents us from the realization of this highest state of bliss. The semi-circle is open at the top, and when ideally drawn does not touch the dot. This means that this highest state is not affected by Maya. Maya only affects the manifested phenomenon. This effect is that of preventing the seeker from reaching his goal, the realization of the One, all-pervading, unmanifest, Absolute principle. In this manner, the form of OM represents both the unmanifest and the manifest, the noumenon and the phenomenon.

As a sacred sound also, the pronunciation of the three-syllabled AUM is open to a rich logical analysis. The first alphabet A is regarded as the primal sound, independent of cultural contexts. It is produced at the back of the open mouth, and is therefore said to include, and to be included in, every other sound produced by the human vocal organs. Indeed, A is the first letter of the Sanskrit alphabet.

The open mouth of A moves toward the closure of M. Between is U, formed of the openness of A but shaped by the closing lips. Here it must be recalled that as interpreted in relation to the three curves, the three syllables making up AUM are susceptible to the same metaphorical decipherment. The dream state (symbolized by U) lies between the waking state (A) and the state of deep sleep (M). Indeed, a dream is but the compound of the consciousness of waking life shaped by the unconsciousness of sleep.

AUM thus also encompasses within itself the complete alphabet, since its utterance proceeds from the back of the mouth (A), travelling in between (U), and finally reaching the lips (M). Now all alphabets can be classified under various heads depending upon the area of the mouth from which they are uttered. The two ends between which the complete alphabet oscillates are the back of the mouth to the lips; both embraced in the simple act of uttering of AUM.

The last part of the sound AUM (the M) known as ma, when pronounced makes the lips close. This is like locking the door to the outside world and instead reaching deep inside our own selves, in search for the Ultimate truth.

But over and above the threefold nature of OM as a sacred sound is the invisible fourth dimension which cannot be distinguished by our sense organs restricted as they are to material observations. This fourth state is the unutterable, soundless silence that follows the uttering of OM. A quieting down of all the differentiated manifestations, i.e., a peaceful-blissful and non-dual state. Indeed, this is the state symbolized by the dot in the traditional iconography of AUM. The threefold symbolism of OM is comprehensible to the most 'ordinary' of us humans, realizable both on the intuitive and objective level. This is responsible for its widespread popularity and acceptance. That this symbolism extends over the entire spectrum of the manifested universe makes it an absolute and authentic source of spirituality. Professor Jayalal Kaul, an outstanding scholar, says in his insightful volume on the saint poetess: "Lal Ded is undoubtedly one of the greatest spiritual geniuses of the world." The sound 'aum' was discovered in India thousands of years ago without actual travel in space...The sacred sound of aum is described in Indian Vedas thousands of years ago.

OM is mentioned numerous times throughout Vedic literature, most commonly in its original form of AUM. In the Vedas, AUM is the sound of the Sun, the sound of Light. It is the sound of assent. OM has an upward movement that uplifts our soul, just like the sound of a divine eagle or falcon. The names of God have been given great sanctity by the Vedas themselves. That is where we find the basic mantras such as Om Namah Shivaya, where the names themselves contribute to the significance of the mantras. Om by itself is the mystic word which is most important for the religious and spiritual search of a Hindu. Without an explanation and understanding of this word no study of Spirituality in Hindu religion may be complete.

In Upanishads Om is spoken of as the primeval, or primitive or basic word which stands for the entire universe permeated by Brahman and therefore Brahman itself. The three sounds that go to make up Om constitute symbolically the entire universe of words. For, 'a' is the sound with which the human mouth is opened to speak any word and 'u' is the sound which allows the tongue all positions from the palate to the lips, and 'm' is the vocal movement one makes to close the lips. Every sound which man can produce is between the extremes of 'a' and 'm' and so; together with the intermediate stage of 'u' it represents everything words represent.

The Chandogya Upanishad opens with the recommendation to "let a man meditate on OM, the essence of all." The same Upanishad also tells us that the gods took the song of OM unto themselves, thinking, "with this [song] we shall overcome the demons," thus implying that OM inspires the good inclinations within each person.

When speaking of OM, the Katha Upanishad says, "this syllable is Brahman (the Absolute), this syllable is the highest, he who knows that syllable, whatever he desires, is his."

OM is a tool of meditation that empowers one to know the God within oneself, to realize one's Atman (Soul, Self)-The Shvetashvatara Upanishad

Adi Shankara said that if you can only study one Upanishad, it should be the Mandukya, which is fortunate because it happens to be the shortest and is devoted entirely to OM. It opens by declaring, "AUM, this syllable is this whole world, all past, present, future, and whatever exists beyond time is AUM." In other words, everything that exists in manifest creation is contained within AUM.

Mysterious significance of 'AUM' or OM

AUM represents the 3-Fold Division of Time

A – is the Waking State
U – is the Dreaming State
M – is the state of Deep Sleep

At the end of AUM is a pause, a silence. This represents the fourth state known as Endless Consciousness. The visual symbol represents the true meaning of AUM

The symbol OM visually consists of three curves, one semicircle, and a dot.

- The large bottom curve symbolizes the waking state, A.

- The middle curve signifies the dream state, U.

- The upper curve denotes the state of deep sleep, M.

The dot signifies the fourth state of consciousness.

The semi-circle at the top represents Maya and separates the dot from the other three curves. It represents an illusion of Maya which is an obstacle to self-realization.

Aum is the sound of infinite. Aum is said to be the essence of all mantras and Vedas, the highest of all mantras or divine word. By sound and form, AUM symbolizes the infinite Brahman and the entire universe.

A stands for Creation.
U stands for Preservation.
And finally, M stands for Destruction or dissolution.

AUM represents the Trinity of God in Hindu dharma (Brahma, Vishnu, and Shiva).

The three portions of AUM relate to the states of waking, dream, and deep sleep and the three guans (rajas, satva, tamas).

The three letters also indicate three planes of existence, heaven, earth, and the netherworld.

OM mantra is a brain stabilizer. By practicing it one can enter deeper and deeper into the own natural state, which is also an energy medicine for human being under stress- so says science.

In one experiment, scientists analyzed functional Magnetic Resonance Imaging scans (f-MRI scans) before and after Om mantra chanting and concluded that regular chanting of Om mantra can treat depression and epilepsy as well.

Based on scientific experiments & research studies, we can confirm the age-old claims made by Yogis that chanting Om mantra reduces mental stress, cures depression, improves focus and concentration, calms the mind, and leads to better well-being, peace, and happiness. When Om Mantra is chanted, the frequency of the vibrations is said to be 432 Hz which happens to be the frequency of everything in the universe. This scientific finding is the justification of the saying in harmony with the being.

The pronunciation of the word "OM" is supposed to symbolize the totality of all sounds as it includes all other sounds that humans can utter. This idea of totality also exists in the English word "Omnipresent" that includes OM as its prefix. We also have words like Omnipotent and Omniscient, all of which have the concept of totality in their meanings.

The ancient Greek alphabet had Omega as its last letter. Omega written in the lower case of the Greek alphabet, if turned to its side, looks quite like the Sanskrit way of writing Om. It is from the Greek alphabet "Omega" that we have the English phrase "the alpha and Omega", which means, "to include everything". It is said that the word Om has been used to make other words. The Christian term "Amen" is said to have some link with "Om" as also the Islamic term "Amin". Both terms are like OM.

Om is a well-known symbol to Indians all over the world. Almost every Indian household owns some sort of Om symbol. The way I was taught Om is a symbol of God.

Om or AUM is not just a sound, but a vibration of the universe. It is a frequency of energy that connects and joins the entire universe together.OM is not just O and M but it is a vibration that lingers and flows like energy itself.

Om is a mantra, or vibration, that is traditionally chanted by Hindus. This mantra is considered to have high spiritual and creative power. This mantra is both a sound and a symbol rich in meaning and depth. When pronounced correctly it is AUM. This syllable is also referred to:

Omkara (oṃkāra); Aumkara (auṃkāra); Pranava (praṇava)

The frequency of Om is the same as the frequency of earth's rotation around its own axis. So, in some sense, earth is saying OM. It is the most universal and spiritual feeling that neither refers to any religion nor any God or religion. Om is said to be the cosmic sound which initiated the creation of universe (big bang theory).OM also has a scientific and practical explanation (based on the physics of sound, vibrations & resonance).

Pranava- the primordial sound: OM, equally common is Pranava (AUM), (ॐ)-, the Sanskrit symbol of the OM, or AUM, the first sound vibrating out of creative void. Chanting this syllable rhythmically drives all evil spirits away and wears down the results of past deeds (karma) that still affect the present. The OM is the first syllable of all the holy mantras and powerful chants, such as Om Namah Shivaya, by which God is invoked.

The Hindu 'OM' Sounds of the Sun has now been confirmed by NASA (USA). **OM (Cosmic sound) and The Big Bang Theory of Modern Sciences.**

Sound is vibration which, as Modern science tells us, is the source of Creation.

AUM or OM as a Sun origin sound:

NASA's (National Aeronautics and Space Administration) findings of interstellar sound picked up by Voyager:

NASA's space physicist Don Gurnett reported at a NASA press conference in Sept. 2013 that he had heard "the sounds of interstellar space," now shown in various YouTube videos as "symphony of the planet and sound of the sun. Mr. Gurnett is the professor of physics at the University of Iowa and the principal investigator for the Plasma Wave Science Instrument in Voyager 1. Strictly speaking, the plasma wave instrument does not detect sound. Instead, it senses waves of electrons in ionized gas or "plasma" that Voyager travels through. No human ear could hear these plasma waves. Nevertheless, because they occur at audio frequencies, between a few hundred and a few thousand thousand hertz. The data that has been collected cannot be played through a loudspeaker and listened. This is what physicist Gurnett has said. "The pitch and frequency tell us about the density of gas surrounding the spacecraft."

Is "AUM" or OM the sound of Sun?

The Sun worshipping is very primordial and found to exist in very ancient civilizations in one form or other. The sound of sun was considered by most ancient religions as the most sacred sound of the universe. It is a sound that cannot be heard by the human ear because the human ear only hears between 20-20,000 Hertz frequency. The sound of sun is really plasma wave data translated into sound and it changes with every solar flares. If we listen to this sound, we can hear and feel the deep vibration.

The sound of the sun recorded by NASA was probably heard or felt by those yogis of India who reached the perfect state of meditation so the spirit or Soul can travel anywhere in the universe and see and hear the things that mortal human cannot hear. This is what the ancient texts describe to us. Those select few who attained omniscient status probably at will leave the body during the meditation and reenter the body during the meditation, as did Lal Ded, thereby breaking time and space barrier in a similar way NASA's deep probe voyager did. Each planet or celestial body makes its own sound and not all of them sound like "AUM" mantra, but they are rhythmic. It is possible that those sages and seers heard these types of sound and introduced as mantra that can be chanted with human speech as "OM" What needs to be conveyed is that OM mantra is exclusively used during meditation and some prayers as repetitive chants. Why this mantra was selected by a yogi is a major mystery. There are plenty of other choices from oldest texts of Veda, but OM is a supreme mantra where all yogis deposit their faith for salvation.

'AUM(ॐ)' is symbol for PARABRAHMA the Supreme Being.

'SHREE (श्री)' is symbol for PARAM Shakti.

At the point of death, the 'yogi' can pronounce 'oṁ, oṁkāra,' the concise form of mystical sound vibration. If the 'yogī' can vibrate this sound, he attains the highest goal. According to Indian spiritual sciences, God first created sound, and from these sound frequencies came the phenomenal world. Our total existence is constituted of these primal sounds, which give rise to mantras when organized by a desire to communicate, manifest, invoke or materialize. Matter itself is said to have proceeded from sound and OM is said to be the most sacred of all sounds. It is the syllable which preceded the universe and from which the gods were created. It is the "root" syllable (mula mantra), the cosmic vibration that holds together the atoms of the world and heavens. Indeed, the Upanishads say that AUM is God in the form of sound. Thus, OM is the first part of the most important mantras in both Buddhism and Hinduism, e.g., "Om Namoh Shivai" – I humbly surrender to the Supreme who blesses all with happiness."

"Bijamantra are sounds of Chakras which are: lam – vam – ram – yam – and ham to become one with God.

OM is associated with Ganesha. The physical form of Lord Ganesha is said to be that of OM. The upper curve, of OM, is identified with the head or the face of

Ganesh. The Lower curve his belly. The twisted curve, on the right side of OM is the trunk.

According to Indian spiritual sciences, God first created sound, and from these sound frequencies came the phenomenal world. Our total existence is constituted of these primal sounds, which give rise to mantras when organized by a desire to communicate, manifest, invoke or materialize. Matter itself is said to have proceeded from sound and OM is said to be the most sacred of all sounds. It is the syllable which preceded the universe and from which the gods were created. It is the cosmic vibration that holds together the atoms of the world and heavens. Indeed, the Upanishads say that AUM is God in the form of sound.

Another ancient text equates AUM with an arrow, laid upon the bow of the human body (the breath), which after penetrating the darkness of ignorance finds its mark, namely the lighted domain of True Knowledge. Just as a spider climbs up its thread and gains freedom, so the yogis climb towards liberation by the syllable OM.

5) *Lal Ded and Cosmic vision*

This knowledge was the legacy she had received from her Guru Sad Mol. He gave her the awareness of life, reality, and their connection to the cosmos. This allowed them to develop a guide and disciple relationship, a way, to behave as influenced by the energy of each day, and this guide affected her future life, till one day she superseded the master. Her Cosmo-vision-that is, her view of time and space based on a philosophy of harmonious coexistence with nature was the truth behind creation, the truth regarding human existence. It teaches us to live in harmony with nature and to respect every little form of life. Natural Order so that both the Earth and humanity can attain the next stage of evolution.

From the beginning Lal Ded had followed the life of discipline and spiritual path.

We are reaching a supreme period as predicted by Lal Ded being one of the world's great visionaries. Now we can ascend spiritually together with Mother Earth.

Lal Ded spoke of such prophetic times when either perfection would be possible or there would be self-destruction.

Her many prophecies of events in future period have been astonishingly exact. The prophecies regarding the bad times to come:

Kokkali sath kula gatchan Patali, Akali zal mal varshun peun,

Mamas tanki ti mus ki piyalai, Brahman ti chrali ikvath khen.

is just an example.

The predictions that have not yet come to pass are even more catastrophic-but there is time to change the outcome! Our grandfathers warn of calamities and the possible destruction of a large part of humankind so that we can change such events. Lal Ded wants to caution us that we must live in harmony, become aware, stop polluting air, earth, and water, and safeguard our natural resources. The damage we have already done to Mother Earth is more than obvious.

6) *Lal Ded as a wandering preacher*

Lal Ded lived as a wandering ascetic, seeking, and seeing God everywhere. She was a seer in the literal sense of the word and laid great stress upon direct seeing and experience: "I have seen the lord"; "I have seen Shiva and Shakti sealed in one"; "I have seen the universe pervaded by Shiva." She often refers to God or the supreme principle as Sahaj which means consciousness of the self. Several her verses point out that God is to be found only within the self: One who knows the heart to be the abode of God, who has experienced the self-created in the life breath Rising from the heart, whose worldly fancies have fled, such an one is God. Whom, then, should such a one worship?

Lal Ded gave up her secluded life and became a wandering preacher. She got rid of from the worldly things and began to wander from village to village singing songs of enlightenment (Vakhs). She passed on moral teachings to the masses during wandering. She explained to her disciples that mental equipoise should not be altered by the manner people greeted or treated a person.

She gave up her comfortable life and began to convey her teachings to the masses. She confined herself to Lord Shiva. She moved from village to village along with her disciples and conveyed her vakhs to thousands of her followers which included Hindus and Muslims. Eventually, Lal Ded became an ascetic. She expressed her thoughts, experiences, and attainments through four liners known as vakh (from Sanskrit meaning a sentence). The vakhs have a rhyme scheme. Pure Kashmiri language has been used in these vakhs. The words used in these vakhs are popular and taken from day-to-day life. The words are musical and soothing to the ears. An example is cited to illustrate the depth of the thoughts. Lal Ded said,

"Larah lazam manz maidaanas, aind aind karmas takiya ta gah.

Swa rooz yati tai bo gayas paanas, vounya gav vaanas phaalav dith."

I constructed a house in the middle of the ground; I decorated it from all side with pillows and beautiful lights; it remained there when I left that place, as if a shopkeeper closed the shutters of his shop. Till today the sayings of Lal Ded are inseparable from the idioms and proverbs of Kashmiri language. These proverbs are a part and parcel of the day-to-day conversation of Kashmiri people. The vakhs of Lal Ded are invariably sung in the beginning of every local classical music. Lal vakhs are among the earliest records in the Kashmiri literature.

Lal Ded says:

Swargas pheeras burgas burgas, Torgus khasith maarim chaiy

That during my wanderings as a particle in Hyperspace I had a chance to go through a belt of heavens including all apparent position of sun and its planets utilising the electromagnetic waves as a steed and galloped through all the belts of stars there in. So, it shows that Lal Ded has observed most of the places in the hyperspace, she felt as if all the objects in nature rejoice in her happiness. She meditated upon the Auspicious light of the suns and those heavenly lights illuminated her thought flow in her intellect.

Lal Ded says:
Neerith gachaan teelith yivaan; Lal bo paanai Daiyee chhas.

I transform myself into vibrational (energy) form and through it I travel beyond cosmos and then come back to my physical body form. And, lo! I am the incarnation of the Lord. I'm a divine spirit in the garb of a human being.

7) Lal Ded and her trials and tribulations

In her verses,

I, Lal, came into the world, Joyful, like a cotton flower- When it blooms on the stem. But the cleaner and the carder-Gave me hard blows and fragmented me into fine strands. Then I was taken to the weaver, and hung, helpless, upon the loom. After this, the washer man -Beat me on the stone, scrubbed me with soap, And the tailor cut me to pieces with scissors. So, finally, I, Lal, Reached the high estate of God.

In another Vakh she says.

The soles of my feet were cut - And shredded on the roads- As I wandered in search of truth.

Finally, the One showed me the way. Those who hear the name of that One, why should they not be mad with joy? From a hundred words Lal has derived the one word, the essence.

Many scholars say that Lal's philosophy was that of a follower of the Kashmir branch of the Shaiva religion.

8) *Lal Ded as social reformer*

Lal Ded was a rebel saint. She opposed idol worshipping openly. During her lifetime she raised her voice against false practices of Hindus of Kashmir. She was a strong believer of Kashmir Shaivism. She advocated for Shiva philosophy which is based on the doctrine of pure monism. This concept of pure monism refers all phenomena to a single ultimate power which is Shiva. Monism is the opposite of dualism. According to Shiva philosophy preached by Lal Ded, the Hindus should follow Vedas. The orthodox practices of idol worshipping, ritualistic practices, false show of religiosity and superstitions were not acceptable to Lal Ded. She revolted against all such false practices. She repeatedly laid stress on the essence of Hindu Dharma and not idol worship.

In one of her vakhs she has said,

"Deev vata deever vata, heri bon chhui ikavata.

Pooz kas karakh hatt Bhatta, kar manas ta pavanas sangatha."

The idol is stone, the temple is stone, the temple above and idol below are made of one material, whom will you worship, O intelligent and well-read pandit, better create harmony between your breath and mind and make union of your mind and soul.

Lal Ded preached the omnipresence of God. She emphasised that rather than going to pilgrimages and far off places in search of God, one should focus on sadhana and self-meditation. God is present everywhere.

Some false rituals were very much prevalent in Kashmir during Lal Ded's time. Sacrificing of sheep at the Hindu shrines was common in her times. This was perhaps due to some tantric practices. She voluntarily opposed this barbaric act by saying in her vakh...

"Yi kamuy vopdesh ditui Bhata, atsiitan vattas dyun satsiithan kath aahaar"

Who gave this absurd advice to you 'O' Pandit, to sacrifice a living sheep for a lifeless stone idol?

Lal Ded criticized the myth that through fasting self-torture and self-denial one can attain God or truth. She suggested people to take proper care of their health during daily life and worships. She said,

"Treshi bochhi mo kreshinavun, yani tchepi taani sandarun deeh; frath choun darun ta parun, kar vopkarun soi chhai krai."

Do not suffer your body from hunger and thirst, maintain yourself by proper eating and drinking, put off you're fasting and religious rites by which you are torturing yourself, help others in their needs, there is no better worship.

Lal Ded laid stress on practical worshipping and search for truth. She advocated on experiencing the truth, rather than reading about the truth in scriptures. For this one should adopt the principles of equality and calmness. She revolted against all the oppressive structures that stifled and killed human spirit. She opposed the critically interrogated practices of inequality and injustice that were prevalent during her lifetime. Lal Ded stressed for searching the God within one's own self.

9) Lal Ded and Shaivism

According to the philosophy of Shaivism Shiva is considered as a supreme being. Shiva is sometimes depicted as God Bhairava. The followers of Shaivism are called Shaivas or Shaivists. They believe that God Shiva is deathless God. Shaivists believe that Shiva is the creator, preserver, and destroyer of all. All the deities from Brahma to Pisachas worship Shiva. He transcends all natural phenomena as well as the absolute spirit. It is Shiva whom the Rishis who practice sadhana and have arrived at truth contemplate. He is indestructible, supreme, wise, and the Brahmin himself. He does not exist and yet exists.

Kashmir Shaivism, a householder religion, was based on a strong monoistic interpretation of the Bhairava Tantras. Those tantras were written by Kapalikas. There was additionally a revelation of the Shiv Sutras to Vasugupta who was a great sage of Kashmir in 8th century. Vasugupta re-established and propounded Kashmir Shaivism. The goal of Kashmir Shaivism is to recognize one's already existing identity with Shiva, the deity who represents universal consciousness. It propounds for recognizing oneself as Shiva, who is the entirety of the universe. For this sadhana and practice are of utmost importance.

Since her childhood Lal Ded was devoted to Lord Shiva. Later she became a practitioner of Shiva philosophy (Kashmiri Shaivism) under the able guidance of her guru Siddha Srikantha. She believed in ultimate merger of the seeker and the Divine through sadhana and yoga. Kashmir Shaivism has become so popular that it has impressed the reputed writers, scholars, and philosophers globally. In testimony of that Rabindra Nath Tagore has once said, "Kashmir Shaivism has penetrated to that depth of living thought where diverse currents of human wisdom unite in a luminous synthesis."

According to Lal Ded 'the conception of Shiva' is the highest happiness of religious consciousness. As per her Sadhna- she urges all the aspirants to be regular in japa, and meditation. This way their doubts will vanish automatically in a mysterious manner.

Lal Ded was a true follower of Kashmir Shaivism which revolutionized the age-old attitude of man and the Brahmins of Kashmir. This philosophy advocates a casteless society. The vakhs of Lal Ded are the Kashmiri interpretation of Shiv Sutras. She valued calmness and a balanced treatment for everything. The most beautiful part of Lal Ded is that while conveying her philosophy through vakhs, she did not invite the wrath of the rulers at that time. While discharging her mission she did not make any enmity out of other faiths. Her appeal was humanistic and not sectarian. Her approach was of positive affirmations and not of negative renunciation. That is why Hindus as well as Muslims became her followers.

It is said that Lal Ded had a big belly, because of this she was called "Lall", this seems to me completely erroneous. The word "Lall" means 'dear' and 'beautiful', such as "Krishan Lalla" and "Ram Lalla". Many scholars are of the opinion that Lal Ded was the reincarnation of 'Sharda Mata'. To match Lal Ded with goddess Sharda Ma may be a great attribute to Lal Ded who was a spiritual saint and was on the true path of a Saadakh. She was goddess "Swarasati" in the human form. Lal Ded had drunk nectar of immortality draught by draught. She saw Shiva face to face-O God destines me to the same fate.

Her Guru was Siddha Srikantha and she learnt yoga from him. Lal Ded propounded the yoga philosophy and high moral truths in Kashmiri verse. These are called Lala Vakh or sayings of Lal Ded. These sayings are the gems of Kashmiri poetry and true knowledge of yoga. These are deep and sublime. She was influenced by Kashmir Shaivism and Shankaracharya's Advaita Philosophy. Lal Ded's God is Nirguna. She wanted to make Shaivism easy for common man. She says that one who thinks himself not different from the other; one who accepts sorrow as good as pleasure; one who frees himself from duality; he and he alone tells the beads of Lord of the Lords-Almighty, and this is the basic thinking of Shaivism. She held a key to many mystic truths. The following stanza illustrates her deep mystic thought:

"So my lamp of knowledge afar,

Fanned by slow breath from the throat of me.

They, my bright soul to my self-revealed.

Winnowed I abroad my inner light.

And with darkness around me sealed,

Did I garner truth and hold Him tight." (Translated by Sir Richard Temple)

10) Lal Ded had three discourses with Guru

[The three A, B, C, should be read together]

    A) *Nabisthans chet zal wani, Brahmasthaanas shishroon moakh,*

        Brahmandas chiiy nad behwani, Tawi hoo gav turoon ta haah gav tote.

The master (Guru) was happy over the originality and creativity of Lal Ded. He in his heart of heart attributed it to the idea that "the younger people show more powerful activity in the memory related areas of the brain than the elderly does". The Guru strongly urged Lalla to condition her brain and the body for experiencing the state of ecstasy.

Then she explains, "The abdomen or the Gut has a brain of its own just like the larger brain in the head. This system sends and receives impulses, records experience and responds to emotions, the nerves in the lining of the abdomen are highly inter-connected and have direct influence on things like the speed of digestion, the movement and contractions of the different muscles and the secretion of various juices in the abdomen."

The brain in the Gut plays a major role in the human happiness and misery. In fact, nearly every substance that helps run and control the brain has turned up in the Gut. That is why she says that the brain in the Gut is very sensitive so it should be kept warm.

Secondly the neurons in the cerebrum the brain proper is to remain cool. The Neurons in the sense organs of the brain are required to create necessary impulse for the emission of the celestial waveband, which is required to synchronize with the waveband which the Almighty Lord is emitting and is spread up in the universe as a thin tenuous web-like thing to acquire the mingling with the Lord and His grace. Thirdly the hormones released by the Ductless glands produce an important role in the realization of ecstasy and spiritual bliss. The air in the breath plays an important role in bringing chemical combination in the internal metabolic activity of the cells in the brain and other parts of the body. That is why Hoo the 'inhale' and Haa the 'exhale' is cold and hot, respectively.

B) Hai Gura Parameshwaraa; Bavtam tee chei chuy andrie veiud

Doshwii wopadaan kandi-puraa; Huh gav turoon ta haa gav tote

Lalla affirms the sutra of Guru Gitta that Guru is Parmeshwara-The True Divine Being. The blissful one is the Guru, to whom she addresses for bestowing her true knowledge, which is natural flow of the AUM –the seed of inner experience.

Lalla requests her Guru "O! Guru, you are as a god to me. Tell me, you know the secret truth. Both Praanas arise from 'Kandapura', the place of the navel region. Kindly tell me as to how the two components of breath in this body complex, "inhale" and "exhale", are cold and hot." Both the 'Ha-Ha and Hoo-Ha' are but 'Pranas' inhaling and Apana (exhaling) forces of life in the yogic processes. The short breath is cold, and the long breath is warm. Why so?

Lala requests her Guru-I entrusted myself to your gracious fold, how marvelously are threads weaving themselves, with the tissue of legend. Please tell me the secrets of esoteric and cryptic discipline about which you have enough of knowledge and realization. Please bring an understanding in me as to how the two components of breath in this body complex, the 'inhale and exhale are cold and 'hot.'

The revered Guru Sidh explains:

In *Tantra Yoga*, there are the ten primary energy channels. They are known as the "ten gates," as it is believed that at death the *jivatman* (soul) and the vital energy abandon the physical body through one of these gates. Out of these ten *nadis* the most important are: **Sushumna, Ida, and Pingala.** Nadi in Sanskrit means 'Channel' or 'Tube'. In yoga, it refers to a network of channels from which energy flows in our bodies. Within the human body, there is a network of 72,000 Nadis that distribute Prana effectively throughout the body. There are three major Nadis that pass through the spinal cord and the intense energy chakras present in our spinal column. By doing asanas, pranayama's, chanting, etc. can be performed to help energy flow through these Nadis. Nadis are the pathways through which Prana flows as per Ayurveda. Prana can only flow through these Nadis when they are clear and strong enough to hold the Prana. Hence, it becomes very important to keep the Nadis unblocked so that Prana can flow through them easily.

The Ida and Pingala represent the basic duality in the existence. It is this duality which we traditionally personify as Shiva and Shakti. Or you can simply call it masculine and feminine, or it can be the logical and the instinctive aspect of you. It is based on this that life is created. Without these two dualities, life wouldn't exist as it does right now. In the beginning, everything is primordial, there is no duality. But once creation happens, there is duality.

Most people live and die in Ida and Pingala; Sushumna, the central space, remains dormant. But Sushumna is the most significant aspect of human physiology. Only when energies enter Sushumna, life really begins. Fundamentally, Sushumna is attribute-less, it has no quality of its own. It is like empty space. If there is empty space, you can create anything you want. Once energies enter Sushumna, we say you attain to Vairagya. "Raga," means color. "Vairag," means no color, you have become transparent. If you have become transparent, if what is behind you is red, you turn red too. If what is behind you is blue, you turn blue too. If what is behind you is yellow, you turn yellow too. You are unprejudiced.

Nadis are like the nervous system in our bodies, but their significance extends beyond the physical realms into the astral and spiritual planes of our existence. Breath plays a really important role in harmonizing and activating these channels. At certain places on our spinal column these Nadis form a Knot known as 'granthi' which is an important point in our spiritual development. When these knots are untied the energy stored in them gives us hidden powers ('Siddhi') such as healing powers, seeing auras, seeing past and future, etc. Hence, Nadis play a very important role in our spiritual existence.

Traditional yogic texts describe their paths.

1. **The Sushumna Nadi** – It is also known as *brahma nadi*. It is the "most gracious energy channel," is the neutral energy channel that passes through the spine in the subtle body. It begins in *muladhara chakra* and goes along the middle of the delicate spine to *brahmarandhra* at the crown of the head.

Sushumna Nadi – Also known as the central channel. It runs straight up the spine from below the root chakra to the crown chakra. This is the Nadi of spiritual awareness and is the most significant aspect of human physiology. For most people this Nadi remains dormant as they do not seek out their spiritual existence

In *yoga,* the person attempts to make *prana* (life force energy) run in *Sushumna nadi*. When energy flows predominantly through *Sushumna* for long periods of time, the person become *"dead to the world,"* and enter *samadhi*. Symbolically, *Sushumna* is associated with the Fire element (*tejas tattva*) and it is considered sattvic (harmonious) in nature.

2. **Ida Nadi** –It is also known as *chandra nadi or* also known as the left channel. It begins at a sensitive level in *muladhara chakra*, goes along the back on the left side of the spine, and intersects with *Pingala nadi*. *Ida nadi* means "comfort energy channel."

It is the passive, feminine, energy channel in the refined body. It lies to the left of *Sushumna nadi*, and its energy is complementary to that of *Pingala nadi*. Symbolically, it is associated with the Moon and is considered tamasic (inert) in nature. It finally flows towards the left and weaves through the other chakras, flowing in and out of them until the left nostril. Our mental energy is represented by this Nadi.

Ida represents the feminine part of the duality. Ida is inward-focused or introverted and is associated with mental work. It is also known as Chandra Nadi. It promotes feelings, love, and attachment.

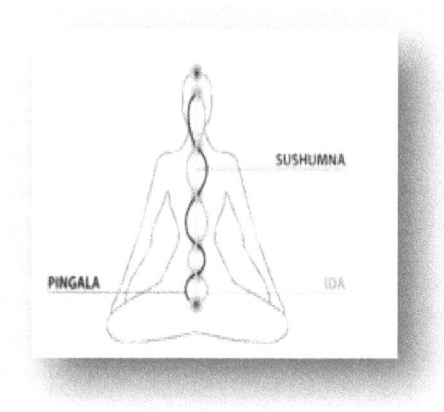

3. Pingala Nadi – It is also known as *Surya nadi and* is the "yellow energy channel." It is the masculine, active, energy channel in the subtle body. It lies to the right of *Sushumna nadi*, and its energy is complementary to that of *Ida nadi*.

Pingla nadi weaves in and out through the rest of the chakras and eventually ends in our right nostril. Pingala Nadi is where the Prana originates. Pingala represents the masculine part of the duality. Pingala is outward-focused or extroverted and is associated with physical work. Symbolically, it is associated with the Sun and is considered rajasic (dynamic) in nature.

C) Sidh Maali Sidho Sedh Kathan Kan Thav; Che doh barith kaal soran kya.

"Balko" tohi ketho dhen raath barev; Kaal aav kuthaan kariv kya

Lal Ded in one of her rare discourses, with, her teacher 'Sidh Mole' says, O Sidh! Since you have attained liberation and your mind shines out in its purity and wisdom, please take me under your fold. I am helpless and I am burning in the love of the Lord, to dissolve in the sea of Bliss. The time is running, and it is difficult to keep pace with it. The life is short lived and then she urges the children, who were watching her meeting with the Guru nearby, not to waste their time unnecessarily. They should try to make better use of time available as hard times are following and there is no way to rescue. Thus, she conversed heart to heart with her master. This eased her mute pain.

11) Lal Ded-14th Century a turning point in the history of Kashmir

The Kashmiri Pandits are the original inhabitants of Kashmir since times immemorial. Though their recorded history is of 5000 years Only, but as per the latest archaeological excavations done at Semthan (near Bijbehara) it is established that the Aadhi Manav (supposed to be the real ancestors of Kashmiri Pundits) were living in Kashmir even 85,000 years ago.

Islam established in Kashmir in 14th century. Much before the arrival of Islam, the saints of both the faiths of Sanatan Dharma (Hinduism) and Buddhism existed in Kashmir. Along with the arrival of Islam several *Sufis* came to Kashmir. They were highly influenced by the prevalent and predominant faith of Kashmir. With the passage of time several Hindu and Muslim saints were produced by Kashmir. Thus, a Rishi cult prevailed in Kashmir that made the lives of its inhabitants to incline towards peace and brotherhood. An atmosphere of composite culture and co-*existence* developed in Kashmir which is perhaps called Kashmiriyat by the political leaders till date.

14th century was a crucial period in the history of Kashmir. As Islam established in Kashmir in this century, and, along with it came the forcible conversions and loss of identity of Kashmiri Hindus. The Hindus were forced to convert to Islam else they were mercilessly killed. There was hue and cry everywhere as most of the outsiders were ruthless. This period was the darkest period of the history of Kashmir. Before this Kashmir was inhabited and ruled by Hindus for thousands of years.

During Mother Lalla's days of youth, Kashmir was in a boiling pot. External invasions and internal chaos, killings, mass-migration, destruction of religious places and forced mass-conversions were order of the day. The Kashmiri society was badly divided among various warring groups, Casteism was playing havoc and at intermittent palaces - revolts had thrown up inexperienced faces to do further damage to the already worn-out political fabric. Corruption was widespread at all levels; lack of foresight and absence of moral values had added fuel to existing inferno. This trend touched its all-time low during the reign of S. Sikandar the iconoclast (1390-1414 A.D.). With the result mass exodus and heavy toll of life took place. Only eleven Pandit families saved themselves by hiding in mountain caves and thick forests, living an unnoticed life there.

It was devastation of un-imagined magnitude. Social consciousness was a far cry. Heroic valour was on wane. The great Philosophical treasure proved of little help. Faith in Divine justice was lost. In such a turmoil a ray of hope appeared on the horizon challenging the forces of darkness and sustained masses by applying balm of love. It ventured to give new direction to the prevailing situation. It was Lalleshwari and her Rishi Movement.

Divine Mother Lalla directed all towards divine love of Shiva. She travelled from village to village and gave encouragement to the masses. She changed the fate of hopeless lot. She changed despair into eternal hope. Wherever she went she strengthened faith in Shiva. This became a regular feature of her mission. The Vaidic, the Saivas, the Vaishnavas, the Buddhists, the Jains, the Shakta's including the converted Kashmiris received love and affection from her. She would recite devotional songs to bless them all. This very approach took form of a movement known as the "Rishi Movement" of Lalleshwari.

The saints who were revered in Kashmir by both Hindus and Muslims include Lal Ded, Nund Rishi, Roopa Bhawani, Krishan Joo Razdan, Parmanand, Swami Nand Lal, Swami Mirza Kak, Swami Alakh Ram, Swami Gopi Nath, Swami Prakash Ram, Rishi Peer, Kash Kak, Arni Mal, Mathura Devi, Shams Faquir, Swash Kral, Shah Gafoor, Nyam Sahib, Wahab Khar, Ahmad Batwari, Manshah Sahib, and others.

12) Lal Ded – The main contribution of Rishi Movement

The inspirers of Rishi movement had to face a devastating problem of forced mass conversions to Islam. In this topsy turvy situation the way out was to unite the broken hearts by offering the love and respect. The invaders had created a permanent rift in the society. It was resultant of hate.

Against this background the Rishis of the day treated the whole society as one whole and offered affection. Lalla in that hour of crisis declared that all paths lead to Shiva. He is present in every creature big and small the Hindu and the Musalman.

Nunda Rishi as the most prominent pillar of this movement cautioned Zealot, thus -

Beware, thee don't Sow seeds of hate. Both are Sons of Shiva's trait.

They are progeny of the same mother. Do good unite them together.

Muslims and Hindus both come from Him. May they be blessed by Him.

Thee wrote books instead. To feed thyself in need.

These sermons don't stop thee. From doing many a sinful deed

This is bad indeed. You, believe you are a chosen seed.

Alas! will not get desired feed. i.e., salvation

Rishis did not spare the Hindus either for their small mindedness, casteism and egoistic approach. This concept of caste superiority had generated falsehood and self-centred existence. This very tendency debarred the Tibetan Buddhist prince Rinchen from accepting the Vaidic faith, and unity of society was further shortened, and door opened for further ruination. This same trend declared Nunda Rishi as a non-Hindu by the mighty pen of the historian Jonaraja. This same trend did not allow both the communities to become one under the patronization of Swami Dayananda Saraswati. Keeping this kind of approach in view Lalla had offered a ray of hope, had given patronization had united the masses through her marvellous way.

She opened doors of Rishi homes for both; offered nectar of cosmic presence of Shiva. This broadmindedness has come down to us from our great saints and seers. This broad mindedness was reshaped and wrapped in false-hood and false show.

In the days of yore, sages and seers of Kashmir applied the same approach to unite the Nagas, the Pishachas and the Madras into one whole. They had established Ashrams at various places. These still carry the word "*home*" like "Dudurhome", 'Humahome", "Khuyahome" etc. This was reasoning that Lalla the greatest of all the sages accepted word Rishi i.e., a Sage for her mission.

There are a few *homes* still alive here and there in the valley of Kashmir. The Rishi tradition is followed as per past practice. Weeklong Rishi festivals are organized, vegetarian food is served, and Rishi devotees adopt the same approach in their respective households during these days. These houses are (1) Rishi Moul Sahib, Anantnag (2) Batmoul Sahib, Srinagar (3) Rishi Sahib, Gulmarg and at many other places also.

The Institution of Moul -Lalla gave further push to this Rishi Movement. She involved another great Rishi 'Nunda' in this venture and established two thousand homes. It was to give a new start, a new life to the DE established order.

The daily routine there, in these homes was recitation of devotional songs, lamps used to be lit, offering of oil for this purpose was accepted, community feasts were held, images installed, daily "Arati" was regularly offered. Devotees would offer donation (Cash and kind) and "Prasad" was received from in charge of a home. Annual festivals used to be celebrated on mass scale and cultural events presented.

The chief of a home was called Moul i.e., a patron saint who was expected to offer fatherly treatment towards one and all. This institution of Moul proved a substitution for spiritual, social, and even political leadership that was done to death by the forces of destruction.

It was a nonviolent approach to solve the burning problems of the day. It is a fact that an order can be established either by an iron hand of a ruthless ruler or by a non-violent approach based on love, service, sympathy, and dedication. Our tradition had been the non-violent approach of the Rishis.

Mother Lalla convinced masses that violence against man amounts to violence against Shiva. She silenced militancy, extremism, and piety. Her impact was visible during her times and after words also. Her approach had left deep imprint on the masses that even the Sultan Badshah accepted Surya Bhatt's all the three demands gladly. These were (1) Return of migrants (2) Establishment of Sanskrit schools and (3) Renovation of Hindu Shrines. Roop Bhavani 1621-1721 A.D. accepted Lalla as her Guru.

Seeing pitiable plight of people i.e., violence, false hood intrigues, immorality etc. Lalla directed all to follow the righteous tracks. She came into prominence during 1344 to 1355 A.D. 'Simpur' i.e., her birthplace had become a famous seat of Shiva leaming.

At the time of Nirvana, a divine light emerged forth of Lalla and entered the etherial sphere. Baba Daud Mishkati writes in his "ASRAR -UL-ABRAR" composed in 1654 A.D. that Lalla spent her days and nights contemplating on SHIVA.

Along with the arrival of Islam several Sufis came to Kashmir. They were highly influenced by the prevalent and predominant faith of Kashmir. With the passage of time several Hindu and Muslim saints were produced by Kashmir. Thus, a Rishi cult prevailed in Kashmir that made the lives of its inhabitants to incline towards peace and brotherhood. An atmosphere of composite culture and co-existance developed in Kashmir which is perhaps called Kashmiriyat by the political leaders till date.

The saints who were revered by both Hindus and Muslims include Lal Ded, Nund Rishi, Roop Bhawani, Krishen Joo Razdan, Parmanand, Swami Nand Lal, Swami Mirza Kak, Swami Alakh Ram, Swami Gopi Nath, Swami Prakash Ram, Reshi Peer, Kash Kak, Arni Mal, Mathura Devi, Shams Faquir, Swash Kral, Shah Gafoor, Nyam Sahib, Wahab Khar, Ahmad Batwari, Manshah Sahib and others.

13) Lal Ded and Yoga (Yogini)

The subject and practice of Yoga is said to have passed down from generation to generation until the great sage Patanjali, codified them in the 196 sutras. The Yoga sutras are the fountain head of all. Yogic teachings Patangali says that Yoga is an eight-fold path "YNAPPDDS".

Yama; Niyama; Asana; Pranayama; Pratyahara; Dharna; Dyana; Samadhi. These are the eight limbs of Yoga.

Yama and *Niyama* are Moral codes. These are controlling moral and descent practices of life.

Asana is physical conditioning. While performing Asana it is important to have a perfect co-ordination in breath senses. Beginning of practice, in meditation should normally always be with the Asanas. The Asanas are the doorway to enter the inner realms of our system. They allow us access to our bones, joints, cells, tissues, and glands. The Asanas refine the body, the soul's abode, so that it serves the human body, an intricate purification process.

Pranayama is the Breath Control.

Pratyahara is the Sense Control. The limbs be able to purify the consciousness.

Dharana is Concentration. *Dhyana* is Meditation. *Samadhi* is state of peace beyond ordinary consciousness.

Aware is the centre of consciousness? It is everywhere. The brain is active when a person is conscious. There are multiple areas, these are somehow working together, and each one has its own signature, its own contribution. So, consciousness grows as brain grows.

Lal Ded had acquired many great Yogic powers with release of Hormones, (Shashikal), to which she has given expression to.

Twai Sheshikal Weglith Vacham; Shunis Shunia Meelith Gav

which means-"I was reduced to nothingness and mingled with nothingness of cosmos. i.e., I was converted into vibration form and mingled with the celestial wave form released by the almighty lord." That is how she could travel to cosmos and come back.

Lal Ded's Philosophical thought moves round the Trika School of the Kashmiri Shaivism. She is accepted as a great Shiva yogini world over. I see no parallel to her in the history of Kashmir. Scholars have yet to access 'Mother Lalla' and her contributions. She was well-versed in the original Shaiva treatise, its classical works, and practical aspects of Shiva yoga. She was embodiment of "jnaana' "Karma" and "Bhakti" all in one. She recites: 'Know thyself. Don't treat yourself inferior and valueless!

About the Kundalini Yoga -

Topped the ladder, reached the goal, Un-expectedly realized my soul.

Physical, mental, worry no more, Lotus came forth from its core.

She was doused in Shiva's love - Went out in search for Reality. Got exhausted singing His beauty. Reached the spot but door was closed Had conquered greed and passion - I knew Shiva in many a previous birth. Have come from original source of Truth. Un-sophisticated can do no harm. Oneness with Shiva is the only charm. Lalla's only mantra was Om. She was embodiment of constant heartfelt Japa. She had obtained salvation while in her mortal coil. It was all due to blessings of Shiva. She became Shiva herself and offered prayers to Shiva as per her own conscience. She recites-

To Gurudeva repeatedly I asked

What is the name of 'NAMELESS'? Got exhausted, totally fed up.

'NOTHING' hinted he, at 'MYSTERIOUS.'

Again, Lalla Sings- Did not long for luxuries. Greed and desire not my soup. Got satisfied with simplicities. Bore brent of worries, reached top.

He who contemplates on Shiva alone. By constant Japa of Homa Shiva. After crossing attachment zone. Gets blessed by Parma Shiva. The transitory world - a petty tank size of a mustard seed. Various creatures come, quench thirst. Deer, jackal, oceanic elephants, other monsters are born, drink and burst, when face to face with Parama-Shiva. I started burning like a substance, Crossed the Sixth wheel. Reached Seventh, it was cool moon shine hence.

Lal Ded's Yoga could very well be the ultimate de-stress technique. It lowers blood pressure and heart rate, decreases stress hormones, and increases relaxation hormones like serotonin, dopamine, and endorphins. Modern science confirms this-You can get the benefits of yoga in a single pose or in a full-fledged class. (p-78 YOU: Staying Young). Meditation and deep breathing help modify the messages sent from the gut and the rest of the body to the brain via the vagus nerve. Controlling the vagus can help with everything from improving the memory to improving the immune system. Now science suggests carving out time each day to breathe deeply and meditate. Before bed is a good time, or else when you're trying to manage stress. Meditation: The goal here is to clear the mind of all thoughts. The first step: silence. Even if you use meditation only to sort out headache issues, discipline yourself to save away five minutes of silence a day. To help clear your mind and meditate, pick a simple word (like Om /ohm) and repeat it to yourself over and over. Focusing on the one word helps keep distracting thoughts from seeping into your gray matter. (Ref: YOU: Staying Young).

14) *Yogic powers of Lal Ded*

The first yogic power of Lal Ded is the superhuman power of becoming as small as an atom (nothingness) or Shuni.

The second is the Yogic power of increasing the size of one's own body, after converting her bodily state to the vibration form at will.

The third is the supernatural power of assuming excessive lightness at will on the conversion to the vibration form and mingling or synchronizing with cosmic wave form which the lord Shiva is emanating.

"SHIV CHUE ZAWIVL ZAAL WAHRAVIT, KRANZAN MANZ CHUI TARITH KATH.

The fourth is the superhuman power of obtaining anything desired.

"CHECHET NOVIE CHANDRAM NOVI JAL MEI DUETHUM NOVUM NOVI

YEN LALLI MEI TAN MAN NAVEI TAN LAL BUI NAWAI NAWAI CHAS."

So, she has acquired the power of becoming something new, than the normal human being.

"All her travels to cosmos & beyond to a place called PRAKASH SATHAN in the hyper space is because of her attaining the Yogic power of irresistible will & superhuman power of commanding the whole set up round her.

The fifth Yogic power is to facilitate the whole world by her vakhs poetic expression.

BODH YELI ZEETHUM MEETHUM KATH

By giving expression to her experiences in a sweet simple and melodious tone as such she fascinates the whole universe by her vakhs (sayings).

The sixth Yogic power she possesses is the unrestrained will viz whatever she wills comes true.

VAKH SAIDI CHUI DITH MOKHAS BIETHAM,

SOKHAS DIETHEM NA ROZANS JAAY,

DOKHAS ANDER NEINDAR MEETHEIM,

BODH YELI ZEETHEIM, MEETHEIM KATH"

15) Lal Ded and Kashmiri language

Lal Ded laid the foundations of Kashmiri language. It is believed that phonetic distortion and decay in Sanskrit gave rise to Apabhramsha followed later by Prakrit. Kashmiri emerged as a language towards the close of the 14th Century when it assumed some form in its original base of Sanskrit. Till then Shaivism had expressed itself as the doctrine of Self recognition. The doctrine had made an appeal with its love and devotion regarded as the two main planks of this faith. Giant intellects like Abhinav Gupta, Utpaladeva, Kshemendra and other seers and scholars had enriched this thought and culture with their admirable contributions. As a doctrine of soothing thought Shaivism inspired love and affection in human hearts discarding all the painful and tortuous methods of seeking God. This soothing faith found a wide appeal across the Himalayan frontiers into Tibet, China, Kabul, Kandhar and Bactria. Intensive intellectual activity covered a vast field of literature in Philosophy, Poetry, Chronicle writing and rhetoric's. Kashmir was not a forgotten land of mountains intellectually and spiritually isolated but an illumined literary heaven shedding light of knowledge and wisdom across its Himalayan borders.

The main language of Kashmir is Kashmiri. It is said that it is a mixed language, and the greater part of its vocabulary is of Indian origin, and it is allied to that of Sanskritic-Indo-Aryan languages of Northern India. Kashmiri poetry begins with the works of great mystic poetess Lalleshwari of 14th century.

Sanskrit suffered change and what followed is known Apabhramsha that followed Prakrit. Philologists traced the merger of languages in time and in Kashmir both Apabhransha and Prakrit ultimately merged into Kashmiri – 'the modern Kashmiri of Lal-Ded.'

Kashmiri, it may be mentioned developed as a language, not as a dialect. It emerged in a scientific manner well rooted as it was in its antecedent Sanskrit. Within the Panjal ranges and Kajinag mountains Kashmiri became the mother tongue of those peace-loving inhabitants who steadily settled to an appreciation of regular phonological correspondences of certain words and syllables which indicate common roots. Sounds may have suffered a little change here and there in certain positions to a degree, but the identity was retained. To mention some of the basic words briefly still in common use among many are Prakash, Sumran, Shabd, Rishi, Sunder, anand, Samaya, Prabhat, etc.

Koshur as Kashmiri is called belongs to the Dardic group profoundly affected by the Indo-Aryan spoken Sanskrit and during over two thousand years a part of the "Sanskrit Culture World" it was Yogeshwari Lalla (Lal Ded) whose Vakh laid a sound foundation of this language. Her Vakh passed from mouth to mouth in the beginning. Her four-line stanza Vakh in Kashmiri poetry forms the base of modern Kashmiri. Her verse was uttered with all seriousness saturated as it is with philosophic thought to be pondered over and sung and enjoyed. These stanzas became food for deep thinking and in the words of Lal Ded herself "My Guru gave me but one precept - from without withdraw your gaze within and fix on the inmost self." It is necessary to mention here that her Guru "Siddha" had an important place in her spiritual attainments.

Lal Ded helped Kashmiris to discover their mother tongue and their soul as a people. She opened new channels of communication between the elite and the common people and, what is more important, among the common people themselves. Her Vakh and their spirit pervade the countryside, and poets and mystics, both Hindu and Muslim, over the last four centuries, have paid tribute to her in their writings. Lal Ded is the first among the moderns, not only chronologically, but in the modern quality of interrogation and expostulation in her poetry. Her poetry is modern because it comes alive for us even today.

Philologists may have taken pains to study the original form of Kashmiri, but the conclusion is accepted by all that Bhaskara's Lalla-vakh in Sharda script is to be taken as authentic in modern Kashmiri. It may not be a departure to say that language has its own rhythm of origin and growth. Time punctuates its pulsation. Nature provides elements for its enrichment. It is then that a language assumes its form. It enters deep into human mind. Some believe, may be rightly too, that the origin of a language is always divine. It flows out or even sprouts forth from the depth of soul destined to be its progenitor. So, has it been with Kashmiri also?

Lal Ded a visionary

In Zen Buddhism, it is said that if you meet the Buddha on the road, kill him, which means that if while walking on the spiritual path you encounter the rigid ideas and fixed laws of institutional Buddhism, you must free yourself from them too. This is also an suitable introduction to the spiritual writer, Lal Ded or Lalleshwari (1320-92), the leading mystic of the fourteenth century. Lal Ded in her spiritual quest confronted many hurdles and in the process was successful in breaking the traditional barriers. Her effort brought difficult Saiva philosophy out from the cocoons of the Sanskrit knowing scholars into the metrical indigenous language of the masses. She opened essential channels of communication between the elite and the common people and more importantly was able to establish connect in the society. That is, perhaps the most substantial contribution to our unbroken heritage of mysticism.

16) *Lal Ded and Lullaby- (Lal Songs)*

Lal Ded has deeply influenced the thought and life of her generation and whose sayings still touch the Kashmiri's ear, as well as the chords of his heart. Her vakhs are freely quoted by Kashmiris as maxims on appropriate occasions. She sang of Siva, the great beloved, and thousands of her followers, Hindus as well as Muslims, committed to memory her famous Vakhs. Her teachings and spiritual experiences reached the masses; she propagated them in their own language Kashmiri. She thus laid the foundations of the rich Kashmiri literature and folklore.

Not only Kashmiris seven foreigners had also collected some vakhs and translated these for utility of all. The first person who translated the vakhs of Lal Ded was a British, Mark Aurel Stein. He had collected sixty of these from a Muslim saint in Kashmir about four hundred years ago. These are preserved in Oxford Museum called Stein Collection. Another foreigner George Ibrahim Grierson also collected 107 vakhs of Lal Ded and translated these in English language. The third foreigner, Richard Temple also collected over 100 vakhs and translated them.

Among Indians, Swami Baskar Razdan of Srinagar, Kashmir translated nearly 60 vakhs of Lal Ded in Sanskrit language. Lakshman Kak a devotee of Lal Ded translated 100 vakhs in Sanskrit language. Master Aftab Koul Wanchoo and master Sarwanand Charagi jointly translated 200 vakhs in Urdu, Hindi, and English languages to express their devotion to the great saint. Pandit Anand Koul Bamzai also translated several vakhs of Lal Ded. In 1920 A.D. Pandit Gopi Nath Kralkhud has translated 250 vakhs of Lal Ded.

In addition to above, many translations are now available. The process of collecting and translating Lal Vakhs continues. The recent books are from Nilakanth Kotru in 1990 and Lal Vakhs by B.N. Sopori.

Mita Vasisht sang some of the poems of Lal Ded without the usual musical accompaniments that enhance the rendering of a song. The songs were as naked as Lal Ded herself had been, but they carried a resonance, rising and falling like a wave — a wave of peace and not destruction. The feeling of that resonance was an extraordinary experience that was both like listening to a lullaby and an awakening song. Imagining and expressing peace in this unusual manner made one feel that this is also a valid way of encountering violence in our lives. If there is a need to tackle it physically, at times, there is also the need to look for peace within.

Lal Song-1

Aanchaar Hanzani Hund Gyome Kanan
Nadir Chiv Tai Haieev Maa
Tee Booz Trukaiv Tim Rood Vanan
Chainun Choi Tai Cheeniv Maa
Aanchari bichari vechar wonoon
Pran Ta Ruhan Haieve Maa
Pranas Buzith Mazza Chahoon
Nadir Chui Tai Haiew Maa
Aanchari bichaari pravad karoom
Nadir Chiv Tai Haieve Maa
Pheerith Dubara Jan Kya Wonum
Pran Ta Ruhoon Haieve Maa
Praan ta rohoon kunooi zonoom
Pranas Buzith Lab Na Sadh
Prans Boozith Kenh Ti Naa Khaizai
Twai Labam Sooham Saadh

Lal Song-2

Kando karakh kandi kanday
Kando karakh kandi velaas
Bhoogie meethe ditim yath kanday
Yeth kandi rozi na soor tai saas
Soman gaaroon manz yeth kanday
Yeth kandi dapaan swroop naav
Loob moh chali shoob yi kanday
Yeth kandi teez tai sori Prakash
Kandyav geh te'zy kandyav vanvaas,
Veyphoal, man na rattith ta vaas;
Deyn-raath gaenzarith panun shwaas,
Yuthuy chukh ta tyuthuy aas
Kandeev grah teez kandan vaanas
Yuthui chook te tethuie aas
Manas dheer rath sapdak suwas
Kyah chui malun soor ta saas

Lal Song-3

Lal bo draayas kapsi poshie sachie
Kade tai doonie karnam echay gath

Tuy yeli kharnas zawiji tuye
Vovurni vana gayam alaanzhie lath

Dhobi yeli chavnas dhobi kani pathie
Saz ta saban machnam yeichey
Saichi yaei firnam hani hani kachey
AdLalli mei pravoom Param gath

Lal Song-4
Kus push tai kus poshaanee
Kam kosam lagizes puuze
Kav goadd deezyas zalchi daani,
Kav sanna manter Shankara swaatma vuze.
Manai push tay yach pushanee
Bhavaki kosam lagizas poozai,
Shisharas goadd deezyas zalchi daani,
Chopi manter shanker su atme-woozai.

Lal Song-5
Sone thaav thaij tai hosh thav phokas
Lolki naar sorus vechaar
Soi ras sarthali waawat paiyee
Adha sone sapdee kundan kaar
Chet chai eernai gyan dokurai
Pati kanas kuneei taar
Sarafas nish kahvacha kharoon
Rachi rachi toulun choni maa haar
Chowoohmi bazara phaa loge
Panchami sapdak kundan kaar
Shat-wuhmi bazara moloom sapdee
Panai graak tai paanai sowarn kaar

Lal Song-6
Lal Ded's Vakhs reveal a quarrel. Lal Ded had become a disciple of an illustrious saint, Sidh Srikanth (Sedha Mol), who belonged to the lineage of the sage Vasugupta. Besides, Siddha Srikanth, also got trained under Swami Paramananda Tirth. The very first emphasis was to interiorize her cognizance using special techniques. Once it so happened that Lalleshwar's husband approached her guru and prayed him to convince her to return home, The guru

agreed and the discussions that took place included an interesting insight and explanation.

Husband:
Sirius Hu Na Prakash Kunay (No light equals the light of the sun)
Gangeh Hu Na Tirth Kanh (No pilgrimage like the Ganges)
Bois Hu Na Bandav Kunay (None dearer than a brother)
Zani Hu Na Sukh Kanh (No comfort like a wife)

Sedha Mol:
Achun Hu Na Prakash Kunay (No, light like the light of One's eyes)
Kothen Hu Na Tirth Kanh (no pilgrimage like the one's own knees)
Chundus Hu Na Bandav Kunay (none dearer than one's own pocket)
Khuneh Hu Na Sukh Kanh *(no comfort like a warm blanket)*

Lal Ded:
Mayas Hu Na Prakash Kunay There is no light like the knowledge of -Brahma)
Lai Hu Na Tirth Kanh (no pilgrimage like the love of God)
Dhayas Hu Na Bandav Kunay (none dearer than the God)
Bayas Hu Na Sukhai Kanh (no comfort like the fear of God)

There is no light like the knowledge of ultimate 'truth', She says there is no pilgrimage-worth the name than the place where one sits to seek His gracious presence. It is the seat of emotions and feeling. It is a place where one gets blissful intoxication; it is a place where one does not have impure thoughts. Further she says no relative like the Lord Himself, and no comfort like the fear of God.

Lal as *Digambara*

Later, in her quest for liberalization, Saivite yogini roamed from place to place naked (Digambara, a Sanskrit term meaning sky-clad) singing Vakhs of enlightenment to remain in freezing mountains and orthodox villages. She sang-

Dance, Lalla, with nothing on

but air: Sing, Lalla,

wearing the sky.

Look at this glowing day! What clothes could be so beautiful, or more sacred?

It is paramount for the devotees to attain the heightened state to realize that Shiva lies within our own consciousness, and it is a soul-searching exercise and there is nothing outside the bounds of the body. For her, Dharma is not a bunch of laws and guidelines. Dharma is logic and reason. With that reasoning, you can achieve nirvana and ultimate union with the supreme. She was vividly conscious about the transience of the mundane worldly things.

Lal Song-7

There is noting that Lal can find that could cling to for security. There is always a change in the universe. A continuous change always goes on. She sees a hearth ablaze but, in a moment, there is neither smoke nor ash. The following Vakhs explain this.

Damiami deunthum gaej dazwani, Dami deunthum deh na ta naar,
Dami deunthum Pandavan henz moji, Dami deunthum Kragi mass.
Dami deunthum nad pakawuni, Dami deunthum sum nah tah taar.
Dami deunthum thar phollawuni, Dami deunthum gul nah tah khar.
Dami deunthum shabnum pyomutt, Dami Deunthum Pewan Suur
Dami Deunthum Anigatti Ratus, Dami Deunthum Dohus Noor
Dami aasis loukuti kura, Dami Sapnees Jawaan Kuur
Dami Aasis Fehran Thoran, Dami Sapnes Dazith Soor
Dami aasis sunderi kur, Dami Sapnes Zaam
Dami Chayes Poffeh Vargas Tai, Dami Gayas Poffeh Nan
Doh Yeli Gai Tai Kaal Aav Kothan, Vaen Chim Vanan Kostaan
Modur Samsar Tavnuk Bazar, Praas Chu Ne Kyazeh Kanseh Dwapaan

Nothing in this world can last. Now I saw the hearth ablaze; now I saw neither fire nor smoke; now I saw the Pandavas mother; now she was but a potter's aunt. Everything changes. At one moment I saw the mother of the five Pandavas, at another moment I saw a potter's wife's aunt. The history of the Pandavas, and how their mother was reduced by misfortune to admit herself a potter's wife's aunt, is fully explained in the Mahabharata.

One moment I saw a little stream flowing, another moment I saw neither a bridge nor its banks were seen. At one time I saw a bush blooming, at another time I saw neither a flower nor a thorn was seen.

Now I saw dew formation; now I saw sleet and precipitation; now I saw darkness of night; now I saw day's sun bright.
Lal sees a continuous change. She says: Now I am a small girl; now I am seen as a grown-up girl; now I was moving around; now left as ash on ground.

Now I am a baby girl, now a sister-in law; as time rolls on, now I am an aunt to my brother's children, and now I become a grand aunt to my own brother's grandchildren; with passage of time, times hardened, and now I am called 'somebody.' Gorgeous and beautiful world, where deceitful things go on, Time does not tell, why! Time hath no stop and brings with it predictable quick and brief changes of life and things, resulting in man's feeling of utter insecurity.

There is not a Kashmiri, Hindu, or Muslim, who does not reverence Lal Ded, the fourteenth century mystic poet, and who has not some of her vakh or verse sayings on his or her tongue. Her work is enshrined in the loving memory of generation after generation of Kashmiris.

She did not write for publication nor was her verse an academic exercise. It was the spiritual outpouring of her soul. Her devotees heard the verses, memorised them and circulated them by word of mouth only to those who were fellow seekers. Someone, perhaps, recorded them, not all of them, but only the few he or she happened to hear or learn from somebody who had heard them. Someone else recorded some of these verses as well as some others he or she happened to have heard or learnt from others and so on and on till they became part of the repertoire of the itinerant village minstrel and, later still, of sofiana kalam, Kashmiri classical music, to be sung as a sacred invocation at the start of an assembly of sufis or spiritual seekers.

As time passed and the language imperceptibly underwent change, many words became difficult to understand. The musicians and minstrels, therefore, took liberties with the text of Lalla's vakh, patching them up, adding to them, and substituting words of their own for the original words which had ceased to have any meaning for them or for most of their listeners.

In later times, verse composed by other pious people began to circulate as Lal Ded's verse, but forgery didn't stand, as Lal Ded's vakhs had their own style. Various scholars have collected her works by putting together the verses found in manuscripts as well as by transcribing verses recited by pious villagers who have learnt them by family tradition. However, the authenticity of some of these verses is still disputed.

17) Lal Ded Ignored by Historians

Lal Ded is not mentioned in well-known Sanskrit historical chronicles like Rajatarangini in which Kalhan recorded events up to 1151 AD and which Jonaraj extended up to 1445 AD and Jaina Rajatarangini which chronicles events from 1459 to 1486 AD. Nor do the chronicles written in Persian during succeeding centuries until about 1746 make any mention of her. It may be that because all these were chronicles of kings and narratives of political events, their scope was limited. They were not history in the modern sense. Lalla too, in her verse, does not mention contemporary political or court events. Probably, as a village woman, she did not know or care about what went on at the palace. Or it may be that Sanskrit chroniclers were disinclined to give Lal Ded a place in their books. She had thrown conventional respectability to the winds and roamed about, careless of dress and decorum. She did not observe the formalities of ceremonial piety. She was vehemently critical of orthodoxy, its dogma and ritual, its hypocrisy and exclusiveness. And they would certainly not have approved of her speaking the secret doctrine in the vulgar language of the masses to all and sundry, disregarding the strict injunctions as to difference in meditative possibilities for people of different mental and moral calibre. Or, perhaps, it took time for her fame to spread, and it was only long afterwards when she became a legend that chroniclers felt it necessary to mention her in their annals. However, that may be, we have no record, contemporary or near contemporary, of Lal Ded in any chronicle. The earliest recorded mention of Lal Ded is in Baba Dawud Mishkati's Asrar-ul-Abrar, 1654 AD, a theological document. There are many widely prevalent legends associated with Lal Ded. All of them may not be factually accurate but they do throw light on the social and communal.

18) New Vakhs

SM322
Dhoori dhoori karitham vooth manzrathai; Nazdeekh vaitith ma sae hetem doorie
Vuch kya Lal chas tari-gaemech, Raat votum meh praran
SM323
Na Lal zayes, Na Lal pyayes; Na Lali khyom na hund na shonth
Ichi Lal aayas tichi Lal bu drayas; Bu Lal maras ti rozes kya

SM 324
Douri rosti yii jehaz torum, marum maya teh beyi panun paan
Sedi daebi roozith yii sahib torum, Gangi manz parzinovum yii panun paan
SM 325
Dhori dhori karan umer mali ravum, Togum na sara karun na zanh
Sonas tii sarteli vavath payem, Saad vuchhum sari tii toreh neh sa kanh
SM 326
Jangalan khasan haba loosum Jawaani, Me che khaber yehi che ibadat
Neh sa baba yi karnum aemi bujeran, Sara aasim karen kunei kath
Kathi kathi nai gachham, bu vanay, Kathi manz chai kunai kath
SM 327
Yiem kor inkaar reshis ti saadas, Sui loug varas ti tas rove gyaan
Tas kya kari chillah ya charas, Yiem na aaram trove aath laar
Moat laagith phaeri garas garas, Tas roov garah tas roov gyan
SM 328
Taqdeeras tadbeer na poshan (Luck, Fortune; beats strategy and planning;)
Bu kar drayes paneh shahi dhoor (I left everything for your sake Lord)
Dopyomi sakia kya yaad chunah (Don't you remember Lord)
Meh keechi ratch ravyum chani bar talai (How long have I been waiting at your doorstep)
SM 329
Bu ches kunai tii saeth gochum yaar (I am alone, keep me with you Shiva)
Bu tas yaaras pateh pateh pakeh ha (Lord! I followed you)
Su yaar na deushum Tii gacha bari (Nobody will care for me Lord)
Yet meuon yaar tati bu (Lord! Keep me with you)
SM 330
Yaar tii panai pujj tii panai kabab (You are the savior; you are the destroyer)
Panai panus chu devan gath (You move over the universe, cosmos)
Panai panus hoat chatnavan (You are the demolisher)
Panai chu maaz tii panai chu shraakh (You are both, rescuer and you are destructive force)
SM 331
Dai di tii vai poshan garah kuthan; Dai nai di tii zal poshi ni sara kui
? Dai yeli di dushman gacha babad bari; Dai nai di doun bachun gacha judai
? Yi dai yeli di katan zan noon zan; Dai yeli ne katas noon mool zan
? Dai yeli di baras...
SM332
Saadha taeri chum yi vav kus chalay; yi faraz meh atha goam nakha kus walay
Resh yeli ruthum; oush wothum chraley; Lobumut chu raavan aasi na ba talay

SM 333
Rindi chuk tai zindai marun -sukhnan karun gaur
Jis padney say Neel milay;Tati chui aasun-pad pad kay giya pathar

Notes

*SM49*The mind is ever new. The ever-changing moon is new. Lalla says that she has seen the ever new 'the shore less expanse of waters. 'Since I, Lalla, have worn my body and mind, (emptied it of dead yesterdays and tomorrows unborn), I live in the ever-present Now. All things always are new to me and forever new and new.
Zalamay or (jal maya), Grierson (LV. 93) explains it as a "waste of waters" at the time of pralaya, destruction of the Universe, therefore, "the universe itself". It may rather be the shore less ocean of existence or of Reality. Whatever the exact meaning, Lal Ded speaks of her complete transformation and `renewal'. Interestingly, the same New Mind here may also be referred to as water of a lake which constantly oozes out, (JK Vakh 120.) By constant tapasya the same mind is transformed to be able to see this new shore less expanse of waters.

*[1]**Cheth Torugh Vagi Hyath Rotom**[1]*
*[1] Lalla expresses the ecstasy at the mass conversion of the state of the body, into the requisite wave form of the realm of celestial energy form or mingling of the spirit with cosmic radiance.
"Reduced to nothingness, I, Lalla, mingled with the nothingness of Cosmos."
Note: - (Gray's anatomy/neurology - Page 763/784)
Morphological, pharmacological evidence points to a multiplicity of transmitters within the central nervous system. Why so many are needed is not clear. DALE of London School formulated a concept that each Neuron Synthesizes, only one transmitter substance, which is then released at all its axion terminals including those of its collaterals.
In addition to Neurons, several varieties of non-excitable cells are present in the nervous system. The functions of glial and ependymal cells appear to be numerous, although not fully explored. They have essential metabolic functions in regulating the bio-chemical environment of Neurons. They may provide transport channels between local Vasculature and Neuropile.
They are involved in hormone collecting factors in the median eminence and Hypo physical stalk. They have also an effect on the ionic environment of Neurons.
*[2]**Chui Kuni Tai Choi Naa Kunai***

*2 In the Taittiriya Upanishad, it has been said "know the Atman as the Lord, who sits in the Chariot of the body, Budhi is the charioteer, mind is the reins, senses and the objects are the Roads."

*3**Kokalee Sath Kol Gachan Paatali***3

*3 on the 27th and the 28th of July 2001, the people in Kerala (India) have witnessed the fall of polluted red rain. So, people have witnessed an untimely fall of polluted rain.

*4Kyaah Kara Paantsan Dahan Ta Kaahan *4

*4Lal Ded shows us how to control the mind. The five human instincts viz. anger, envy, greed, attachment, and ego, along with five senses i.e., seeing, hearing, smelling, taste and the touch. The five human instincts (anger, envy, greed, attachment, and ego) helped by five senses (seeing, hearing, smelling, taste and the touch), controlled by 'mind' as their master are individually responsible for keeping away man from the real path of spiritual development. This reminds of Arjun and Lord Krishna in the Chariot with five pair of horses.

The animal instincts keep a person busy in body pleasures and the collection of material benefits. Five sense organs keep him busily involved in the pleasures of the world and keep him glued to the world. The great advanced souls have all these senses and instincts in control, and it is because of this capacity that they enjoy the grace of the Lord. A person who has full control on instincts like anger, greed and above all ego naturally gets detached from the attractions of the world. Some great souls who have their five senses in control cannot differentiate between tastes, for them sweet and sour is the same; they do not get attracted to any kind of human beauty as their eyes are indifferent to any kind of beauty except the beauty of their Lord. Lalleshwari says these powerful human attributes pull on the thought in different directions thus stopping all opportunities of thinking worthwhile. She says -- had these instincts and senses and their respective organs in the body along with their master 'the mind' joined together in good faith, to pull on the boat of this existence, why should all the eleven pulling on together have lost the cow, i.e., the essential spirit of the body. "Eleven people desperately looking for a lost cow' is a very popular Kashmir proverb and Lalleshuri has used it appropriately in case of a desperate search of eleven human capacities for the search of their lost grace of the Lord. All human consciousness is stopped in the first instance by these five instincts followed by the senses and the mind.

*5Tanthur Gol Ta Manther Mochai*5

*5 for seeking truth, the blessed saints resorted to various feats. For acquiring that state of consciousness and morality the fires of greed, hatred, delusion, and flames of passions needed to be extinguished. One such method was to meditate with the recitations of strange utterances or words of incantations, spells and charms and hymns of devils and demons, which are called Tantras. The knowledge was called Tantric (Science) or Krya.

With the incoming of new knowledge, it lost it utility. Followed by Mantras, which were words selected, to produce sounds and prayers in set forms by the old sages for the performance of sacrificial rites and ceremonies, the Vedas and other sacred books transmitted truth through Mantras and regarded as divine revelations. With the evolution of new thoughts and knowledge of spiritual science these Mantras also lost its effectual use due to wrong recitation and loss of morality of the people at large. Gradually the awareness of Mantras and the actual text fell into forgetfulness. With the growth of intellectual perception and with the intense practice of Meditation and thought, the concept of Mantras also faded away and the sages experienced oneness with the universe. Since meditation produces physiological changes, which include reduced, heart rate, blood pressure, as well reduces oxygen consumption, reduced blood lactate level and reduced respiratory rate, the body feels deeply relaxed, and the mind remains alert. This relaxation response counteracts with states of fear, anger, and anxiety. As such the aspirants observe the ways of those saints that are virtuous and righteous. They thus follow the path laid by the high sages. That is the path which leads to happiness.

*6Chowoohmi bazara phaa loge*6
Panchami sapdak kundan kaar

*6From all the authoritative statements of the great sages, the Vedic hymns, and the aphorisms of the Vedānta-sūtra, the components of this world are earth, water, fire, air, and ether. These are the five great elements (mahābhūta). Then there is false ego, intelligence and the unmanifested stage of the three modes of nature. Then there are five senses for acquiring knowledge: the eyes, ears, nose, tongue, and touch. Then five working senses: voice, legs, hands, the anus, and the genitals. Then, above the senses, there is the mind, which is within, and which can be called the sense within. Therefore, including the mind, there are eleven senses altogether. Then there are the five objects of the senses: smell, taste, warmth, touch, and sound. Now the aggregate of these twenty-four elements is called the field of activity. If one makes an analytical study of these twenty-four subjects, then he can very well understand the field of activity. Then there is desire, hatred, pleasure, and pain, which are interactions, representations of the five great elements in the gross body. The living symptoms, represented by consciousness and conviction, are the manifestation of the subtle body-mind, ego, and intelligence. These subtle elements are included within the field of activities.

The five great elements are a gross representation of the subtle false ego. They are a representation in the material conception. Consciousness is represented by intelligence, of which the unmanifest stage is the three modes of material nature. The unmanifest three modes of material nature is called pradhāna.

One who desires to know the twenty-four elements in detail along with their interactions should study the philosophy in more detail. In Bhagavad-gītā, a summary only is given.

The body is the representation of all these factors, and there are changes of the body, which are six in number: the body is born, it grows, it stays, it produces by-products, and then begins to decay, and at the last stage it vanishes. Therefore, the field is a non- permanent material thing. However, the knower of the field, its owner, is different.

¹Karam Zai Kaaran Trai Ta Kombai¹

**¹ there are two types of actions performed by the persons of vision and stature; first the action that leads to immortality, second the action that binds one to life and death cycle. Then further, the frontier of human mind knows no barriers.

Action or KARMA emanates from energy in the human body and the struggle through life is to restore equilibrium of characteristics or Gunas inherently present in the body, controlled by the elementary, electronic configuration of various elements present in the body like SATUGAN = Purity; TAMUGUN=Inertia & RAJUGUN=Activity. The man with more stable elements or SATWEK characteristics can see the celestial light in its pure form and will bind man for happiness and longing for Truth.

So with stable equilibrium developed gain full control over the sense of breathing in the body, thereby releasing the celestial wave form by the mind in calm and composed environment when the release of Hormones/SHASHIKAL comes about in the brain it reduces the body to insignificance or nothingness; reduced to nothingness body mingles with the nothingness or infinite, of the Cosmos after piercing through the galaxies and milky way's, enters into the portals of Cosmic radiance and thus enjoys the thrill of immortality so gained.

So, it is the re-union of Potential energy or Psychic energy in the human body in its purest state of enlightenment, with the cosmic energy. This probably is the ultimate end of Einstein's relativity law: -

Energy=mass x (velocity of light) ^{2} or $E=mc^2$

Or $E/m = c^2$

Or $m = E/c^2$

Or $E/mc^2 = 1$

$E/mc^2 = 1$ = Immortality

$E - mc^2 = 0$ = Death

The basic purpose of human life which LAL-DED has realized by following the ESOTERIC Discipline or Mystic Truth appears to be True when the Einstein's equation is followed in the true sense. So, it is characterised by omniscience transcending all knowledge.

2Maarith Panch Boot Tim Phal Handi2

**2. Here Lalla says: First feed the Five Bhuutas on the grain and cates of self-awareness; thus fed, offer these fatted rams as sacrifice unto the Lord. Then you will know, O restless one, the abode of the Supreme. Ceremonial rites and pieties will cease to be binding on you; and even the 'left-handed' practices will bring no harm to you (Reference to Vaamamaarga ritual). The five bhuuta-s, mahaabhuuta-s, are the five factors constituting the principles of experience of the sensible universe, viz., solidity, liquidity, formativity, aeriality and vacuity.

**3Manai dengi tai akul zaagi

**3It is the mind that falls into a light sleep unintentionally during the sermon, or, when the mind in the body is absorbed in worldly actions, it is asleep for the divine impulses. It becomes inactive to the cosmic impulses. It is the Akula that is (ever alert), when the mind is absorbed in meditation and turns within, it becomes sensitive to all the cosmic radiations. The mighty senses are the lake constantly oozing out, constantly filled again. The constant awareness of the Self is worship befitting the Lord, and Siva hood the supreme station man should gain. The five senses in the body are always emanating five different frequencies or wave forms. The sense organs are always tempted by their desires.

The frequency emanated by uttering the Sacred letter 'OM' or Pious thought should be offered to the Lord unto His worship to bring the tuning of the celestial waves, in the mind by virtue of which glimpse of the ecstatic bliss will be realized. Thus, human body which is made up of MATTER becomes of ENERGY form and it attains the velocity of light. If human being travels at the speed of light, the body will attain immortality or agelessness. That is as per EInstein:

Energy=mass x (velocity of light) ^{2}

$E=mc^2$

or $c^2 = E/m$ ----------->Immortality

Death is the Energy leaving the body $mc^2 - E = 0$

Immortality is the attaining of the speed of light and merger with the cosmic radiance.

Thus, one will attain the height, where in the mind tunes (with the uttering of the sacred letter), with the wave form of celestial waves and with the concentration and control of mind, thoughtless condition of mind is automatically restored which is the highest order of sublime ambition realized.

**5Tana mana gayas Bo TAS kunai

Lalla says: I turned to Him heart and soul. He listened to the warm murmur of my prayers. I did this in the calm and silent environment. Lo! I heard the ringing of the Bells of Truth. The bells of holiness were booming the whole environment round me. There, in meditation, I fixed my thought. My heart rejoiced with pleasure and bliss. I got absorbed in the flashes of truth. I got thrilled and realized the depths of my joy. I was in the sky and far beyond in the regions of light. I had the experience of Aakasha and Prakasha. Lalla heard the ever unobstructed (anahata) sound of AUM (The Bell of Truth); and, in her deep concentration, became absorbed in the Impersonal Transcendent (the Sky, the Void). But she went beyond, ascending to the abode of Paramashiva who, according to Trika Darshana, is Prakasha and Vimarsha, Light and Self-Awareness.

**6Yemai Shei Chei Timay Shei Mei **6

**6Yemai Shei chei Timay Shei mei

Lalla says: 'Lord SHIVA', thou art in control of five senses and the mind, like those you have blessed me with such senses and organs too. You have a Dark Blue throat which I have not. The main difference between you and me is that you have complete control over your five senses and the mind and possess all the six divine virtues, but I am entrapped by all the six invisible sinful instincts and thus have little control over the senses and the mind.

Lord! I wonder why I suffer misery.

Explanation:

Thou art the master of the Six (Sovereign power, omnipotence, omniscience, All-inclusiveness, eternality, All-pervasiveness, that is, in Trika: maya Shakti, sarvakar-tritva, sarvajnatva, puurnatva, nityatva, and vyaapakatva respectively).

By the Six I have been robbed (The six kancuka-s, coverings of limitation, viz., maya, kala, vidya, raga, kal, niyati).

Six divine virtues- Love, Mercy, Purity, Justice, Knowledge and Truth.

**7 Mansur Al-Hallaj (A Sufi saint) **7

**7 Mansur Al-Hallaj (A Sufi saint)

In Vakh SM 82, Lal Ded had spoken about this Mansur. Here is the full story.

Mansur was the most controversial figure in the history of Islamic mysticism. He had travelled widely to Baghdad, Mecca, India, Turkestan, and other places. On reaching Baghdad, he declared himself to be God. On this he was arrested and condemned to death. He was later cruelly executed on (28 March 9I3). He wrote several books and a significant poetry. He passed into Muslim legend as the prototype of the intoxicated lover of God.

Mansur was also called Hallaj (the Wool carder). B*orn in 858AD in a small village in southern Persia. He became a travelling preacher, crossing Persia and Turkestan and even venturing into India; he also made the holy pilgrimage to Mecca.*

At Basra, he stayed for some time and got married there. His time did not pass well there. He left Basra and came back to Baghdad. There he met another famous Sufi called Jonaid. The Sufi advised Mansur to keep calm and loneliness. He remained in Jonaid's company for some time and went to Mecca for one year. Later, he returned to Baghdad. This time with a group of other Sufis he met Jonaid and put several questions to him. Jonaid remained silent and gave no reply.

As time passed, Jonaid predicted that Mansur would face some problem in near future. Soon some leading scholars gave a judgment that Mansur be executed. This judgement was to be signed by Jonaid who was wearing the Sufi robe that day. Jonaid did not sign the warrant. The caliphs said that Jonaid's signature was necessary. So Jonaid put on the academic turban and gown, went to the madrasa, and sanctioned the warrant. On the warrant he wrote "We judge according to externals, as for the inward truth, that God alone knows".

This indirectly meant that he did not sign the death warrant of Mansur. After that, Mansur left for some other place where he was highly praised. He dressed himself in the ragged dervish robes and set out for Mecca. Some people accompanied him in like attire. At Mecca, he was denounced as a magician. Then he went to India and China, calling men to call him God. When he returned the peoples of those regions wrote him letters and appreciated his ideas. Many tales about Mansur began to circulate. He set out for Mecca where he resided for two years. His situation was much changed. He was a different man. It is said that he was expelled from many cities. In their confusion the people were divided in opinion about him. His detractors were countless, his supporters innumerable. They witnessed many wonders performed by him. All his words were carried to the caliph. Finally, all were united in the view that he should be put to death because of his saying, I am the Truth."

On this he was charged that his words have a mysterious meaning. When Jonaid heard about this he pronounced - Let Mansur be killed. Some people favoured him. The caliph ordered that he should be thrown into prison. There he was held for a year. But people would come and consult him on their problems. Soon they were prevented from visiting him.

It is said that on the first night of his imprisonment the gaolers came to his cell but could not find him in the prison. They searched through all the prison but could not discover a soul. On the second night they found neither him nor the prison, for all their hunting. On the third night they discovered him in the prison. Where you were on the first night and where were you in the prison on the second night? They demanded. Now you have both reappeared. What fact is this?"

On the first night, he replied, I was in the Presence; therefore, I was not here. On the second night the Presence was here, so that both of us were absent. On the third night 1 was sent back, that the Law might be preserved. Come and do your work!"

When Mansur was first restricted there were three hundred souls in the prison. That night he addressed them.

Prisoners, shall I set you free?"

Why do you not free yourself? They replied.

I am God's captive. I am the guard of salvation, he answered. If I so wish, with one signal I can lose all bonds."

Mansur made a sign with his finger and all their bonds burst apart.

Now where are we to go?

The prisoners demanded.

The gate of the prison is locked."

Mansur signaled again, and cracks appeared in the walls.

"Now go on your way", he cried.

"Are you not coming too?" They asked.

"No," he replied.

I have a secret meet with Him which cannot be told save on the gallows."

"Where have the prisoners gone?" the warders asked him next morning.

"I set them free,"" Mansur answered.

"Why did you not go?" they enquired.

"God has cause to blame me, so I did not go," he replied.

This story was carried to the caliph.

"There will be a riot," he cried.

"Kill him or beat him with sticks until he retracts.""

They beat him with sticks three hundred times. At every blow a clear voice was heard to say, "Fear not, son, o' Mansur!" "

Then they led him out to be crucified. Loaded with thirteen heavy chains, Mansur strode out proudly along the way waving his arms.

Why do you walk so proudly? They asked him.

"Because I am going to the slaughterhouse," he replied.

And he recited in clear tones; my companions are not to be accused of mean inequity.
And when the round was quite complete, he called for sword and shroud.
When they brought him to the base of the gallows, he kissed the wood and set his foot upon the ladder.
"How do you feel?" They taunted him.
The rise of true men is the top of the gallows, he answered.
He was wearing a loincloth about his middle and a mantle on his shoulders.
Turning towards Mecca, he lifted his hands and communed with God.
What He knows, no man knows, he said. Then he climbed the gallows.
What do you say, asked a group of his followers, concerning us who are your disciples, and these who condemn you and would stone you?
"They have a double reward, and you a single," he answered. "You merely think well of me. They are moved by the strength of their belief in One God to maintain the rigor of the Law."
They plucked out his eyes. A roar went up from the crowd. Some wept, some flung stones. Then they made to cut out his tongue.
Be patient a little; give me time to speak one word. Then he said, "O God, he cried, lifting his face to heaven, do not exclude them for the suffering they are bringing on me for Thy sake, neither deprive them of this happiness. Praise be to God, for that they have cut off my feet as I trod Thy way. And if they strike off my head from my body, they have raised me up to the head of the gallows, contemplating Thy majesty."
Then they cut off his ears and nose. An old woman carrying a pitcher happened to see Mansur, she cried, Strike, and strike hard and true. What business has this pretty little Wool carder to speak of God?
The last words Mansur spoke were these. Love of the One is isolation of the One. This was his final utterance. They then cut out his tongue. It was the time of the evening prayer when they cut off his head. Even as they were cutting off his head, Mansur smiled. Then he gave up the ghost.
A great cry went up from the people. Mansur had carried the ball of destiny to the boundary of the field of resignation. From each one of his members came the declaration, I am the Truth..." Next day, they declared, this scandal will be even greater than while he was alive. So, they burned his limbs. From his ashes came the cry, I am the Truth, even as in the time of his slaying every drop of blood as it trickled formed the word Allah. Dumbfounded, they cast his ashes into the Tigris. As they floated on the surface of the water, they continued to cry, I am the Truth." Now Mansur had said, when they cast my ashes into the Tigris, Baghdad will be in peril.

**8 Black Holes **8

**8 Black Holes

Astronomers discover biggest black holes ever   PhysOrg - December 5, 2011
University of California, Berkeley, astronomers have discovered the largest black holes to date two monsters with masses equivalent to 10 billion suns that are threatening to consume anything, even light, within a region five times the size of our solar system. These black holes are at the centers of two galaxies more than 300 million light years from Earth.

A black hole is a region of space-time from which gravity prevents anything, including light, from escaping. The theory of general relativity predicts that a sufficiently compact mass will deform space-time to form a black hole. Around a black hole, there is a mathematically defined surface called an event horizon that marks the point of no return. The hole is called "black" because it absorbs all the light that hits the horizon, reflecting nothing, just like a perfect black body in thermodynamics.

Objects whose gravity fields are too strong for light to escape were first considered in the 18th century by John Michell and Pierre-Simon Laplace. The first modern solution of general relativity that would characterize a black hole was found by Karl Schwarzschild in 1916, although its interpretation as a region of space from which nothing can escape was first published by David Finkelstein in 1958. The concept of black hole was known to spiritualist Lal Ded, a mystic 14th century saint of Kashmir who had wandered into space giving the description of what she had seen.

Machih kya zanih pampurin gat?

Will the fly understand the revolutions of the moth (around the light)? A place for every man and every man in his place.

Azapa Gyatari Hamsa Hamsa Zapith

The Gayatri mantra, a prayer to the Divine light.

Om bhur bhuvah svah; tat savitur varenyam; bhargo devasya dhimahi; dhiyo yo nah prachodayat.

It means: The eternal, earth, air, heaven; That glory, that resplendence of the sun; May we contemplate the brilliance of that light; May the sun inspire our minds.

History and Meaning of the Gayatri Mantra: The Gayatri mantra first appeared in the Rig Veda, an early Vedic text written between 1800 and 1500 BCE. It is mentioned in the Upanishads as an important ritual and in the Bhagavad Gita as the poem of the Divine. In the Rajanaka yoga tradition, the Gayatri is the most sacred phrase uttered in the Vedas. "It doesn't get more ancient, more sacred, than this. It's an ecstatic poetic moment."

The mantra is a hymn to Savitur, the sun god. The sun in the mantra represents both the physical sun and the Divine in all things. "The Vedic mind doesn't separate the physical presence of the sun from its spiritual or symbolic meaning," he says.

Chanting the mantra serves three purposes. The first is to give back to the sun. "My teacher used to say the sun gives but never receives. The mantra is a gift back to the sun, an offering of gratitude to refuel the sun's gracious offering." The second purpose is to seek wisdom and enlightenment. The mantra is a request to the sun: May we meditate upon your form and be illumined by who you are? (Consider that the sun offers its gift of illumination and energy to all beings, without judgment and without attachment to the outcome of the gift.) Finally, the mantra is an expression of gratitude, to both the life-giving sun and the Divine. It's an offering, a way to open to grace, to inspire oneself to connect to the ancient vision of India. Its effect is to inspire modern yogis to participate in the most ancient aspiration of illumination that connects modern yoga to the Vedic tradition.

Brahman-is other than the universe. There exists nothing that is not Brahman. If any object other than Brahman appears to exist, it is unreal like a mirage.

What is sixfold path? -They are Sham, dam, uparam, titiksha, shraddha, and samadhna.

What is sham? -It is control or mastery over mind.

What is dam? It is control of the external sense organs such as eyes, etc.

What is upram? It is the strict observance of one's own dharma (duty)

What is titiksha? It is stamina of heat and cold, pleasure and pain etc.

What is shraddha? Faith in the words of guru and Vedanta (scriptures)

What is samadhana? It is the single pointedness of mind.

Lal Vakhs have been translated by many renowned persons like Sir Richard Temple, Pandit Jia Lal Killam, Coleman Bards, Jaishree Odin, Dr. Grierson, Anand Koul Bamzai, Prof B.N. Parimu, Dr. Bernett Shiela Trisal.

About The Author(s)

Sham S. Misri

Born, brought up, educated, lived, and married in Kashmir, one of the beautiful places in the world. In my mind this best place in the world is Mother Kashmir, which is what I call home. Everyone knows everyone because we have the same mother.

I did my master's degree in science from Kashmir University. Initially worked in a college as a lecturer where I was familiar with the children and the staff. I later switched over my job to Central services where I joined as a scientist and retired from the same organization as a senior level officer. Over the years of my active career a lot has been contributed to the cause of Education and science in my own field. There have been many publications in various scientific journals and magazines.

Circumstances forced me and my family to flee from my native place because of barbaric acts of the militants over there in the valley, thus, leaving us as migrants. My mother conquered a great deal in her life, but she can do nothing about her heartbreak and her longing for her home in Kashmir, her routine, her vendors, and her neighbors. She is gone now, having died peacefully in Jammu, surrounded by her children, all sons and daughters, sons-in law, and daughter –in laws. She was reassured at the sight of her children who had collected at her bedside; yet her face betrayed the homesickness that was eating away at her. She would have given anything to go home just once. She, always house proud, used to say that she would like to go home at least once to pour water out of her brass pot on Shiv Linga, have the furniture dusted the house cleaned, and to have everything sorted out. We could not let her go, as old and delicate as she was. We did not want her to find out what we had hidden from her all these years that her house had been robbed bare by militant crowds out on a rampage against the homes of Kashmiri Pandits. The neighborhood she wanted to go back is now a battlefield. We lived at Baghat, Barzulla, Srinagar, with a big chunk of land and a huge building, now raised to ground. The city is familiar with firearms and weapons.

Foreigners have cropped up everywhere, like unfamiliar trees and no one asks who sent them or why they came.

I have my wife Sarla with me. She is M.A. B Ed. and has done a lot for the cause of good Education in the state. She has cooperated with me through thick and thin, and she bore me three beautiful children Sandeep, Sanjla and Sumeet. All of them have been given superior higher education at a time when the conditions in Kashmir were extremely bad. I along with my wife had to prove in harder times how to keep the crucial education of our children going. We Kashmiri Pandits have a belief, that, our wealth is to give education to our children. In difficult times our children co-operated with us. They perhaps put in extra hours of labour and got admissions in various professional colleges on their own steam. They are doing very well in their jobs. They have a strong educational background. They are all married and are happy with their spouses.

I, along with my wife and small children left Kashmir valley, the valley of my ancestors, looking for safety wherever I could find it. A proud and highly civilized race has been beaten, defeated, and driven out of our birthplace- "Kashmir valley." The cruel militants have evicted us and made us homeless. They humbled and disgraced and finally ejected us systematically. The Muslim neighbors could not help me even if they wanted to do so. For the first time in Kashmir the veil and the bindi became weapons of communal division in the hands of the militants.

Many of my community, the Kashmiri Pandits, a "Kashur Batta" left Kashmir. I became a migrant in my own country. Lakhs of Kashmiri Pandits had to flee from Kashmir. We Kashmiri's call ourselves the children of Rishis; we learnt from them how to live with harmony and in tranquil. Now our pride is lost, our houses razed to ground, and the people of my community live in refugee camps, some under tents and some near the graveyards.

We had a modest library with more than thousand books. The books were priceless and a treasure. The Book of Knowledge, Several Encyclopaedias, books on science, Mathematics, religion and what not. All the books were in hard bound. All the books catalogued in the library and pasted oval printed bookplates inside the covers. The labels bore catalogue numbers and a famous quote:

"My library was dukedom large enough"-The Tempest.

I along with my wife and children have widely travelled to various countries like United States of America, the United Kingdom, India, and Canada. Now we belong to all worlds, and all men are our brothers.

I am here at Seattle, Washington as of now. This I had never thought. For me, being from Kashmir it is a dream. Had we been here under normal circumstances things would have been different, anyway, a dream is a dream which has come true. We meet here often, Hindus Kashmiri Battas, the children of Rishi Var, the valley of our common sages, and there are many of us in the United States now. We have get-togethers; we have Kashmiri food and talk to each other in Kashmiri, something we cannot share with anyone else. A single sentence in Kashmiri can reduce us to tears or laughter as no other language can. Even if we live in the calm of Washington, USA, all of us are thrashing about internally, for different reasons, redoing our inner maps. We do not talk much about the current situation in Kashmir, what we talk is about our past culture, we carry on as if nothing had happened.

Ours was a big family tree. The thick branches of that grand tree have borne the fruit. The new branches will go on adding, with more fresh leaves and flowers every now and then. We are all passengers together aboard this spaceship earth. We are all closely related to each other, but time has drifted us a part, we are scattered all along the earth now.

"The truth is one; the wise call it by various names" ... Rig Veda

Sham S. Misri
Claremont Avenue, New Malden
London UK

About The Book

The main purpose of writing this book is to raise awareness of young Kashmiri Pandit generation, the migrants, about the rich culture and heritage material that may not get lost in wilderness. Kashmiri Pandits are faced with decimation of their culture and history. More than the loss of their ancestral homeland and other material possessions, it is the looming loss of the identity that perturbs the exiled Kashur Batta. To fortify the identity, ethos, and culture of the exiled Kashmiri Pandits it is vital to know what the great saint poetess, has said for sake of national integrity. I would reiterate that there is certainly something great, rather spiritual in Lal Ded's poetry that it has withstood the onslaught of history and has become a part of the life of every Kashmiri speaking person today, as it was some 600 years back. This book has been created by the process of shake-up of a lot of literature books and other source material. Care has been taken not to violate the spirit of the original Vakh and its meaning though some corruptions of words appear from source to source. In this book the authors have tried to consolidate all the available vakhs and prepared a first catalogue of more than 315 vakhs of the great saint poetess Lal Ded. Some of the vakhs have their source as audio recordings and some including the word of the mouth. Often to be frank, I as an author have been grappling with the cryptic and linear meaning of some vakhs. I humbly acknowledge myself to be a student and shall remain content with that name. With my many years of research I have been able to compile the book "Lal Ded of Kashmir- Saint Poetess" A Catalogue of Lal Vakhs.

Android App

We have also developed an android app which has all the Vakhs in audio format. The app is free of cost.
You can look at the app by following Lal Vakhs link:
https://play.google.com/store/apps/details?id=com.misri.lalvakhs

References

1) Bhatt, S. Environment Protection and International Law, Radiant Publishers, 1985, p. 20, Margaret Mead, "Anthropology Today",
2) Bhatt, S, Prof. LAL DED - Her spiritualism and present scientific world order
3) Bhatt, S. Kashmiri Pandits: A Cultural Heritage, Lancers Book,
4) Dhar Triloki Nath (1 January 2006). Kashmiri Pandit Community: A Profile. Mittal Publications.
5) Raina, Krishna Dr. Mystic Trends in Kashmiri Poetry Koshur Samachar.
6) Raina, Chaman Lal. Prof.Icons of Kashmir, Shiva Yogni Lalleshvari, Sanjeevani Sharda Kendra, Anand Nagar, Bohri, Jammu.
7) Lal Ded www.radiokashmir.org.
8) Einstein, Albert, Ideas and Opinions, ed. Car Sealing, 1995,
9) Bohemia K. All for theatre. The Hindu, 7 November 2011.
10) Lalleshwari: Forerunner of Medieval Mystics Kashmiri Herald,
11) Mystic insights Abdullah Khan's review of I, Lalla by Ranjit Hoskote in The Hindu
12) Remembering Lal Ded in Modern Times National Seminar by Kashmir Education, Culture and Science Society, 2000.
13) Kashmir's wise old Grandmother Lal Aditi De's review of I, Lalla by Ranjit Hoskote
14) Lal Ded's Vakhs
15) Raina, Krishna Dr. Mystic Trends in Kashmiri Poetry Koshur Samachar.
16) Barks, Coleman (1992). Naked Song. Maypop Books
17) Hoskote Ranjit in Hindustan Times Words are floating Jerry Pinto's review of I, Lalla
18) Lal Ded www.poetry-chaikhana.com.
19) Lal Ded www.radiokashmir.org.
20) Lal Vakh online
21) Lalla and Kabir, resurrected Niranjani S. Roy's article on Ranjit Hoskote I, Lalla, and Arvind Krishna Mehrotra's Songs of Kabir
22) Songs of a mystic The Hindu, 1 May 2005.
23) Temple, Richard Carnac (1 August 2003). Word of Lalla the Prophetess. Kessinger Publishing.
24) Toshkhani, S.S. (2002). Lal Ded: the great Kashmiri saint-poetess. New Delhi: A.P.H. Pub. Corp.
25) Bamzai, P.N. Kaul. Lal Ded – Lalleshwari; Forerunner of Medieval Mystics; Koshur Samachar.
26) Chitkara, M. G. (1 January 2002). Kashmir Shaivism: Under Siege. APH Publishing.
27) Coleman Barks, (1992). Naked Song. Maypop Books.
28) Dhar Triloki Nath (1 January 2006). Kashmiri Pandit Community: A Profile. Mittal Publications.
29) Dhar, K. N. Lalleshwari; An apostle of Human values.
30) Grierson Lall Vakyani 1920
31) Hoskote Ranjit, Kashmir's wise old Grandmother Lal Aditi De's review of I, Lalla by Hoskote Ranjit in The Hindu/ Business Line

32) Hoskote's. Ranjit. I, Lalla, and Arvind Krishna Mehrotra's Songs of Kabir in The Caravan
33) I, Lalla: The Poems of Lal Ded, translated by Ranjit Hoskote with an Introduction and Notes, Penguin Classics
34) KOUL, M.L. PROF.Bhakti and Worship in Scriptures in Kashmir Shaivism and Lal Ded Vakh
35) Lal Ded www.poetry-chaikhana.com.
36) Lal Ded by Jayalal Kaul, 1973, Sahitya Akademi, New Delhi.
37) Lal Ded: Her life & sayings, by Swami Laldyada. Utpal Publications, 1989,
38) Lal Ded: Her life and sayings by Nil Kanth Kotru, Utpal publications, Srinagar,
39) Lalla Yogeshwari, Anand Kaul, reprint from the Indian Antiquary,
40) Lalla-Vakyani, Sir George Grierson and Dr. Lionel D. Barnett Litt. D.
41) Lalleshwari: spiritual poems by a great Siddha yogni, by Swami Muktananda and Swami Laldyada. 1981,
42) Naked Song, by Laldyada, Lalla, Coleman Barks
43) Siddha Yogni, A Kashmiri Secret of Divine Knowledge. By Ghauri, Laila Khalid.
44) Sopori, B.N. Lal Ded -The Greatest Lady of last Millennium
45) The Ascent of Self: A Reinterpretation of the Mystical Poetry of Lalla-Ded by B. N. Parimoo, Motilal Banarsidass, Delhi.
46) The Hindu, 1 May 2005. Songs of a mystic
47) Toshkhani, S.S. (2002). Lal Ded: the great Kashmiri saint-poetess. New Delhi:
48) Vakh Lalla Ishwari, Parts I and II (Urdu Edition by A. K. Wanchoo and English by Sarwanand Chaaragi, 1939).
49) Warikoo, K. (1 January 2009). Cultural Heritage of Jammu and Kashmir. Pentagon Press
50) http://dsal.uchicago.edu/dictionaries/grierson/
51) http://koausa.org/lalded2/3.html
52) https://www.facebook.com/
53) https://www.facebook.com/media/set/...
54) https://www.facebook.com/pages/Lalleshuri-Lal-Ded-of-Kashmir/247354993652
55) https://www.google.co.uk/?gfe_rd=cr&ei=oP1EVeP2FdOq8wey14CICA#q=Life+Sketch+of+Lalla+Yogishwari+-+A+great+Hermit+of+Kashmir.++SHEILA+TRISAL+
56) http://dsal.uchicago.edu/dictionaries/grierson/http://www.koausa.org/Saints/LalDed/article3.html
57) "Om." Encyclopædia Britannica (2007). Encyclopædia Britannica Online.Nitin Kumar, "Om." Exotic India Arts.
58) http://themodernvedic.com/science-vedas/science-om-aum-mystery
59) https//www.academia.edu/14412717/Mystery and Origin of Aum_OM_Mantra
61) Trailblazer Lal Ded, daily Excelsior Magazine-Dr. Vinay Thusoo.
62.Nadis- Functions & Importance in Human Body || Three Major Nadis for Yoga Sadhana (himalayanyogaashram.com)
63.www.ishahathayoga.com or mail info@ishahatayoga.com
64.The Three Fundamental Nadis - Ida, Pingala and Sushumna (sadhguru.org)

Other Books by The Same Author(s)

1. Kashmir Shaivism and Modern Science
2. Kashmir - A Concise History: Mahabharata Epoch 3067 BCE to Modi Era 2016 A. D
3. The Aryan Invasion Theory - A Subterfuge: A Scientific Look
4. Tibet: Earthly Paradise
5. Kali Maa: The Dawn of Woman and Beyond
6. Maa Ganga: Mythology, Mystery and Science
7. Shiv and Shakti: A Journey of Life
8. The Ten Departures of Kashmiri Pandits
9. Tales from Kashmir, Part-1
10. Tales from Kashmir, Part-2
11. Tales from Kashmir, Part-3
12. Tales from Kashmir, Part-4
13. Tales from Kashmir, Part-5
14. The Wandering Pandit
15. Wonderful Stories for Children, Book-1
16. A Peep into America's Past
17. Silkworm Breeding Made Easy
18. Collected Poems of Pt. Krishen Joo Razdan, By J. N. Misri, Vol. 1, 2,3,4,5 and 6[Edited and Published]
19. Travels Through America and Canada
20. When I Met Her
21. The Ultimate Fishing Rod
22. Kashmir: The Book of Anecdotes
23. Tour to 5 Countries in Europe
24. Cleopatra-Harmachis-Part-1-Love-Lord
25. Cleopatra and Harmachis - Part-2: The Finding of Treasure
26. Amorous Ancient Mythological Tales
27. The Sleeping Eyes
28. Human Evolution-Science and Vedic Antiquity
29. Bharatvarsha-The Cradle of Civilization (A Story of Ancient India)
30. Buddha And Buddhism in Kashmir: Buddhism Spread Without Conquest

Acknowledgements

This book is a thank you to my parents who were powerful role models. They were very much God fearing and loved to recite Lal Vakhs, mostly my mother, while my father would recite the poems of Krishen Joo Razdan. All this had a great impact on the entire family. They taught love and kindness.

Yet, the people most directly responsible for this book becoming a reality include my wife, Sarla, who makes my life complete. Sarla Gurtoo is my partner in marriage and life. Without her I would be lost. To Sarla's parents, Mohini and P. N Gurtoo, for raising such a great daughter. The first author gives special thanks to Mrs. Sarla (Gurtoo), Misri, MA. B.Ed., coauthor, for her copious assistance in proof reading, and giving useful suggestions while compiling the book.

My extraordinary thanks are to Sh. B.L. Misri, Ex. C.E. and to Sh. A.K. Misri, Ex. Jt. Dir. for giving some valuable source material for reading and reference.

My individual thanks are to Mr. Sandeep Misri, MS. Texas (A&M), who has been always keen and motivating me to write about Lal Ded, as he himself had listened to the great vakhs from his grandmother to whom he would cling during his childhood.

My singular thanks are to Suprigya Babu B Tech, Mr. Sumit Nautiyal, MCA and Mrs. Sanjla Nautiyal, MCA for their valuable suggestions while compiling the book.

My special thanks are to Sumeet Misri B.E. Information Technology for picking up the pieces of this book in my computer and putting them together. He, under the guidance of Sandeep Misri has solely edited the book and given it a fine shape. They along with Mrs. Priyanka Sharma have developed the cover page of the book.

My grand-children, Parum, Neel, Shivam, Ishan, Aarna, and Aadya have been an inspiration to me and their presence around me has helped me immensely in writing these books. They have memorized close to 50 Vakhs and those videos can be found at Misri Library YouTube Channel *https://www.youtube.com/channel/UCy7qLofBIj8XM2v2bCzfB7g/videos*

Milton Keynes UK
Ingram Content Group UK Ltd.
UKHW021358141023
430596UK00024B/601